LIFE HISTORIES OF *ETNOS* THEORY

Life Histories of *Etnos* Theory in Russia and Beyond

Edited by David G. Anderson, Dmitry V. Arzyutov and Sergei S. Alymov

OpenBook Publishers

https://www.openbookpublishers.com

ISBN Paperback: 978-1-78374-544-9
ISBN Hardback: 978-1-78374-545-6
ISBN Digital (PDF): 978-1-78374-546-3
ISBN Digital ebook (epub): 978-1-78374-547-0
ISBN Digital ebook (mobi): 978-1-78374-548-7
ISBN Digital (XML): 978-1-78374-685-9
https://doi.org/10.11647/OBP.0150

Cover image: S. M. Shirokogoroff, *Psychomental Complex of the Tungus* (London: Kegan Paul, 1935), p. 36. Cover design: Corin Throsby.

All paper used by Open Book Publishers is SFI (Sustainable Forestry Initiative) and PEFC (Programme for the Endorsement of Forest Certification Schemes) Certified.

Printed in the United States, United Kingdom and Australia by Lightning Source for Open Book Publishers (Cambridge, UK)

Contents

Notes on Transliteration and Place Names

This volume references texts published in a number of languages, and often the names of the cities where those works were printed were changed. Throughout the text, we have transliterated Russian and Ukrainian Cyrillic text using the Library of Congress system complete with diacritics. Chinese names have for the most part been transliterated using the Hanyu Pinyin system. We refer to cities as they were known during the exact year that is under discussion in that section or paragraph. In the first instance, we put the modern name of the city in square brackets. Thus,

- St Petersburg — Petrograd — Leningrad — St Petersburg
- I͡Ur'ev — Tartu
- Beiping [Peiping] — Běijīng
- Amoy — Xiàmén
- Canton — Guǎngzhōu

We have used the same Library of Congress transliteration standard for both Russian language categories and the surnames of Russian language authors with two exceptions. The key term of this book *этнос* is properly transliterated as *ėtnos*. Given the density of reference to the term, and the fact that the term is widely mentioned in European languages, we have transliterated it in the text as *etnos*, although it remains correctly transliterated in the reference lists. The surname of Sergei Shirokogorov is most widely known by his French-inflected transliteration 'Shirokogoroff' and we use that version in the text. The other published variants of his surname are Shirokogorov (Широкогоров), Chirokogoroff, Śirokogorov, Shǐ lù guó (史禄国), Shokogorov (シロコゴロフ). These versions can all be found in the reference lists.

Quoted texts and bibliographic references use the transliteration system in the original published text, which may differ from the system in this volume.

Notes on Referencing Archival and Museum Collections

This volume references American, British, Estonian, Polish, Russian and Ukrainian archives.

The references to the collections of Russian and Estonian archives are organised as follows: a collection is divided into the inventory lists of documents which in their turn are divided into folders. For example, the reference SPF ARAN 282-2-319 reads as: St Petersburg Filial of the Archive of Russian Academy of Sciences, collection (*fond*) 282, inventory list (*opis'*) 2, document (*edinit͡sa khranenii͡a* or *delo*) 319.

Russian museums with archival collections use two different systems: one for museum objects and artefacts and one for the museum archive. A combination of the abbreviation and item number refers to the collection of photographs or artefacts. The same system is used in institutions storing phonograph wax cylinders. The abbreviation of a museum starting with "A" refers to the museum archive. Some institutions have their internal departmental archive which has only numbers of folders (*papki*) following the abbreviation of an institution [The Phonograph Archive of the Institute of Russian Literature (Pushkin House) of Russian Academy of Sciences, St Petersburg]. For example, Peter the Great Museum of Anthropology and Ethnography, Russian Academy of Sciences, St Petersburg uses the abbreviation MAĖ for photographic and museum collections, and the abbreviation AMAĖ RAN for the archival collections. For an example of the archeographic work with Russian archival documents, see the appendix to chapter 5.

American, British, Polish and Ukrainian archives use the system of classifying archival documents as follows: abbreviation of an archive, collection, box and sometimes folder. In addition to this system, some archives use the year category (The Archive of Lucy Cavendish College, Cambridge) or the Russian *opisi* (Museum of Russian Culture in San Francisco).

The references to photographs of the Museum of Anthropology and Archaeology in Cambridge includes the type of images (film or negative), the number, and first letters of a collector's surname. For example, F.126021.LIN reads as a film (F.) under the number 126021 which was delivered to the museum by Ethel J. Lindgren (LIN).

Chinese archives use only the number of file (*yuan/juan*).

And finally, the personal archives that are used in this book do not have any internal system of classifications, with the exception of the collection of Donald Tumasonis [TumA], who personally numbered his incoming and outgoing correspondence.

Contributors

David G. Anderson holds the Chair in the Anthropology of the North at the University of Aberdeen. He is the author of *Identity and Ecology in Arctic Siberia* (2000) and editor of several volumes in northern anthropology, the most of recent of which was *About the Hearth* (2009). He recently completed a large international project funded by an ERC Advanced Grant called *Arctic Domus* (2012–2018). His most recent research in the history of anthropology includes an overview of the human-animal relationships in the circumpolar north for *Annual Reviews of Anthropology* (2017) and an article co-authored with Dmitry V. Arzyutov on Sergei Shirokogoroff in *Current Anthropology* (forthcoming 2019).

Sergei S. Alymov is a Researcher at the Institute of Ethnology and Anthropology, Russian Academy of Sciences and an Honorary Research Fellow at the University of Aberdeen. He is an author of the monograph *P. I. Kushner i razvitie sovetskoĭ ėtnografii v 1920–1950-e gody* (2006) and a number of articles on the history of social sciences and humanities in Russia and the Soviet Union. His recent publications include '"This is Profitable for All": Agrarian Economists and the Soviet Plan-Market Debate in the Post-Stalinist Period' in *Jahrbucher fur Geschichter Osteuropas* (2017), and 'Activating the "Human Factor": Do the Roots of Neo-Liberal Subjectivity Lie in the "Stagnation"?' in *Forum for Anthropology and Culture* (2018).

Dmitry V. Arzyutov is a doctoral student at KTH Royal Institute of Technology (Stockholm) and Honorary Research Fellow at the Department of Anthropology, University of Aberdeen. He holds a doctorate in anthropology (Kunstkamera, St Petersburg) and is working on his second doctorate in the History of Science and Environment. He has published extensively in Russian, English, and French on indigenous religions in South Siberia, environmental anthropology and history of the Russian Arctic, the history of Russian/Soviet anthropology in a transnational context, and visual anthropology. He is also the author of the documentary film *Samoyedic Diary* (2016), which is based on early Soviet visual archival documents from the north. His most recent publications include the special issue entitled 'Beyond the Anthropological Texts: History and Theory of Field Working in the Nort' in *Sibirica* (2017), and the edited volume *Nenet͡skoe olenevodstvo: geografii͡a, ėtnografii͡a, lingvistika* (2018).

Jocelyne Dudding is the Manager of Photographic Collections at the Museum of Archaeology and Anthropology, University of Cambridge. She is interested in the history of expedition photography in the South Pacific and in Inner Asia and their use in subsequent re-presentation by originating communities. She is the author of *River, Stars, Reindeer* (2015), the catalogue relating to the co-curation of a multi-voice exhibition on a historical set of photographs with Evenki and Orochens from, and academics in, Inner Mongolia and Eastern Siberia. Jocelyne's ongoing research focuses on photographs as objects of cultural property, and their positioning in museums and by source communities. As such she is currently participating in a number of collaborative museum projects to re-connect dispersed photographic collections and improve their access and agency for all stakeholders.

Nathaniel Knight is an Associate Professor of Russian and East European History at Seton Hall University in New Jersey. He has published extensively on the history of the human sciences in Russia and concepts of identity in Russian culture. His most recent article is 'Geography, Race and the Malleability of Man: Karl von Baer and the Problem of Academic Particularism in the Russian Human Sciences' in *Centaurus* (2017). He is currently writing a monograph on the history of Russian ethnography.

Svetlana V. Podrezova is a Senior Researcher at the Institute of Russian Literature (Pushkin House) of the Russian Academy of Sciences and the Leading Curator of the collections at St Petersburg State Conservatory named after N. A. Rimsky-Korsakov. Her research interests include the history of Russian folklore and ethnography, Russian musical folklore, pragmatics and the musical poetics of revolutionary, street, and mass songs in Russia in the nineteenth and twentieth centuries. She is currently preparing a monograph on the Easter troparion 'Christ is Risen' as a folklore phenomenon in Russian culture.

Masha Shaw (formerly Maria Nakhshina) holds a doctorate in social anthropology from the University of Aberdeen. She carried out multiple research projects in the northwest of Russia, particularly in coastal villages along the White Sea coast. Her research interests include small-scale fisheries and fishing collective farms, rural migration and lifestyle, sense of home and local identity, resource governance and indigeneity movements in post-Soviet Russia, and more recently research ethics. She currently works as a Researcher Development Adviser at the Postgraduate Research School at the University of Aberdeen, looking after professional development training of doctoral students across disciplines.

Natalie Wahnsiedler is a doctoral student of anthropology at the University of Aberdeen, interested in questions of identity, indigeneity and the history of ethnography in Northwest Russia. She holds a Master of Arts degree in social and cultural anthropology from the University of Marburg (Germany). Prior to starting her doctoral project, she also completed a one-year Master of Arts programme in Russian and Eurasian studies at the European University in St Petersburg.

Acknowledgments

A great many colleagues and friends have helped us to assemble the research that has gone into this book. First of all, we express our gratitude to Donald Tumasonis of Horten, Norway, a man who has spent more than forty years of his life compiling the archive of Sergei M. Shirokogoroff. He generously shared his collection with us, which helped us enormously in the reconstruction of Shirokogoroff's biography that deeply intertwined with the biography of *etnos* theory.

Our archival research would never have been successful without the help and recommendations of our colleagues from different countries. Rusana Cieply (Berkley), Elena Davydova, Evgenii͡a Zakharova, Ekaterina Kapustina, Aleksandra Kasatkina, Natal′i͡a Komelina, Ksenii͡a Radetskai͡a, Sergeĭ Shmykov, Dari͡a Vakhoneva (St Petersburg) and Dari͡a Tereshina (Halle) all helped us identify and transcribe a vast collection of archival documents in St Petersburg.

Tanzila Chabieva, Anna Gromova, Svetlana Koni͡aeva, Olga Shemi͡akina, Tamara Tsareva (Moscow) professionally and incessantly helped to catalogue and interpret the archives of contemporary Soviet ethnographers in Moscow.

We are thankful to Dr. Olena Braichenko (Kiev) who worked extensively in the archives in Kiev, and helped us identify secondary literature in Ukrainian.

Laura Siragusa (Helsinki) helped us navigate and transcribe the documents from The National Archives of Estonia (Tartu).

Prof. Roberte Hamayon (Paris) and Dr. Aurore Dumont (Paris/Sha Tin) shared their contacts and expertise to try to find the archival records of the Shirokogoroffs in Paris. Dr. István Sántha (Budapest) helped us to classify the collection of Ethel J. Lindgren. Dr. Elena Volzhanina (Ti͡umen′) spent many hours and days with the manuscripts of Sergei M. Shirokogoroff, making them publishable. We are also grateful to Prof. Hitoshi Yamada (Sendai) for his work transcribing the Shirokogoroff archive in Taipei. Finally, we would like to thank Yuanyuan [Kathy] Xie (Běijīng) and Kun-hui Ku (Běijīng) for helping us to navigate and interpret the Chinese language literature on Shirokogoroff; and Yves Franquien (San Francisco) and Patricia Polansky (Honolulu) for their help and recommendations with archival research in the US.

We gratefully acknowledge the generosity of the relatives of Shirokogoroff-Robinson — Elena Robinson (St Petersburg), Vladimir Shirokogorov (Moscow) and Dr. Natalia Shirokogorova (Saratov) — who shared their family archives with us. We would also like to thank Nikolaĭ Kradin (Vladivostok) for sharing his personal archive with us.

We also thank all the archivists in the over thirty archival institutions and libraries where we worked for their generous support of our research.

Our special thanks go out to our colleagues who helped us with the interpretations of huge archival collections at our research meetings and through email correspondence: Dr. Martin Beisswenger (Moscow), Dr. Uradyn Bulag (Cambridge), Dr. Vladimir Davydov (St Petersburg), Prof. Bruce Grant (New York), Prof. Nathaniel Knight (New York), Dr. Jeff Kochan (Konstanz), Prof. David McDonald (Wisconsin-Madison), Prof. Serguei Oushakine (Princeton), Prof. Peter Schweitzer (Vienna), Dr. Christoph Seidler (Freiburg), Dr. Joshua Smith (Victoria), Prof. Sergeĭ Sokolovskiĭ (Moscow), Dr. Khristina Tur′inskai͡a (Moscow), Prof. Nikolaĭ Vakhtin (St Petersburg).

We are grateful to our colleagues from the Department of Anthropology at the University of Aberdeen and Peter the Great Museum of Anthropology and Ethnography (Kunstkamera) and especially Dr. I͡Uriĭ Chistov for their support and advice over the course of our work on this project.

We would also like to thank three anonymous reviewers who helped us restructure the manuscript, and especially Olga Pak (Karlsruhe) for translating some chapters of the volume from Russian into English and Dr. Marionne Cronin (Winnipeg) who helped us with the copy-editing.

A special word of thanks is due to Prof. Aleksandr Semyonov from the Higher School of Economics in St Petersburg for his invitation to publish an earlier version of chapter 2 in the journal *Ab Imperio*. We are also grateful to the journal *Ėtnograficheskoe obozrenie* for publishing abridged Russian-language versions of chapters 3, 4, 5 and 6 in a special issue guest edited by Dr. Sergei S. Alymov: "The Invention of *Etnos*: The Unknown History of a Well-known Theory" (no. 5, 2017).

All images reproduced in this book have permission from their archival institutions.

This book would not have been possible without the financial support of The Economic and Social Research Council (ESRC ES/K006428/1) "*Etnos*: A life history of the *etnos* concept among the Peoples of the North" (2013–2017). This project also benefited from earlier sponsored research from the Leverhulme Trust "*Etnos* and *minzu*: The histories and politics of identity governance in Eurasia" (IN-2012-138) (2012–2017) and the Wenner Gren Foundation "The concept of *etnos* in post-Soviet Russia: The ethnogenesis of the Peoples of the North" (ICRG 103) (2011–2013).

1. Grounding *Etnos* Theory: An Introduction

David G. Anderson, Sergei S. Alymov and Dmitry V. Arzyutov

This book, based both on extensive archival research and on field research in Russia and China, presents an account of *etnos* thinking — the attempt to use positivistic and rational scientific methodologies to describe, encapsulate, evaluate, and rank *etnoses*[1] across Eurasia. Our central argument is that the work of professional ethnographers created a powerful parallel language to the political vocabulary of "tribes", "nationalities", and "nations" that was hitherto thought to have structured Eurasian space. We develop an understanding of how these technocratic Eurasian states engaged with national identities.

The *etnos* concept, with its radical primordialism, has been associated strongly with Soviet state-building, creating the unspoken assumption that the theory crumbled along with Soviet institutions. It has been one of the surprises of the post-Soviet transition that *etnos*-style arguments not only persist, but are a vibrant part of regional anthropological traditions in Russia, Central Asia, and China. Given that European and North American anthropologists have traditionally interpreted *etnos* theory as a sort of deserted island, isolated from the main currents of

1 The plural of the Russian term would be *etnosy*, but we have chosen to use the more intelligible (to an English ear) *etnoses*, and italicised the term so it is consistent with its singular form.

 https://doi.org/10.11647/OBP.0150.01

the discipline, this volume aims to rewrite the concept in an active mood demonstrating its evocativeness both to contemporary Russian society and to the discipline as a whole.

The book has three main themes that run throughout the volume, but they are concentrated in several key chapters. First, we give a chronological historical development of *etnos* thinking from the mid-nineteenth century up until the present day. Chapter 2 provides the majority of the evidence for this theme. Second, we develop the idea of a "life history" of *etnos* theory through biographies and through an examination of the fieldwork of several of its key proponents. The life histories of the *etnos* concept are developed primarily in chapters 3 through 6. Finally, we present our contemporary ethnographic research in two opposing corners of Eurasia — the Russian north and the Manchurian south — to illustrate the way that the archives of the early *etnos* pioneers continue to structure the lives of people across the region.

Defining *Etnos*

The term around which this volume revolves — *etnos* — is likely not familiar to most readers. Incorrectly glossed as "ethnicity", it refers to a somewhat transhistorical collective identity shared by people speaking a common language and sharing a set of traditions, and often said to possess a "common psychology" and certain key physiognomic attributes.

Etnos theory is often associated with the stodgy and essentialist school of ethnography led by the former Director of the Institute of Ethnography, I͡Ulian Bromleĭ [Yulian Bromley] (1921–1990). Bromleĭ promoted his theory internationally as a non-racial, anti-colonialist identity theory for anthropology (Bromley 1969, 1974, 1979). The concept was (re-)introduced prominently, if not theatrically, to a western European audience in 1964 during the VII International Congress of Anthropological and Ethnological Sciences (IUAES) held in Moscow (Anderson and Arzyutov forthcoming). Following this event, the term was queried and to some extent promoted by three British scholars — Ernest Gellner (1975, 1980, 1988), Teodor Shanin (1986, 1989) and Marcus Banks (1996). In all three cases, they drew attention to the fact that this was "non-relativistic" theory of identity. Their enthusiasm was fuelled by a certain dissatisfaction with post-structuralist arguments suggesting that ethnic identities could be freely invented independently of historic or cultural circumstances. In Shanin's intriguing turn of phrase, *etnos* was the "missing term" that leant depth, context and coherence to an identity marker that was sometimes employed loosely (Shanin 1986).

At first glance, the term reads as a biologically anchored definition of collective identity. It is distinctive since it diverges from the standard, post-war north Atlantic definition of ethnicity (Lachenicht 2011), which stresses that an individual might choose to belong to one or many social, linguistic, or confessional groups. Peter Skalník, an expert observer of the history of Soviet ethnography, distinguishes *etnos* as "a reified substance" distinct from "relational" north Atlantic understandings of ethnicity (Skalník 2007: 116). In other words, if modern European and North American analysts see ethnicity as a bundle of qualities any one of which an individual might cite to describe his or her identity, to a Russian or Kazakh ethnographer an *etnos* exists as a coherent and enduring set of traits that only knowledgeable experts can see. Circulating around this single term are a number of powerful assumptions about the durability of identities over time; the role of the expert in assigning identity; and the importance of physical bodies to stabilize and reproduce identities over the short term.

The fact that almost all proponents of *etnos* theory understand it to be embodied means it often seems to be a biological or even a racially inflected theory. This quality is perhaps best caught by Serguei Oushakine's (2010) observation that the term reflects a type of "somatic nationalism". This interpretation is one of the greatest stumbling blocks that every student, or experienced researcher, confronts when trying to understand what Eurasian ethnographers mean when they use the term. While it is true that the main *etnos* theorists each took a great interest in physical form, it is also true that each at different times made strong statements against the conviction that physical form could determine human behaviour. Thus, on the one hand, prominent *etnos* theorists are comfortable discussing "behavioural stereotypes" (Gumilëv), group identity built upon group intermarriage (Bromleĭ), or the prevalence of certain "physical types" among a specific ethnolinguistic group (Shirokogoroff). On the other hand, the same theorists will also chart how one *etnos* replaces another over long historical epochs (Gumilëv), how intermarriage promotes the "coming together" of nations (Bromleĭ), or how ecological conditions promote the "growth and decline" of *etnoses* (Shirokogoroff). *Etnos* identities may be stable and coherent, but they are never eternal. They may be embodied, but they also merge, change, evolve and "degrade". The craftsmen of this concept wield the organic metaphor not to imply that *etnoses* are pre-programmed to react to their environment, but instead to emphasise that they are functional and coherent forms of social life. One objective of this volume is to try to illustrate, through citations from archival sources and ethnographic examples, the way that physiological arguments are combined with symbolic arguments within each *etnos* school. In so doing, we hope to "ground" *etnos* theory by giving a long overdue and detailed account of the social conditions that encouraged the growth of this idea.

Before we start out on our overview of the history of *etnos* thinking in chapter 2, it would be helpful to have a crisp and clear definition of what an *etnos* is. This is not as easy a task as it might first seem. In contemporary Russia, the term is so pervasive, and considered to be so self-evident that it sometimes seems to be part of the air one breathes. Some scholars, such as Bromleĭ, wrote entire monographs on how the concept could be applied to Soviet society, but struggled to give a concise definition of the term. For many, it seems that one belongs to an *etnos* as self-evidently as one has a defined gender or belongs to a specified profession.

Although strands of *etnos* thinking can be traced to the seventeenth century, the first scholar to employ the term as a stand-alone, compact concept was Nikolaĭ M. Mogilīanskiĭ (1871–1933), a curator at the Russian Ethnographic Museum in St Petersburg. His life and fieldwork is analysed in great detail in chapter 3 of this volume. His 1916 published definition reads as follows:

> The ἔθνος [*etnos*] concept — is a complex idea. It is a group of individuals united together as a single whole [*odno tseloe*] by several general characteristics. [These are:] common physical (anthropological) characteristics; a common historical fate, and finally a common language — which is the foundation upon which, in turn, [an *etnos*] can build a common worldview [and] folk-psychology — in short, an entire spiritual culture (Mogilīanskiĭ 1916: 11).

His off-the-cuff rendering was published in the context of a wide-ranging debate on the institutionalization of ethnography within Russia, which in particular stressed the role of expert scientists in investigating and setting public policy. The role of experts in identifying *etnoses* is one of the theory's defining features.

An émigré ethnographer, Sergei M. Shirokogoroff (1887–1939), who is widely credited for being the first to publish a book-length monograph on the topic of *etnos*, captures many of the same attributes in one of his published definitions:

> [An] *etnos* is a group of people, speaking a common language who recognise their common origin, and who display a coherent set [*kompleks*] of habits [*obychai*], lifestyle [*uklad zhizni*], and a set of traditions that they protect and worship. [They further] distinguish these [qualities] from those of other groups. This, in fact, is *the ethnic unit* — the object of scientific ethnography (Shirokogorov 1923: 13) (emphasis in the original).

Shirokogoroff's fieldwork, academic and political writings are examined in considerable detail in chapters 5, 6 and 7 of this volume. Here we will show that while in his fieldwork he was to a certain degree obsessed with measuring skulls, or even harvesting skulls from Evenki burials, his conclusions were much more focussed on cultural potentialities and what one might define today as a form of resilience of indigenous societies against those of settlers. His engagement with *etnos* theory is of a particularly unusual kind — that of an iconoclastic émigré who befriended Siberian minorities living at the frontiers of two crumbling empires. This is reflected in his definition of *etnos*, with its references to a protected or cherished lifestyle.

Bromleĭ, who is most closely associated with *etnos* theory today, struggled to define the term, instead preferring to signal his interest by placing the term in the titles of his books and articles. His authoritative monograph, *Ėtnos i ėtnografii͡a* (1973) arrives at a prosaic definition over several pages, in comparison to competing denominations (Bromleĭ 1973: 37–39). He first employed the term in 1968 without defining it whatsoever — presumably relying on the fact that everybody already understood it implicitly (Alekseev and Bromleĭ 1968). In English, his most concise formulation is in his edited book *Soviet Ethnology and Anthropology Today* where he almost accidently defines the concept by noticing that his life-long competitor Lev N. Gumilёv (1912–1992) ignores it:

> Attention has long been drawn to the fact that none of the elements of *ethnos* such as *language, customs, religion, etc.* can be regarded as an indispensable differentiating feature. This is sometimes used as a reason for ignoring these elements as expressions of the essence of *ethnos* (Gumilёv 1967: 5, emphasis added) (Bromley 1974: 66).

In a much later wide-ranging Russian-language encyclopaedia article on *etnos* theory, he stressed that *etnos* includes the concepts of common descent, self-appellation, and a shared region with the following definition:

> An *Etnos* […] is [made up of] the totality [*sovokupnost'*] of individuals [living] on a defined territory, who demonstrate common and relatively stable linguistic, cultural and psychic qualities. [This group] also recognizes their uniqueness and distinguish themselves from other similar groups (self-identity) and represent this [recognition] through a self-appellation (an ethnonym) (Bromleĭ 1988).

Bromleĭ's reference to an all-inclusive, integral "totality" (*sovokupnost'*) is a third important defining feature of the term — and one that points to the way that embodied organic terms are used. His evocation of "totality" builds upon Mogilı͡anskiĭ's "single whole" (*odno tseloe*) and Shirokogoroff's "coherent set" (*kompleks*).

Bromleĭ's sparring partner, the Leningrad-based geographer Gumilёv, made a career out of promoting and distinguishing his own theory of *etnos* in a series of historical monographs, many of which became bestsellers in the late Soviet period. Substantively, however his definition of *etnos* did not differ greatly from that of Bromleĭ (Bassin 2016: 171–76). In an early article, he argued that *etnos* should not belong to ethnography but to historical geography. In his view the concept was composed of language, habits (*obychai*) and culture, ideology, and an account of a common of origin (Gumilёv 1965). Albeit a geographer, his examples of *etnos* were often the most ethnographic — he saw *etnos* evident in the small bodily actions or reactions which he described as "persistent behavioural models" (*stereotipy povedenii͡a*) when they manifested on a small scale, or as ethnic "passions" (*passionnarnost'*) on a large scale (Bassin 2016: 24–26; 55–59). As is characteristic of this entire school, only experts would be able to identify these archetypes or emotions.

Building on these four definitions, each based on fieldwork from different corners of Eurasia, we can identify the followng five qualities, which are associated with *etnoses*:

- a collective identity;
- a common physical anthropological foundation;
- a common language;
- a cherished set of traditions or "historical fate"; and
- a common worldview, "folk psychology", or behavioural archetype.

Perhaps the most influential part of the definition, implied rather than stated, was that this was a specialised *scientific* term for expert use and not necessary caught up in popular definitions of nations or people (*narod*).

Empires, Scientific Traditions, and *Etnos*

The relationship between science and identity politics is a classic long-running issue, and never more so than in the history of the Eurasian states. This particular space is hampered by a general stereotype that scientists and citizens alike respond to authoritarian directives, and that there is little variety or subtlety in scientific thought. In grounding *etnos* theory, we would like to draw attention to the political and environmental controversies that went into the building of this theory. As chapter 2 shows, we see the theory as a "biosocial compromise" between humanistic and positivistic modes of discovery, as well as between inward and outward looking social research.

As will become abundantly clear in this volume, the most significant influence on the development of *etnos* theory was the Russian Empire, or more accurately the Russian Empire at the point of its dissolution. As with many empires in the mid- to late-nineteenth century, the Russian Empire struggled with the challenge of modernization. If, in western Europe, modern nation-states arose out of the toil of capitalist industry, conscripted armies, bureaucracy, and the development of mass education and publishing, the Russian Empire famously lagged behind in all these respects (Lieven 2006). The formation of a single Russian nation out of a "core" population of various Slavic-speaking local communities was hindered by the dynastic and autocratic nature of the regime and the notorious gap between educated elites and peasant masses (Hosking 1997). As Vera Tolz pointed out, "in the prerevolutionary period, intellectuals were virtually the sole nation-builders" among Russians (Tolz 2001: 8). This gave historians and ethnographers a remarkable amount of social influence.

During the late-nineteenth century, the empire faced the development of numerous nationalist movements, especially on its western periphery. Following its painful defeat in the Crimean War (1856), the Polish uprising (1863), and the liberal reforms of Alexander II (1861–1881) the imperial state sought to unify the government of its territories and enhance their integration. This led to a series of measures to bring about the "Russification" of the populations of the western provinces, including the ban on publishing in Ukrainian and Belorussian, the discrimination against the Catholic Church, and state support for Orthodoxy and Russian-language education. The "forced integration" of Ukrainians drew on a perception that they could easily form part of a large Russian nation (Kappeler 2001: ch. 7). This political assimilative pressure, as we show in chapter 3, played an important role in the upbringing of early *etnos* thinkers who were motivated to identify difference among the southern and northern Slavic peripheries. The diversity of points of view over ethnic consolidation was made visible during the revolution of 1905–1907, which was, according to Andreas Kappeler, the Russian Empire's "spring of nations". The first state Duma or parliament, elected in 1906, included numerous regional, confessional and national parties, such as the Polish *Koło*, Ukrainian *Hromada*, Estonian, Armenian, and other groups. This motley composition of the Duma inspired one politician to characterize it as a "live ethnographic map of Russia" (Semyonov 2009). The contradictions generated by ethno-national consolidation and separatism to a large degree set the stage for the two subsequent revolutions, and the eventual founding of the Soviet Union.

The Russian Empire was not the only empire driving the development of this theory. As chapters 5 and 6 show, much of the promotion and lobbying for the definition of a state-led policy on ethnic consolidation was launched within a series of modernizing fragments of former empires along the Pacific Rim. To a large degree, *etnos* thinking cannot be understood in isolation from the breakaway Far Eastern Republic, the nationalist Chinese state created in the wake of the first Chinese revolution, or the paradoxical and ill-fated Manchukuo republic in Manchuria. Although not the focus of this volume, early *etnos* pioneers took inspiration from Russian and Soviet state building "on the edge of Empire" in the Caucasus and in Central Asia (Mühlfried and Sokolovskiy 2011; Gullette 2008; Abashin 2014).

It was within this ethno-political maelstrom that key thinkers such as Fëdor Volkov (1847–1918), Sergeĭ Rudenko (1885–1969), Mogilīanskiĭ and Shirokogoroff tried to advance a scientific account of the growth and decline of ethnic units. To better understand how these thinkers reasoned during the conflicts of the *fin-de-siècle* period, we have placed an emphasis in this volume on examining their day-to-day work in their amateur societies, their museum collections, and their efforts in the field collecting artefacts and measurements among the population of the Russian Empire. In this volume, we make a strong argument that the biosocial quality of *etnos* thinking can be read through the "paleoethnographic" collecting practice of Volkov and Mogilīanskiĭ (chapter 3), the applied physiognomic programmes of Rudenko and Shirokogoroff (chapters 4 and 5), the questionnaires and ethnographic "index" of Dmitriĭ Zelenin (1878–1954) (chapter 4), and the ethnographic mapping of Pavel Kushner (1889–1968) (chapter 2).

The far-eastern legacy of *etnos* thinking underpins the biography of Sergei Shirokogoroff — arguably one of Volkov's students in St Petersburg — who, for a variety of reasons, decided to emigrate from Russia to the Russian Far East, and then to a variety of locations in China. Although Shirokogoroff is thought of as a Russian scholar, from 1923 until his death in 1939 he lived and worked in China. All of his mature works were published there. He participated in setting the foundation for anthropology in China, and likely the worldview and attitudes of the Far East also influenced him and his thinking. After a brief association with the Far Eastern University in Vladivostok, Shirokogoroff found several academic homes for himself within nationalist China in both Amoy [Xiàmén] and Canton [Guǎngzhōu]. The new nationalist administration began to build a new cohort of scholars, educated overseas, who worked under the supervision of a remarkable collective of intellectuals from around the world (Yen 2012; Glover et al. 2012; Guldin 1994). In reaction to the administrative dominance of Manchus during the Qing Empire, local intellectuals began indigenizing foreign concepts of identity such as *ethnie* or nation. They countered Manchu ethnic hegemony with the idea that China hosted a number of independent, hierarchically-organized nationalities. These were described through varyingly inclusive definitions of *mínzú* (民族) — a pair of characters imported from Japanese, which signified a type of "nation-lineage" (Leibold 2007). In Weiner's (1997) account, these characters fused together the European notions of "race", "ethnie", and "nation", creating a truly biosocial way of ascribing group membership.

Shirokogoroff wrote many of his mature works on *etnos* during this time, but it is not clear if he imported his Siberian-based ideas of *etnos* to China, or if he became one of the most prominent exporters of early biosocial *mínzú*-talk to Russia and western Europe. One of Shirokogoroff's lasting legacies was his role as a teacher to Fèi Xiàotōng (1910–2005) and Yáng Chéngzhì — two scholars who had an extraordinary impact on the formation of anthropology in China (Anderson and Arzyutov forthcoming). Given Shirokogoroff's prominent role in developing anthropology across several modernizing Eurasian states, chapters 4, 5, 6 and 7 examine his work in some detail.

Life Histories, and Field Histories, of *Etnos* Thinking

Although the precepts of *etnos* theory make it sound like any other abstract system derived from first principles, it is a little-known fact that the first *etnos* pioneers devoted years, and sometimes their entire lives, to testing and tinkering with their theory in field conditions. When Gellner first (re-)directed the attention of north Atlantic scholars to *etnos* theory he described the work of Bromleĭ as a "minor revolution" (Gellner 1988: 116) which stood in defiant contrast to the dry and scholarly evolutionary models for which Marxism had been famous. A key platform of this revolution was the use of fieldwork to specify and elucidate the details of particular *etnoses* — a feature that defined *etnos* thinking across Eurasia. Rather than compressing ethnocultural diversity into one set of pre-determined moulds, *etnos* investigation explored the local practices that revealed the growth and decline of group identities. Researchers travelled long distances and brought back stacks of glass plate negatives, tables of measurements, and shelves full of artefacts to demonstrate incremental differences between neighbouring communities.

It may not be insignificant that much of the work of *etnos* exploration was done at the frontiers of the Russian and Qing empires. A heavy debt is owed by Sergei Shirokogoroff to Evenkis, Orochens, and Manchus living on the borderlands along the Amur [Hēilóng Jiāng] River (chapters 5 and 7). Further insights were generated by Sergeĭ Rudenko in Bashkirii͡a at the frontier of Slavic and Turkic settlements (chapter 4). Few *etnos* studies were done in the Russian heartlands. Instead, Volkov, Mogili͡anskiĭ, and their students developed most of their theories along the Slavic borderlands in contemporary Ukraine and the Russian north (chapters 3 and 8). These ideas were forged at the frontiers of empires.

It is possible to sketch out a continental map of how fieldwork influenced central *etnos* precepts. The mapping of the border between "Great Russians" and "Small Russians" (Ukrainians) in the southern reaches of the empire provided important evidence for what a proper *etnos* should be. Similarly, the charting of the northern boundary of Slavic identity on the coasts of the frigid White Sea fuelled a debate in the Soviet period about of the existence of so-called *subetnoses* — a type of evolving or consolidating identity, which was distinct but not yet complete in itself. In contrast, many of the classic examples of ethnic resilience and assimilation came from Russian-occupied territories far to the east. In examining the fieldwork that went into these influential cases, we can see that the *etnos* and *subetnos* concepts themselves balanced central and peripheral experiences and in its own way lent a sense of unity to the empire. The role of these Siberian and pan-Slavic conversations has never been documented in existing accounts, giving the impression that the *etnos* concept appeared out of thin air.

In drawing attention to the scholarly networks and the concrete fieldwork that led to *etnos* theory, we are making a heavy investment in what Nathaniel Knight (2017) describes as "academic particularism" within the Russian Empire. His broad definition focusses on the roles of geographical factors and interpersonal contacts in the formation of a uniquely Russian perspective on the nature of mankind. While historians of science often nest their analysis in "styles" or even "ecologies" of knowledge, our research tends to support the idea that the encounter between Siberian indigenous peoples and the foreign-trained scholars working for the Russian Academy of Sciences generated a special type of ethnographic and political thinking that became refined as *etnos* thinking. We suggest that the investment these expatriate scholars made in exploring the frontiers of empire spurred them to develop this essentialist theory.

One of the major contributions of this volume is to elucidate the various life histories of the *etnos* concept. With this turn of phrase, we have made use of our own ethnographic skills to try to reconstruct the stories and biographies of some of the key figures in the development of *etnos* theory. Further, we have done our own fieldwork among the peoples in the same borderlands that gave rise to this ethnographic dialogue. The crafting of life histories is a common method in the ecological and health sciences and is used to understand the everyday practices that lead to resilience (or illness) in communities of all types. Our method arguably goes one step further, by touching on the personal and interpersonal dynamics that influence the careers of a group of scholars. Our inspiration comes from the movement in science studies that tries to contextualize the history of ideas in the local interpersonal and environmental conditions in which people worked and interacted.

With the term "life history" we risk implying that *etnos* thinking was the work of erudite pioneers lighting out on horseback for the territory. We have been careful to contextualize the fieldwork of *etnos* thinkers within their institutions. As described in the previous section, the institutional academic configurations of the crumbling Romanov and Qing empires left few official spaces for academic action. The polymath scientists who conducted physiognomic measurements, ethnographic cartography, and who organized public exhibits all worked within the embrace of a small face-to-face community of intellectuals. Institutional affiliations often overlapped. The work done in informal amateur societies was also injected into the minutes of formal academic structures. Chapter 2 places a heavy emphasis on the institutionalization of ethnography in the late imperial period and the start of the Soviet period. The success of *etnos* theory — and its remarkable resilience — is largely due to the way that classic proofs from the field, such as the physical types of Bashkirs and Zabaĭkal Orochens, shaped the curriculum of future generations of scholars. The heavy interpenetration of Russian scholars in nationalist — and communist — China also lent a stabilizing role, as *etnos* and *mínzú* came to represent one another and a continent-wide paradigm of identity governance was thus created.

Our life-history method leads to some untraditional ways of illustrating the development of this case. In a purely chronological and institutional frame, *etnos* thinking can be rooted in the geographic particularism of the research of Karl von Baer (1792–1876) — also based in the Russian North — in the middle of the nineteenth century (Knight 2017) as well as in the paleoethnographic work of Fëdor Volkov, which bridged the nineteenth and twentieth centuries (chapter 3). Both scholars had one foot in and one foot out of Russian scholarly networks, and each was a key figure in the institutionalization of ethnography within the Academy of Science and the universities respectively. However, the relatively marginal and contentious émigré scholar Sergei Shirokogoroff likely did the most to popularize and distribute the *etnos* concept. Aside from conducting ambitious and to some extent unrivalled fieldwork in Zabaĭkal'e and Manchuria with his wife and intellectual partner Elizaveta Shirokogoroff (née Robinson), the Shirokogoroffs implemented a wide programme of correspondence, circulating (often self-published) copies of their work internationally in several European languages. Indeed, until recently, very little of Shirokogoroff's work was available in Russian. This, however, did not stop several generations of Soviet scholars from incorporating many of his ideas into their own works, sometimes unattributed, relying on unpublished translations or precis passed down orally from colleague to colleague. Due to the wide influence of his thinking, and to some degree the paucity of any reliable information about his life, three of the chapters in this volume focus on the legacy of this remarkable ethnographic couple (chapters 5, 6, and 7).

The use of life histories also helps us to resolve a long-standing controversy about how to classify *etnos* theory. Marcus Banks captures the consensus of many north Atlantic anthropologists that *etnos* theory is a "most strongly primordialist" theory (Banks 1996: 17). In using this pejorative term Banks was referencing an argument common in the late 1980s and early 1990s that theories of identity can be placed on a continuum between "romantic, essentialist, and primordialist" on the one hand, and "modernist, constructivist and instrumentalist" on the other.[2] Yet at the same time *etnos* commentators, including Banks, are quick to note that ethnographic fieldwork done using *etnos* theory seems to be "relatively synchronist" (Gellner 1988: 118) or harbouring elements of transactionalism (Banks 1996: 23). The paradox of the theory is best captured by the fact that Soviet Marxist theorists understood *etnos* identities to persist across historical stages, and yet they felt that the term was not essentialist or romantic but materialist. The best example was the often quoted example of Bromleĭ that Ukrainians remained Ukrainians under feudalism, capitalism and socialism (qtd. in Gellner 1977: 213). By examining the fieldwork of *etnos* pioneers in detail, we can see how some of these paradoxes unfold in practice — although admitedly some of their field methods seem today to be unusual or non-standard.

Thus we learn in chapter 5 that Shirokogoroff employed physiometry in order to map cultural resiliance, or in chapters 3 and 4, that Volkov used linguistic data to understand how physical types were formed. To capture this ambiguity we have employed the term "biosocial" — a term that admitedly for some might imply that *etnos* thinking was more racial than constructivist. With this term we are trying to capture a recent change in Euro-American science, which is exploring new ways of melding the biological and social. These range from the realm of "nature-culture" in Haraway (1991), to "biosociality" (Rabinow 2010), and "biosocial becomings" (Ingold and Palsson 2013). From this point of view, the unique geographically-inflected way that early Russian scholars approached physical and cultural identities appears to be ahead of its time. By "biosocial" we refer to an approach that understands that group identity embodies the landscapes, languages and material technical objects around it. This is the reverse of a racial hypothesis, which would assume that certain physical traits set limits on how individuals can cope with their environment.

---

2 In Russian-language translations of English-language research in history and political science, the term *ethnie* championed by Anthony Smith (1986) is overwhelmingly translated as *etnos*. Smith's *ethnie* is often cited as a hallmark case of primordialism. See for example Kappeler (2000: 11) and Khosking (2001).

Etnos and Contemporary Identity Movements

Although this book is primarily based on archival and historical research, it has been motivated to a great extent by our awareness that *etnos* thinking plays an important role in Eurasian societies today. Each of the co-editors have conducted fieldwork across Russia — sometimes in the same communities where Shirokogoroff, Mogilīanskiĭ, and Rudenko worked (Anderson 2000; Anderson 2011; Alymov 2011; Arzyutov 2017; Arzyutov 2018). To signal the contemporary importance of this biosocial theory we have included two ethnographic case studies to conclude the volume.

In chapter 7, Jocelyne Dudding describes her experiences, and those of our group, in sharing the fieldwork images collected both by the Shirokogoroffs and the British-trained social anthropologist Ethel Lindgren in the former Manchurian highlands of what is now China. The descendants of the contemporary Evenkis and Orochens who once spoke with Shirokogoroff and Lindgren have been resettled several times since then, and now live in communities quite far from the larch forests of the "Three Rivers Region". Given the tumultuous modern history of the People's Republic, these black and white images provide a rare and tangible insight into a proud past. The Shirokogoroffs, and Lindgren, selected the subjects for their portraits based on the cultural evolutionary assumptions of their fieldwork projects, which aimed on the whole to document types of adaptation and levels of culture. One hundred years later, as Dudding notes, these images have become "reanimated" both with remembered stories and new narratives of community resilience. Likely neither Lindgren nor Shirokogoroff anticipated that their fieldwork tools would come alive for future generations. This remarkable example demonstrates how this fieldwork-driven science of mapping *etnoses* has created an archive that enlivens and recreates those same identities.

In the final substantive chapter to the volume, chapter 8, Masha Shaw and Nathalie Wahnsiedler return to one of the imperial frontiers where the definition of concrete *etnoses* was never clear. Working among modern Pomors, a newly "indigenous" Russian-speaking group along the coasts of the White Sea, Shaw and Wahnsiedler document how *etnos* thinking is mobilized by contemporary political activists to defend the subsistence rights of local Pomors. The chapter examines how Pomor identity has always been a challenge for imperial, Soviet, and post-Soviet scholars. In different contexts, the unique dialect and ways of life of this maritime people have been described as being, variously, a "most authentic", example of Russian-ness, a creole mixture of indigenous "Chud'" and Finno-ugric people, a *subetnos*, which never seems to achieve the status of being a "big" *etnos*, or the markers of an indigenous people in their own right. This concluding chapter demonstrates how Pomors have served as an important limiting case to illustrate *etnos* thinking. When read together with southern Russian or Ukrainian examples, this northern outlier helps to frame the identity of Russians living in the central regions of the Russian Federation.

This volume presents 150 years of *etnos* thinking in a variety of contexts. The chapters take us between urban seminar rooms to nomadic camps, from dusty archives to remote villages. Despite being at times a controversial theory with its insistence on a bodily coherence to cultural identity, *etnos* theory has proven to be remarkably resilient. During the early Soviet period — when it was officially discouraged — *etnos* thinking lived a hidden life in discussions of nationality. After the collapse of the Soviet Union, the concept took root outside of the walls of the Academy, and has become one of the key terms of public debate over identity governance in Russia and in China. Using a variety of sources, from the archival to the ethnographic, this volume tries to build an alternative history of a relatively unknown and sometimes unloved concept, which plays an important role today in revitalizing societies throughout Eurasia.

Published References

Abashin, S. N. 2014. 'Ethnogenesis and Historiography: Historical Narratives for Central Asia, 1940s-1950s', in *An Empire of Others*, ed. by R. Cvetkovski, and A. Hofmeister (Budapest: CEU Press).

Alekseev, V. P., and I. U. V. Bromleĭ. 1968. 'K izucheniîu roli pereselenii narodov v formirovanii novykh ėtnicheskikh obshchnosteĭ', *Sovetskaîa Ėtnografiîa* 2: 35–45.

Alymov, S. S. 2011. 'On the Soviet Ethnography of the Soviet Life: The Case of the "Village of Viriatino"', *Histories of Anthropology Annual* 7: 23–48, https://doi.org/10.1353/haa.2011.0011.

Anderson, D. G. 2000. *Identity and Ecology in Arctic Siberia: The Number One Reindeer Brigade* (Oxford: Oxford University Press).

—. 2011. 'Shamanistic Revival in a Post-Socialist Landscape: Luck and Ritual among Zabaikal Orochen-Evenkis', in *Landscape and Culture in Northern Eurasia*, ed. by P. Jordan (Walnut Creek, CA: Left Coast), 71–95.

—. and D. Arzyutov. Forthcoming. 'The Etnos Archipelago: Sergeĭ M. Shirokogoroff and the Life History of a Controversial Anthropological Concept', *Current Anthropology*.

Arzyutov, D. V. 2017. 'Oleni i/ili benzin: ėsse ob obmenakh v severo-îamal'skoĭ tundre', in *Sotsial'nye otnosheniîa v istoriko-kul'turnom landshafte Sibiri*, ed. by V. N. Davydov (St Petersburg: MAĖ RAN), 314–48.

Arzyutov, D. V. 2018. 'Voices of the Land, Samizdat, and Visionary Politics: On the Social Life of Altai Narratives', *Anthropology & Archeology of Eurasia* 57 (1): 38–81, https://doi.org/10.1080/10611959.2018.1470426.

Banks, M. 1996. *Ethnicity: Anthropological Constructions* (New York: Routledge).

Bassin, M. 2016. *The Gumilev Mystique: Biopolitics, Eurasianism, and the Construction of Community in Modern Russia* (Ithaca, NY: Cornell University Press).

Bromleĭ, ÎU. V. 1973. *Ėtnos i ėtnografiîa* (Moscow: Nauka).

—. 1988. 'Teoriîa ėtnosa', in *Svod ėtnograficheskikh poniatiĭ i terminov. Vyp.2: Ėtnografiîa i smezhnye dist͡sipliny*, ed. by ÎU. V. Bromleĭ (Moscow: Nauka), 41–53.

Bromley, Y. V. 1969. 'Major Trends in Ethnographic Research in the USSR', *Soviet Anthropology and Archeology* 8 (1): 3–42, https://doi.org/10.2753/AAE1061-195908013.

—. 1974. 'The Term Ethnos and its Definition', in *Soviet Ethnology and Anthropology Today*, ed. by Yu. Bromley (The Hague: de Gruyter), 55–72.

—. 1979. 'Subject Matter and Main Trends of Investigation of Culture by Soviet Ethnographers', *Arctic Anthropology* 16 (1): 46–61.

Gellner, E. 1975. 'The Soviet and the Savage', *Current Anthropology* 16 (4): 595–617.

—. 1977. 'Ethnicity and Anthropology in the Soviet Union', *European Journal of Sociology* 18 (2): 201–20.

—. 1980. 'A Russian Marxist Philosophy of History', in *Soviet and Western Anthropology*, ed. by E. Gellner (London: Duckworth), 59–82.

—. 1988. 'Modern Ethnicity', in *State and Society in Soviet Thought*, ed. by E. Gellner (Oxford: Blackwell), 115–36.

Glover, D. M., S. Harrell, C. F. McKhann, and M. B. Swain. 2012. *Explorers and Scientists in China's Borderlands, 1880–1950* (Seattle, WA: University of Washington Press).

Guldin, G. E. 1994. *The Saga of Anthropology in China: From Malinowski to Moscow to Mao* (London: Sharpe).

Gullette, D. 2008. 'A State of Passion: The Use of Ethnogenesis in Kyrgyzstan', *Inner Asia* 10 (2): 261–79, https://doi.org/10.1163/000000008793066768.

Gumilëv, L. N. 1965. 'Po povodu predmeta istoricheskoĭ geografii: (Landshaft i ėtnos): III' *Vestnik Leningradskogo universiteta* 3 (18): 112–20.

—. 1967. 'O termine "ėtnos"', in *Doklady otdeleniĭ komissiĭ Geograficheskogo obshchestva SSSR*, ed. by V. A. Beli͡avskiĭ (Leningrad: Prezidium GO SSSR), 3–17.

Haraway, D. 1991. *Simians, Cyborgs and Women: The Reinvention of Nature* (London: Free Association).

Hosking, G. A. 1997. *Russia: People and Empire, 1552–1917* (Cambridge, MA: Harvard University Press).

Ingold, T., and G. Palsson. 2013. *Biosocial Becomings: Integrating Social and Biological Anthropology* (Cambridge: Cambridge University Press).

Kappeler, A. 2000. *Rossii͡a — mnogonat͡sional'nai͡a imperii͡a. Vozniknovenie, istorii͡a, raspad* (Moscow: Tradit͡sii͡a).

—. 2001. *The Russian Empire: A Multi-Ethnic History* (New York: Pearson).

Khosking, D. 2001. *Rossii͡a: narod i imperii͡a (1552–1917)* (Smolensk: Rusich).

Knight, N. 2017. 'Geography, Race and the Malleability of Man: Karl von Baer and the Problem of Academic Particularism in the Russian Human Sciences', *Centaurus* 59 (1–2): 97–121, https://doi.org/10.1111/1600-0498.12154.

Lachenicht, S. 2011. 'Ethnicity', in *Oxford Bibliographies Online* (Oxford: Oxford University Press), https://doi.org/10.1093/OBO/9780199730414-0022.

Leibold, J. 2007. *Reconfiguring Chinese Nationalism: How the Qing Frontier and its Indigenes Became Chinese* (Basingstoke: Palgrave).

Lieven, D. 2006. 'Russia as Empire and Periphery', in *The Cambridge History of Russia: Volume 2, Imperial Russia, 1689–1917*, ed. by M. Perrie, D. Lieven, and R. G. Suny (Cambridge: Cambridge University Press), 9–26.

Mogil͡anskiĭ, N. M. 1916. 'Predmet i zadachi ėtnografii', *Zhiva͡ia starina* 25: 1–22.

Mühlfried, F., and S. Sokolovskiy. 2011. *Exploring the Edge of Empire: Soviet Era Anthropology in the Caucasus and Central Asia* (Berlin: Lit).

Oushakine, S. A. 2010. 'Somatic Nationalism: Theorizing Post-Soviet Ethnicity in Russia', in *In Marx's Shadow: Knowledge, Power, and Intellectuals in Eastern Europe and Russia*, ed. by C. Brădățan and S. Oushakine (Plymouth: Lexington), 155–74.

Rabinow, P. 2010. 'Artificiality and Enlightenment: From Sociobiology to Biosociality', *Politix* 2: 21–46.

Semyonov, A. 2009. '"The Real and Live Ethnographic Map of Russia": The Russian Empire in the Mirror of the State Duma', in *Empire Speaks Out: Languages of Rationalization and Self-Description in the Russian Empire*, ed. by I. Gerasimov, J. Kusber, and A. Semyonov (Leiden: Brill), 191–228.

Shanin, T. 1986. 'Soviet Theories of Ethnicity: The Case of a Missing Term', *New Left Review* 158: 113.

—. 1989. 'Ethnicity in the Soviet Union: Analytical Perceptions and Political Strategies', *Comparative Study of Society and History* 31: 409–38.

Shirokogorov, S. M. 1923. *Ėtnos — issledovanie osnovnykh prin͡tsipov izmenenii͡a ėtnicheskikh i ėtnograficheskikh i͡avleniĭ* (Shanghai: Sibpress).

Skalník, P. 2007. 'Gellner vs Marxism: A Major Concern or a Fleeting Affair?', in *Ernest Gellner and Contemporary Social Thought*, ed. by S. Malešević, and M. Haugaard (Cambridge: Cambridge University Press), 103–21.

Smith, A. D. 1986. *The Ethnic Origins of Nations* (Oxford: Blackwell).

Tolz, V. 2001. *Russia: Inventing the Nation* (London: Bloomsbury).

Weiner, M. 1997. 'The Invention of Identity: Race and Nation in Pre-War Japan', in *The Construction of Racial Identities in China and Japan: Historical and Contemporary Perspectives*, ed. by F. Dikötter (Honolulu, HI: Hurst), 96–117.

Yen, H.-P. 2012. *Constructing the Chinese: Paleoanthropology and Anthropology in the Chinese Frontier, 1920–1950* (unpublished doctoral dissertation, Harvard University).

2. *Etnos* Thinking in the Long Twentieth Century

Sergei S. Alymov, David G. Anderson and Dmitry V. Arzyutov

In *The Age of Extremes*, the historian Eric Hobsbawm (1995) argued that "the short twentieth century" ended with the breakup of the Soviet Union. This epoch-defining event cast into doubt major ideologies such as the Soviet-led communist movement, as well as *laissez-faire* free-market capitalism — but it also called into question the effectiveness of expert knowledge. Unprecedented nationalist unrest preceded the fragmenting of the Soviet Union into a collage of new European and Eurasian republics. Another historian dubbed this fragmentation "the revenge of the past" (Suny 1993), as if long-term pre-existing ethnic identities had somehow outlived and triumphed over a centralized and technocratic state. In the mid-1990s it seemed impossible to gain a long-term perspective over this explosive part-century, but it now seems self-evident that ethnic and national identities have held, and continue to exercise a hold, on social order in this region, if not elsewhere. If the end of the short twentieth century is marked by the collapse of the Soviet national project, the long twentieth century can be associated with the uneven and discontinuous growth of the use of *etnos* categories within the Soviet/Russian academy, the government, and finally throughout civil society.

 https://doi.org/10.11647/OBP.0150.02

This chapter provides a detailed overview of the development of *etnos* thinking from the end of the nineteenth century, through its various incarnations in the Soviet period, to the present day.[1] A difficult and to some degree clumsy part of this story has been the uneven valences of the *etnos* term itself. Aside from the fact that *etnos* was always the defining prefix in words like *ėtnografia*, there were periods of time when the use of the substantive term was discouraged, if not banned outright. Unlike other investigators, such as the cultural historian Han Vermeulen (2015; 1995), we do not place primacy on the prefix itself. Instead, we locate *etnos* thinking in the contexts where expert observers attribute to themselves the ability to discern long-term yet flexible biosocial identities within the matrix of everyday life. In certain periods of time, most significantly in the late nineteenth century, and during the Stalinist academy, the *etnos* term was completely absent — but *etnos* thinking was tangible in the way that terms like *narodnost'* (nationality) or *narod* (people) were used. As outlined in the introduction, we concur that I͡Ulian Bromleĭ led a "minor revolution" in reintroducing the term in the late Soviet period. In short, *etnos* thinking is not only present when then the term is used overtly. It is also recognizable when more familiar terms such as "tribe", "nationality", or "nation" are applied by experts.

In perhaps the most authoritative study of the cultural technologies of rule at the beginning of the Soviet period, Francine Hirsch describes how the "vocabulary of nationality" allowed two different groups to use "the same words to talk about different things" (Hirsch 2005: 35–36). In Hirsh's view, this shared paradigm permitted Tsarist intellectuals to negotiate an alliance with the rising Soviet state, allowing them to launch long-sought-after projects such as a modern census or a Union-wide mapping project. We argue that talk about nations and about *etnoses* are often two sides of the same coin — where one face is an unrooted scientific discourse while the other is its complement of engaged ethnographic action in building or rebuilding ethnic communities.

Etnos thinking, therefore, is obvious when it is overtly discussed, as in Bromleĭ's multiple monographs in the 1970s and 1980s. It is also implicit in the way that expert ethnographers in the late 1880s and the early Soviet period assumed the existence of discrete nations and

1 An earlier draft of this chapter was published in *Ab Imperio* 19 (1) 2018 as "Life Histories of the *Etnos* Concept in Eurasia".

nationalities. However, there are very few pithy definitions of the term. In the introduction to this volume we specified five key qualities of *etnos* thinking that one can extract from a variety of different definitions of the term, and here we provide a map of how *etnos* thinking has developed in the Russian academy. The structure of this chapter is therefore formally chronological, conveying, perhaps, a misleading impression that *etnos* thinking unfolded logically and inevitably within several Eurasian states. However, our intention here is simply to provide a set of guideposts to the development of Eurasian anthropology. In the sections that follow, which on the whole focus on the biographies of particular individuals and the life histories of their concepts, we hope to convey the contingency of the development of this sometimes controversial concept.

What's in a Term?: The *Etnos* Term and the Institutionalization of Ethnography in Russia

Anthropology has had a complicated and entangled history, which is evident in the variety of terms by which different regional traditions describe the ways that they study peoples, cultures, and societies. George Stocking, in his survey of western European traditions, identified three discourses that contributed to the formation of anthropology: biological discourse or "natural history", humanitarian discourse rooted in philology, and a social science that drew on the philosophical thought of the French and Scottish Enlightenments containing within it a strong interest in environmental determinism (Stocking 1992: 347). Eurasian anthropological traditions draw generally on the same trinity for inspiration.

The reasons for this shared history are understandable. In the late nineteenth and early twentieth centuries, many local scholars in St Petersburg, Moscow, Tōkyō, and Běijīng often received their training in one of the capitals of early anthropological thinking within western Europe or North America. Nevertheless, local idioms of identity also pull and reshape this common foundation in different ways. One of the most distinctive qualities of Eurasian anthropological thinking is that many competing strands of thought are bound into a single compact term. For example, as mentioned in the introduction, a single character — *mínzú* — is said to fuse together European notions of "race", *ethnie* and nation (Weiner 1997). In Russia, the Greek-inflected neologism *etnos* is commonly said to represent a *sovokupnost'* (a single totality of many parts). In this section we will explore how different biological, geographical, and humanitarian arguments came to be bound together into a single toolkit represented by one word. This word, in turn, structured the way that ethnographic description was incorporated into Russian universities and museums, and in so doing created several generations of academics skilled in employing it.

The institutionalization of Russian ethnography is commonly associated with the establishment of the Imperial Russian Geographical Society (IRGO) in 1845, which at its very outset included a subdivision of ethnography (Knight 1995: 8; Semënov 1896: 37–40; Raĭkov 1961: 343–48). Imperial Russian practice did not diverge substantially from that in Europe at the time, with the Société Ethnologique being founded in Paris in 1839, and the Ethnological Society being established in London in 1842 (Vermeulen 1995: 39–40). Justin Stagl (1995) argues that, up until that time, travellers and other reporters demonstrated a "curiosity" about cultural difference without establishing a coherent methodology for documenting it. Vermeulen (2015; 2008), in his masterly overviews of the history of Eurasian anthropologies, links the ethnographic intuition to the very first published appearances of what he calls "ethnos-terms" (or, perhaps more accurately, ethnos prefixes) within the words *ethnologie, ethnologia,* and *ethnographie* between 1770 and 1780. A key actor in this late eighteenth-century movement was August Ludwig Schlözer (1735–1809), whose work was influenced by the descriptive "folk typologies" of Gerhard Friedrich Müller (1705–1783), which built heavily on reports from Russia, Siberia and Mongolia.

It is our contention that with the founding of the Ethnographic Division of the IRGO in 1845, Russian ethnographic practice took a slightly different trajectory than the other European societies. Struggling to place itself within the visions of two influential individuals, and thereby define itself as the study of Slavic peoples, or non-Slavic peoples, Russian ethnographers gradually adopted what we describe as a biosocial quality, which distinguished their work from the then-developing European and North American traditions. To be clear, we do not read into this biosocial turn a conviction that biophysically-defined races of people were forever propelled (or limited) by their mental capacity, or physical stamina. Instead, we argue that several generations of scholars distilled an *etnos* concept that mixed together biophysical and humanitarian arguments to create a vision of human communities that were enduring, internally consistent, and yet open to change.

Much as Stocking (1971) tells the story of the founding of the Royal Anthropological Society as the struggle between two men, the Ethnographical Division of the IRGO also structured its work around two individuals (Knight 1995; Tokarev 1966): the anatomist and embryologist Karl Ernst von Baer (1792–1876) and the philosopher Nikolaĭ I. Nadezhdin (1804–1856). Following Nathaniel Knight, we will argue that their approaches can be distinguished by their "imperial" and "nationalistic" interests.

Von Baer's imperialistic vision can be read in his original application to the emperor to establish an ethnographic section within the IRGO. His appeal emphasized the importance of "preserving" historical information, of discovering "ethnographic laws", and of updating imperial knowledge of all of the peoples inhabiting this vast continental empire (Knight 1995: 22). Von Baer's vision of ethnography was inspired by the need to link race and geography to human diversity, and this naturalistic vision steadily gathered adherents. As early as 1852, Timofeĭ I. Granovskiĭ (1813–1855) — a historian known as the "leader of the Westernizers" — argued the need to make an alliance between history and the natural sciences in order to specify the effect of geography on the human form (Levandovskiĭ 1989: 211–12). Meanwhile the most prominent Russian historian of the mid-nineteenth century, Sergeĭ M. Solov'ëv (1820–1879), embraced the geographical determinism of German geographer Carl Ritter (1779–1859) and the positivistic "organismic metaphor", i.e. a view of societies as "biological organisms" (Bassin 1993).

Granovskiĭ and Solov'ëv were among the first Russian scholars inspired by naturalistic approaches to history and society, an enthusiasm that was connected to the growing popularity of the concept of race. By the 1860s, famous Russian historians and thinkers, such as Ivan S. Aksakov (1823–1886), Nikolaĭ I. Kareev (1850–1931), and many others, experimented with the concept, although using it rather unsystematically to denote "linguistic races", tribes and "breeds" of people. Vera Tol't͡s argues that even Nadezhdin mentioned the importance of studying the physical characteristics of human "breeds", although she notes that the popularity of the concept increased only in the 1880–1890s (Kholl 2012; Tol'ts͡ 2012).

Nadezhdin is credited with developing the first published research programme to document Eastern Slavic/Russian identity (Nadezhdin 1847). He was strongly influenced by the German romantic historians Johann Herder and Friedrich Schelling as he strove to define "a unique and immutable essence which revealed itself first and foremost in the creative expression of the common folk" (Knight 1998: 120). His work centred around the category *narodnost'* — a word introduced into Russian at the beginning of the nineteenth century to translate the French term *nationalité* (Miller 2015). In Nadezhdin's usage, however, the term came to mean the qualities of what make up the Russian people "a totality" (*sovokupnost'*) of "what makes a Russian Russian" (Knight 1998: 118).

This term eventually took on a rich set of meanings that extended well beyond its original usage. At the height of its influence in the mid-nineteenth century, *narodnost'* became incorporated as one of the three central pillars that defined autocracy — a gloss often described as "official nationality" (Riasanovsky 1959; Zorin 2004). Nadezhdin and his colleagues searched for national essences broadly in the oral traditions, folklore, and songs of Russian peasants. The victory of the "Russian faction" at the IRGO inspired local citizen-scientists to collect vast amounts of material on local lifeways and folklore through responding to questionnaires. The search for *narodnost'* at the IRGO resulted in such publications as Vladimir Dal's *Dictionary of the Great Russian Language* and Aleksandr N. Afanas'ev's collection of Russian folktales, which were fundamental for the Russian nation-building project (Tokarev 1966: 233–42).

The fault lines that initially ran through the institutionalization of ethnography within the IRGO are to some extent familiar to historians of western European anthropology. The division of effort between the study of one's own nation and the traditions of foreigners duplicates the German-language division between *Volkskunde* and *Völkerskunde* (Fischer 1970; Vermeulen 2015; Stagl 1998). However, unlike in western Europe, these branches of ethnography did not sit as two solitudes. As Knight points out, von Baer's wide-ranging, survey-generated positivism was an artefact of the imperial imagination of Russian ethnography:

> [...] the Russia [von Baer] had in mind was a vast and largely unexplored territory populated by a multitude of diverse nationalities some of whom were in danger of disappearing off the face of the earth. [...] He viewed it as the representative of general European civilization bringing 'enlightenment' to the primitive peoples under its domain. Ethnography, Baer suggested, could play an important role in ameliorating [...] destructive processes. By studying the natural processes of development at work among primitive peoples, scientists could determine the proper level of outside intervention [...] (Knight 1995: 90–91).

Thus, from the outset, scientistic, imperial ethnography had an applied edge that would only become accentuated in Soviet times. The hierarchical and applied ethnography of von Baer falls "within the boundaries of Western European ethnology" with its interest in developing so-called savage peoples (Knight 1995: 99).

Similarly, the "nationalist" and philological approach of Nadezhdin and his followers can be understood to be inward looking only at first glance. It must be remembered that Nadezhdin also proposed that ethnographers study a wide variety of "Russians", including Slavic peoples whom we today divide off as separate nations such as Belorussians and Malorussians (Ukrainians). He also stressed the importance of studying Russians beyond the Russian Empire in Galicia and Hungary (Nadezhdin 1847). In so doing, his nationalist project shaded into a transnational, imperial project. As Steven Seegel argues:

> Essentially, the society was an intelligence-gathering colonial institution and "think tank" for Russian empire building. Under the auspices of tsarist rule through the Ministry of Internal Affairs (MVD), Russian state scientists such as Pyotr Keppen and Pyotr Semyonov adopted German geographic and ethnographic models and found professional positions as academic and bureaucratic proponents of state modernization and empire building (Seegel 2012: 19).

One of the key functions of the IRGO was producing maps and cartographic knowledge of the borderlands and peripheries of the empire. The western border was especially important because of the need to legitimate the European periphery as an inseparable part of the imperial state and to neutralize the possibility of Polish and Malorussian demands for autonomy. The founding member of the IRGO, Pëtr Keppen, produced an Ethnographic Map of European Russia (1851) that implemented Germanic ideals of cultural nationalism. The map united Malorussians, Belarusians, and Russians by linguistic kinship and initiated a long series of maps that classified borderland identities according to languages, "tribes", and confessions. Thus, Russian imperial science actively opened the gates to the "floods of ethnographic maps, in which nationalities were postulated to hold a delicate imperial balance or make national-territorial claims by language, confession, culture, and history itself" (Seegel 2012: 134).

Despite these differences in constituency, and in methodology, both imperial and nationalist ethnologists each argued that ethnography should be much more closely integrated with the state than would have been the case in Europe or the Americas. This search for an imperial toolkit — still without a unifying term — would strongly influence the flavour of Russian ethnography. Arguably, it was the initial "organicistic" curiosity of Russian ethnographic science that opened an intellectual space where biologists, geographers, and linguistic could agree. The "races" of Granovskiĭ, Solov'ëv, and arguably von Baer (Knight 2017) were never the stiff biophysical containers of early twentieth-century racism, but instead were complex and coherent assemblages of perception, geographical condition and physical possibilities. Knight describes this constellation as a "particularistic strain within the Russian human sciences [that arose] out of a cluster of interrelated postulates concerning the sources of human diversity and the place of humanity in relation to the natural world" (Knight 2017: 115).

The next stage in the distillation of this concept came through the institutionalization of the discipline within Russian universities and museums. The government University Charter of 1884 included provision for "geography and ethnography". At the beginning, this dual-discipline sat within either the Faculty of History or the Faculty of Philology — somewhat reflecting the earlier ambivalent debates within the IRGO. In 1888, however, at the request of Moscow University, ethnography was reframed as a natural science within the Faculty of Physics and Mathematics (Alekseeva 1983). A key figure in this new development was the highly influential polymath scientist Dmitriĭ N. Anuchin (1843–1923), who taught ethnography alongside geography and physical anthropology at Moscow University. He wrote an important programme defining anthropology (as opposed to ethnography) as a broad discipline that incorporated ethnology among a range of topics, including the comparative anatomical and psychological study of human types, anthropogenesis, and an account of diversity (Anuchin 1889; Alymov 2004: 18–20). Anuchin's vision was reinforced in St Petersburg through the work of its first lecturer in geography and anthropology, Ėduard I͡U. Petri (1854–1899). Petri, whose life and work is described in more detail in chapter 3 of this volume, believed in a strong link between physiognomy and ethnography.

Nikolaĭ N. Kharuzin (1865–1900) provided an important counterbalance to the dominance of the naturalist outlook within the universities. Lecturing both at Moscow University and the Lazerev Institute of Oriental Languages, he distinguished ethnography as a science that "studies the way-of-life (*byt*) of tribes and peoples and strives to ascertain the laws of the development of humanity on the lowest stages of culture" (Kharuzin 1901: 37). He was a widely experienced fieldworker publishing ethnographic studies on Sámis (*Lopari*) and the Finno-Ugric peoples of Siberia. Kharuzin's approach staked out a middle ground between the nationalist focus on Slavic peoples and a more general interest in non-Russian peoples. This was reflected in the way that he packaged his ideas using the *etnos* term, written out using Greek letters, which he explained should be "understood not as a people in general, but in the sense of uncivilized, primitive nationalities, who constituted the subject of ethnography" (Ibid: 27). After his untimely death at the age of thirty-four, his lecture course at Moscow University was published by his sister and students in a four-volume set (Kerimova 2011: 143–315).

It is significant that those scholars who were inspired by Nadezhdin's humanist investigation of national spirit also organized within museums. Of particular importance was Lev I͡A. Shternberg (1861–1927), based in the Museum of Anthropology and Ethnography in St Petersburg, who was enthusiastic about the "humanistic" potential of ethnography, which he considered "the best teacher of civic consciousness" (Kan 2009: 177–80). As was the fashion of the time, he set out his vision in a long and heavily referenced encyclopaedia article (Shternberg 1904). This article, aside from decrying the terminological "chaos" caused by the continual renaming of ethnographic research across Europe, also made a strong case for a division of labour between physical anthropologists, archaeologists, and ethnographers. The latter he distinguished by their methods, using a rather modern description of what we would today call participant observation combined with what could be described as a unique interest in the "cultural production" (*dukhovnoe tvorchestvo*) of primitive peoples. It is an interesting footnote that Shternberg, following Kharuzin, also cited the Greek language roots of ethnography in his 1904 encyclopaedia article; however unlike Kharuzin, he put the emphasis on the descriptive (*-graphii͡a*) portion of this key term.

It is important to mention that the naturalists fought their corner within the museum sector as well. Nikolaĭ M. Mogili͡anskiĭ (1871–1933), who is often cited as the first to distinguish *etnos* as a standard object of scientific research, raised his objections to the humanist programme while working as curator in the Russian Museum. In a lecture read out at a meeting of the Anthropological Society of St Petersburg University in 1902 (published later in 1908), he reviewed Kharuzin's posthumous volume *Ėtnografii͡a* with an eye to defining ethnography as a distinct science subsumed within (physical) anthropology. He saw ethnography as documenting the intellectual and spiritual achievements of distinct races and peoples, which were adapted to a defined geographical space (Mogili͡anskiĭ 1908: 12). Later, as he became the head of ethnography at the museum, he reworked his earlier review into a broad outline of concepts of ethnology. Here we have an early formulation of the now ubiquitous definition of *etnos* (spelled with Greek letters [ἔθνος]) as

> [...] a group of individuals united together as a single whole [*odno tseloe*] by [...] common physical (anthropological) characteristics; a common historical fate, and finally a common language. These are the foundations upon which, in turn, [an *etnos*] can build a common worldview [and] folk-psychology — in short, an entire spiritual culture (Mogili͡anskiĭ 1916: 11).

A particularly strong statement in the title of this article distinguishes *etnos* as *the* "object" of ethnography. Given Mogili͡anskiĭ's career as a museum ethnographer, and his fieldwork as a collector of evocative items that represent the heart of a nation, it is tempting to read his bookish definition as a statement that ethnography can be read through objects.

After 1916, the five core elements of Mogilı͡anskiĭ's diffuse, prosaic definition (a single collective identity; a physical foundation; a common language; a common set of traditions or destiny; and a common worldview) would appear in successive descriptions of Russian and Eurasian *etnos* theory for the next 100 years. In particular, the pamphlets and book-length monograph published by Sergei Shirokogoroff in China and the Russian Far East (described in more detail in chapter 5) would be built around these same five elements (Shirokogorov 1922a, 1923).

It would not be entirely accurate to say that the nationalists and the imperialists reached a rapprochement through their common search for a single toolkit to describe both Slavic and non-Slavic peoples within the empire. From the start of World War I, and then during the two Russian revolutions, one can only describe a discordant collage of competing techniques. During the war, the newly appointed liberal minister of education, Pavel N. Ignatiev (1870–1945), initiated a fresh debate on the institutionalization of ethnography with his unsuccessful attempt to standardize university education (Dmitriev 2010). A revealing set of memoranda in the Archive of the Russian Geographical Society (NA RGO 109-1-15) gives an insight into the range of the debate. Elements of this debate can also be tracked in a published summary of a meeting of the Society (Zhurnal zasedanii͡a 1916).

Shternberg, representing the humanists, called for a clear division between anthropologists, who should study the science of the human body, and ethnographers, whom he saw as studying the history of the human spirit and culture (Kan 2009: 232–37). As Sergei Kan writes in his detailed biography of Shternberg, the war years were the period when Shternberg was able to articulate his long-standing ideas publicly. Thus, Shternberg expressed his dissatisfaction with the fact that ethnography was still taught in some institutions by naturalists, and described this as:

> [...] a survival of the distant past when anthropologists, educated mostly as zoologists, followed their lead in studying the way of life of species [...] [They] considered ethnography to be the description of the way of life of primitive peoples, which was supposed to be an appendix to anthropological morphology of human varieties (NA RGO 109-1-15: 3).

It was not the first time that Shternberg called for an improvement in the organization of Russian ethnography. The same problem had been discussed during the Twelfth Congress of the Russian Natural Scientists, held in Moscow from December 1909 until January 1910. In his presentation at the Section of Geography, Ethnography, and Anthropology, Shternberg suggested establishing a centralised ethnographic bureau and chairs of ethnography in historical-philological divisions of major universities. Even as he presented his proposals at that meeting, other members of the Ethnographic Division of the IRGO challenged his ideas. As Kan summarizes the results of the discussions, "there was no agreement on the question of which department — a scientific or a humanistic one — such *kafedras* should be affiliated with, nor was there much consensus on their curriculum" (Kan 2009: 185).

The disagreement was resumed in 1915–1916. Our erstwhile inventor of *etnos* theory, Mogili͡anskiĭ, countered Shternberg's claim and defended the role of the naturalism in ethnography:

> A naturalist should in no way refuse to study the everyday life [*byt*] [of people]. He cannot limit his task to the morphology of the brain. He must trace its functions to their ends (psycho-physiology) and to their final results be they articulate speech, [or] the experience of the sacred [*kult*] stemming from a worldview and religious consciousness. [He must study] clothing as a material object and as the final result of complex intellectual and physical labour (NA RGO 109-1-15: 11).

In Mogili͡anskiĭ's view, every ethnographer needs a solid training in the natural sciences, including training in morphology, physiology, and psychophysiology, as well as geodynamics, geomorphology and paleontology (NA RGO 109-1-15: 12).

Mogili͡anskiĭ's view was buttressed by the elderly statesman of physical anthropology and ethnography in St Petersburg, Fëdor Volkov (Vovk), whose work is discussed in detail in chapter 3. In his own memo, Volkov concluded in a somewhat irritated manner that "there has been no doubt, so far, that ethnography belongs to the anthropological and, hence, natural sciences both [in Russia] and in Western Europe" (NA RGO 109-1-15: 5). He continued to make sarcastic remarks about the mistakes that historians make when they try to do archaeological and ethnographic research by applying an "elastic" concept of the history of culture that included "not only ethnography, but astronomy, canonical law, veterinary and what not" (Ibid: 8). In their arguments both Volkov and Mogili͡anskiĭ relied on the model of the Société d'anthropologie de

Paris, established by Paul Broca in 1859. Broca's "general anthropology", which he defined as "the biology of human species", was divided into six subfields, which included demography, ethnology, and linguistic anthropology, and thus "subsumed the cultural study of man within the physical study of man" (Vermeulen 2015: 7–8; Conklin 2013).

This debate led to no conclusive result. The 1917 revolution shifted the agenda, if not the opponents. Volkov and Mogilianskiĭ, who strictly opposed the Bolsheviks, moved to Kiev in 1918. Volkov died the same year. Mogilianskiĭ soon found himself as an émigré in Paris. Shternberg and Vladimir Bogoraz, who supported the revolution, opened a historically and philologically minded faculty of ethnography within the State Institute of Geography in December 1918. In a few years' time, the Institute became the Faculty of Geography of Leningrad State University, wherein Shternberg and Bogoraz established the Leningrad school of ethnography (Gagen-Torn 1971; Ratner-Shternberg 1935). Although at first glance it would seem that the evolutionist and humanist view of the discipline prevailed over the naturalists, it should be remembered that Volkov's students, Sergeĭ Rudenko, David Zolotarëv (1885–1935), and arguably Sergei Shirokogoroff, occupied prominent positions in Russian anthropology and ethnography until the late 1920s when a new cultural revolution moved the goalposts once again.

The institutionalization of ethnography in Russia in the second half of the nineteenth century rehearsed several themes common to the history of ethnographic and ethnological thought across Europe and North America. From 1840–1920 there was an ongoing debate as to the extent to which ethnographers should document little-known, non-industrial societies, and the extent to which they should uncover the hidden psychological spirit of their own people. Scholars also diverged on the extent to which physiognomy and physical geography could be credited in the production of culture. However, perhaps in a manner that diverged from the early ethnographic debates in western Europe and in the Americas, early Russian ethnographers produced programmes that fed into state-controlled projects for improving the lives of non-Russian nationalities and for defining the imperial state. This political pressure, which only increased after the revolution, created an imperative to come up with a single term — a single object of ethnographic analysis — which Mogilianskiĭ had already baptised as *etnos*. Although debates continued, this single compact term began to unite diverging opinions into what can be identified as a biosocial synthesis.

Etnos and Biosocial Science in Russia

At the turn of the twentieth century, there was marked disagreement among Russian scholars about the extent to which geography and biology should be seen to structure the science of man. However, there was a remarkable agreement that ethnographers should study *etnoses*, and that therefore *etnoses* were to some extent tangible units. There remained considerable variety over the types of data that practitioners collected. Volkov and his students placed their energy on documenting anthropological types, but as chapter 3 shows, they felt that linguistic and cultural data gave important clues as to how physical forms changed. Shternberg and his students placed their emphasis on documenting language and material culture, but they felt that cultural patterns were grounded in organic national psychologies that could be linked to specific regions. There was broad agreement that social agency was packaged biologically.

What we identify as a biosocial synthesis is not simply a compromise between warring schools, but instead reflects a particular epistemic constellation in Russia at this time that asserted that advances in biology and the life sciences could promote social and spiritual progress. As Mark B. Adams (1990) has argued, the period of 1900–1930 in Russia was characterized by "an almost unparalleled profusion of new interdisciplinary theories and fields", including Vladimir I. Vernadskiĭ's "biogeochemistry", Pëtr P. Lasarev's "biological physics", Nikolaĭ I. Vavilov's "science of selection", and even a proposal for the creation of a "plant sociology" (Adams 1990: 158). Daniel Beer (2008), who studied the development of Russian psychiatry and life sciences from 1880–1930, describes this development as follows:

> Building on the traditional association between the body and society in Christianity, the life sciences were particularly well equipped to offer indirect commentaries on the nature of Russia's social relations and its evolution as a state. The two paradigms — biological and social — merged, and the object of medical science and the object of social science were defined in the course of mutual projection (Beer 2008: 29).

Beer also shows that in fin-de-siècle Russia the biosocial alliance also led to theories of degeneration, criminal anthropology, and crowd psychology. Neo-Lamarckian theories of heredity flourished instead of Darwinian analyses of struggles for existence (Graham 2016). Anthropology was among the disciplines that found itself right at the epicentre of this movement.

The debates surrounding the foundation of the Russian Anthropological Society of St Petersburg University in 1888 nicely illustrate this dialogue. One of the society's first meetings was devoted to the discussion of Pëtr F. Lesgaft's presentation "On the Methods of Anthropological Research". He criticized the inaccuracy and fruitlessness of craniological and other anthropological measurements and offered instead a complex social model wherein the physical environment and a child's upbringing created certain "character types" (Russkoe Antropologicheskoe Obshchestvo 1889: 13). Although this project was criticized by Anuchin, and ultimately abandoned, the themes of "degeneration" and "criminal types" continued to be discussed during the early years of the society's existence.

These debates were carried out as part of the process of the institutionalization of physical anthropology — perhaps the most biological of the "biosocial" sciences. The first professional Russian physical anthropologists like Anuchin, Anatoliĭ P. Bogdanov, and Petri made their careers within learned societies (such as Moscow's Society for Enthusiasts (*li͡ubiteli*) of Natural Sciences, Anthropology, and Ethnography, established in 1863) and in universities (the first chair of anthropology was established in Moscow in 1879). In her recent cultural history of Russian physical anthropology, Marina Mogilner defines this science as a "hybrid field of knowledge that exemplified the highest ambitions of modern natural and social sciences to uncover objective laws governing both nature and societal organisms and to influence both" (Mogilner 2013: 3).

Mogilner's study suggests an ambiguous position of race and race science in the Russian Empire. On the one hand, race was more widespread as a category than has been observed by the research paradigm that stressed the empire's uniqueness or backwardness. On the other hand, "this empire was reluctant to offer its anthropologists unambiguous political support and to make physical anthropology an official science of imperialism" (Mogilner 2013: 5). Russian physical anthropologists, meanwhile, demonstrated a variety of approaches to conceptualizing race. Mogilner distinguishes the dominant liberal approach, with its central category of mixed racial type and clear distinction between race and culture (led by Anuchin, the dean of Russian anthropology); the anthropology of the Russian imperial nationalism of Ivan A. Sikorskiĭ (1842–1919), who tried to equate the "Russian race" and nation; and the anthropology of various non-Russian national projects, which tended to connect a "physical type" to a "nation", exemplified, among others, by Volkov's anthropology of Ukrainians (Mogilner 2013: 202).

Another source of biosocial ideas lay in ethnography's close alliance with geography. As outlined above, ethnography was often combined with geography within a single department — and the section was distinguished within the IRGO. The German geographer and anthropologist Friedrich Ratzel (1844–1904) was widely read and appreciated in turn-of-the-century Russia. Ratzel was an honorary member of the Russian Anthropological Society and corresponded with Russian anthropologists through his student Bruno Adler (1874–1942). One of Ratzel's most notorious concepts, which informed *etnos* thinking, was that of the *lebensraum* (living space), which he applied equally to plants, animals, and peoples (*Volker*). As the historian of German science Woodruff D. Smith (1980: 54) puts it: "the Lebensraum concept, [...] was the idea that, like a plant, a *Volk* had to grow and expand its *Lebensraum* or die". As outlined in chapter 5, the territorial quality of cultural adaptation was a motif that attracted many *etnos* pioneers such as Sergei Shirokogoroff.

Another powerful source of geographical thinking came from several early proto-Eurasianist thinkers. Slavophile philosophers like Nikolaĭ I͡A. Danilevskiĭ (1822–1885) and Vladimir Lamanskiĭ (1833–1914) fought with modernizers who felt that Russia should adopt European institutions. Instead, they argued that culturally, and racially, Russia gained its social and political strength from its deep roots in the unbroken continental landmass of Asia flowing into Europe and thereby held a separate destiny (Bassin 2003). The anthropological study of Siberian peoples was an important part of their argument (Bassin 1991). The historian and philologist Lamanskiĭ was an especially important actor in this movement, since he served as the head of the Ethnographic

Division of the IRGO and edited its flagship ethnographic journal *Zhivaı͡a starina*. Among other things he was also active in stabilising the regional classification of the Russian Empire for the authoritative ethnographic expositions in the Russian Museum (Cvetkovski 2014).

The most ardent proponent of Ratzel's anthropogeography was prominent statistician and geographer Veniamin Semënov-Tı͡an'-Shanskiĭ (1870–1942). In a widely cited paper entitled "The Power of Russia's Territorial Possessions" he mapped out a programme for documenting all botanical, zoological and social phenomena (Semënov-Tı͡an'-Shanskiĭ 1915). Perhaps sensing the power and evocativeness of Mogilı͡anskiĭ's distillation of the *etnos* concept, he presented a detailed criticism of Mogilı͡anskiĭ's published paper "The Object and Tasks of Ethnography", arguing that the ethnographic division of the IRGO should be renamed the Anthropogeographical Division (Zhurnal zasedaniı͡a 1916: 4).

Etnos and Soviet Marxism

There can be no clean break between the imperial-era reflections on biosocial science and Soviet social theory. Marxist and Proudhon-influenced socialist thinking was a strong feature of debates within intellectual circles throughout the turn of the century. Of particular interest — especially in Soviet-era histories of science — was the way in which Marx and Engels themselves used ethnography from the Russian Empire to think through examples of "primitive communism". In terms of this volume, it is interesting that these reflections were drawn from the very same regions that inspired *etnos* theorists — from descriptions of the Russian peasant commune (*mir*) (Watters 1968; Mironov 1985) or from Shternberg's writing on the Nivkh fishing and hunting society from the far east of Siberia (Grant 1999). A key concern of both the naturalist and philological strains within imperial ethnography was to understand how historical laws, destinies, and social evolution could be harnessed to improve the lives of impoverished peoples along the edges of empire. This liberal conviction folded easily into Soviet Marxist-Leninism.

The Bolshevik faction within the first post-revolutionary state Duma (parliament) was primarily focussed on taking state power in order to better distribute land and capital for the benefit of the peasants and the then small urban proletariat in cities. Their thinking was strategic, and they invested a great deal of effort in trying to understand how different nations within the empire could be co-opted into supporting the revolution. Their key term was not *etnos* but nation (*natsiia͡*).

The Russian Bolshevik notion of the nation was heavily influenced by European debates, and defined itself in opposition to the ideas of Austrian political thinkers Otto Bauer (1881–1938) and Karl Kautsky (1854–1938) in particular. The Austrian Social Democrats and the Jewish Socialist Party were among the first to realize the importance of "cultural-national autonomy". They argued for the recognition of a cultural autonomy for minorities regardless of the fact that they may not live in compact or easily defined territories (Bottomore and Goode 1978). Their argument based itself around an understanding of the nation that stressed the "personality principle", wherein the nation is constituted "not as a territorial corporation, but as an association of persons" (Bauer 2000 [1907]: 281). The Bolshevik's objection to this voluntaristic vision was sketched out in Iosif Stalin's famous pamphlet "Marxism and the National Question" (Stalin 1946 [1913]). Characteristically, Stalin outlined a much more holistic and territorially anchored definition of a nation than the Austrians, wherein a nation was seen as inhabiting a defined region (*oblast'*). Although he used the same Austrian lexica of nation and nationality, Stalin re-employed many of the key ideas of the imperial biosocial compromise — an awareness of a common language, culture, and psychological character — as well as a passing reference to the physiognomy of the nation. A little-noticed but significant turn of phrase was Stalin's reference to a type of "stable collectivity" (*obshchnost'*) (literally "the quality of being the same"). For almost sixty years *obshchnost'* would come to serve as a circumlocutory expression for all ethnic qualities which were persistent but could never really be called by their proper name. To a great extent, *etnos* thinking found a refuge for itself within this term for the many decades at the start of the Soviet period when it was officially discouraged.

It is important to remember that Stalin's 1913 intervention at first was just one minor voice in a symphony of discussion about ethnic identity. Mogilia͡nskiĭ first published his *etnos* concept in 1908 (Mogilia͡nskiĭ 1908) (see chapter 3). Shirokogoroff started developing his *etnos* concept between 1912 and 1914 — before first publishing it in a pamphlet form in 1922, alongside his parallel pamphlet on the nation (Shirokogorov 1922a, 1922b) (see chapter 6). However, by the late 1920s, as the Soviet state achieved hegemony, there was a movement to standardize thinking about the nation although even then there was more than one Marxist position. "Mechanists", like the naturalists before them, believed that the natural sciences can explain all social and geophysical phenomena. The "Bolshevisers" favoured the philosophical conviction that science should not measure nature but change it — perhaps staking out a position that was much more radical than that of the philological faction in imperial times (Bakhurst 1991: 28–47).

This relative pluralism ended with what Stalin himself labelled "the great break" (*velikiĭ perelom*) in an article in 1929 (Joravsky 1960). Among other disruptions, such as the restructuring of the Academy of Sciences and the acceleration of the collectivization of rural communities, there came a firm philosophical dictate that social laws should be shown to work independently of natural laws. Within ethnography, and the description of national policy, this placed a taboo on any direct reference to the social structures being linked to biological processes. As Adams has observed, this was epitomised by the emergence of a new pejorative term *biologizirovat'* (to biologize). He further reflected that "no field that linked the biological and the social survived the Great Break intact" (Adams 1990: 184). The sudden ideological turn of the late 1920s and early 1930s led to a devastating critique of "bourgeois" science, purges of many prominent ethnographers, and the creation of a new Marxist ethnographic literature that used only "sociological" or historical concepts (Alymov 2014; Slezkine 1991; Soloveĭ 2001).

The standardization, or purging, of bourgeois science occurred within prominent public meetings that were often thickly documented with sheaves of stenographic typescripts. For ethnographers, the two most important events were the Colloquium (*soveshchanie*) of Ethnographers of Leningrad and Moscow (held in Leningrad in April 1929) (K[oshkin] and M[atorin] 1929; Arzi͡utov, Alymov and Anderson 2014), and the All-Russian Archaeological-Ethnographic Colloquium (held in Leningrad in May 1932) (Rezoli͡ut͡sii͡a 1932). The resolutions of the first meeting signalled a determination to build a materialist Marxist ethnography on the basis of classical evolutionism and the notion of social-economic formations. The conclusion of the second meeting proclaimed that ethnography and archaeology could no longer exist as independent disciplines and subsumed both within the discipline of history — or to be more specific, the Marxist-Leninist study of the succession of socio-economic stages. The need to subsume ethnography under history was stated in particularly militant terms:

> [The proposal] that there exists a special "Marxist" ethnography is not only theoretically unjustified, but is deeply harmful, disorientating, and uses a leftish expression to cover up its rightist essence — that it is a type of bourgeois and petty-bourgeois adaptability and eclecticism (Rezoli͡ut͡sii͡a 1932: 13).

Ethnographers were now to study the "social laws" of pre-capitalist formations and create histories for the numerous nationalities of the USSR.

Each of these meetings sent a chill over biosocial research in the Soviet Union, and in particular, the overt use of the term *etnos*, which came to be associated with émigré and presumed anti-Soviet intellectuals. By this time both Mogili͡anskiĭ and Shirokogoroff had fled the Soviet Union and could be easily classified as "bourgeous" scholars. I͡An Koshkin, a Tungus linguist and ethnographer, specifically singled out Shirokogoroff's book on *etnos* during the Leningrad symposium as "antischolarly" (Arzi͡utov, Alymov, and Anderson 2014: 411). The young Sergeĭ Tolstov, who would later head the Institute of Ethnography of the Academy of Sciences, declared that:

> It is unfortunate that there is a tendency to associate with an *etnos* some sort of special meaning or to define ethnography as the science of the *etnos*. This is [a] harmful tendency and one we should fight. "Etnos" as a classless — or perhaps un-classlike (*vneklassovoe*) — formation is exactly what could serve as a banner [uniting] bourgeois and petty-bourgeois ideologists (Arzi͡utov, Alymov, and Anderson 2014: 142).

Nevertheless, even within these authoritative settings the transcripts show that others contradicted Tolstov and promoted opposing views. Some were recorded as stating that *etnos* and "ethnic culture" could be usefully confined to a particular historical stage of development, and that they therefore still remained the proper subject of ethnographers (Arzi͡utov, Alymov, and Anderson 2014: 149, 196, 199).

These sharp methodological strictures on biosocial thought had a very profound effect on physical anthropologists, whose discipline, by definition, sat on the border between the social and the biological. The editorial of the first issue of the new *Anthropological Journal* noted that the years 1930–1932 were "a time of intensive reorganization", and of "the revaluation of values". It called for a fight against racist "anthroposociology" and, in particular, against fascist theories that ignored the social essence of humans by transferring "biological laws to human society" (Za sovetskui͡u 1932: 2–3). A significant marker of the restructuring of physical anthropology came in an article in the same issue by Arkadiĭ I. I͡Arkho (1903–1935) who placed considerable distance between Soviet physical anthropologists and foreign racialists and eugenicists. Here, he explained that the development of the human form followed a different path than that of animals, wherein the importance of biological factors and "racial instincts" became muted and replaced by the influence of social formations (I͡Arkho 1932: 11–14).

Despite these proscriptions, *etnos* thinking incubated itself within applied studies of "stable collectivities". There are several clear examples of these holistic studies. During this period, work began on a four-volume encyclopaedia sketching out the qualities of the component peoples of the Soviet Union (Struve 1938; Anderson and Arzyutov 2016). In the surviving drafts of the unpublished volume there was a heavy emphasis on durable cultural traits that spilled over from one historical stage to another. There were also numerous single-author ethnographies published at this time on Siberian ethnography, folklore, and material culture — many of which are still respected today (Popov 1937; Okladnikov 1937; Vasilevich 1936; Vasil'ev 1936; Anisimov 1936; Vasilevich 1934; Terlet͡skiĭ 1934; Meshchaninov 1934; Dolgikh 1934). The focus of these works was on defining the qualities of smaller, "less-developed" peoples with an eye to improving their lives. The newly appointed director of the Institute of Ethnography, Vasiliĭ V. Struve (1889–1965), justified the applied work on specific peoples using Stalin's dictum that research on the "tribe" was work on "an ethnographic category", while work on the nation was an historical one (Struve 1939: 5). Struve felt that ethnographers should document not only primitive rituals but also the process of transformation of peoples into socialist nationalities (Struve 1939: 8). Ethnographic work thereby went hand-in-hand with the crafting of new territorial divisions that accentuated national differences between peoples (Terlet͡skiĭ 1930). Mark Bassin, in his survey of Eurasianism and biopolitics, attributes "equivocal essentialism" to the Stalinist thinking on identity (Bassin 2016: 146ff). He notes that though, in principle, Stalin insisted that human nature (as physical nature) was infinitely malleable, the centralized rural developmental initiatives were nested within regional political and territorial units defined by one "leading" nationality. The pragmatic and applied reality of wielding state power opened a space where biosocial thought could continue — even if it could not name itself as such.

The outbreak of World War II provided a further impetus to the development of an applied ethnography that rooted coherent groups of people in time and place. In 1942 Moscow-based geographers and ethnographers received an order from the General Headquarters of the Red Army to prepare maps of all of the nationalities of the USSR — as well as maps of nationalities living within Germany and its occupied territories. Following this directive, intense work in the Moscow branch of the Institute of Ethnography led to the production of more than thirty large-scale maps, as well as historical, ethnographical and statistical memos and reviews. The result of three years of work was entitled "A Study of Ethnic Composition of Central and South-Eastern Europe". The work was never published, and the original documents are probably kept to this day in the army's archives. The principal aim of this wartime project was to provide diplomats with arguments about the "ethnic composition" of European territories to aid them in the redrawing of state borders. The issue of how to define ethnic differences became once again a top priority, and older models of biosocial continuity were dusted off and re-launched to aid in the war effort.

One of the key actors of this new movement was Pavel I. Kushner (Knyshev) (1889–1968). In March 1944, he became head of the Department of Ethnic Statistics and Cartography at the Institute of Ethnography in Moscow. He defended his dissertation entitled *The Western Part of the Lithuanian Ethnographic Territory* in 1945 and published parts of his doctoral work, as well as his wartime work, in an influential book entitled *Ethnic Territories and Ethnic Borders* (Kushner [Knyshev] 1951). Significantly, Kushner reintroduced the term *etnos* into post-war

Soviet ethnography, although in his reintroduction he acknowledged both history and geography — and ignored physical form. In his view, "ethnic phenomena":

> distinguish the everyday life [*byt*] of one people from another. The set of such special markers include differences in language, material culture, customs, beliefs, etc. The sum-total [*sovokupnost'*] of such specific differences in everyday lives of peoples, preconditioned by the history of those peoples, and the effect of the geographical environment upon them is called "etnos" (Ibid: 6).

In his book he placed great stress on the theme of stable and long-term continuities. He saw cultural judgements about beauty, and "proper form" as markers of ethnic traditions which had been "formed over centuries" (Kushner [Knyshev] 1949: 7).

The geographical reinvention of national identity played itself out in a number of other venues. Ethnographers were recruited to aid in the rapid modernization and development of Siberian peoples — many of whom were often thought to subsist at the stage of primitive communism. With the application of "all-sided assistance" by the socialist state it was felt that these people could "skip" all historical stages of development and progress directly to communism. This programme, which was standardized by Mikhail A. Sergeev (1888–1965) as the "non-capitalist path to socialism" (Sergeev 1955), was significant since it became a model for international developmental assistance in Africa and southeast Asia (Graf 1987; Thomas 1978). Within the conditions of the Cold War, the Soviet state felt compelled to show that it could modernize rural societies more efficiently than the United States. The first step to modernization was often the standardization and rationalization of identities. The science of ethnic classification was one of the main exports of the mature Soviet state to China following the second Chinese revolution (Mullaney 2010).

These territorial and political involutions, apart from playing on Cold War anxieties, also built upon the "ethnogenetic turn" of Soviet ethnography (Anderson and Arzyutov 2016). Perhaps influenced by their forced cohabitation with historians, ethnographers became interested in tracing the path by which modern nations were formed (Shnirel'man 1993). Ethnogenetic theorists squared their interest in long-term, seemingly ahistorical stability with Marxist-Leninist thought by treating the term *etnos* as a generic category for Stalin's triad of the tribe, nationality, and nation. For example, an early theoretical work of this time argued that even though *etnos* should be the main subject matter of ethnography, "there are no special 'etnoses' as eternal unchanging categories, which are so dear to bourgeois science" (Tokarev and Cheboksarov 1951: 12).

It is perhaps important to emphasize at this point the very special way that print culture worked during the height of Stalinist science. Printed scientific works represented the consensus view of groups of scholars and were not used to present minority opinions or debates. However, there was room for non-standardarized terms to be discussed verbally during seminars or privately in the corridors between official meetings. For example, the ethnographer Vladimir V. Pimenov (1930–2012) recalls that he was introduced to the work of Shirokogoroff and the concepts of *etnos* during a course of lectures on China by Nikolaĭ N. Cheboksarov (1907–1980) at Moscow State University in 1952–1953. Pimenov directly cites the cautious and hushed manner that Cheboksarov spoke about the concept (Pimenov 2015: 115). Our own interviews with elderly and retired ethnographers in the Institute of Ethnology and Anthropology confirm that in the 1950s there was a wide discussion of biosocial and ethnogenetic ideas in the corridors despite the fact that Stalin's text on nationalities might be the only required reading for a particular course.

An oblique marker of the spaces of freedom within the late Stalinist academy is the fact that Stalin's definition of nation barely survived the dictator's death. In 1955, the Department of Historical Sciences of the Academy was already debating Kushner's memo about types of ethnic communities. Sergeĭ A. Tokarev (1899–1985), one of the most authoritative and prolific ethnographers of the Soviet period, spoke up against Kushner (Kozlov and Puchkov 1995: 225). He himself began toying with non-standard models of national identity. According to his diary, Tokarev sketched out an outline for a future paper that suggested that different vectors of kinship and language formed the foundation for identity at different stages of history (Tokarev 1964; Kozlov and Puchkov 1995: 252–63). These tentative debates in the corridors were the main point of reference for a generation of students who were to change the face of Russian ethnography.

Among those post-war students was Viktor I. Kozlov (1924–2012), who was to become one of the most important *etnos* theorists in the 1970–1980s. Having acquired some experience in cartography during the war, he became a professional cartographer in the 1950s. He finished his postgraduate studies in ethnic statistics and cartography at the Institute of Ethnography in 1956 with his dissertation "On the Settlement of the Mordovan people in the mid-19th — beginning of the 20th centuries" (Kozlov 1956). Despite this narrow title, Kozlov followed Kushner's methodology closely, attempting to outline the continuity in Mordva's occupation from the beginning of the second millennium to the present day. Nevertheless, Kozlov was eager to contribute somewhat heretical ideas to theoretical discussions of the day. In 1960 the party cell of the Institute of Ethnography lambasted one of his papers as revisionist and accused him of reviving Kautsky's idea that personal national affiliations constitute the only characteristic of nationhood. It is significant that the archival transcript of the discussion notes that high-status luminaries of the Institute, such as Georgiĭ F. Debet͡s (1905–1969) and Tokarev, spoke in defence of his views (TsGAM P7349-1-13: 10–11).

Despite earlier criticisms of eclecticism in bourgeois science, late Stalinist ethnographers and physical anthropologists began to argue strongly for multidisciplinary studies of identity. Debet͡s and his co-authors argued that physical anthropological measurements could ascertain degrees of homogeneity and diversity among speakers of certain linguistic groups as a sort of independent measure of ethnogenetic progress (Debet͡s, Levin, and Trofimova 1952: 28–29). Although there was no citation to this effect, this idea describes very well the older methodology espoused by Volkov and by his students Rudenko and Shirokogoroff (see chapters 4 and 5). Valeriĭ P. Alekseev (1929–1991) epitomized this resumption of a multidisciplinary approach by the new generation. He started his post-doctoral studies at the Institute of Ethnography in 1952 as a student of Debet͡s, but was also influenced by other prominent anthropologists of the Institute such as Bunak, Cheborsarov, and Levin. His doctoral dissertation, defended in 1967, was published a few years later as *The Origins of the Peoples of the Eastern Europe* (Alekseev 1969). He used craniological research to balance arguments about ethnogenesis. In particular, in his review of physical anthropological research among Eastern Slavic populations since the

1930s, he noticed that the tendency to deny distinct anthropological types among these peoples was an ideological reaction to previous studies (Alekseev 1979: 49–52). He supported the idea that Great and White Russians displayed evidence of a significant Baltic and Finnish "substrate" while Ukrainians displayed a different anthropological type (Alekseev 1969: 208; Alekseeva 1973). It is interesting that his book partially "rehabilitated" Volkov's earlier views on the distinctiveness of Ukrainians (Alekseev 1969: 164). Later in his career Alekseev invoked the idea of "ethnogeneseology" (*ėtnogenezologii͡a*) as a field in itself that combines the approaches of history, anthropology, ethnography, linguistics, and geography (Alekseev 1986: 6–7).

The death of Stalin and the reconstitution of Soviet science under Nikita Khrushchëv created an unusual opportunity for *etnos* entrepreneurs. Contrary to the assumptions of adherents of the totalitarian hypothesis, the relaxing of a possible threat to one's career and wellbeing did not simply open a window onto what people "really" believed. It also created an opportunity for imaginative and aggressive intellectual actors to pose new theories and inevitably to create a new orthodoxy — or in our case, orthodoxies. The post-Stalinist "thaw" opened a space for the expansion of multiple theories of identity, many of which had for a long time been implicit in the way that scientists and government agents interacted with society. In a strange recapitulation of the 1840s, the revitalization of *etnos* theory was to a great extent the story of the competition between two men: Bromleĭ and Lev N. Gumilëv. Looking at their work is like staring through both ends of the same telescope. Each vehemently differentiated his work from that of the other, despite the fact that their conclusions and examples were broadly similar. Even their formal educational backgrounds were similar. Both were strangers to ethnography, each arriving to the discipline through ethnography's "parent" discipline of history. Untangling the theoretical work of the two men is next to impossible since it was determined by the tenor of the times.

It is not often recognized that de-Stalinization was a planned process led by the state. In 1963, the Soviet Academy of Sciences reflecting an instruction from the Plenary Meeting of the Central Committee of the Communist Party in June of that year, mandated a wide-ranging debate on methodological experimentation in the humanities and social sciences

(Markwick 2001: 156). Academicians Pëtr N. Fedoseev (1908–1990) and Ĭ͡Uriĭ P. Frantsev (1903–1969) wrote a sort of instruction manual for de-Stalinization, which encouraged social scientists, including ethnographers, to rewrite sociological and historical laws and to embark on interdisciplinary research (Akademii͡a nauk SSSR 1964: 16, 37). As with all centrally planned and managed initiatives, academies had to report on their progress. Thus in 1966, the leading journal *Voprosy istorii* proudly reported that they had published 34 methodological papers since the instruction had been issued (ARAN 457-1 (1953–2002)-527: 5).

Of those papers, a seminal publication by the philosopher Ĭ͡Uriĭ I. Semënov (b. 1929) had far-reaching impacts on Soviet ethnography. Semënov argued for the need for a new bridging concept, which he called the "social organism", that would allow scientists to elevate a single society as the leading force of history. Ernest Gellner, who was enthralled by Semënov's work, dubbed this chosen society a "torch-bearer" in a "torch-relay vision of history" (Gellner 1980b: 114; Skalník 2007). Semënov's innovation allowed ethnographers to map the broad utopian vision of Marxist evolutionary theory onto a particular point in time without having to fudge the details of their expeditionary field findings. In the theoretical spirit of Hirsch's "vocabularies of identity", he uncovered a way to allow teleological categories such as tribe — nationality and nation — to sit above and alongside ethnographic facts (Semënov 1966).

The mandated methodological discussion also touched upon the definition of the "nation" and in particular Stalin's authoritative formula. This special debate was no doubt spurred on by the new Program of the Communist Party of the Soviet Union, accepted in 1961, which spoke about "erasing national differences" and contained a further directive to create "a new multinational collectivity (*obshchnost'*)" (Shnirel'man 2011: 251). The editors of the journal *Voprosy istorii* encouraged a brave revision of the Stalinist definition of a nation (without, however, putting their weight behind any one suggestion). In 1966 they wrote:

> In the course of the discussion, there were many suggestions concerning refining and modification of the definition of nation. Participants argued for or against such attributes of nation as "common psychic make-up", "national statesmanship", different views were pronounced about the types of nations. The relations between such concepts as "nation" and

> "ethnic collectivity", nation and nationality are discussed (ARAN 457-1 (1953–2002)-527: 18).

This discussion prompted a parallel set of meetings among ethnographers. At least three meetings of the theoretical seminar of the Institute of Ethnography in 1965 were devoted to the concept of ethnic group and nation. A number of positions were presented and argued. One influential paper by Kozlov, which was published two years later, linked Semënov's social organism to the concept of an ethnic collectivity (*obschnost'*):

> An ethnic collectivity is a social organism which forms on a certain territory out of groups of people who possessed or developed a common language, common cultural characteristics, social values and traditions, and a mixture of radically varied racial components (Kozlov 1967: 111).

Participants at the seminar questioned many of Kozlov's arguments, but the majority supported his challenge of Stalin's "simplified schemes". His paper inspired enthusiasm from a younger generation of scholars. Even a spokesperson of the older generation — Tokarev, one of the most prolific and authoritative writers among Soviet ethnographers — summed up the mood of the meeting positively:

> The debate has shown that there are many [different] opinions, but I have compiled several conclusions [*tezisy*] which [I believe] everyone can sign up to:
>
> 1) the theory of ethnic collectivity [*obschchnost'*] is in need of revision;
>
> 2) there is a need for further [field] research — and not only within Europe;
>
> 3) ethnic communities are real, but we lack a definition of them;
>
> 4) it is still not clear what types [of ethnic communities] exist;
>
> 5) is there law governing the transformation from one to another type? It is not clear what type of law this would be. It is [further] unclear if social-economic formations also follow the same law (ARAN 142-10-522: 29–30).

These new terms, ranging from the "social organism" to the "ethnic community" to the "ethnic group", did not wander far from the biosocial consensus that had been built up in Russia for over eighty years. Viktor A. Shnirel'man also observed two characteristic trends that emerged out of the discussions of the 1960s–1970s. On the one hand, there was a wide consensus among Soviet intellectuals that such things as a "national character" or "national psychological make-up" (*sklad*) existed. On the other hand, there was a renewed interest in and enthusiasm for linking human behaviour to genetic heredity (Howell 2010; Shnirel'man 2011: 252–80). The search for a new synthesis between the social and natural sciences was proclaimed by no other than the president of the Academy of Sciences, Mstislav V. Keldysh (1911–1978). In his speech at the general meeting of the Academy in October 1962 he declared:

> We cannot leave the social sciences with the task of developing themselves [in isolation]. There is no clear-cut division between the social, natural, and technical sciences. [...] The interrelation between the social and natural sciences plays a key role in [the expression of] ideology [and] in the strengthening of a materialist worldview (Keldysh 1962: 6).

It was in this newly "thawed" yet strangely familiar landscape that both Bromleĭ and Gumilëv sought to make careers for themselves.

Bromleĭ, who was appointed director of the Institute of Ethnography in January 1966, was trained as a historian of medieval Croatia. He had served as a secretary of the Department of History of the Academy of Sciences since 1958. Here he would have silently watched or participated in all of the abovementioned theoretical developments. After his appointment, he found himself in a position where he was forced to adjudicate the raging theoretical debates in order to earn respect among his peers. His authoritative reaction to the 1965 disputation was telling. Capturing its spirit, he declared:

> We need a common set of tools [*instrumentariĭ*]. We must speak in a language using one and the same understanding. And at some stage, we need [to stop and] agree what is our working [*sovremennyĭ*] definition of the nation (ARAN 457-1(1953–2002)-529: 50).

Upon becoming the institute's director, Bromleĭ set about the task of producing a common definition. To compensate for his lack of training, he surrounded himself with a group of talented contemporaries such as Kozlov, Valeriĭ P. Alekseev, and Sergeĭ A. Arutiunov. According to a posthumous biography by one of his circle, he also took care to distance himself from the old "masters" Cheboksarov and Tokarev so as not to appear to be taking on the role of a pupil. He also read ethnography avidly after work at night (Kozlov 2001: 5–6).

Bromleĭ chose to write his maiden article together with one of his hand-picked comrades on the topic of ethnogenesis. In the article, entitled "On the Role of Migration in the Formation of New Ethnic Communities", they pondered the role of indigenous populations and newcomers in the formation of new *etnoses* in the first millennium AD across Eurasia (Alekseev and Bromleĭ 1968). A distinctive feature of this article was the use of the term *etnos* when describing tribal and early-state societies. The *etnos* term was (re-)used casually without a formal definition. Nevertheless, its sudden appearance in print was unusual. Likely, the lack of citations and a definition signalled that the term was already in broad circulation.

Gumilëv followed a different path than Bromleĭ in making a name for himself during this time of experimentation. His chequered record as a political prisoner — he had served over thirteen years in various Stalin-era prisons — made it difficult for him to be fully accepted by Soviet academic institutions (Bassin 2016: 10–11). Gumilëv was never appointed as a professor and was officially employed throughout his life as a research associate in the Faculty of Geography at Leningrad State University. However, as Mark Bassin notes, Gumilëv also deliberately cultivated his image as an independent-thinking dissident — a move that made his unorthodox ideas highly popular among the intelligentsia (Bassin 2016: 17). Needless to say, he was much less constrained by official doctrines of Soviet Marxist-Leninism than Bromleĭ, who headed an official governmental research institute.

Of the two men, Gumilëv was the first to place the stamp of *etnos* upon his broad vision of the interdependence of peoples, "passions", and landscape. In a likely little-read journal with a low print-run, published by the Institute of Geography in Leningrad, he wrote a short article, "About the Object of Historical Geography", in 1965 — a full two years before Bromleĭ's first published intervention (Gumilëv 1965). It is an interesting footnote that this early contribution was almost immediately translated into English in one of the Cold War journals of translation (Gumilëv 1966). Two much more detailed articles were to follow in 1967 (Gumilëv 1967c, 1967b). Later, a set of high profile articles in the mass-circulation periodical *Priroda* (Gumilëv 1970) cemented his name as a charismatic Soviet public intellectual. While official ethnographers gingerly felt their way towards making connections with geography and physical anthropology, Gumilëv drew inspiration from a wide range of disciplines, including ecology and earth sciences, genetics, biophysics, and Vernadskiĭ's holistic vision of the biosphere.

It is difficult to write the history of the development of Gumilëv's thought, both because of the severe hiatus imposed by his long prison sentences and because of his own tendency to create a myth out of his own life. In an interview given shortly before his death he rooted his unique *etnos* theory in a vision that he had while in a prison cell in Leningrad in 1939 (Bassin 2016: 43). Shnirel'man speculated that Gumilëv may have been influenced by "antisemitic and Nazi sentiments" which were often present in the camps, as well as a "neonazi racist ideology" promoted by several underground right-wing thinkers with whom he was allegedly acquainted in the late 1960s and early 1970s (Shnirel'man 2011: 281–82). He may have been introduced to Eurasianism by Pëtr N. Savit͡skiĭ (1895–1968), with whom he established an intellectual friendship and correspondence in the late 1950s–1960s (Beisswenger 2013). However, scattered unpublished documents suggest that his self-styled arcane ideas were part of a broader contemporary interest in enduring, biophysical identities. Rudenko, a student of Volkov and fellow sufferer of the Stalinist repressions, helped Gumilëv re-establish his career in Leningrad (pers. comm. I͡A. A. Sher 2016) (Bassin 2016: 160). Rudenko wrote a little-known unpublished manuscript entitled "*Etnos* and Ethnogenesis" at some point in the mid-1960s where he alluded to his discussions with the young historian. The archivists at the St Petersburg Filial of the Archive of the Russian Academy of Sciences assert that Gumilëv's handwriting can be identified in the margins of the typescript — suggesting that he was familiar with the text (SPF ARAN 1004-1-118: 8–14). Rudenko's thinking and fieldwork is discussed in more detail in chapter 4.

At the heart of Gumilëv's theory of *etnos* was a traditional definition connected to language, traditions, and biology. However, he also sketched out the careers of world-historical *etnoses* into millenial cycles powered by an undefined cosmic energy. If, like Bromleĭ, he made a symbolic break with the Stalinist theory of nations, he nevertheless reintroduced the theme of what Bassin identifies as an "ethnic hierarchy" (Bassin 2016: 62–67) by describing sub-regional and super-regional units known as the *subetnos* and the *superetnos*. A unique element of his vision of *etnos* was his insistence that ethnic phenomena manifested themselves according to the laws of the natural sciences, while the history of human societies followed a different set of laws within the social sciences. Thus, like Semënov, he was able to speak in the characteristic dual voice of the era, accepting a formal Stalinist progression from tribe to nation within social history while documenting eternal, passionate, and stable ethnic forms within natural history. In a formal sense his *etnos* theory was not biosocial since he insisted that it was profoundly biological and *not* social (Bassin 2016: ch. 6). Several of the millennial *superetnoses* that he identified conveniently tended to overlap with the boundaries of the Soviet Union (Bassin 2016: 70–71). Unlike Bromleĭ, Gumilëv appealed to wider audiences through his historical monographs about various historical and ancient Turkic peoples such as *The Unveiling of Khazarii͡a* (Gumilëv 1967d) or *The Ancient Turks* (Gumilëv 1967a). These popular-scientific works on exotic peoples were published before his key theoretical works and served to illustrate the evocativeness of his *etnos* perspective.

Bromleĭ also followed up his early interest in the socio-genetic origins of identity in his now infamous article "*Etnos* and Endogamy" (Bromleĭ 1969). There he claimed that endogamy — the tendency for members of one group to prefer to marry partners of their own group — was a "mechanism of ethnic integration". This direct reference to a biological foundation to ethnicity quickly got the new director into trouble. The head of the Department of the Near and Middle East, Mikhail S. Ivanov (1909–1986) started a campaign of attacks against Bromleĭ. Ivanov claimed that if *etnoses* are "stabilized" by endogamy this not only negated the Marxist formations of Bromleĭ's thinking, but made *etnos* a biological category (Bromleĭ 1970: 89; Tumarkin 2003). This debate was perhaps a defining moment of this period of experimentation. The records show that all other members of the institute, with one exception, rose to speak in support of the new director. On the one hand, a moment of liberal experimentation was preserved — on the other hand, a new orthodoxy of *etnos*-talk was imposed from this time onwards, at least within ethnographic circles.

Perhaps over conscious of the popularity of Gumilëv's work, Bromleĭ followed Gumilëv along a similar Byzantine path of devising increasingly complex systems and subsystems by which to describe *etnos*. In his mature works, Bromleĭ introduced his own notion of a *subetnos*, as well as the super-regional "metaethnical community" (*metaėtnicheskaia͡ obshchnost'*). Unlike with Gumilëv, his sub-regional or meta-regional units were defined by classical ethnological paramaters such as language or material culture, and not energy or "passions". Nevertheless the geopolitical effect was the same through the delibrate rationalizaiton of existing blocks of political affinity at the height of the Cold War. In a nod towards Euro-American thinking about ethnicity, Bromleĭ also introduced the adjectival form of the Greek word *etnos* — *etnikos* — in order to refer to a subjective quality of belonging. It is difficult to draw sharp lines between Bromleĭ's *subetnos* and Gumilëv's *subetnos*, let alone the pantheon of their parallel sets of concepts. What does seem clear from this inflationary expansion of the *etnos* enterprise is that this forest of terms created a rich plantation for a new generation of ethnographers and social geographers, while ironically not really threatening the geoterritorial foundation of state power within the former Soviet Union.

Marcus Banks in his overview of *etnos* theory wonders "how can [it] be made into a virtue"? He posits a widely held view that the late 1960s search for a pillar of identity helped scientists avoid the "trap" of orthodox Marxist five-stage evolutionary theory. In his view:

> *Etnos* theory provides a bridging mechanism, by positing a stable core which runs through all the historical stages any society will undergo. It therefore acts as a tool for diachronic analysis (Banks 1996: 22).

In the same work he is one of the first to label the theory as being an important example of "primordial ethnicity" — but one that nonetheless admits that there are scattered elements of transactional and relational historical factors that give every concrete ethnographic case its particular shape (Banks 1996: 23). As Gellner (1988: 118) wrote, in his pithy and economical prose, *etnos* theory was "*relatively* synchronist" (emphasis in the original), opening the door to applied fieldwork within a tradition that had been obsessed with formal, off-the-shelf models. As strange as it may sound, in the late 1960s the theory sounded innovative and radical. The unique nature of the approach was probably never appreciated by North American and European anthropologists who, in the 1960s, were preoccupied by different issues. As Gellner (1980a: x) again observes, "It is ironic that at the very moment at which anthropology in the west is finding its way back to history, not without difficulty, Soviet anthropology is in part practicing a mild detachment from it". Bassin goes one step further. He sees in Gumilëv's rendition of *etnos* a radical reassertion of Stalinist national essences, which he describes as "the Stalinist accommodation". Within the fog created by Gumilëv's invisible eternal energies, levels and sublevels of ethnicity, he reads an impassioned defence of local communities against the assimilatory force of the post-war Soviet industrial state (Bassin 2016: 163–71). He associates this impassioned voice for ethnic difference with the near-hero status that Gumilëv achieved amongst non-Russian nationalities in the Soviet Union and within the Russian Federation today (Bassin 2016: ch. 10). Bromleĭ in this respect continued to serve as an ideologist advocating assimilation, intermarriage, and the creation of seamless, political-territorial communities. During perestroika, Gumilëv controversially linked the strained ethnic tensions in the crumbling Soviet federation to Bromleĭ's misguided theories. Bromleĭ retaliated by labelling Gumilëv's distinction of "passionate" and "sub-passionate" peoples as covert racism (Vaĭnshteĭn 2004: 624–27).

The revival of *etnos* theory during the early Brezhnev period reveals several things. The first is that this "relatively" primordialist theory could support multiple variants and multiple accommodations with the late Soviet state. Further, despite surface expressions of "revolution" and "dissidence", the theory in all its variants remained steadfastly loyal to the vision of a hierarchy of nations led by the world-historical Russian state. One proof of this loyalty might be the failed attempt by Valeriĭ A. Tishkov (b. 1941) — the first post-Soviet director of the Institute of Ethnography — to entomb *etnos* theory through his book *A Requiem to Etnos* (Tishkov 2003). This wide-ranging summary of theories of ethnicity and a call to reinvent sociocultural anthropology in Russia made a strong argument that the Russian academy should reject collectivist and essentialist theories of belonging in favour of a relational definition that is juggled and negotiated by individuals. To underscore the point, he changed the name of the Institute of Ethnography to the

Institute of Ethnology and Anthropology. In a recent retrospective on his *Requiem*, he takes credit for introducing North American cultural anthropology to Russia and loosening the hold of *etnos* theory on the academy (Tishkov 2016: 6).

The surprise of the epoch was the fact that even if the *Requiem* was perhaps sung by a handful of central ethnographers, it by and large went unheeded across Eurasia within regional colleges, newspapers, and the programmes of various regional nationalist political parties. In the tumultuous post-Soviet present, local intellectuals and political actors alike reject liberal individual models of ethnic management and have turned once again to powerful and very old models of biosocial identity.

Etnos in the Long Twentieth Century and Beyond

Hobsbawn's "short twentieth century" was strongly associated with a single world-historical state promoting a vision of emancipation and modernity that served to inspire several generations. His somewhat nostalgic account mourns the waning of the ideological certainties that defined that era. Our overview of the origins of *etnos* thinking suggest that that the Soviet state was perhaps not so exceptional, but instead drew upon very widely held convictions that collective identities were durable — and perhaps was eventually entangled by them. Our argument is that *etnos* thinking, and its brief association with Soviet modernity, was rooted in a biosocial compromise between competing camps. We thereby run the risk of suggesting (alongside many *etnos* entrepreneurs) that persistent identities are somehow mystically natural or fixed. That would misrepresent the debates, the lack of agreement, and the general untidiness of this story — a flavour of which is clearly visible in the following chapters in this book. The moral of this story is that collective identities seem to enjoy their own histories, much like individual biographies. The story of *etnos* thinking is that there needs to be a way of speaking about contextualized identities — and to some extent *etnos*-talk addresses, if not solves, Shanin's (1986) "case of the missing term".

If the height of the Soviet period was marked by Bromleĭ's "minor revolution", the beginning of the post-Soviet period is marked by

Tishkov's counter-revolution. He highlighted his transformation by identifying a "crisis" in Soviet ethnography in a prominent article in the American journal *Current Anthropology* (Tishkov 1992). Like his predecessor Bromleĭ, Tishkov was trained as a historian — only in this case not of the Balkans but of the 1837–1838 "revolutions" in British North America. Having written several books on the history of Canada, American historiography, and on Native Americans, he came to the Institute of Ethnography in 1981 to lead its Department of the Peoples of America. After briefly serving as Bromleĭ's deputy, he took over the institute in 1989 and led it up until 2015. In his numerous publications, including the *Requiem,* Tishkov propagated an individual-oriented approach to the study of ethnic identity, stressing the situational and processual character of ethnic identification. He relied almost exclusively on North American and European sources, hoping to invigorate the field with new perspectives. He harshly criticised the ossified nature of Soviet ethnography's hierarchy of *etnoses, sub-etnoses, etnikos,* and *superetnoses,* as well as what he described as the "étatisation" of ethnicity by the Soviet state. In one of our interviews, he dismissed Bromleĭ as "building forts and barricades" (*gorodushki gorodit'*) out of his Byzantine ethnic superstructures — a reference to the modern Russian adolescent practice of wreaking havoc on long summer nights. In his work, Tishkov stressed the way that state actors used narrow classificatory state practices to construct ethnicity, which he insisted might present itself in multiple forms:

> If Soviet *etnos* theory had never existed, people would never have been inscribed as parts of the collective torso [*telo*] known as an *"etnos"*. [...] And, if there had never been a long-standing Soviet practice of registering a single nationality in one's passport — a nationality which necessarily had to correspond to that of one's parents, then people might have realized and have been able to publically declare [that they held multiple identities]. A person could be at any one time a Russian and a Kazakh, a Russian and a Jew, or they [might have been able to express] a "vertical" stack of various senses of belonging [*prinadlezhnosti*] such as being an Andiets and a Avarets, a Digorets and an Osetian, an Erzarian and a Mordovan [...] a Pomor and a Russian [...] etc. (Tishkov 2005: 167).

In another book he criticized the way that state policies ironed out the diversity of a region he described as the "Russian-Ukrainian-Belorussian cultural borderland" (Tishkov 1997: 56). As an academic, and a public intellectual, for several decades Tishkov has been the most vocal proponent of the idea that there is a Russian Federative civic identity that transcends the Russian ethnic identity as a *Rossiĭskiĭ narod* (Tishkov 2010, 2013).

Although Tishkov takes credit for steering Soviet ethnography out of its crisis by encouraging professional ethnographers to abandon *etnos*, he admits that the *etnos* concept is very much alive and well outside of the academy:

> Indeed, today in [the] Russian public sphere the idea of "etnos" is very much alive, probably due to the fact that it wandered [*perekochevalo*] from ethnology to different spheres of social and humanitarian research. [...] *Etnos* and *etnichnost'* which had until recently been notably absent from the work of Russian humanists has now appeared in multiple variants such as with historians of the 'ethnocultural history of Ancient Rus' or [the debate on] "etnoses in the early Middle Ages", or among the pseudophilosophers with their concept of the "philosophy of the *etnos*". [...] *Etnos* has been abandoned by the language of ethnologists (that is, if we exclude the few researchers teaching in colleges who do not keep up with contemporary developments) (Tishkov 2016: 5–6).

In our view, he underestimates the broad influence of the term within the public sphere today.

While it might be true that *etnos* is no longer used widely by state ethnographers within the Academy of Sciences, an unreconstructed vision of Bromleĭ's *etnos* can be widely found in state-sanctioned textbooks used in introductory level cultural studies courses (Pimenov 2007; Sadokhin 2006; Arutiunov and Ryzhakova 2004).

The *etnos* term also lives on, quietly, in the pages of ethnographic encyclopaedias. One of the best illustrations is the series entitled *Peoples and Cultures*, which is currently running at 25 volumes. This series does not use *etnos* in its title, but the term appears within its pages quite regularly. Being a rebranding of the well-known Soviet-era series *Peoples of the World* (Anderson and Arzyutov 2016), the new series presents ethnographic snapshots from across Russian regions, such as the "northeast", and documents former Soviet republics. Occasionally it features volumes on single peoples such as the Tatars or Buriats. The volumes' internal structure is hauntingly familiar, dissecting *etnoses* by their "folklore", "occupations", "ethnogenesis", and "technology". An important new feature of this series is the respect and encouragement afforded to members of the regional intelligentsia outside of Moscow and St Petersburg. Many volumes include chapters by local authors, which immediately made the series a focal point for ethnonationalist reflection. The volume *The I͡Akuts (Sakhas)* (Alekseev 2012) was issued in conjunction with a national festival in Moscow organized by the I͡Akut national intelligentsia. The same strategy was repeated in St Petersburg with the publication of the volume *The Ingushes* (Albogachieva, Martazanov, and Solov'eva 2013). In our interviews, one of the editors confessed that they hoped that the volume itself would calm the tension between Ingush and Chechen scholars in these republics (pers. comm. M. S.-G. Albogachieva, 2014). The example of Altaians is perhaps one of the best for illustrating the way that the *etnos* term has been appropriated to defend local identity claims. In the volume published within the central series, entitled *The Turkic Peoples of Siberia* (Funk and Tomilov 2006), the Altaians were treated in a series of *chapters* among many other peoples. This troubled the local Altaian intelligentsia, who rushed to prepare their own competing volume, entitled *The Altaians* (Ekeev 2014), where they presented the complex and detailed history of the many identity groups in the region as a single history of a single *etnos* formed under the influence of the Russian Empire and Soviet Union.

The passion with which regional scholars have taken up the cause of essentialist and enduring identities is likely the most tangible artefact of the reincarnation of *etnos* theory today. These works have a distinctive quality that one might identify as a type of indigenous-rights discourse. The *etnos* term itself appears directly in the title of a number of regional collections in order to emphasize their sense of pride and their expectation of respect for their nationality. Volumes such as *The Reality of the Etnos* (Goncharov, Gashilova and Bali͡asnikova 2012) or *The Etnoses of Siberia* (Makarov 2004a; 2004b) emphasise the longevity, energy, and persistence of cultural minorities. These works have manifesto-like qualities in that they insist on the vibrancy of cultural difference. Even Tishkov, in his retrospective review of his *Requiem*, was forced to acknowledged that "etno-" identities are characteristic of Russia now, and likely "forever" (*navsegda*) (Tishkov 2016: 17–18). The role of regional elites in developing *etnos* theory was a major theme in the analysis of Bassin (Bassin 2016). Ranging from the nostalgia for Stalinist essentialism to the Eurasian geopolitics of the twenty-first century, he sees this "biopolitical" term being able to stand in for concerns about modernization and environmentalism, cultural survival, and the strengthening of the newly independent Turkic states.

Regional nationalism is not the only magnetic pole that has attracted contemporary enthusiasts of *etnos* thinking. Perhaps the most startling appropriation of *etnos* is by the neo-Eurasianist political philosopher, Aleksandr Dugin. Dugin has become the focus of a plethora of European and American studies who posited him at one time as a sort of philosopher or central ideologist of the Putin administration (Shlapentokh 2017; Umland 2016; Laruelle 2006). One of his bestselling books, *The Foundations of Geopolitics* (Dugin 1997), excited concern about its declaration that it is the fate of Russia to annex and incorporate most of the former Soviet republics as well as significant parts of Manchuria and Inner Asia. In 2001 he established the political movement "Eurasia", thus making his murky geopolitical ideas visible beyond the subculture of right-wing radicals (Umland 2009). It is not well known amongst these political scientists that he also used ethnographic arguments to underpin his political arguments. His interests in *etnos* theory began in 2002 when he participated in a conference dedicated to the memory of Gumilëv (Dugin 2002). He then presented a series of lectures, published online in 2009, on the "sociology of the *etnos*" which drew heavily from Shirokogoroff's and Gumilëv's work (Dugin 2009). These were assembled together and published as a textbook in 2011 (Dugin 2011). Here he redefines *etnos* as an organic unit: "a simple society, organically (naturally) connected to the territory and bound by common morality, rites and semantic system" (Dugin 2011: 8). Drawing on a selective reading of anthropological literature of the nineteenth and twentieth centuries, he decorates this definition with evocative examples of mythological thinking, shamanism, standardized "personas", and cyclical time. Shirokogoroff's ethnographic work among Manchurian Tunguses even plays a cameo role in Dugin's description of Eurasian societies. Some nationalist commentators have taken his vision even further. While Dugin rejects overt biological or racial interpretations of the *etnos*, the historian and political commentator Valeriĭ D. Soloveĭ uses genetics and Jungian psychology to define *etnos* as "a group of people, differentiated from other groups by hereditary biological characteristics and archetypes" (Soloveĭ 2008: 68). This type of racist essentialist appropriation of *etnos* is characteristic not only of the Russian far right, but also of a wide range of post-Soviet intellectuals of various nationalities (Shnirel'man 2011: 328–60).

As Serguei A. Oushakine (2009; 2010) has shown, *etnos* was used extensively by Russian nationalists to create the peculiar genre of "The Tragedy of the Russian People", popular in the 1990s–2000s. In his analysis of a series of texts of this kind, he describes the common theme of suffering, demographical decline, and the erosion of the national values of the Russian people both during the Soviet and post-Soviet periods. According to Oushakine, by deploying the *etnos* concept these authors "were able to introduce a clear-cut split between the Russian '*etnos* proper' and institutions of the Soviet and post-Soviet state whose politics was deemed to be non-Russian or even anti-Russian" (Oushakine 2009: 81). He claims that the theories of Bromleĭ and Gumilëv were instrumental in this regard as they had already distilled *etnos* away from the socio-political realm where constructivist terms of identity were widely used (Oushakine 2009: 86–95). Extracting an essentialist "bio-psycho-social ethnic body" from history, theories of *etnos* produced a post-Soviet "patriotism of despair", but they also generated a resource for reinventing a sense of national vitality such as the Altai "school of vital forces" (Oushakine 2009: 127).

The demographic health of the Russian *etnos* is also one of the main concerns of the Russian nationalists. For example, a demographic chart depicting the increase in the death rate and the declining birthrate is commonly dubbed the "Russian cross" in the mass media. In the conclusion to his volume *A History of the Tragedy of a Great People* (Kozlov 1996), Kozlov determined that the Russian *etnos* had lost its vitality by the end of the twentieth century. Among the reasons for its decline he listed Soviet ethnic policy and the market reforms of the 1990s, which led to the degeneration and "de-ethnization" of Russians (Kozlov 1996: 274). Although he was an old opponent of Gumilëv's theories, he was forced to admit that his pessimistic picture strongly reminded him of the 1200-year life cycles of an *etnos* hypothesized by Gumilëv (Kozlov 1996: 283).

These demographic disaster narratives contrast strongly with the position of Tishkov, who repeatedly criticized not only "demographic myths" of this kind, but also the "crisis paradigm" in general. He asserted that Russian population figures would stabilize due to immigration and the "drift of identity" through "a free choice [of identity] and the ability to shift from one ethnic group to another" (Tishkov 2005: 174). Tishkov's optimism extended to his evaluation of the role of civic experts, and of state power. If *etnos*-nationalists like Kozlov asserted that the Russian state often acted against the interests of the Russian people, Tishkov praised the post-Soviet state for promoting civic nationalism and market reforms (Tishkov 2005: 189–207). If Tishkov's optimism could be reduced to a headline, it would be "We have all begun to live better" — a slogan which served as a title of one of his many public outreach articles in the daily newspaper *Nezavisimaia͡ Gazeta* (Tishkov 2000).

The nostalgia for essentialist and enduring identities has led to a renewed interest in the works of the pioneers of *etnos* theory. Sergei Shirokogoroff's few Russian-language studies were republished for the very first time within Russia by a scientific collective based in Vladivostok (Kuznet͡sov and Reshetov 2001–2002). Recently, the Institute of Ethnology and Anthropology has (re)launched an early Soviet project to translate and publish Shirokogoroff's *Social Organization of the Tungus* in Russian (Sirina et al. 2015), correcting the historical oddity that translations of this work have long been available in Japanese and Chinese. Dugin supported this movement by writing the forward to the Moscow edition of Shirokogoroff's *Etnos* (Dugin 2010).

Larisa R. Pavlinskaia͡, former head of the Siberian Department in the Museum of Anthropology and Ethnography, wrote one of the first book-length ethnographies to redeploy *etnos*-theory overtly. Her richly detailed ethnography entitled *The Buria͡ts: Notes on their Ethnic History* (Pavlinskaia͡ 2008) was based on several decades of fieldwork in the same East Siberian landscape that inspired Sergei and Elizaveta Shirokogoroff. Sharing perhaps the puzzlement the Shirokogoroffs experienced in the multilingual and multicultural diverstity of these communities (see chapter 5 and 7), she tracked the process by which diverse groups split and merged into a single *etnos*. The volume quotes extensively from Shirokogoroff's newly republished texts, in part advocating for and explaining his biosocial theory of the *etnos* for those who may not have read this émigré's work (Pavlinskaia͡ 2008: 53–6). She then moves on to merge Shirokogoroff's interest in leading *etnoses* with

Gumilëv's description of the "persistent behavioural models" that fuel ethnogenetic progression. The book covers a wide expanse of time from the seventeenth to the nineteenth centuries and includes significant archival examples. For example, she cites the case of the Russian *voevoda* I͡Akov Khripunov, whose predatory military campaign of 1629 she interprets (via Gumilëv) as "the result of the work of an individual who [had been excited into] a higher nervous state triggered by a certain stage of ethnogenesis" (Pavlinskai͡a 2008: 106). Pavlinskai͡a perhaps goes further than Shirokogoroff himself by stressing the biological component of ethnogenesis. She postulates that there must exist a genetic "passionarity mutation" (*mutat͡sii͡a passionarnosti*) (Pavlinskai͡a 2008: 57), which, once activated in an individual's DNA, has a ripple effect on the people around that individual, gradually transforming a collage of local groups into a single *etnos*. This frames Shirokogoroff's interest in mixed-blood Tungus individuals, as discussed in chapter 5, in a completely new light:

> The metisification (*metisat͡sii͡a*) of the Russian and aboriginal population is one of the mainstays of new etno-formation processes (*ėtnoobrazovatel'nye prot͡sessy*) in Siberia, and particularly in the Baikal region. It has been repeatedly noted in the [academic] literature that the majority of the Russian population [in Siberia] were men. [This was the case] not only in the 16th century but also in the 17th and 18th centuries. One should point out that these men were [likely] the most "passionary" representatives of the Russian *etnos*. They settled on new lands in Siberia and temporarily or permanently married members of the native peoples. [They therefore] passed on this quality — the passionary gene — thus initiating ethnic development among the local population. These individuals, [in turn,] played an important role in the formation of today's Siberian *etnoses*. This is especially the case in the forested areas where the Russian population was particularly numerous. It follows that the impact of Russians on the native people of Siberia even led to a change in the gene pool, which is the most important element within any etno-formation process (Pavlinskai͡a 2008: 160).

Through works like Pavlinskai͡a's ethnography we can follow the transformation of over a century of *etnos* thinking from an interest in persistent identity types to a fully molecular genetic theory of identity.

At the start of the twenty-first century we can observe a subtle transformation of the word *etnos* from a somewhat scholastic scientific term used primarily by experts to a widely quoted expression in the public sphere that touches upon the destiny of peoples. Of particular interest to political actors, be they neo-Eurasianists or members of the regional intelligentsia, is the way that a single compact term can denote a vibrant and biologically anchored quality. According to Shnirel'man, "during the last 15–20 years, an appeal to genetics has firmly entered the popular discourse, [leading] some authors [to begin] to abuse the term" (Shnirel'man 2011: 354). This process can be followed right up to the office of the president. Just before the 2012 presidential election, Vladimir Putin published an article devoted to the "national question" (Putin 2012). There he used the term *etnos* as a category for understanding how post-Soviet migrants from Central Asia and the Caucuses were guided by the leading vision of the Russian people. He noted, "The self-determination of the Russian people [hinges] on a poly-ethnic civilization strengthened with Russian culture as its foundation". In this article he coined the phrase a "single cultural code" (*edinyĭ kul'turn'yĭ kod*), which elaborates a sort of centralized version of multiculturalism wherein Russia is seen as a multinational society acting as a single people (*narod*). Originally, his ideas seem to have been aimed at creating a law that would protect the identity of this single people. Tishkov's earlier argument for a *Rossiĭskiĭ narod* undoubtedly echoed this proposal (Tishkov 2010). This idea revived the discussion among some lawmakers of resurrecting Soviet-era nationality registers that tracked the *etnos* identity held by each individual — although in the abovementioned article Putin then distanced himself from that decisive step. More recently, Putin argued that his ethnocultural definition of the *Rossiiskiĭ narod* should be militarized. In his speech at the 9 May 2017 celebrations, he spoke of the need to deploy military strength to protect the "very existence of the Russian people (*Rossiĭskiĭ narod*) as an *etnos*" (*Pravda.ru* 2017). Here we witness a slippage from the use of *etnos* to denote non-Russian migrants, to the use of *etnos* to diagnose a possible life-threat to the biological vibrancy of a state-protected people. This led to a further controversy in October 2017 when Putin expressed concern about foreign scholars collecting genetic samples from "various *etnoses*" across Russia. Spokespersons from the Kremlin further speculated that by holding this "genetic code", foreign interests might be able to build a biological weapon (Zyri͡anova 2017).

By stressing an accommodation that we describe as a "biosocial synthesis", we try to express that there remains a wide range of debate within the academy and within the public sphere on the relative role of biological heritage in producing stable collective identities. We have indicated that the particular synthesis that stabilized within Russia, as well as other Eurasian states, seems "primordialist" when compared to a slightly different weighting of factors that one might find in Europe or America. As the following chapters will show, much of this peculiar Eurasian accommodation was in constant dialogue with traditions overseas, and should really be viewed as a sibling to north Atlantic theories of identity (and not an orphan). Although we have demonstrated that *etnos*-talk is always somewhere near the corridors of power, we have tried to show that it still cannot be equated with a single state ideology. Its persistence well into the twenty-first century clearly shows that *etnos* theory was not a monster sewn together and animated by Soviet-era *apparatchiki*, but an intellectual movement that has been relatively stable over 150 years.

Published References

Adams, M. B. 1990. *The Wellborn Science: Eugenics in Germany, France, Brazil, and Russia* (New York: Oxford University Press).

Akademiîa nauk SSSR. 1964. *Istoriîa i sotsiologiîa* (Moscow: Nauka).

Albogachieva, M. S.-G., A. M. Martazanov, and L. T. Solov'eva, eds. 2013. *Ingushi* (Moscow: Nauka).

Alekseev, N. A., Romanova, E. N., Sokolova, Z. P., ed. 2012. *ÎAkuty (Sakha)* (Moscow: Nauka).

Alekseev, V. P. 1969. *Proiskhozhdenie narodov Vostochnoĭ Evropy* (Moscow: Nauka).

—. 1979. 'Antropologicheskie dannye o proiskhozhdenii narodov SSSR', in *Rasy i Narody*, ed. by I. R. Grigulevich (Moscow: Nauka), 42–66.

—. 1986. *Ėtnogenez* (Moscow: Vysshaîa shkola).

Alekseev, V. P., and ÎU. V. Bromleĭ. 1968. 'K izucheniîu roli pereseleniĭ narodov v formirovanii novykh ėtnicheskikh obshchnosteĭ', *Sovetskaîa Ėtnografiîa* 2: 35–45.

Alekseeva, L. D. 1983. 'Moskovskiĭ universitet i stanovlenie prepodavaniîa ėtnografii v dorevoliûtsionnoĭ Rossii', *Vestnik Moskovskogo universiteta* 8 (Istoriia) 6: 54–62.

Alekseeva, T. I. 1973. *Ėtnogenez vostochnykh slavîan po dannym antropologii* (Moscow: Izdatel'stvo MGU).

Alymov, S. S. 2004. 'Dmitriĭ Nikolaevich Anuchin: "estestvennaîa istoriîa cheloveka v shirokom smysle ėtogo slova"', in *Vydaîushchiesîa otechestvennye ėtnologi i antropologi*, ed. by V. A. Tishkov, and D. D. Tumarkin (Moscow: Nauka), 7–48.

—. 2014. 'Ethnography, Marxism and Soviet Ideology', in *An Empire of Others*, ed. by R. Cvetkovski, and A. Hofmeister (Budapest: CEU Press), 121–43.

Anderson, D. G., and D. V. Arzyutov. 2016. 'The Construction of Soviet Ethnography and "The Peoples of Siberia"', *History and Anthropology* 27 (2): 183–209, https://doi.org/10.1080/02757206.2016.1140159.

Anisimov, A. F. 1936. *Rodovoe obshchestvo Ėvenkov* (Leningrad: Izd-vo Instituta Narodov Severa).

Anuchin, D. N. 1889. 'O zadachakh russkoĭ ėtnografii', *Ėtnograficheskoe obozrenie* 1: 1–35.

Arutîunov, S. A., and S. I. Ryzhakova. 2004. *Kul'turnaîa Antropologiîa* (Moscow: Ves' mir).

Arzi͡utov, D. V., S. S. Alymov, and D. D. Anderson. 2014. *Ot klassikov k marksizmu: soveshchanie ėtnografov Moskvy i Leningrada (5–11 aprelia 1929 g.)*. Serii͡a "Kunstkamera — Arkhiv" 7 (St Petersburg: MAĖ RAN).

Bakhurst, D. 1991. *Consciousness and Revolution in Soviet Philosophy: From the Bolsheviks to Evald Ilyenkov* (Cambridge: Cambridge University Press).

Banks, M. 1996. *Ethnicity: Anthropological Constructions* (New York: Routledge).

Bassin, M. 1991. 'Inventing Siberia: Visions of the Russian East in the Early Nineteenth Century', *The American Historical Review* 96 (3): 763–94.

—. 1993. 'Turner, Solovev, and the Frontier Hypothesis: The Nationalist Significance of Open Spaces', *Journal of Modern History* 65 (3): 473–511.

—. 2003. '"Classical" Eurasianism and the Geopolitics of Russian Identity', *Ab Imperio* 2: 257–66.

—. 2016. *The Gumilev Mystique: Biopolitics, Eurasianism, and the Construction of Community in Modern Russia* (Ithaca, NY: Cornell University Press).

Bauer, O. 2000 [1907]. *The Question of Nationalities and Social Democracy* (Minneapolis, MN: University of Minnesota Press).

Beer, D. 2008. *Renovating Russia: The Human Sciences and the Fate of Liberal Modernity, 1880–1930* (Ithaca, NY: Cornell University Press).

Beisswenger, M. 2013. 'Was Lev Gumilev a "Eurasianist"?: A New Look at his Post-War Contacts with Petr Savitskii', *Ab Imperio* 1: 85–108, https://doi.org/10.1353/imp.2013.0004.

Bottomore, T. B., and P. Goode. 1978. *Austro-Marxism* (Oxford: Clarendon).

Bromleĭ, I. U. V. 1969. 'Ėtnos i ėndogamii͡a', *Sovetskai͡a ėtnografii͡a* 6: 84–91.

—. 1970. Obsuzhdenie stat'i I͡U. V. Bromlei͡a ""Ėtnos i ėndogamii͡a' *Sovetskai͡a Ėtnografii͡a* 3: 86–103.

Conklin, A. L. 2013. *In the Museum of Man: Race, Anthropology, and Empire in France, 1850–1950* (Ithaca, NY: Cornell University Press).

Cvetkovski, R. 2014. 'Empire Complex: Arrangements in the Russian Ethnographic Museum, 1910', in *An Empire of Others: Making Ethnographic Knowledge in Imperial Russia and the USSR*, ed. by R. Cvetkovski and A. Hofmeister (Budapest: CEU Press), 211–52.

Debet͡s, G. F., M. G. Levin, and T. A. Trofimova. 1952. 'Antropologicheskiĭ material kak istochnik izuchenii͡a voprosov ėtnogeneza', *Sovetskai͡a ėtnografii͡a* 1: 22–35.

Dmitriev, A. N. 2010. 'Po tu storonu "universitetskogo voprosa": pravitel'stvennai͡a politika i sot͡sial'nai͡a zhizn' rossiĭskoĭ vyssheĭ shkoly (1900–1917 gody)', in *Universitet i gorod v Rossiĭ v nachale XX veka*, ed. by T. Maurer and A. N. Dmitriev (Moscow: Novoe literaturnoe obozrenie), 105–204.

Dolgikh, B. O. 1934. *Kety* (Irkutsk: OGIZ).

Dugin, A. G. 1997. *Osnovy geopolitiki (geopoliticheskoe budushchee Rossii)* (Moscow: Arttogei͡a).

—. 2002. 'Ėvoli͡ut͡sii͡a nat͡sional'noĭ idei Rusi (Rossii) na raznykh istoricheskikh ėtapakh', in *Teorii͡a ėtnogeneza i istoricheskie sud'by Evrazii: Materialy konferentsii, posvi͡ashchennoi 90-letii͡u so dni͡a rozhdenii͡a vydai͡ushchegosi͡a evraziĭt͡sa XX v. – L. N. Gumileva*, ed. by L. R. Pavlinskai͡a (St Petersburg: Evropeĭskiĭ Dom), 9–36.

—. 2009. 'Lekt͡sii͡a №7 Sot͡siologii͡a ėtnosa (Strukturnai͡a sot͡siologii͡a)', T͡Sentr Konservativnykh Issledovaniĭ, http://konservatizm.org/konservatizm/sociology/220409204809.xhtml

—. 2010. 'Sergeĭ Mikhaĭlovich Shirokogorov: vozvrashchenie zabytogo klassika', in *Ėtnos. Issledovanie osnovnykh print͡sipov izmenenii͡a ėtnicheskikh i ėtnograficheskikh i͡avleniĭ*, ed. by N. V. Melenteva (Moscow: Librokom), 5–8.

—. 2011. *Ėtnosot͡siologii͡a* (Moscow: Akademicheskiĭ Proekt).

Ekeev, N. V., ed. 2014. *Altaĭt͡sy: Ėtnicheskai͡a istorii͡a. Tradit͡sionnai͡a kul'tura. Sovremennoe razvitie* (Gorno-Altaĭsk: NII altaistiki im. S. S. Surazakova).

Fischer, H. 1970. '"Völkerkunde", "Ethnographie", "Ethnologie": Kritische Kontrolle der frühesten Belege', *Zeitschrift Für Ethnologie* 95 (2): 169–82.

Funk, D. A. and N. A. Tomilov, eds. 2006. *Ti͡urkskie narody Sibiri* (Moscow: Nauka).

Gagen-Torn, N. I. 1971. 'Leningradskai͡a ėtnograficheskai͡a shkola v dvadt͡satye gody (u istokov sovetskoĭ ėtnografii)', *Sovetskai͡a ėtnografii͡a* 2: 134–45.

Gellner, E. 1980a. 'Preface', in *Soviet and Western Anthropology*, ed. by E. Gellner (London: Duckworth), ix–xvii.

—. 1980b. 'A Russian Marxist Philosophy of History', in *Soviet and Western Anthropology*, ed. by E. Gellner (London: Duckworth), 59–82.

—. 1988. 'Modern Ethnicity', in *State and Society in Soviet Thought* (Oxford: Blackwell), 115–36.

Goncharov, S. A., L. B. Gashilova and L. A. Bali͡asnikova, eds. 2012. *Real'nost' ėtnosa: obrazovanie i ėtnosot͡sializat͡sii͡a molodezhi v sovremennoĭ Rossii* (St Petersburg: RGPU im. Gertsena).

Graf, W. 1987. '"The 'Non-Capitalist Road" to Development: Soviet and Eastern European Prescriptions for Overcoming Underdevelopment in the Third World', in *The Political Economy of North/South Relations*, ed. by M. Toiva (Peterborough: Broadview).

Graham, L. R. 2016. *Lysenko's Ghost* (Cambridge, MA: Harvard University Press).

Grant, B. 1999. 'Foreword', in *The Social Organization of the Gilyak*, ed. by L. I. Shternberg (New York: American Museum of Natural History), xxiii–lvi.

Gumilëv, L. N. 1965. 'Po povodu predmeta istoricheskoĭ geografii: (Landshaft i ėtnos): III', *Vestnik Leningradskogo universiteta* 3 (18): 112–20.

—. 1966. 'On the Subject of Historical Geography (Landscape and Ethnos, III)', *Soviet Geography* 7 (2): 27–36.

—. 1967a. *Drevnie Tı͡urki* (Moscow: Nauka).

—. 1967b. 'Ėtnos kak ı͡avlenie', in *Doklady otdeleniĭ komissiĭ Geograficheskogo obshchestva SSSR*, ed. by V. A. Belı͡avskiĭ (Leningrad: Prezidium GO SSSR), 90–107.

—. 1967c. 'O termine "ėtnos"', in *Doklady otdeleniĭ komissiĭ Geograficheskogo obshchestva SSSR*, ed. by V. A. Belı͡avskiĭ (Leningrad: Prezidium GO SSSR), 3–17.

—. 1967d. *Otrkrytie Khazarii: Istoriko-geografincheskiĭ ėtı͡ud* (Moscow: Nauka).

—. 1970. 'Ėtnogenez i ėtnosfera', *Priroda* 2: 43–50.

Hirsch, F. 2005. *Empire of Nations: Ethnographic Knowledge and the Making of the Soviet Union* (Ithaca, NY: Cornell University Press).

Hobsbawm, E. 1995. *Age of Extremes: The Short Twentieth Century 1914–1991* (London: Abacus).

Howell, Y. 2010. 'The Liberal Gene: Sociobiology as Emansipatory Discourse in the Late Soviet Union', *Slavic Review* 69 (2): 356–76.

I͡Arkho, A. I. 1932. 'Protiv idealisticheskikh techeniĭ v rasovedenii SSSR', *Antropologicheskiĭ zhurnal* 1: 9–23.

Joravsky, D. 1960. 'Soviet Scientists and the Great Break', *Daedalus* 89 (3): 562–80.

K[oshkin], I. A. and N. M[atorin]. 1929. 'Soveshchanie ėtnografov Leningrada i Moskvy (5/IV – 11/IV 1929 g.)', *Ėtnografiı͡a* 8 (2): 110–14.

Kan, S. 2009. *Lev Shternberg: Anthropologist, Russian Socialist, Jewish Activist* (Lincoln, NE: University of Nebraska Press).

Keldysh, M. V. 1962. 'Stroitel'stvo kommunizma i zadachi obshchestvennykh nauk: (Rech' na Obshchem sobranii AN SSSR)', in *Stroitel'stvo kommunizma i obshchestvennye nauki. Materialy sessii Obshchego Sobraniı͡a Akademii Nauk SSSR 19–20 oktı͡abrı͡a 1962 g. Moskva* (Moscow: Izdatel'stvo AN SSSR), 5–8.

Kerimova, M. M. 2011. *Zhizn', otdannaı͡a nauke. Sem'ı͡a ėtnografov Kharuzinykh. Iz istorii rossiĭskoĭ ėtnografii (1880–1930-e gody)* (Moscow: Vostochnaı͡a literatura).

Kharuzin, N. N. 1901. *Ėtnografiı͡a: lekt͡sii, chitannyı͡a v Imperatorskom Moskovskom universitete* (St Peterburg: Gosudarstvennaı͡a tipografiı͡a).

Kholl, K. 2012. 'Rasovye priznaki koreniı͡atsı͡a glubzhe v prirode chelovecheskogo organizma": neulovimoe poniı͡atie rasy v Rossiĭskoĭ imperii', in "*Poniı͡atiı͡a o Rossii": K istoricheskoĭ semantike imperskogo perioda*, ed. by A. Miller, D. A. Sdvizhkov, and I. Shirle (Moscow: Novoe literaturnoe obozrenie), 194–258.

Knight, N. 1995. *Constructing the Science of Nationality: Ethnography in Mid-Nineteenth Century Russia* (unpublished doctoral disseration, Columbia University).

—. 1998. 'Science, Empire, and Nationality: Ethnography in the Russian Geographical Society, 1845–1855', in *Imperial Russia: New Histories for the Empire*, ed. by J. Burbank and D. L. Ransel (Bloomington, IN: Indiana University Press), 108–41.

—. 2017. 'Geography, Race and the Malleability of Man: Karl von Baer and the Problem of Academic Particularism in the Russian Human Sciences', *Centaurus* 59 (1–2): 97–121, https://doi.org/10.1111/1600-0498.12154.

Kozlov, S. I͡A and P. I. Puchkov, eds. 1995. *Blagodarim sud'bu za vstrechu s nim: O Sergee Aleksandroviche Tokareve — uchenom i cheloveke* (Moscow: Institut etnologii i anthropologii).

Kozlov, V. I. 1956. *Rasselenie mordovskogo naroda v seredine XIX–nachale XX vv.* (unpublished doctoral dissertation).

—. 1967. 'O poni͡atii ėtnicheskoĭ obshchnosti', *Sovetskai͡a Ėtnografii͡a* 2: 100–11.

—. 1996. *Istorii͡a tragedii velikogo naroda* (Moscow: [no pub.]).

—. 2001. 'Ob akademike I͡Uliane Vladimiroviche Bromlee - uchenom i cheloveke', Ėtnograficheskoe obozrenie 4: 3–9.

Kushner (Knyshev), P. I. 1949. 'Uchenie Stalina o nat͡sii i nat͡sional'noĭ kul'ture i ego znachenie dli͡a ėtnografii', *Sovetskai͡a ėtnografii͡a* 4: 3–19.

—. 1951. *Ėtnicheskie territorii i ėtnicheskie granit͡sy* (Moscow: AN SSSR).

Kuznet͡sov, A. M. and A. M. Reshetov, eds. 2001–2002. *Etnograficheskie issledovaniia v 2-x kn.* Izbrannye raboty i materialy / S. M. Shirokogorov (Vladivostok: Izdatel'stvo Dal'nevostochnogo universiteta).

Laruelle, M. 2006. 'Aleksandr Dugin: A Russian Version of the European Radical Right', *Kennan Institute Occasional Papers* 294 (Washington, DC: Woodrow Wilson International Centre for Scholars).

Levandovskiĭ, A. A. 1989. *T. N. Granovskiĭ v russkom obshchestvennom dvizhenii* (Moscow: Izdatel'stvo MGU).

Makarov, N. P., ed. 2004a. *Ėtnosy Sibiri. Proshloe. Nastoi͡ashchee. Budushchee*, vol. 1 (Krasnoiarsk: Krasnoiarskii kraevoi kraevedcheskii muzei).

—. ed. 2004b. *Ėtnosy Sibiri. Proshloe. Nastoi͡ashchee. Budushchee*, vol. 2 (Krasnoi͡arsk: Krasnoi͡arskiĭ kraevoĭ kraevedcheskiĭ muzeĭ).

Markwick, R. D. 2001. *Rewriting History in Soviet Russia: The politics of Revisionist Historiography, 1956–1974* (Basingstoke: Palgrave).

Meshchaninov, I. I. 1934. 'I͡Azyk i myshlenie v doklassovom obshchestve', *Problemy istorii dokapitalisticheskikh obshchestv* 9–10: 18–44.

Miller, A. I. 2015. 'The Romanov Empire and the Russian Nation', in *Nationalizing Empires*, ed. by A. I. Miller and S. Berger (Budapest: CEU Press), 309–68.

Mironov, B. 1985. 'The Russian Peasant Commune after the Reforms of the 1860s', *Slavic Review* 44 (3): 438–67.

Mogilîanskiĭ, N. M. 1908. 'Ėtnografiîa i eë zadachi', *Ezhegodnik Russkogo antropologicheskogo obshchestva* 3: 1–14.

—. 1916. 'Predmet i zadachi ėtnografii', *Zhivaîa starina* 25: 1–22.

Mogilner, M. 2013. *Homo Imperii: A History of Physical Anthropology in Russia* (Lincoln, NE: University of Nebraska Press).

Mullaney, T. S. 2010. *Coming to Terms with the Nation: Ethnic Classification in Modern China* (Berkeley, CA: University of California Press).

Nadezhdin, N. I. 1847. 'Ob ėtnograficheskom izuchenii narodnosti russkoĭ', *Zapiski Russkogo Geograficheskogo Obshchestva* (St Petersburg: Tipografiîa Imperatorskoĭ Akademii Nauk), 61–115.

Okladnikov, A. P. 1937. *Ocherki iz istorii zapadnykh buriat-mongolov* (17–18 vv) (Leningrad: Gos.sotsial'no-ekonom. izd-vo).

Oushakine, S. A. 2009. *The Patriotism of Despair: Nation, War, and Loss in Russia* (Ithaca, NY: Cornell University Press).

—. 2010. 'Somatic Nationalism: Theorizing Post-Soviet Ethnicity in Russia', in *In Marx's Shadow: Knowledge, Power, and Intellectuals in Eastern Europe and Russia*, ed. by C. Brădățan and S. Oushakine (Plymouth: Lexington), 155–74.

Pavlinskaîa, L. R. 2008. *Buriaty: ocherki ėtnicheskoĭ istorii (XVII–XIX vv.)* (St Peterburg: Evropeĭskiĭ Dom).

Pimenov, V. V., ed. 2007. *Osnovy Ėtnologii: Uchebnoe Posobie* (Moscow: Izd-vo MGU).

Pimenov, V. V. 2015. *Moîa professiîa — ėtnograf* (Moscow: Avrora).

Popov, A. A. 1937. *Dolganskii fol'klor* (Leningrad: Sov. pisatel').

Pravda.ru 2017. 'Putin predlozhil tost v chest' Dnîa Pobedy: "Za pobediteleĭ, za mir na nasheĭ zemle, za velikuîu Rossiîu!"', Pravda.ru, 9 May. https://www.pravda.ru/news/society/09-05-2017/1333337-putin-0.

Putin, V. 2012. 'Rossiîa: nat͡sional'nyĭ vopros', *Nezavisimaîa gazeta*, 23 January.

Raĭkov, B. E. 1961. *Karl Bėr. Ego zhizn' i trudy* (Moscow: Izdatel'stvo AN SSSR).

Ratner-Shternberg, S. A. 1935. 'L. ÎA. Shternberg i Leningradskaîa ėtnograficheskaîa shkola 1904–1927 (po lichnym vospominaniîam i arkhivnym dannym)', *Sovetskaîa Ėtnografiîa* 2: 134–54.

Rezolîut͡siîa. 1932. 'Rezolîut͡siîa Vserossiĭskogo arkheologo-ėtnograficheskogo soveshchaniîa 7–11 maîa 1932 g. po dokladam S. N. Bykovskogo i N. M. Matorina' *Sovetskaîa ėtnografiîa* 3: 4–14.

Riasanovsky, N. V. 1959. *Nicholas I and Official Nationality in Russia, 1825–1855* (Berkeley, CA: University of California Press).

Russkoe Antropologicheskoe Obshchestvo. 1889. *Protokoly zasedaniĭ Russkogo Antropologicheskogo Obshchestva pri Imperaterskom Sankt-Peterburgskom universitete za 1888 god* (St Peterburg: [no pub.]).

Sadokhin, A. P. 2006. *Ėtnologii͡a: uchebnik* (Moscow: Gardariki).

Seegel, S. 2012. *Mapping Europe's Borderlands: Russian Cartography in the Age of Empire* (Chicago, IL: University of Chicago Press).

Semёnov, I͡U. I. 1966. 'Kategorii͡a "sot͡sial'nyĭ organizm" i eё znachenie dli͡a istoricheskoĭ nauki', *Voprosy istorii* 8: 88–106.

Semёnov, P. P. 1896. *Istoriia poluvekovoi dei͡atel'nosti Russkogo geograficheskogo obshchestva: 1845–1895* (St Peterburg: [no pub.]).

Semёnov-Ti͡an'-Shanskiĭ, V. P. 1915. 'O mogushchestvennom territorial'nom vladenii primenitel'no k Rossii', *Izvestii͡a Imperatorskogo Russkogo Geograficheskogo Obshchestva* 51 8: 425–57.

Sergeev, M. A. 1955. *Nekapitalisticheskiĭ put' razvitii͡a malykh narodov Severa* (Moscow: Izdatel'stvo AN SSSR).

Shanin, T. 1986. 'Soviet Theories of Ethnicity: The Case of a Missing Term', *New Left Review* (158): 113–22.

Shirokogorov, S. M. 1922a. *Mesto ėtnografii sredi nauk i klassifikat͡sii͡a ėtnosov* (Vladivostok: Izdatel'stvo "Svobodnai͡a Rossii͡a").

—. 1922b. *Zadachi Nesot͡sialisticheskogo dvizhenii͡a: doklad, prochitannyĭ na otkrytom zasedaniĭ Soveta S"ezda Predstaviteleĭ nesotsialisticheskago naselenii͡a Dal'nego Vostoka 26 marta 1922 goda* (Vladivostok: Tip. Voennoĭ akademiĭ).

—. 1923. *Ėtnos — issledovanie osnovnykh print͡sipov izmenenii͡a ėtnicheskikh i ėtnograficheskikh i͡avleniĭ* (Shanghai: Sibpress).

Shlapentokh, D. 2017. 'Alexander Dugin's Views of Russian History: Collapse and Revival', *Journal of Contemporary Central and Eastern Europe* 25 (3): 331–43, https://doi.org/10.1080/25739638.2017.1405491.

Shnirel'man, V. A. 1993. 'Zlokli͡uchenii͡a odnoĭ nauki: ėtnogeneticheskie issledovanii͡a i stalinskai͡a nat͡sional'nai͡a politika', *Ėtnograficheskoe obozrenie* 3: 52–68.

—. 2011. *"Porog tolerantnosti". Ideologii͡a i praktika novogo rasizma* (Moscow: Novoe literaturnoe obozrenie).

Shternberg, L. I͡A 1904. 'Ėtnografii͡a', in *Ėnt͡siklopedicheskiĭ Slovar' F. A. Brokgauza i I. A. Efrona*, ed. by I. E. Andreevskiĭ, K. K. Arsen'ev, and F. F. Petrushevskiĭ (St Peterburg: [no pub.]), 180–89.

Skalník, P. 2007. 'Gellner vs Marxism: A Major Concern or a Fleeting Affair?', in *Ernest Gellner and Contemporary Social Thought*, ed. by S. Malešević and M. Haugaard (Cambridge: Cambridge University Press), 103–21.

Slezkine, Y. 1991. 'The Fall of Soviet Ethnography, 1928–38', *Current Anthropology* 32 (4): 476–84.

Smith, W. D. 1980. 'Friedrich Ratzel and the Origins of Lebensraum', *German Studies Review* 3 (1): 51–68.

Soloveĭ, T. D. 2001. '"Korennoĭ perelom" v otechestvennoĭ ėtnografii (diskussii͡a o predmete ėtnologicheskoĭ nauki k. 1920-kh - n. 1930-kh gg.)', *Ėtnograficheskoe obozrenie* 3: 101–20.

Soloveĭ, V. D. 2008. *Krov' i pochva russkoĭ istorii* (Moscow: Russkiĭ mir).

Stagl, J. 1995. *A History of Curiosity: The Theory of Travel 1550–1800* (Amsterdam: Harwood).

—. 1998. 'Rationalism and Irrationalism in Early German Ethnology: The Controversy between Schlözer and Herder, 1772/73', *Anthropos* 93 (4/6): 521–36.

Stalin, I. V. 1946 [1913]. 'Marksizm i nat͡sional'nyĭ vopros', in *Sochinenii͡a, t. 2 (1907–1913)*, ed. by Institut Marksa — Ėngel'sa — Lenina pri T͡SK VKP(b) (Moscow: Gosudarstvennoe izdatel'stvo politicheskoĭ literatury), 290–367.

Stocking, G. W. 1971. 'What's in a Name?: The Origins of the Royal Anthropological Institute', *Man* 7: 369–90.

Stocking, G. W. 1992. *The Ethnographer's Magic and Other Essays in the History of Anthropology* (Madison, Wisconsin: University of Wisconsin Press).

Struve, V. V. 1938. 'Chetyrekhtomnik "Narody SSSR"', *Leningradskai͡a Pravda*, 28 Jan. 7210 (22).

—. 1939. 'Sovetskai͡a ėtnografii͡a i eë perspektivy', in *Sovetskai͡a ėtnografii͡a. Sbornik stateĭ*, ed. by Institut ėtnografii Akademii nauk SSSR (Moscow: Izdatel'stvo Akademii nauk SSSR), 3–10.

Suny, R. G. 1993. *The Revenge of the Past: Nationalism, Revolution and the Collapse of the Soviet Union* (Stanford, CA: Stanford University Press).

Terlet͡skiĭ, P. E. 1930. 'Nat͡sional'noe raĭonirovanie Kraĭnego Severa', *Sovetskiĭ Sever* 7–8: 5–29.

—. 1934. 'K voprosu o parmakh Nenet͡skogo okruga', *Sovetskiĭ Sever* 5: 35–44.

Thomas, C. Y. 1978. 'The Non-Capitalist Path As Theory and Practice of Decolonization and Socialist Transformation', *Latin American Perspectives* 5 (2): 10–28.

Tishkov, V. A. 1992. 'The Crisis in Soviet Ethnography', *Current Anthropology* 33 (4): 371–94.

—. 1997. *Ocherki teorii i politiki ėtnichnosti v Rossii* (Moscow: Russkiĭ mir).

—. 2000. 'My stali zhit' luchshe. Vvedenie v obshchepartiĭnuiu izbiratel'nuiu programmu', *Nezavisimaia gazeta — Stsenarii,*, 12 Jan, 2000 (3).

—. 2003. *Rekviem po etnosu* (Moscow: Nauka).

—. 2005. *Ėtnologiia i politika. Stat'i 1989–2004 godov* (Moscow: Nauka).

—. 2010. *Rossiĭskiĭ narod. Kniga dlia uchitelia* (Moscow: Prosveshchenie).

—. 2013. *Rossiĭskiĭ narod: istoriia i smysl natsional'nogo samosoznaniia* (Moscow: Nauka).

—. 2016. 'Ot ėtnosa k ėtnichnosti i posle', *Ėtnograficheskoe obozrenie* 5: 5–22.

Tokarev, S. A. 1964. 'Problema tipov ėtnicheskikh obshchnosteĭ (k metodologicheskim problemam ėtnografii)', *Voprosy filosofii* 11: 43–53.

—. 1966. *Istoriia russkoĭ ėtnografii (Dooktiabr'skiĭ period)* (Moscow: Nauka).

—. and N. N. Cheboksarov. 1951. 'Metodologiia ėtnogeneticheskikh issledovaniĭ na materiale ėtnografii v svete rabot I. V. Stalina po voprosam iazykoznaniia', *Sovetskaia ėtnografiia* 4: 7–26.

Tol'ts, V. 2012. 'Diskursy o rase: imperskaia Rossiia i Zapad v sravnenii' in: *Poniatiia o Rossii: k istoricheskoĭ semantike imperskogo perioda*, ed. by A. Miller, D. Sdvizhkov, I. Shirle. vol. 2. (Moscow: Novoe literaturnoe obozrenie), 145–93.

Tumarkin, D. D. 2003. 'IU. V. Bromleĭ i zhurnal "Sovetskaia ėtnografiia"', in *Akademik IU. V. Bromleĭ i otechestvennaia ėtnologiia. 1960–1990-e gody*, ed. by S. IA Kozlov (Moscow: Nauka), 212–27.

Turaev, V. A. 2008. *Dal'nevostochnye ėvenki: ėtnokul'turnye i ėtnosotsial'nye protsessy v XX veke* (Vladivostok: Dal'nauka).

Umland, A. 2009. 'Formirovanie pravoradikal'nogo "neoevraziĭskogo" intellektual'nogo dvizheniia v Rossii (1989–2001 gg.)', *Forum noveĭsheĭ vostochnoevropeĭskoĭ istorii i kul'tury* 1: 93–104.

—. 2016. 'Alexander Dugin and Moscow's New Right Radical Intellectual Circles at the Start Of Putin's Third Presidential Term 2012–2013: The Anti-Orange Committee, The Izborsk Club And The Florian Geyer Club In Their Political Context', *Europolity–Continuity and Change in European Governance-New Series* 10 (2): 7–31.

Vaĭnshteĭn, S. I. 2004. 'IUlian Vladimirovich Bromleĭ: chelovek, grazhdanin, uchenyĭ', in *Vydaiushchiesia otechestvennye ėtnologi i antropologi*, ed. by V. A. Tishkov and D. D. Tumarkin (Moscow: Nauka), 608–27.

Vasil'ev, I. A. 1936. 'Transportnoe sobakovodstvo Severa', *Sovetskaia Arktika* 4: 78–88.

Vasilevich, G. M. 1934. *Ėvenkiĭskie skazki* (Leningrad: Izd-vo detskoĭ literatury).

—. 1936. *Sbornik materialov po Ėvenkiĭskomu (Tungusskomu) fol'kloru* (Leningrad: Izdatel'stvo Instituta narodov Severa).

Vermeulen, H. F. 1995. 'Origins and Institutionalization of Ethnography and Ethnology in Europe and the USA, 1771–1845', in *Fieldwork and Footnotes: Studies in the History of European Anthropology*, ed. by H. F. Vermeulen and A. A. Roldan (Routledge: London), 39–59.

—. 2015. *Before Boas: The Genesis of Ethnography and Ethnology in the German Enlightenment* (Lincoln, NE: University of Nebraska Press).

Watters, F. M. 1968. 'The Peasant and the Village Commune', in *The Peasant in Nineteenth Century Russia*, ed. by W. S. Vucinich (Stanford, CA: Stanford University Press), 133–57.

Weiner, M. 1997. 'The Invention of Identity: Race and Nation in Pre-War Japan', in *The Construction of Racial Identities in China and Japan: Historical and Contemporary Perspectives*, ed. by F. Dikötter (Honolulu, HI: Hurst), 96–117.

Za sovetskui͡u. 1932. 'Za sovetskui͡u antropologii͡u', *Antropologicheskiĭ zhurnal* 1: 1–8.

Zhurnal zasedanii͡a. 1916. 'Zhurnal zasedanii͡a Otdelenii͡a ėtnografii IRGO 4 marta 1916 goda', *Zhivai͡a starina* 2–3: 1–11.

Zorin, A. 2004. *'Kormi͡a dvuglavogo orla'. Literatura i gosudarstvennai͡a ideologii͡a v Rossii v posledneĭ treti XVIII–pervoĭ treti XIX veka* (Moscow: Novoe literaturnoe obozrenie).

Zyri͡anova, A. 2017. '"Utechka biodannykh": kto i zachem sobiraet biomaterialy rossii͡an', *Russkai͡a sluzhba Bi-Bi-Si*, 9 Nov.

Archival References

ARAN: Archive of the Russian Academy of Sciences, Moscow

ARAN 142-10-522. Protokoly i stenogrammy zasedaniĭ gruppy obshcheĭ ėtnografii IĖ AN SSSR. 1965 g. 299 folios.

ARAN 457-1(1953–2002)-527. Protokoly № 1–19 zasedaniĭ Bi͡uro otdelenii͡a istorii AN SSSR. 1967 g. 179 folios.

NA RGO: Scientific Archive of the Russian Geographical Society, St Petersburg

NA RGO 109-1-15. L. I͡A. Shternberg, F. K. Volkov, N. M. Mogili͡anskiĭ. Zapiska ob ėtnografii i antropologii [undated]. 13 folios.

TsGAM: Central State Archive of [the City of] Moscow

TsGAM P7349-1-13. Protokoly zasedaniĭ partiĭnoĭ organizat͡sii Instituta ėtnografii, 1960 g.

SPF ARAN: St Petersburg Filial of the Archive of the Russian Academy of Sciences

SPF ARAN 1004-1-118: 8–14. Rudenko, Sergeĭ I. [Ėtnos i ėtnogenez: po povodu odnoĭ diskussii v otdelenii ėtnografii VGO]. Typescript with the handwritten annotations of Lev N. Gumilëv.

3. Ukrainian Roots of the Theory of *Etnos*

Sergei S. Alymov

The aim of this chapter is to contextualize the first appearance of *etnos* as a principal object of ethnographic research. This Greek-derived term was first elevated to a central theoretical concept by Nikolaĭ Mikhaĭlovich Mogilı̑anskiĭ in 1916 in an article titled "The Object and Tasks of Ethnography" (Mogilı̑anskiĭ, 1916).[1] At that time, Mogilı̑anskiĭ was a comparatively young thirty-year-old scholar who had recently taken up the post of curator at the newly created Russian Museum. That fact alone makes one curious as to how the term *etnos* "suddenly" emerged. This chapter examines its appearance and the theoretical thinking behind it not as the creation of an individual mind, but rather as a product of the activity of a network of intellectuals that exchanged ideas and were influenced by contemporary trends in European science. Mogilı̑anskiĭ, as well as the author of the first detailed book-length exposition of *etnos*, Sergei Shirokogoroff (1923), was certainly a part of this circle of turn-of-the-century scholars and his work reflected ideas that were "in the air".

The intellectual tradition that produced *etnos* theory was formed around such institutions as the Department of Geography and

1 As outlined in Chapter 2, the term first appeared in 1908 in Mogilı̑anskiĭ's review of the first volume of N. Kharuzin's (1901) *Ethnography* (Mogilı̑anskiĭ, 1908) but that text did not contain a detailed definition of *etnos* as a theoretical concept. According to this published text, Mogilı̑anskiĭ first presented his review of Kharuzin in 1902 at a meeting of the St Petersburg University's Russian Anthropological Society.

 https://doi.org/10.11647/OBP.0150.03

Ethnography of St Petersburg University, the Russian Anthropological Society of St Petersburg University, the Russian Museum, and the Museum of Anthropology and Ethnography (Kunstkamera, or MAĖ) of the Academy of Sciences. The main features that characterized their thinking were:

1) a training in natural sciences and to an extent a shared positivistic idea of biosocial laws that govern society as a "natural" phenomenon;
2) an interest or training in physical (biological) anthropology;
3) a connection to the discipline of geography and sometimes geographical determinism;
4) borrowings from contemporary French and German anthropology;
5) a vision of anthropology as an umbrella natural science of "man" that stemmed mainly from the French tradition. Ethnography was seen as one of its sub-disciplines.

Apart from these common traits, there was one characteristic that Mogilı͡anskiĭ shared with his older friend and teacher Fëdor Kondratievich Volkov [Khfider Vovk]: their Little Russian/Ukrainian origins and active involvement in the Ukrainian national movement and Ukrainian politics. This chapter will deal mainly with the influence of this movement on *etnos* theory. It will argue that Mogilı͡anskiĭ and Volkov's involvement in a movement with the main aim of formulating and defending its program in ethnic-national terms made these anthropologists particularly mindful of ethnic divisions while their scientific anthropological outlook contributed to the way they naturalized these differences. The appearance of "*etnos* thinking" should be considered not as an invention of pure scientists, but in the political context of the turbulent last years of the Russian Empire, "replete with national parties and movements" at the age of collapsing empires and rising nation-states (Semyonov and Smith 2017: 373).

Since the following text is an attempt to reconstruct the context and genealogy of Mogilı͡anskiĭ's thinking and the origins of *etnos* theory, a short outline of his biography is necessary. Nikolaĭ Mogilı͡anskiĭ was born in 1871 in Chernigov in Malorossii͡a. His father was the son of a priest, but received a juridical university education, served as an investigator and a judge, and was granted personal nobility. In 1889 Nikolaĭ entered the natural sciences division of St Petersburg University, where he attended the lectures of the anthropologist and geographer Ėduard Petri (1854–1899) and the anatomist Pëtr Lesgaft (1837–1911) amongst others (TsGIA SPb 14-3-26932: 32–37, 41). He became interested in anthropology, but was not satisfied with Petri's teaching, and in 1894 he went abroad to continue his education in Paris. During his stay there, Mogilı͡anskiĭ studied anthropology at L'École d'anthropologie under Paul Broca's disciple, Léonce Manouvrier (1850–1927). He also attended Gabriel de Mortillet's (1821–1898) lectures on archaeology and comparative ethnography, as well as lectures by Charles Létourneau (1831–1902) and others. In Paris he became close friends with Volkov, a more experienced anthropologist and compatriot who would have an important influence on him:

> For a start of my studies I needed no better guide [than Volkov]. During the days we listened to lectures together, in the evenings we discussed them, delved into the literature and made plans for the future [...] F. K. Volkov taught me the basics of photography, and I tried to make photos for scientific purposes (GARF R-5787-1-17: 83).

Upon returning to St Petersburg, Mogilı͡anskiĭ became a professional anthropologist and ethnographer (Fig. 3.1). He worked for a time at the Museum of Anthropology and Ethnography and in the Russian Museum until 1918. He also lectured in anthropology and geography in several educational institutions. After the Bolshevik revolution, Mogilı͡anskiĭ moved to Kiev, where he held high posts in the government of the recently independent Ukraine under Hetman Pavlo Skoropadskiĭ (1873–1945). In 1920, he immigrated to Paris and in 1923 he moved to Prague, where he resumed his teaching and research. Mogilı͡anskiĭ died in Prague in 1933. As can be seen from this short biography, Mogilı͡anskiĭ lived most of his life in St Petersburg, the capital of the Russian Empire and Russian intellectual life, at the same time retaining the sympathies and connections of his south Russian background. But, before turning to the Ukrainian roots of *etnos* per se, we need a short overview of the St Petersburg anthropological scene, of which Mogilı͡anskiĭ and his friend and colleague Volkov were both a part.

Fig. 3.1 Nikolaĭ Mogilīanskiĭ upon his return from Paris with the employees of the Mobile Museum of Teaching Aids, St Petersburg, 1898. Mogilīanskiĭ is standing at the far right (no. 6). Sitting at the far left (no. 1) is Aleksandra Kollontaĭ, future People's Commissar of Social Welfare in the first Soviet government. Commenting on this photo in his diary, Mogilīanskiĭ wrote in 1920 "[…] A. M. Kollontaĭ was not yet a People's Commissar, i.e. narkom, but a nice, charming lady, a wife of an officer of the Guards. I came back from Paris in the spring and in the autumn took part in the organization and work of the Mobile Museum of Teaching Aids" (GARF R-5787-1-6-83; GARF R-5787-1-6-84). © State Archive of the Russian Federation, Moscow

St Petersburg Anthropology before Volkov

A paradigm that saw ethnography as a sub-discipline of the natural science of man was predicated upon its institutional position in the university curriculum. The department of geography and ethnography was opened at St Petersburg University in 1887 as part of the division of natural sciences in the faculty of physics and mathematics. The department's first professor was Ėduard Petri (Fig. 3.2), a Baltic German who received his degree in medicine from the University of Bern in 1883 (Tikhonov 2003: 109–12; Mogil'ner 2008: 112–20). He was an anthropologist and started his teaching at St Petersburg with a lecture titled "Human Races and their Significance in Science and Life" (TsGIA SPb 14-1-8843: 6). His two-volume coursebook, *Anthropology*, published in 1890 and 1895, is the main source of information about his teaching and views (Petri 1890, 1895).

Fig. 3.2 Portrait of Ėduard Petri. Photographer unknown. *Ezhegodnik Russkogo antropologicheskogo obshchestva*, vol. 4, 1913, insert 2

Petri saw anthropology as the study of the natural history of "man", which was further subdivided into sciences that studied "man" as an individual organism (anatomy, physiology and psychology) and as a "social organism" (ethnography, ethnology, and sociology, each of them having a homological relation to the disciplines in the first set). Petri conceived of ethnography as the comparative anatomy of various peoples or description of their appearances, while ethnology studied their "life" and dealt with material and spiritual culture (Petri 1890: 42–43). Petri was sceptical about dividing the human race into neat categories based only on physical characteristics. The generalized "types" of European, African, and Mongol man he described in his textbook had both physical and psychological characteristics. Arguing against Friedrich Muller's vision of nationalities as differing only in language and ways of life, he claimed that nations are basically smaller subdivisions of races that could be grouped together on the basis of all "anthropological data" about them (Petri 1890: 107).

In 1892, Petri published a short program, "Anthropological Collections and Observations", which was intended to become a guideline for a truly scientific fieldworker. The program illustrated his idea of the "division of labour" between ethnography and ethnology; it also reflected his conceptualization of nationality. He divided the program into ethnographical and ethnological parts. The ethnographical section contained detailed instructions concerning the measurement and preservation of all body parts, skeletons, and skulls, i.e. manipulations that later were routinely seen as referring to the field of physical anthropology. Introducing his methodological recommendations, Petri noted that when encountering a new *narodnost'* the researcher must first determine the characteristics that differentiate this group from others, observing somewhat melancholically that "to find at least one specimen of a certain variety of mankind alive or in a complete state is a rare happy occasion" (Petri 1892: 5). A few lines later, he added that the researcher can "diagnose" nationality based on one skull only in an extreme case and needs a collection of skulls to make a sure judgment. The ethnological half of the program contained entries covering material culture, social life, and spiritual culture. The final paragraph of the latter read: "Perceptivity to the higher culture. Attitudes to schooling. Future prospects" (Petri 1892: 20). Thus, the paradigm of seeing ethnic differences in biological terms while at the same time rejecting the epistemological validity of the idea of race was in place in Petri's writings and was further elaborated by his followers.

Petri's immediate successor, Dmitriĭ Andreevich Koropchevskiĭ (1842–1903) (Fig. 3.3), is quite remarkable in this regard. Born in Moscow and educated at Moscow University, he became interested in anthropology and prehistoric archaeology under the influence of his tutors: zoologist and anthropologist Anatoliĭ P. Bogdanov (1834–1896), and geologist and palaeontologist Grigoriĭ E. Shchurovskiĭ (1803–1884). In the 1860–1880s he worked as a journalist and authored many popular science books and articles, including reviews of Petri and Paul Topinard's anthropology textbooks. He probably edited most of the translations of foreign anthropological literature, including the works of Edward B. Tylor, John Lubbock, Élisée Reclus, Karl W. Bücher, and many others, such as the English social Darwinist Walter Bagehot.

In 1899 he started teaching at St Petersburg University with a course on anthropogeography (TsGIA SPb 14-2-1390: 11–12). This was not a random topic. Fridrich Ratzel's work had exercised a formative influence on Koropchevskiĭ's thinking. In addition to editing Ratzel's Russian translations, Koropchevskiĭ published *An Introduction to Political Geography* (Koropchevskiĭ 1901) which popularized Ratzel's concept of anthropogeography and outlined "the newest geographical ideas about the significance of surrounding nature for the physical, mental and social development of humanity" (Ibid: vii). In this work he came quite close to evaluating the laws governing correlations between the density of population, territory, and "the level of culture" obtained by certain peoples or states. Their viability, in his opinion, heavily depended on their ability to expand, increase in population, and encourage the population's activity. This led Koropchevskiĭ to portray colonialism as a natural phenomenon that demonstrated the internal weaknesses and "unhealthy basis" of the colonized (Ibid: 134–36).

Fig. 3.3 Portrait of Dmitriĭ Koropchevskiĭ. Photographer unknown. *Ezhegodnik Russkogo antropologicheskogo obshchestva*, vol. 4, 1913, insert 2

Koropchevskiĭ presented his most pronounced presentation of peoples as the important collective actors in his dissertation, *The Significance of "Geographical" Provinces in Ethnogenetic Processes*, published soon after his death in the first volume of *The Annual Review of the Russian Anthropological Society*. Koropchevskiĭ began his study with a critique of the concept of race, which he, following French anthropologists Topinard and Deniker, saw as an abstract and subjective collection of physical characteristics. Instead, he credited only peoples and ethnic groups with real existence. These, in his view, constituted the proper object for ethnology:

> Theoretically, the main object of ethnologist's research is the ethnogenetic (*narodoobrazovatel'nyĭ*) process [...] Practically the task of the ethnologist boils down to defining to which stage of ethnogenetic process one or another ethnic group can be assigned (Koropchevskiĭ 1905: 27).

Ethnic groups or types, Koropchevskiĭ argued, should be studied in connection with the geographical milieu that gave birth to them. He saw the ethnogenetic processes in naturalistic terms as defined by Ratzel and the German naturalist Moritz Wagner, who discovered the main evolutionary mechanism in migration and isolation of species. Thus, Koropchevskiĭ followed Petri's line of argument in preferring ethnic terms to racial ones and, at the same time, introduced Ratzel's concept of geographic determinism and the term "ethnogenesis", which would have a long career in twentieth-century Russian-Soviet science.

As one can see from this brief overview, the fledgling discipline of anthropology in St Petersburg can be described as the "science of race" only with an important qualification. Their main representatives were rather sceptical of this concept. Instead, they often spoke about human "types", distinguished on the basis of various physical and non-physical characteristics, which they tended to equate with peoples or "nationalities".

The Ukrainian National Movement and the Definition of Nationality

Defining nationality as a natural unit was not the only prerequisite for the birth of *etnos*. Ideological motivation and national fervour were also ingredients that contributed to this complex notion. As has been already noted, Mogilîanskiĭ, who coined the term in its modern usage, and Volkov, an older friend and colleague who influenced Mogilîanskiĭ's thinking, both came from what was known at the time as southern or Little Russia (Malorossiîa) — modern Ukraine. Although they both became cosmopolitan intellectuals who published and worked in several countries, they never lost touch with their motherland and promoted the Ukrainian cause in various ways.

Mikhaĭlo S. Hrushevs'kiĭ [Mikhaĭl S. Grushevskiĭ] (1866–1934) called Ukrainian ethnography "a martial science" that dominated Ukrainian studies throughout the nineteenth century. For the Ukrainian public, the richness of folklore constituted "one of the major signs attesting to the value of the Ukrainian element and its rights to development and national culture" (Grushevskiĭ 1914: 15). Nevertheless, until the middle of the century Ukrainian ethnography had a predominantly antiquarian character and consisted mainly in collecting and publishing folksongs. Idioms of "academic Ukrainianness", as Serhiy Bilenkyi has put it, reflected Herderian ethnolinguistic understanding of nationality, and were based on ethnography, language, mentality and history (Bilenkyi 2012: 285). The historiographic and literary activity of Little Russian patriots was in no way incompatible with the appreciation of the Russian Empire or an "all-Russian identity".

> The cultural and historical particularity of Little Russia, as well as the special regional patriotism of the Little Russians, were quite acceptable to the advocates of the All-Russian nation concept. Moreover, in the first half of the nineteenth century Little Russian specificity evoked lively interest in St. Petersburg and Moscow as a more picturesque, romantic variation of Russianness (Miller 2003: 27).

Things began to change by the mid-1840s, the period which saw "the beginning of modern Ukrainian nationalism" (Ibid: 247). The first semi-organized nationalist movement with clear political aims — the Sts. Cyril and Methodius Brotherhood (1845–1847) — appeared on the eve of the European Spring of Nations (1848) and was harshly put down by the Tsarist government. Mykola [Nikolaĭ] I. Kostomarov (1817–1885), the leader of the Brotherhood and author of its programmatic statements was arrested, removed from his position as a professor of history at Kiev University, and after a year in prison, was sent into exile. Returning to public activity in the 1860s, he became a prolific historian and ethnographer who, as the *Encyclopedia of Ukraine* puts it, "argued for the national distinctiveness of the Ukrainian people and the uniqueness of their historical development, which [...] was manifested in the Ukrainian freedom-loving, democratic, and individualistic spirit" (Zukovsky 1988).

"Spirit" was indeed at the centre of his thoughts about nationality, expressed in an essay, "Two Russian Nationalities" (Kostomarov 1861), that became a key text of Ukrainian nationalism. He wrote that while "external" differences between Great and Little Russians in appearance, customs and language are obvious, all these features arise from the depth of their souls, and one has to reveal their "spiritual essence" to understand the source of these differences. National character and attitudes are formed, according to Kostomarov, at the very beginning of the history of these nationalities, and the unfolding of history reveals rather than moulds them. In his account, in the twelfth and thirteenth centuries southern and eastern-northern Slavs were already opposites in their attitudes to authority, spirituality, and social life. Great Russians, Kostomarov contends, tend to be authoritarian state-builders who have no poetic sensibility and are not able to penetrate beneath the ritualistic surface of religion. Little Russians, on the other hand, are sensitive, religious, and democratic people, incapable of real politics and state building. Thus, Kostomarov perceived nationality as a person, whose character could be best known by the study of their collective poetry, i.e. folklore (Bilenkyi 2012: 293). Other prominent members of the Brotherhood Panteleĭmon Kulish and Taras Shevchenko shared Kostomarov's views:

> Modern Ukrainian nationality as envisioned by the Sts. Cyril and Methodius Brotherhood was based on ethnography, language, history, and egalitarian sociopolitical values that sharply contrasted it with the dominant visions of Russianness (Ibid: 300).

During the following decades the Ukrainophile movement experienced several ups and downs. During the liberal reforms of Alexander II, members of the Brotherhood were allowed to the imperial capital. In the early 1960s, Ukrainophile activists organised their circles (*hromadi*) in major cities of southern Russia. In St Petersburg they founded a journal *Osnova* which discussed the independent status of Ukrainian language, history and identity (including the abovementioned Kostomarov's article) and championed the idea of the federation of southern and northern Rus'. This short period was followed by the closure of *Osnova* and the Valuev Circular (1863), forbidding to publish grammars and elementary reading books in the Little Russian language. A revival of the movement occurred during "the Kiev Period of Ukrainophilism" which Alekseĭ Miller dates 1872–1876 (Miller 2003: 155–77). The Kiev Hromada renewed its activity under the leadership of historians and ethnographers Volodimir Antonovich [Włodzimierz Antonowicz] (1834–1908), Pavlo P. Chubins'kiĭ [Pavel P. Chubinskiĭ] (1839–1884) and philologist and critic Mikhaĭlo [Mikhail] Dragomanov (1841–1895). They were connected to the short-lived south-western branch of the Russian Imperial Geographic Society. The branch collected and published historical and ethnographical material and was closed down in 1876 by the authorities. The crackdown was accompanied by another restriction on teaching in the Ukrainian language ("the Ems edict")[2] and the exile of the leaders of Hromada.

While Kostomarov's thinking still conceived of nationality in romantic terms as "the spirit of the people" or people's character, with the advent of positive science these arguments would be supported by more "solid" and "objective" evidence. This was evident in a synopsis of the lectures on Ukrainian anthropology and ethnography Volodimir Antonovich delivered in Kiev in the 1880s and early 1890s. Antonovich taught history at Kiev University from 1870 until his death. He influenced a whole generation of historians, the most well-known among them being the leader of Ukrainian historiography and its national movement, Hrushevs'kiĭ (Līaskoronskiĭ 1908). But Antonovich was also well prepared to embrace the new spirit of positivism emerging at the turn of the century. His first education was in medicine and natural sciences. While in Paris he studied anthropology under Topinard (Korotkiĭ and Ul'īanovs'kiĭ 1997: 27). A polymath scholar, Antonovich also pioneered archaeological excavations in the Kiev area. So, his interests were quite close to anthropology, in the broad sense of the term, while his historical writings were also much more positivistic and based on extensive archival research, in contrast to Kostomarov's literary romantic style.

2 This decree, signed by Alexander II in Bad Ems (Germany), forbade the publication of books in Ukrainian and the use of the language in education in the Russian Empire.

Antonovich gave private lectures on anthropology, ethnography, and archaeology at his home, lectures that sometimes resulted in police intervention (Korotkiĭ and Ul'îanovs'kiĭ 1997: 431–32). He had good reasons to be wary of the police and their actions: he was deeply involved with the Khlopomany, the populist movement of the 1860s. He also severed his connections with his aristocratic Polish milieu and became one of the founders of Hromada, an organization of nationally minded Ukrainian intellectuals. The synopsis of his lectures on anthropology and ethnography was published in Lvov in 1888 under the title "Three National Types of Peoples" which referred to the "types" of the Little Russians, Great Russians, and the Poles. In these lectures he defined nationality as the sum of the characteristics that differentiate one group of people from another. These characteristics are of two kinds: some are given by nature and are primordial; others are "developed on the basis of the first ones" and are shaped by a nation's history and culture.

The most important primordial characteristics, according to Antonovich, were to be found in the data of physical anthropology, particularly measurements of the skull. Craniological data he provided attested to significant differences in the shapes and other indicators of the skulls and faces of Great Russians, Ukrainians and Poles. The peoples' characters, in Antonovich's interpretation, not only exhibited differences similar to those described by Kostomarov; these differences had a natural basis in what he called the "functioning of the nervous system of a people" whereby the nervous system of a Muscovite was of a phlegmatic type, the Poles were sanguine, and the Ukrainians-Russians were melancholic (Antonovich 1995: 90–100). According to one memoirist, Volkov was not satisfied with this publication by Antonovich. Nevertheless, it was he who continued Antonovich's positivistic approach to the "national question" in Ukrainian science (Ibid: 755).

Volkov and the Politics of Ukrainian Identity in the Russian Empire

As we have seen in Antonovich's case, historians who embraced positivism tended to become interested in physical anthropology and were ready to see nationality not only as an incarnation of national spirit expressed through folklore and literature, but also as a natural phenomenon that has to do with the bodily characteristics of the population in question. One scholar who probably did most to elaborate on this approach was Khfider Vovk, known in Russian literature as Fëdor Kondrat'evich Volkov (Fig. 3.4). Volkov was an anthropologist, ethnographer, and archaeologist who, as a preface to a post-Soviet Ukrainian reissue of a collection of his works put it:

> [...] refuted fabrications of Russian imperial historians that Ukraine is only "South Russia" and "a periphery" [...]. In his archaeological, anthropological and ethnographical works [...] the scholar convincingly proves that Ukrainians are a separate and distinct kind among neighbouring Slavic peoples, an anthropological type that possesses entirely original ethnographic characteristics (Ivanchenko 1995: 3).

Born into the family of a poor official in the Poltava region, Volkov studied at the natural sciences departments in the faculties of physics and mathematics at the universities of Odessa and Kiev. Although he studied mainly botany and chemistry, he also had a long-standing interest in folklore. Being an active member of Kiev's Hromada, he also took part in the ethnographic research activities of the south-western branch of the Russian Geographical Society and in Antonovich's archaeological excavations. He published a program for ethnographic research in Ukraine (1875) and a study of specific features of Ukrainian ornaments (1878) (Franko 2000a: 177).

In the early period of his life, Volkov was influenced by Antonovich, Chubins'kiĭ, and Kostomarov, as well as by contemporary socialist populist theories. As a result of the increasing persecution of members of the Ukrainian national movement, Volkov left the Russian Empire. In 1876, he moved to Geneva, where he worked on Hromada's publications. In 1887, after a peripatetic period involving many cities and countries of residence, he finally settled in Paris, where he attended lectures of leading French anthropologists, including Léonce Manouvrier, Paul

Topinard, and others, and was on the editorial board of the journal *L'Anthropologie*. Between 1901 and 1905 he lectured on anthropology and ethnography at the Russian High School of Social Sciences in Paris at the invitation of its organizers, Ivan I. Mechnikov and Maksim M. Kovalevskiĭ. In 1905 he received a master's degree in natural sciences for his dissertation, *Skeletal Variations of Feet among the Primates and Races of Man* (Taran 2003; Volkov 1905).

Fig. 3.4 Fëdor Kondratievich Volkov (RĖM IM9-93). © Russian Ethnographic Museum, St Petersburg

Volkov's biographer, Oksana Franko, came to the conclusion that "Volkov's social-political activity is inseparably connected with his scientific work, and it is often difficult to see where the first one ends and the second one begins" (Franko 2000b: 26). Franko distinguishes two periods in Volkov's ideological development. During the first, she argues, he can be characterized as a proponent of Mikhaĭlo Dragomanov's ideas of federalist socialism. Dragomanov was an influential Ukrainian critic, historian, folklorist, and activist who struggled to combine socialist views with Ukrainian patriotism and folklorism, opposing both the centralist tendencies of Russian populists and extreme Ukrainian nationalists. Volkov's views evolved in the state-building direction as a result of his collaboration with Galician colleagues who "formulated the idea of political independence as an ultimate goal of Ukrainian movement" (Franko 2000a: 302–03). Volkov supported Hrushevs'kiĭ in his efforts to establish the T. Shevchenko Scientific Society as a centre of Ukrainian studies and an ideological centre designed to unite Ukrainians from the Austro-Hungarian and Russian empires. He was active in organizing the society's ethnographical publications and saw it as a unit for consolidating Ukrainian ethnography.

After the Russian revolution of 1905, Volkov returned to Russia, and in 1907 was appointed a curator at the Russian Museum thanks to Mogil͡anskiĭ's efforts. The same year he also started teaching at St Petersburg University. The very beginning of his teaching there was marked by an incident that involved a police investigation. On 4 February the police arrested several non-students at a "gathering" in a university lecture room. In his statement, one of them explained that he had been invited to Volkov's lecture on "The Ethnography of Ukraine" by the Ukrainian scientific educational society. Volkov, in his turn, did not deny the fact of the lecture, but pointed out that this was a "private meeting aimed at introducing my listeners to the current state of Ukrainian ethnography". The university's rector stepped in to protect Volkov and pointed out that the Ukrainian scientific circle was in the process of formation, its charter would be considered by the university, and its meeting had taken place with the rector's permission (TsGIA SPb 14-1-10085: 7–10).

This small incident was only the beginning of Volkov's intense pro-Ukrainian activity. Franko notes that "The Petersburg period is characterized by a synthesis of his scientific and civic activity: the publishing of *Kobzar* and *Drawing by Taras Shevchenko*, and [the] organization of Shevchenko's jubilees in 1911 and 1914, establishing of [the Ukrainian] Political club and publishing the first Ukrainian encyclopaedia and essays about Galicia, Bukovina and Transcarpathia in protest against the destruction of the region during the First World War" (Franko 2000a: 26). The Petersburg period, which lasted almost until Volkov's death in 1918, was, in Franko's assessment, the peak of his "state-building activity", and his "scientifically-grounded concept of the individuality of the Ukrainian people that differs from all other peoples in its physical, material and spiritual features, laid a solid foundation for state-building" (Ibid: 28).

After the declaration of civil liberties and the convening of the first parliament (Duma), Ukrainian nationalists could finally engage in public politics. The Ukrainian group of the Duma's deputies (which shared its name, Hromada, with the group of Ukrainian intellectuals) had several dozen members, including the famous sociologist and ethnologist Maksim M. Kovalevskiĭ (1851–1916). The intellectual leader of the group was the historian Hrushevs'kiĭ, who prepared the group's programmatic documents that demanded territorial autonomy and self-government for all nationalities of the Russian Empire. The group's mouthpiece was a weekly journal, *Ukrainskiĭ vestnik* (Ukrainian Herald), published "with the close participation" of south Russian academics Hrushevs'kiĭ, Dmitriĭ N. Ovsi͡aniko-Kulikovskiĭ (1853–1920), and Aleksandr A. Rusov (1847–1915). Apart from them, the journal also cooperated with Maksim Kovalevskiĭ, philologist and historian academician Alekseĭ A. Shakhmatov, Mikhaĭlo Mogili͡anskiĭ (Nikolaĭ Mogili͡anskiĭ's brother), Volkov, and many others. The journal's aim, in Hrushevs'kiĭ's words, was "to clarify the Ukrainian national question from historical, cultural (*bytovoĭ*), social and economical sides; to point at the place and importance of Ukraine among other regions of the new democratic Russia, and to contribute to a solution of the national and regional question in general" (Hrushevs'kiĭ 1906: 6). The periodical published only fourteen issues and was closed later the same year after the dissolution of the First Duma in July 1906.

It is obvious that most of the contributions to this journal dealt either with Ukraine and its political and social situation, or with the theory of the "national question" and nationality. The most visible example of the latter was a long essay by the historian of literature, Khar'kov University professor Dmitriĭ Ovsi͡aniko-Kulikovskiĭ, "What is Nationality?", published in parts across almost all issues of the *Ukrainskiĭ vestnik*. This essay was an attempt to define nationality as a complex of psychological characteristics, evident in the mental and volitional spheres of the most "developed" personalities (for example, talented writers) who, according to Ovsîaniko-Kulikovskiĭ, most explicitly revealed national traits; these traits, however, were almost absent among peasants and "savages". This approach could not be more different from that offered by Volkov on the pages of the same journal.

Volkov's contribution was titled "Ukrainians from the Anthropological Point of View" and was published in the journal's seventh issue. This is in fact a short summary of what would later become his definitive work, published in the two-volume edition *Ukrainian People in the Past and Present.* Volkov began his text from a statement about the racially mixed character of all peoples, including Ukrainians. But he then proceeded to deny the language the role of an "ethnic indicator" and claimed that

> [...] the successes of somatic anthropology revealed the complete worthlessness of this indicator and urged [scholars] to look for other, more lasting ones, which happen to be purely physical indicators like the colour of bones, hair and eyes, proportions and forms of various parts of the body and, predominantly, its skeleton (Volkov 1906: 418).

The major characteristics that he then considered were height, "head index" (cranial measurements) and the colour of hair and eyes, all of which he labelled "ethnic indicators". Volkov argued that they all showed a similar pattern of geographic variation along a northeastern-southwestern axis from a comparatively short, blonde, long-headed type to the brachycephalic population of tall stature, dark hair and eyes and a straight and narrow nose that he believed to be "the main Ukrainian type". This type was somewhat "softened" on its northeastern borders due to an increased admixture of Great Russians who, in their turn, had undergone very significant admixture with the Turks and the Finns. Volkov's main conclusions were as follows:

1) Ukrainians belonged to the anthropological type of western and southern Europe and are its eastern extension;
2) the influence of the Turks and Mongols on Ukrainians was minimal;
3) the ethnic affinity between Great Russians, Belorussians, and Ukrainians, although "preserved in the language, to a large extent is lost because of too-significant admixture of Finns

> and other eastern elements among Great Russians, Finnish and Lithuanian elements among Belorussians, and those and probably German ones among the Poles" (Ibid: 426).

Ironically, he concluded the article with the note that, although this could not have any political consequences as long as "race and nation are not the same thing at all", they should "once and for all" stop all reference to Ukrainians as "Polonized" Great Russians or "Moscovized" Poles. This peculiar combination of "ethnic indicators" predicated on characteristics drawn from physical anthropology and the denial of any equation between race and nation are characteristic features of Volkov's thinking that would be passed on to his younger colleagues and students like Nikolaĭ Mogilīanskiĭ.

The Ukrainian People in its Past and Present as a Joint Project of the Russian and Ukrainian Liberal Intelligentsia

Volkov's views on the anthropology of Ukrainians can be traced back to his presentation at the Anthropological Society of Paris in 1897, where he spoke of Ukrainians as "a nation, whose ethnic character can be defined by anatomic, ethnographic and linguistic characteristics" (qtd. in Taran 2003: 53). From 1898 until 1909, the scholar headed the Ethnographic Commission of the T. Shevchenko Scientific Society, which functioned as a budding Ukrainian Academy of Sciences. In 1900, the head of the Society, Mikhaĭlo Hrushevs'kiĭ, suggested the idea of an anthropological expedition to Ukraine and asked Volkov to provide a set of instructions for collecting measurements. The expedition was partly sponsored by the Austrian government, which financed all the society's activities, and Volkov spent four summers, from 1903–1906, measuring the populations of western Ukraine (Taran 2003: 54–55).

The final, classic version of Volkov's studies of Ukraine were published in the second volume of a rich and well-illustrated edition, *The Ukrainian People in its Past and Present*, published in St Petersburg by Maksim A. Slavinskiĭ (1868–1945), the same journalist who edited *Ukrainskiĭ vestnik*. The first volume came out in 1914, the second one in 1916. The book's editorial board was quite remarkable. It included anthropologist and ethnographer Volkov, historian Hrushevs'kiĭ, sociologist and ethnographer Kovalevskiĭ, philologists Fëdor E. Korsh (1843–1915) and Agafangel [Agatangel] E. Krymskiĭ (1871–1942), economist Mikhail I. Tugan-Baranovskiĭ (1865–1919), and philologist and historian Alekseĭ A. Shakhmatov (1864–1920). All of them were professors, two were academicians, and some of them (e.g. Kovalevskiĭ, a prominent Kadet and member of State Duma) were influential in politics. All of them, except Korsh and Shakhmatov, were born in the part of the empire that would later become Ukraine. Volkov, Hrushevs'kiĭ, and Krymskiĭ were actively involved in Hromada and the Ukrainian national movement as well as in Ukrainian state-building and culture during the Civil War (1918–1922) and later (except Volkov, who died in 1918). From 1917–1918 Tugan-Baranovskiĭ, a constitutional democrat, served as a minister of finance for the Ukrainian Republic, which had proclaimed its autonomy in 1917 and independence in January 1918.

Kovalevskiĭ, also a constitutional democrat and deputy of the First and Third Dumas and State Council, was directly involved in the Ukrainian movement. He was the head of the T. Shevchenko Society, Society, whose main purpose was to help Ukrainian students in St Petersburg. His deputy in this society was Volkov (Franko 2000a: 305). During his days as the head of the Russian School of Social Sciences in Paris, Kovalevskiĭ had invited Volkov and Hrushevs'kiĭ to give lectures on anthropology and Ukrainian history. In the First Duma he also sided with the Ukrainian group. It is not clear whether all of these abovementioned academics who were born in "South Russia" identified as "Little Russians" or as Ukrainians. Almost all of them, except Hrushevs'kiĭ, made their careers in the imperial capital or returned to St Petersburg after years living outside of Russia. Overall, they were very closely connected with the Russian life and envisioned Ukraine's future as an autonomous region in the democratic Russia of the future.

Korsh and Shakhmatov, the two editors of *The Ukrainian People* who were not born on Ukrainian soil were far from accidental members of this "team". Korsh was an expert on classic and Slavic languages who expressed sympathy with the Ukrainian movement and he became a chairman of the Society for Slavic Culture, founded in Moscow in 1908. The society's aim was the study of all Slavic cultures, "valuing individual traits of every nationality". In 1912, the first issue of a journal *Ukrainskai͡a zhizn'* (Ukrainian Life) was published in Moscow, featuring a report from the first meetings of the Ukrainian section of the Society for Slavic Culture (the journal's editorial board included, among others, Volkov, Hrushevs'kiĭ, Korsh, Krymskiĭ, M. Mogili͡anskiĭ, and Rusov). The section declared its intention to propagandize the Ukrainian national cause among the Russian public and to prove to it "that Ukrainians constitute a quite independent nation in the historical and ethnographic sense, that the Ukrainian language is not a dialect, but a language with the right to develop on par with Great Russian" (Al. S. 1912: 124).

Korsh was the only *kat͡sap* [Great Russian] present at this meeting of the Ukrainian section of the Society for Slavic Culture. He expressed his total sympathy with the movement and his belief that Ukrainians "like other nations will get what they have the full right to have, and this will tie them to Russia not with coercion but with voluntary bonds and reasons of their self-interest" (Al. S. 1912: 125). His speech, published under the title "Ukrainian People and Ukrainian Language", was his most fully developed statement on this subject. As a linguist he devoted most of his attention to the history of language. Following the academicians Shakhmatov and Sobolevskiĭ, he dated the appearance of the first phonetic peculiarities of the south Russian language to as early as the twelfth century and the formation of "a totally specific, quite distinct Little Russian language" to the fourteenth century. He defined language as "a means of expression of thoughts and feelings of a people, which has a distinctive culture and history and constitutes a certain ethnographic entity". He also pointed to psychological differences between Great and Little Russians, following an already familiar trope of juxtaposing passionate, sensitive, and romantic southerners with harsh northerners. At the same time, he preferred the term "Malorossii͡a" to "Ukraine" and was convinced that Great and Little Russians were "the closest" in all regards (Korsh 1913: 24–40).

Academician Alekseĭ Shakhmatov, a pupil of Korsh and a leading Russian linguist and historian, was probably the most influential expert on the history of the Russian language and early Slavic history. In 1899 he published a concise leaflet, "On the Question of [the] Formation of Russian Tongues and Russian Nationalities" based on Shakhmatov's vast knowledge of East Slavic dialectology and medieval history.

Juxtaposing the information about Slavic tribes and their migrations with differences in dialects, he distinguished four major groups of tribes and dialects (southern, northern, middle-western, and middle-eastern). This division, he argues, dated back to at least the beginning of the second millennium and the dialect groups coalesced into three major "Russian" tongues. Shakhmatov contends that the formation of the Great Russian and Belorussian nationalities dates back to the fourteenth and fifteenth centuries, when the centralized Muscovite and Lithuanian states stimulated the formation of comparatively unified languages. The language of the south Russian *narodnost'*, according to Shakhmatov, corresponds quite neatly to the group of dialects of the south Russian tribes that were already in place circa the tenth century (Shakhmatov 1899).

At the end of 1904, the minister of people's education assigned the Academy of Sciences the task of validating its intention to cancel the prohibition on publishing and distributing any print material in the Malorussian language, imposed by the infamous Ems Edict (1876). The academy convened a special commission chaired by Korsh and consisting of six members, including Shakhmatov. The latter authored one of the commission's concluding documents, titled "About the Abolition of Restraints of the Malorussian Printed Word". He reviewed the history of this printed word, beginning in the sixteenth century, and reiterated his conclusions concerning the diverging development of the Great and Little Russian languages and nationalities since the early Middle Ages, especially after the Tatar invasion (1237–1240). He found no justification for suppressing the Malorussian language and no danger of separatism in its unimpeded development. The only consequence of the oppressive policy, according to Shakhmatov, was the reinforcement of the anti-Russian Galician political forces and their increased influence on Ukrainians in the Russian Empire (Shakhmatov 1905: 16–23).

Finally, one of the leading editors of this volume, Volkov was influenced by the historian Mikhaĭlo Hrushevs'kiĭ, who was by far the most important leader of the Ukrainian national movement and the creator of Ukraine's national historical narrative. Hrushevs'kiĭ and Volkov were both pupils of Antonovich and were deeply involved in the activities of Ukrainian political and scientific organisations. The correspondence between these scholars, which started in 1895 and spans for almost twenty years, reveals their support for the T. Shevchenko Society and the development of Ukrainian studies in Europe and the Russian Empire (Vovk 1997). In his monumental ten-volume *History of Ukraine-Rus* which was published between 1898 and 1936, Hrushevs'kiĭ offered a definition of the Ukrainian people, which came close to that of Volkov. In 1913 he wrote:

> The Ukrainian population differs from its closest neighbours both in anthropological characteristics — i.e., in body build — and in psychological features: in individual temperament, family and social relationships, way of life, and in material and spiritual culture. These psychophysical and cultural characteristics, some of which emerged earlier than others, are all the result of a lengthy process of evolution and quite clearly unify the individual groups of the Ukrainian people into a distinct national entity that differs from other such national entities and possesses an unmistakable and vital national personality — that is, comprises a separate people with a long history of development (qtd. in Plokhy 2005: 176).

Nevertheless, as Plokhy stresses, Hrushevs'kiĭ regarded the distinctiveness of the Ukrainian nation "not so much as the product of any racial distinctiveness (he believed that the Ukrainian nation was racially mixed) as of long historical evolution" (Plokhy 2005: 176). Indeed, in the same introduction to the first volume of his history, he stated that Ukrainians had a "mixed" physical type, and the modern population has different craniological characteristics from their archaeological predecessors (Hrushevs'kiĭ 1904: 3).

As noted above, the ultimate product of the pro-Ukrainian activity that united Great Russian liberal intellectuals and the Ukrainophiles, was the two volume edition *The Ukrainian People in its Past and Present*. The first volume was written exclusively by Hrushev'skiĭ and consisted of his "History of Ukrainian People", along with a historiographical introduction. The second volume consisted of geographic surveys of Ukraine, of the Russian Empire, Galicia, Bukovina, and Carpathian Ruthenia, and an anthropological section that included Volkov's "Anthropological features of the Ukrainian people" and "Ethnographic features of the Ukrainian people", as well as "Custom law of the Ukrainian people" by Aleksandra I͡A. Efimenko, and "A brief outline of the history of the Malorussian (Ukrainian) language" by Alekseĭ Shakhmatov. In his first article Volkov reiterated his conclusion concerning "the anthropological type" of Ukrainians. He also found support in Shakhmatov's thesis about the continuity of the southern Russian dialects' development. "Translating this opinion from linguistic language into an anthropological one", Volkov claimed a greater "purity" of Slavic type among the Ukrainians, unlike the "mixed" population of Great Russians and Belorussians (Volkov 1916a: 453–54).

The second article was an impressive compendium of Ukrainian ethnography, starting with hunting, agriculture, and other means of subsistence, and technology, and concluding with beliefs, customs, and folk knowledge. Volkov claimed that "under the influence of various factors — race, environment, culture, every people creates these items and these phenomena in its own way, the more so, the more integral it is as a racial and social group" (Volkov 1916b: 455). Concluding this 200-page encyclopaedia of Ukrainian ethnography were five clauses that sounded like a credo of Ukrainian nationalism, but that Mogilîanskiĭ, however, referred to as "objective conclusion of impartial science" (Mogilîanskiĭ 1917: 138; 2014: 583–86):

1) The Ukrainian people on the entire territory it occupies is distinguished by a range of common ethnographic characteristics, which leaves no doubt that it constitutes an ethnic unity that definitely stands out among other Slavic peoples.

2) The Ukrainian people preserved in its ethnographic way of life a considerable number of vestiges from the past, proving that it had not undergone very deep ethnic influences from outside, and, in spite of its eventful history, developed its ethnographic characteristics consistently and quite uniformly.

3) As all other peoples, it was exposed to a certain extent to external ethnographic influences and assimilated some alien forms, but not to a degree that could alter its main ethnographic characteristics and remove it from a common Slavic type.

4) In particulars of its ethnographic way of life the Ukrainian people manifests the closest similarity with its Western neighbours — Southern Slavs, such as Bulgarians and Serbs,

as well as Romanians, who remain a quite Slavic people ethnographically. Poland was the main conduit of cultural diffusion from the European West.

5) Ethnographic characteristics of Belarusians and Great Russians in their most ancient form are close if not identical to those of Ukrainians (Volkov 1916b: 647).

Etnos, the St Petersburg Paleoethnological School, and the Teaching of Ethnography

Volkov was a devoted researcher in all branches of the "umbrella" science of anthropology, but his role as a teacher was no less important. Under rather Spartan financial conditions, he managed to attract and nurture a group of talented students who would create what could be described as the "paleoethnological school". His students Pëtr S. Efimenko (1835–1908), Aleksandr A. Miller (1875–1935), Sergeĭ I. Rudenko (1885–1969), and others were responsible for what the historian of archaeology Nadezhda I. Platonova considers to have been a breakthrough in Russian archaeological thought in the 1920s (Platonova 2010: 149). Volkov's students were by no means exclusively archaeologists (Fig. 3.5). Rudenko and David A. Zolotarëv (1885–1935) were primarily physical anthropologists, although both also did ethnographic research. Mogilîanskiĭ, who can be considered Volkov's student, was mainly an ethnographer, but he also taught physical anthropology and geography. This was absolutely natural, since Volkov was very clear about his vision of anthropology as a single science that studies:

> 1) [the] position of man in the line of all mammals (zoological anthropology), 2) anatomical characteristics of different ages, races, sexes etc. (anatomical anthropology), 3) physiology of races, sexes etc. (physiological anthropology), 4) origins and development of human race before the historical record begins (prehistoric anthropology or paleoethnology), 5) study of peoples, their ethnic composition, origins, material and psychological *byt* (culture) (ethnological anthropology or ethnology), 6) study of forms of *byt* and their development (ethnographical anthropology or comparative ethnography), 7) history and laws of origins and development of social groups and relations (sociological anthropology) (Volkov 1915: 100).

Fig. 3.5 Fëdor Volkov during his lessons with students in the Cabinet of Geography and Ethnography, St Petersburg University (SPF ARAN 1004-1-467: 1). © St Petersburg Filial of the Archive of the Russian Academy of Sciences

Volkov offered to divide the department of geography and ethnography into two independent departments and establish an anthropological institute with departments of physical anthropology, prehistoric anthropology, and ethnography. The model for this institute was L'École d'anthropologie in Paris, the only place, where, according to Volkov, anthropological sciences were taught "in their entirety" (Volkov 1915: 102). French anthropology had, however, developed in a rather peculiar way. The term "anthropology" was used to denote "a natural science devoted to "positive" investigations into human anatomy, the variety of human physical types, and "man's place in nature" (Williams 1985: 331).

That understanding was associated with anatomist and anthropologist Paul Broca (1824–1880) who played a key role in establishing the Société d'anthropologie (1859) and the École d'anthropologie (1876). Although Broca and his school ascribed to the most encompassing definition of anthropology, in practice they saw anthropometry, physical anthropology, and "racial science" as their main vocation. Broca was a world-acclaimed leader and innovator in the sphere of anthropometry, but these innovations were put in the service of "racial science", which, in Alice L. Conklin's words, "tried to sort humans neatly into racial categories in which intelligence correlated with skin color, on the basis of increasingly precise measurements of body parts, usually skulls" (Conklin 2013: 5). After Broca's death in 1880, his pupils were generally loyal to the mentor's project, although some of them — for example, Broca's last student Léonce Manouvrier — distanced themselves from biological and racial reductionism.

French *fin de siècle* ethnography was primarily the science of classification of museum objects. The key figure in its development was the first curator of the Musée d'Ethnographie, the museum's chair in anthropology, and the supervisor of Volkov's dissertation, Ernest-Théodore Hamy (1842–1908). With his mentor Armand de Quatrefages he authored a compendium on skull shapes tellingly entitled "Crania ethnica". Although Hamy did not challenge the biological definition of anthropology, his activity as museum curator, according to Conklin, tentatively moved in the direction of the study of cultures in historical rather than evolutionary terms (Conklin 2013: 46). Nevertheless, the aims of ethnology were defined by Broca's students as late as in 1907 in the following way:

> The scientific objective of ethnology is to draw a profile of each race, and then order all the human races in an ascending series, that is to say from the simian point of departure to the most intellectually and socially endowed (qtd. in Ibid: 53).

Volkov's abovementioned suggestion was his contribution to an ongoing discussion about the establishment of the proper teaching of ethnography in Russian universities. In 1911 Mogilīanskiĭ was already complaining that, unlike in France, where an entire school of anthropology existed and "ethnography is taught along with its nearest and inseparable disciplines like prehistoric archaeology and anthropology, linguistics and sociology", none of the abovementioned disciplines found their way into Russian high schools (Mogilīanskiĭ 1911: 474).

In his famous 1916 article, "The Object and Tasks of Ethnography", which introduced the neologism of *etnos* as a theoretical concept to the Russian literature and also laid out his views on the establishment of a department of ethnography, Mogilīanskiĭ closely followed

Volkov's understanding of the relationship between anthropology and ethnography. Understanding ethnography as a part of the natural science of anthropology, he presented *etnos* as its main object:

> The ἔθνος [*etnos*] concept — is a complex idea. It is a group of individuals united together as a single whole [*odno tseloe*] by several general characteristics. [These are:] common physical (anthropological) characteristics; a common historical fate, and finally a common language — which is the foundation upon which, in turn, [an *etnos*] can build a common worldview [and] folk-psychology — in short, an entire spiritual culture (Mogilîanskiĭ 1916: 11).

Mogilîanskiĭ was emphatic about the distinction between the history of culture, which has as its object human culture in general, and ethnography, which deals with *etnos* and its specific features. He suggested establishing two departments — anthropology and ethnography — in the faculty of natural sciences, and a separate department of history of culture in the faculty of history and philology.

The discussion that followed revealed serious disagreement among Russian anthropologists. Two famous experts on the peoples of the north, Lev [Leo] ÎA. Shternberg (1861–1927) and Vladimir I. Iokhel'son [Waldemar Jochelson] (1855–1937), argued that there was no sense in this kind of division and that individual features in any nationality do not exist on their own, but are part of a general evolution of culture (Zhurnal zasedanîîa 1916: 5–9). They both advocated that ethnography be affiliated with the humanities and saw culture as its main object of study, but they both failed to recognize that Mogilîanskiĭ's insistence on the discipline's natural science affiliation revealed a different approach to the question of the nature of ethnic differentiation. Ten days after reading his paper, Mogilîanskiĭ wrote a letter to Shakhmatov in which he expressed the wish to "speed up the business with the commission on the issue of new departments of ethnography and cultural history that I brought up". He also voiced his dissatisfaction with the fact that this commission happened to consist of only those who participated in the debates (Iokhel'son, Semënov-Tîan'-Shanskiĭ and Shternberg) and suggested that its membership should be expanded to include his university colleagues Fëdor A. Braun (1862–1942) and Fëdor K. Volkov (SPF ARAN 134-3-998: 7). He also reiterated his principal idea that,

> ethnography, as a science that has to do with analysing phenomena related to ethnogenesis, cannot be separated from anthropology as a natural discipline and should be taught at the faculty of natural science, because naturalists will not tear off this study from its root, from its ethnic substrate. For historians, philologists and linguists there remains a vast field in ethnography, and they will approach it with their methods and instruments. Anthropologists will always owe them for their analysis, which builds on studying language, mythology, folklore and history. They must elucidate and deepen the very idea of culture in its high philosophical sense and its objectified process of development. They are exactly historians of culture; they will posit the data of ethnography in another scheme, according to another plan and will process them with their methods. That is why I insist on the department of cultural history and not ethnography for historic-philological faculty (Ibid: 8).

Mogili͡anskiĭ's ideas of structuring the material of ethnography according to the principles of the natural sciences and humanities found their best expression in his own lectures. Mogili͡anskiĭ taught courses of geography and anthropology in several institutions. At first, he earned his living as a lecturer in geography at the Teachers' Institute and at the Kadet's Corpus. In 1907, he was elected to the department of geography and ethnography of the private *Vysshie Zhenskie Estestvennonauchnye Kursy M. A. Lokhvit͡skoĭ-Skalon* (High Natural Sciences Courses for Women by M. A. Lokhvitskai͡a-Skalon) where he was teaching "with satisfaction and passion". The courses prepared students for work in primary and secondary schools. He was also employed at the College for Teachers in Military Schools where he taught the basics of anthropology and ethnography. In his memoirs, he refers to his students as "an outstanding audience" consisting of university and military academy graduates or pedagogues who aspired to teaching positions in military education.

The Bolsheviks, according to Mogili͡anskiĭ, ruined this institution by appointing as its director "the only person during its entire history to be expelled from the courses for unspeakable insolence". Instead of reading his paper about Jean-Jacques Rousseau's pedagogy, this person declared that Rousseau was "a fool and idiot" whose theories need not be considered (GARF R-5787-1-23: 140). Mogili͡anskiĭ continued his teaching in exile, where he wrote down or published his lectures. As a result, we can have a clear idea of his concept of a full course of anthropological science.

The manuscript of his course "The Basics of Anthropology" is dated "Paris, 1921" and is dedicated to his students at all three of the abovementioned institutions. In the introduction he defined the tasks of the complex discipline of anthropology:

> the science that studies "types, races, tribes and peoples of the Earth" is called "racial anthropology or ethnology"; ethnography studies *byt* (everyday life), material and spiritual culture of these peoples; and the "relations" inside groups such as families, clans or states is the subject of the last anthropological sub-discipline — sociology (GARF R-5787-1-23: 5).

Following this understanding of the discipline, the first part of the course discussed the classification of races (based on physical traits) and peoples (based on language). The second and third sections discussed cultural and social life in a manner quite consistent with evolutionism and that ignored the ethnic divisions laid out in the first part of the course.

Mogiliânskiĭ's course presented the material in the following order. The first chapters were devoted to ontogenesis and phylogeny of humans, anthropoid forms, and racial classification. Mogiliânskiĭ presented evidence in support of Darwinism and "transformism" of human types and races under the influence of their environment. His understanding of sexual selection and survival of the fittest might be identified as Social Darwinism as he referred to interracial selection: "a constant progressive elimination of the weak by representatives of higher races" as a well-known "general tendency" (Ibid: 59). In the debate between monogenists and polygenists, Mogiliânskiĭ was on the side of the first, although he admitted that the final proof of this theory belonged to the future.

The chapter on racial classification introduced a student into the entangled relationships between such terms as "race", "type", "species", and "tribe". Mogiliânskiĭ acknowledged the lack of agreement among scholars about the nature and quantity of "races". Still, in this part of the course he was rather straightforward in equating "race" with ethnicity or language groups: "one however insignificant but hereditary and durable feature is sometimes enough to distinguish between 'races'. For example, all ethnologists, historians, whether polygenists or monogenists, claim that the Irish belong to a different race than the English. Germans, Slavs, Jews, Celts, Arabs — all these are 'races', more or less different and more or less easily characterized" (GARF R-5787-1-23: 82). At the same time, taking into account "the most important characteristics", these races can be classified into several groups that Mogilı͡anskiĭ also calls races (Caucasian, Mongolian, Ethiopian, etc.), reserving the term "type" to denote "a sum of common characteristics of this group".

The "types" are mere abstractions or "ideal descriptions" that do not exist empirically. Thus, Mogilı͡anskiĭ continued, the two distinct meanings of "race" should not be conflated. The first one denotes "a set of individuals similar enough to theorize about their descent from common parents" (like Celts, Germans, Tasmanians, Papuans, etc.). The second signifies 'a set of individuals with a certain number of common characteristics, although belonging to different proper "races" and having more morphological similarities than other humans' (GARF R-5787-1-23: 87). The terminological mess is complicated in Russia, commented Mogilı͡anskiĭ, by the tendency to use the word "tribe" to refer to the same realities that are denoted by "race" and "type".

In the second part of the course, entitled "Ethnological anthropology", the professor discussed the methods of physical anthropology and prehistoric archaeology and then proceeded to classify the peoples of the world. Starting with the Old World, he relied on J. Deniker's six races of Europe and classified European peoples strictly according to linguistic principles. He made it very clear that linguistic and physical anthropological characteristics systematically contradict each other, and all linguistic groups are very diverse in their culture and appearance (Ibid: 156–60). The last two sections of the course were titled "Ethnography" and "Sociology" and, as was already mentioned, had their material arranged in a traditional evolutionary manner. "Ethnography" included chapters on such diverse topics as food and cooking, husbandry, agriculture, anthropophagy, pottery, dwellings, dressing and finery, beliefs (animism, fetishism, ancestors' cults, etc.), science, medicine, art, and geographical ideas. This second section's keyword — culture — was defined as "an accumulated mental power of previous generations" and a "result of [the] collective thought of humankind" without much reference to ethnic cultures or *etnos* (Ibid: 201–4). This was also the case with the sociological part, which discussed family, law, taboos, and international relations.

Mogili͡anskiĭ stated that modern science had given up attempts to classify peoples according to the stage of development they achieved, and no single factor was found to account for any of these "stages" (Ibid: 205). Nevertheless, the general ideological attitude of his course can be described as progressive and optimistic. In the conclusion he agreed with "a young Russian scholar", Nikolaĭ S. Trubet͡skoĭ's critique of the idea of "pan-human civilization" as merely disguising "a certain ethnographic notion" of the Romano-Germanic culture, but he disagreed that "Europeanization" is an absolute evil. European culture, in his view, was exceptional because it had developed modern science: "In any case, there is no sign of regress in humankind, which in general moves steadily forward, and one cannot set limits to this progressive movement [...]" (Ibid: 304–05).

In 1928 Mogili͡anskiĭ wrote another manuscript, entitled "The System of Anthropology", that summarized his vision of this science and its sub-disciplines in the following scheme (Table 3.1):

Table 3.1: "The System of Anthropology", 1927 (GARF R-5787-1-93: 10).

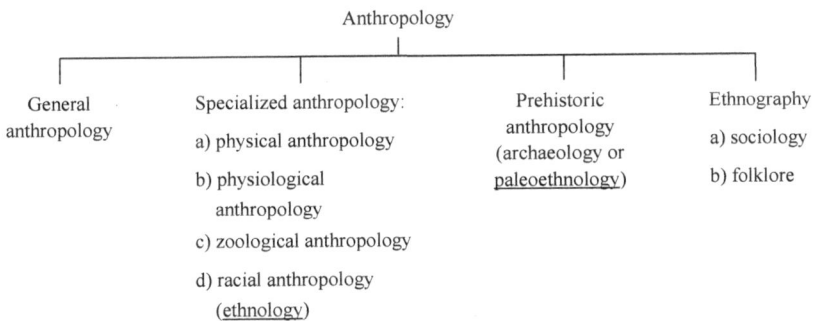

Anthropology

General anthropology	Specialized anthropology:	Prehistoric anthropology (archaeology or paleoethnology)	Ethnography
	a) physical anthropology		a) sociology
	b) physiological anthropology		b) folklore
	c) zoological anthropology		
	d) racial anthropology (ethnology)		

Mogili͡anskiĭ subscribed to Paul Broca's definition of anthropology as a "science that studies the human group in its entirety, its details, and its relations to nature" (GARF R-5787-1-93: 2). The most interesting aspect of this scheme is, of course, Mogili͡anskiĭ's concept of a relationship between racial anthropology (ethnology) and ethnography that reflected his vision of the nature of ethnic differences. Just as in his general course, tribes and peoples were defined as "lesser units" within a few large racial groups that "differ from each other by secondary characteristics". As an example, he cited the visible physical differences between a tall, blonde, and blue-eyed Norwegian and a brown, dark-eyed, and dark-haired Portuguese, both of whom would be classified within a single "white race" (GARF R-5787-1-93: 4).

Ethnography, for Mogilîanskiĭ, is a "science that has as its object of study the evolution of human thought (culture) within the limits of ethnic groups, ascertained by ethnology" (Ibid: 8). Reiterating his early twentieth-century critique of evolutionism, he took Kharuzin and Shternberg to task for "tearing off ethnographical facts from ethnological substrate" and considering them as parts of the cultural evolution of undifferentiated humanity. This, according to Mogilîanskiĭ, would abolish ethnography and turn it into the history of culture. In several of his manuscripts he provided the reason why this should not be done, which must have seemed obvious to his audience, who had recently gone through the Great War:

> Ethnographers cannot ignore the fact that with the disappearance of a certain ethnic group, its culture also disappears, and its remnants become no more than museum material. But no matter how much they destroy objects of culture (during the World War whole villages, cities and regions were wiped off), nevertheless, until the people is alive, it will reconstruct everything according to its knowledge, habits, its unique aesthetics of everyday life (GARF R-5787-1-93: 9).

Museum, Fieldwork, and *Etnos*: The Role of Ethnographic Exhibits

Teaching anthropology and creating university departments were not the only important practices that led to the emergence of *etnos*. Mogilîanskiĭ was an experienced and devoted museum worker. He started his museum career soon after his 1896 return to St Petersburg when he was employed by the MAĖ to sort out its collections. In 1902, he took up a post as a curator in the Russian Museum's ethnographic department. He became the department's head in 1910 and stayed in office until his move to Kiev and his subsequent emigration in 1918.

The Russian Museum of Alexander III was founded in 1895. According to its founding statute, the museum aimed not only to commemorate the deceased emperor, but also "to give a clear idea of Russia's artistic and cultural situation" (Mogilîanskiĭ 1911: 475). The organization of the ethnographic department's exhibition was the subject of a series of meetings that involved the elite of St Petersburg anthropology and related disciplines, including the head of the MAĖ, Vasiliĭ V. Radlov [Friedrich Wilhelm Radloff] (1837–1918); the head of the Imperial Russian Geographical Society (IRGO) ethnographic department, Vladimir I. Lamanskiĭ; academicians Aleksandr N. Pypin (1833–1904) and Vladimir V. Stasov, (1824–1906); anthropologist Dmitriĭ A. Koropchevskiĭ; and others. Two main questions were debated: the geographical area the exhibition would cover and whether the exhibition should be divided along ethnic or geographical lines. While the majority agreed that the planned exhibition should encompass the Russian Empire, Slavic territories, and neighbouring countries, the second question provoked disagreement. A special commission — consisting of Dmitriĭ A. Klemen͡ts (1848–1914), Dmitriĭ A. Koropchevskiĭ (1842–1903), Vladimir I. Lamanskiĭ (1833–1914), and Pëtr P. Semënov-Ti͡an'-Shanskiĭ (1827–1914) — proposed a draft list of 21 provinces (the territory of modern Ukraine was evidently cut into Malorossii͡a and Novorossii͡a). This division appeared too minute and unfit for museum purposes.

Klemen͡ts himself wrote against this plan in his "Separate opinion". In place of the 21 provinces, Klemen͡ts suggested only five zones, determined by the relations between "nature and man": "From times immemorial, even beyond the limits of history, nature determined man's way of life". Culture, continued Klemen͡ts, can be basically defined as an "elementary adaptation to natural conditions" (AIVR 28-1-197: 6–8). Klemen͡ts' "cultural-geographical regions" — such as the tundra and the regions of settled life and agriculture, nomadism, etc. — were defined both by the environment and the ways of life conditioned by it. In his "Separate opinion" he cited the example of the nomadic Kirgiz and Kalmyks, who had similar ways of life, although separated by religion and ethnic origin.

Mogili͡anskiĭ believed that Klemen͡ts' opinion was based on an "anthropogeographical principle", a comment that brings us back to Ratzel's influence on the circle of St Petersburg anthropologists. Klemen͡ts was in personal contact with Ratzel through the latter's student, Bruno Adler (1874–1942), who was employed by the museum in 1910 as a result of Klemen͡ts's influence. In his letters to Klemen͡ts, Adler mentions Ratzel several times. He made arrangements to meet at Ratzel's villa to create a plan of the museum (AIVR 28-2-1: 11–12). In another letter he informed Klemen͡ts that "I will talk with Ratzel about nomad *byt* (way of life) and will do everything to prepare him for a talk with you" (Ibid: 21).

While Ratzel's influence on Koropchevskiĭ and, to a lesser extent, Klement͡s, is quite obvious, Mogili͡anskiĭ's attitude to anthropogeography is ambiguous. During the debates about the ethnographic exhibition, Lamanskiĭ offered his own vision. His version had only thirteen regions and they were defined by a combination of geographic and ethnic-historical characteristics. The regions were named in a purely geographic manner (north, north-west, central Russia, Caucasus, etc.), each one was meant to illustrate the relations between Great Russians (and in the case of the "West" and "South-West", Belorussians and Little Russians) with the non-Slavic nationalities of the region in question (Semënov-Ti͡an-Shanskiĭ 1915: 16–17). Lamanskiĭ's purpose was to emphasize the role of the Russians as an empire-building nation and Russia as a "living historical entity".

When Lamanskiĭ died in 1915, Semënov-Ti͡an'-Shanskiĭ published an article titled "V. I. Lamanskiĭ as an anthropogeographer and political geographer" where he claimed that this scheme was a "purely anthropogeographical partition of Russia" (Ibid). Mogili͡anskiĭ did not agree with that assessment. In a letter to Shakhmatov, who apparently wanted to see Lamanskiĭ's original maps, Mogili͡anskiĭ reported that he was unable to find them. He also wrote:

> Having attentively looked at Lamanskiĭ's memo one more time, I did not find, by any stretch of imagination, the grounds for Semënov-Ti͡an'-Shanskiĭ's definitive statements that Lamanskiĭ drew on the idea of modern anthropogeography. Although not myself a follower of Ratzel's, from whom the word "anthropogeography" originated, I think, the late Lamanskiĭ had little relation to the main ideas of this school (SPF ARAN 134-3-998: 5–6).

As will be discussed later, in spite of his declaration that he was not a follower of Ratzel, Mogili͡anskiĭ mentioned Ratzel with respect and used the term anthropogeography to organize the material in his lectures on the geography of Russia. It also should be borne in mind that he formulated his views on *etnos* for the first time during these debates at the museum, which he witnessed as a newly appointed member of this nascent institution.

The museum had another important impact on Mogilīanskiĭ's career: he became a true fieldworker. The responsibility for different geographic zones of the Russian Empire and neighbouring countries was divided between the department's ethnographers. Mogilīanskiĭ's share was a vast space of central and eastern European Russia, Malorossiīa, Novorossiīa, and Bessarabiīa (Mogilīanskiĭ 1910: v). Between 1902 and 1909 he devoted three to four months a year in the spring and summer to expeditions across this territory. Their main purpose was to collect items of material culture for the museum. Mogilīanskiĭ's fieldwork was a classical example of salvage ethnography. In a published report about his travels in Tula and Orel oblasts in 1902 he tried to refute a "commonplace opinion that factory and seasonal work wiped out all 'ethnography'", and that old characteristics of everyday life (*byt*), dresses, and ornaments were not to be found (Mogilīanskiĭ 1910: 1–2). He used the same salvage rationale while convincing peasant women to sell him their old garments: "Things, 'customs' vanish, and our grandchildren will not know how their grandparents lived and dressed. I will buy these things and they will be kept forever in St Petersburg as a keepsake for our descendants" (Ibid: 6). Aleksandr M. Reshetov estimated that the ethnographer contributed sixteen collections containing 572 items to the museum (Reshetov 2002: 149). Regarding interpretations, Mogilīanskiĭ mentioned in his report that it would be fruitful to analyse the geographical diffusion and terms for women's headwear, *soroki*, spread among Russians and Finns, as well as the "eastern influence" in Russian ornaments.

The beginning of Mogilīanskiĭ's fieldwork trips coincided with the rise of peasant unrest, which developed into open mass revolts during the revolution of 1905. This obviously affected both his relations with local authorities and peasants. Sometimes he felt he was under close police surveillance, the house that he stayed in a village was monitored, and peasants were afraid to talk to him (GARF R-5787-1-17: 100). Visiting Russian villages also made the ethnographer reflect upon his hybrid identity, the differences between Russians and Ukrainians, and their relations: "Educated in a Russian school, in Russian literature and history, in a society that considered itself Russian, I never felt myself more of a Little Russian or Ukrainian than here, in this unfamiliar ethnographic environment" (Ibid: 99).

This important statement in Mogilîanskiĭ's memoirs should be read in the context of his earliest childhood memories. While the Russian language was for Mogilîanskiĭ the language of education and, apparently, his mother tongue, beginning at the age of four he had a nanny who most likely spoke Ukrainian. At the age of six she passed him on to a German "bonne", who in a few years taught him fluent German. Aside from the Ukrainian "ethnographic environment" that stretched out in the country outside Chernigov, young Nikolaĭ saw portraits of Kostomarov and Shevchenko and forbidden books written by Ukrainian activists in his father's study — "the traces of influence" that Hromada and "the 1860s in the Kiev University" had had upon him (GARF R-5787-1-17-100: 2).

Moreover, since his early childhood, the future ethnographer had travelled throughout central Ukraine, at first with his parents and, since the age of thirteen, with school and university friends. He loved Ukrainian nature and country life and had known them intimately, so when he became a museum worker he often returned to his native places (GARF R-5787-1-38). The fieldwork obviously played an important part in Mogilîanskiĭ's conviction that

> […] those who speak about *khokhly* and Ukrainomania with contempt, who do not accept the existence of non-Great Russians, and think that Little Russians and Belorussians are equally Russian and consider the Ukrainian movement an intrigue of Russia's enemies, are foolishly wrong. The Ukrainian element (*stikhiîa*) exists and it attracts, captures in its nets and holds firmly the souls of people of even non-Little-Russian origin. The example of professor V. B. Antonovich, a Pole by origin is not the only one, and there are a lot of Great Russians who, having lived in Ukraine, unwittingly fell under the spell of this element (GARF 5787-1-17: 99).

Things were quite different in the Great Russian regions that were equally important parts of the ethnographer's zone of responsibility. The Great Russian countryside that Mogilîanskiĭ encountered looked extremely poor and backward compared to the Ukrainian regions (Fig. 3.6). The contrast between them obviously made a very important impression on Mogilîanskiĭ, and he returned to this issue several times in his unpublished works and memoirs. He could remember his astonishment at his first visit as an ethnographer to the Great Russian village in Tul'skaîa guberniîa where he could see neither fences nor trees or yards in their familiar form (Fig. 3.7).

Fig. 3.6 A village. Russians, Kaluga gubernii͡a. Photo by Nikolaĭ M. Mogili͡anskiĭ, 1903 (RĖM 758-12). © Russian Ethnographic Museum, St Petersburg

Fig. 3.7 A view of the *sloboda* (a quarter of a village) "Bugor". Russians, Tula gubernii͡a. Photo by Nikolaĭ M. Mogili͡anskiĭ, 1902 (RĖM 757-2). © Russian Ethnographic Museum, St Petersburg

The feeling of discomfort turned into disgust when he stepped inside houses that were dirty and heated by an open fire without a chimney (*po-chernomu*). They were so full of insects that the ethnographer would meet children whose ear edges were bitten off by cockroaches.

> The contrast between two cultural types is striking. The difference between cultural habits is evident. [...] This impression permeates everything from top to bottom. [...] In dress, manner of eating and cooking, in trappings and ornaments, in family and social relations, a Ukrainian substantially differs from his Great Russian brother (GARF 5787-1-34: 31).

A published fieldwork report contains the ethnographer's musings about the correlation between the planning of Great and Little Russian villages and the psychology of their dwellers. The southern Great Russian villages consisted of chaotically positioned houses without fences between them, while in Mogilīanskiĭ's native Chernigov province "each farm is a self-contained whole, fenced off from all sides and accessible for the eyes of only [its] closest neighbours" (Mogilīanskiĭ 1910: 3) (Fig. 3.8). Thus, he muses, the public nature of life in the Great Russian village naturally accustoms dwellers to collectivism, while the planning of Ukrainian villages itself conveys the idea of individualism (Fig. 3.9, 3.10).

Fig. 3.8 An *izba*, covered with reeds. Ukrainians. Bessarabskaīa guberniīa. Photo by Nikolaĭ M. Mogilīanskiĭ, 1906 (RĖM 851-3). © Russian Ethnographic Museum, St Petersburg

Fig. 3.9 "A khata". Ukrainians of the Volynskaîa guberniîa. Photo by Fëdor K. Volkov, 1907 (RĖM 3747-43). © Russian Ethnographic Museum, St Petersburg

Fig. 3.10 "A street". Ukrainians of the Volynskaîa guberniîa. Photo by Fëdor K. Volkov, 1907. RĖM 3747-64. © Russian Ethnographic Museum, St Petersburg

In his unpublished writings Mogilîanskiĭ was much more explicit about the realities he witnessed during fieldwork and with which side of this contrast he sympathized. For example, he noted important differences between the groups' family relations. According to his "Ukraine and Ukrainians, ethnological and historical-cultural essay" (1921), Ukrainians are "gentle and deeply humane" in their family life, and women hold a very high position in society. Great Russians, on the contrary, despise, oppress, and regularly beat their wives. The nature of religious dissidence is also different: while Great Russians usually "cling to the letter" of religious dogma or choose fanatical "unhealthy" sects, Ukrainians prefer rational doctrines of baptism and its like (GARF 5787-1-34: 33).

This dualistic scheme, apparently, was an intellectual tool quite characteristic of Mogilîanskiĭ's thinking. A few years later he applied it to the situation of Russian emigrants in France. In 1922 he published a short newspaper article titled "Liquids that do not mix (An essay in social psychology)" in which he argued that there was no "diffusion" or adaptation of Russian emigrants in Paris. Instead, the French and the Russians stayed "liquids that do not mix, two elements, two races and two psychologies — products of different ethnic origins, different climates and different cultures". Interestingly, he blamed the émigré's lack of curiosity about the achievements of French culture and society as well as their psychological characteristics for this situation, but did not discuss their social circumstances. He claimed that "alongside the challenging, active, and scheduled-by-the-minute life of a European we managed to preserve our disorderly way of life". In the ethnographer's account, "we" despise the French for their thrift, coldness, and standoffishness, but at the same time make no efforts to enter the "depth of life" of Paris to understand the "language of the spirit of the people, its highest psychological origin" (GARF R-5787-1-13: 136). Thus, in a manner somewhat anticipating of Shirokogoroff's "psychomental complex", Mogilîanskiĭ often appealed to psychological and "spiritual" differences, even while borrowing the "hard" data of physical anthropology from Volkov. The latter argument, nevertheless, did not go unchallenged in the Russian scholarship.

Physical Anthropology and *Etnos*: Dmitriĭ Anuchin Challenges Volkov's Ukrainian "Anthropological Type"

Upon his move to St Petersburg, Volkov taught anthropology and archaeology at St Petersburg University, chaired the Russian Anthropological Society, and worked for the Russian Museum and the Russian Geographical Society. His unique position in the centre of imperial science enabled him to train a host of students who formed the "Volkov school" in archaeology and anthropology (Tikhonov 2012). Volkov and his students (some of whom, like Pëtr Efimenko and Sergeĭ Rudenko, were Ukrainians) organized anthropological research in many regions, but the Ukraine was a priority. During the pre-war period they managed to organize anthropological research covering all corners of the Ukrainian territory.

Physical anthropology, as we have already noticed, played a crucial role in the multidisciplinary project of St Petersburg anthropologists. Ukrainian anthropological material, collected and analysed by Volkov, became a crucial case study for debating important theoretical questions, such as the relations between physical type and culture, and the homogeneity and variety of anthropological type within ethnic groups. Volkov started collecting physical anthropological data on Ukrainians in his 1903–1906 expeditions to Galicia, Bukovina, and Trans-Carpathian Ukraine, conducted under the aegis of the Ethnographic Commission of the T. Shevchenko Scientific Society. It was in the publication of the results of these expeditions that he first described the Ukrainians as a tall, brachycephalic, dark-haired and dark-eyed anthropological type (Taran 2003).

Debates about the methods of defining anthropological groups were among the central issues in early twentieth-century Russian anthropology. Two main centres of anthropological research, St Petersburg and Moscow, were in complex relationships of partnership and competition. This can be illustrated by the correspondence between their long-time leaders, Volkov and Dmitriĭ N. Anuchin (1843–1923).

Anuchin's first letter to Volkov is dated March 1895 and contains an offer to become a translator of *Liudstvo v době předhistorické ze vlăštním zřetelem na země slovanské* (Humanity in Prehistoric Times with a Special Attention to Slavic Lands) by the Czech archaeologist and historian Lubor Niederle [Niderle] (1865–1944), the first archaeological compendium that paid attention to the question of Slavic antiquities and the origins of the Slavs. The edition was published in Russian in 1898 using Volkov's translation and with a preface by Anuchin (Niderle 1898). Discussing the edition's preface in 1897, Volkov shared with Anuchin his concerns about the declining interest in the natural sciences in Russia and his view of archaeology as a natural science, and asked Anuchin to send him copies of his entries in the Brokgauz and Efron encyclopaedia about the anthropology of the Great Russians and Little Russians (OR RGB 10-20-135: 14).

The correspondence became active again in the early 1910s. In 1911, Volkov reported that, amidst the students' strike, he had a consolation: results of the recent anthropological investigations allowed the publication of an anthropological survey and maps of both Galician and Malorussian Ukraine (OR RGB 10-20-138: 20). In March 1915, he announced to Anuchin that *The Ukrainian People* was moving forward after the delay caused by the war and "the Judaic fear in expectation of the persecution of *mazepinstvo*".[3] He promised that Anuchin would be the first to receive proofs, but warned that he had to conform to the popular character of the whole edition.

In fact, this article was just an extract of a much more elaborate *zapiska* (note) on the anthropological map of Ukraine that was to be published by the IRGO. An ethnographic map of Ukraine was also almost complete: it was compiled on the basis of answers to a questionnaire that had been sent to all regions of Ukraine. The plan was to publish six maps, including those of variations in Ukrainian dwellings, household constructions, male and female clothing, etc. The answers to a similar Belorussian questionnaire had been also received, while a Great Russian one had only been sent, and a Siberian questionnaire was in the process of development (OR RGB 10-20-139: 25–26).

3 This comment is based on a saying that refers to one of Jesus's disciples, who hid his beliefs because he was afraid of persecution. The saying refers to the fear of being oppressed by any authorities. "Mazepinstvo" comes from the Ukrainian hetman Ivan Mazepa, who betrayed Peter the Great. It refers to the fear of betrayal that the Russians have towards Ukrainians.

While sending the newly published articles to Anuchin, Volkov asked Anuchin to give his opinion about the proofs of Volkov's manuscript, "Ethnographical Features of the Ukrainians", considering it "the first attempt at scientific analysis of Malorussian ethnography" based on French and, partly, American anthropological ideas and written in opposition to Ratzel, Schurz, and Kharuzin. As to the anthropological part of his work ("The Anthropological Features of the Ukrainians"), Volkov referred to it as having only a popular and descriptive character (OR RGB 10-20-142: 30–31).

Anuchin's reaction was quite the reverse. He replied:

> I studied this article ["The anthropological features of the Ukrainians"] in the first place and I must state it very clearly that I strongly disagree both with its conclusions, and its whole composition. The fact that it has a "popular and descriptive character" urges me to pay it special attention, as it is desirable to popularize what is well known and certain, but not something that is doubtful and can provoke rightful objections (NAIA NANU 1/B-156: 1–2).

In the next letter he expounded his critique: Anuchin was upset with Volkov's denial of the correctness of Russian anthropologists' measurements, he protested against Volkov's tendency to lump together the "Adriatic" anthropological type with the Slavic linguistic group. He stressed that the author of this concept, Joseph Deniker, extended it to the territories populated not only by southern Slavs, but to Switzerland, Italy, France and even Great Russia. He also countered Volkov's claims about the homogeneity of Ukrainians and their essential difference from neighbouring Great Russians, Belorussians, and Poles (NAIA NANU 1-B-158: 1–2).

Anuchin's 1918 review of "The anthropological features of the Ukrainian people" was rather devastating. He stated that, even using Volkov's own figures, one can see the tendentiousness of his characteristics. Ukrainians were no more dark-haired, straight-nosed and brachycephalic than their neighbours. Using only averages, Anuchin pointed out, Volkov ignored any geographical variation and explained all features that did not fit his ideal type as ethnic admixtures on the borders of Ukrainian territory with Great Russians, Poles, Germans or even Mongols (Fig. 3.11). In this context, Anuchin formulated his own understanding of *etnos*:

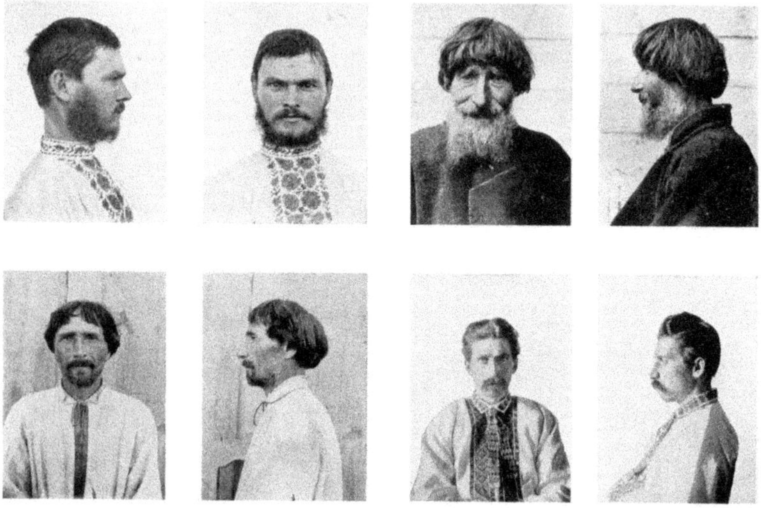

Fig. 3.11 "Types of the Ukrainian population: a) Psarovka, Chernigovskaia gubernia (slightly mongolised), b) Kroveletskiĭ uezd, Chernigovskaia gubernia, c) Obruchskiĭ uezd, Volynskaia gubernia, d) Pavlogradskiĭ" (Volkov et al. 1914–1916: 400)

> Mr Volkov constantly speaks about "ethnic" influences, "ethnic" admixtures etc., but the Greek word *etnos* — the people (*narod*) has to do with a spiritual essence of the people, and not with its bodily features. Ethnic influence can be felt in language, way of life (*byt*), folklore, customs, costume, ornaments etc., but not in the height, the length of legs or the shape of noses' (Anuchin 1918: 54).

Thus, Anuchin strongly objected to Volkov's claims about the homogeneity of Ukrainians, their essential difference from neighbouring peoples, and claims to some "pure" Slavic type that other linguistically Slavic peoples had lost due to mixing with non-Slavs. It is worth mentioning, nevertheless, that this devastating review was published in the same issue that contained birthday congratulations to Volkov from his Moscow colleagues. It is not clear if Volkov was able to read this journal as he died in 1918, on his way from St Petersburg to Kiev.

Correspondence between Anuchin and Volkov shows that, although they both were quite explicit about their disagreement, they never severed personal relations. Moreover, in view of the probable establishment of a separate department of ethnography at St Petersburg University, Volkov was planning to obtain a doctoral degree from a

Russian university, which he needed in order to take up the chair of anthropology. Volkov enjoyed teaching and wanted to become a full professor, but he doubted that he could defend his French dissertation in Russia or present his recent articles on "The Ukrainian People in its Past and Present" as a new dissertation (OR RGB 10-20-142: 29–30). In spite of their disagreement, Anuchin wrote a letter to St Petersburg University in support of granting Volkov the degree, *honoris causa*. In his last letter to Volkov, written half a year before Volkov's death, Anuchin expressed his satisfaction with the university's decision and his respect, while at the same time promising to counter Volkov's anthropological conclusions in print:

> [...] I have always regarded you with esteem, respect and readiness to be of service, and if I disagreed with you, it was only in scientific opinions and arguments. But you know the saying: Amicus Plato, *sed magis amica veritas* (NAIA NANU 1/B-159: 1).

Anuchin's critique of Volkov's anthropological methods and conclusions appeared in the context of a long-running critical campaign that was waged against Volkov's students, Sergeĭ Rudenko and David Zolotarëv, by another Moscow-based physical anthropologist, Efim Chepurkovskiĭ [Ethyme Tschepourkowsky] (1871–1950). He denied the reality of anthropological types that they ascertained, basing his critique on the statistical inadequacy of their methods. As Maksim G. Levin summarized his critique: "E. M. Chepurkovskiĭ showed with a maximum persuasiveness that the types, thus ascertained, as a rule, are not real; that in any however homogeneous group, due to variability of features one can distinguish a certain per cent of more or less pigmented, more or less tall or possessing certain cephalic index individuals, and one can also create different combinations using different traits" (Levin 1960: 132). Chepurovskiĭ's and Anuchin's critique of Volkov's and his students' methods of ethnic anthropology were accepted as generally correct by Soviet anthropologists (Alekseeva 1973: 8–10). Nevertheless, Volkov's conclusions became a dogma for Mogili͡anskiĭ, who often referred to them in his post-1917 writing as purely objective scientific results, obtained by the most recent and accurate methods (Mogili͡anskiĭ 2014: 584–85).

Mogilânskiĭ in Exile: Political Activism and Teaching

Mogilânskiĭ was a liberal who could not accept the Bolshevik revolution and, soon after it took place, the Russian Museum sent him to Kiev. In the summer of 1918 he informed the museum of his resignation and his decision to remain in Kiev (Dmitriev 2002: 152). Meanwhile, Ukraine was going through an extremely turbulent period. In November 1917, the Central Rada proclaimed the autonomous Ukrainian People's Republic in a federation with Russia. After a failed Bolshevik coup in Kiev in January 1918, the Central Rada proclaimed full independence and invited the German army to protect the country from the Bolshevik invasion. Within only months, the Germans occupied the country, disbanded the Rada and, on 29 April, Pavlo Skoropadskiĭ was elected the *hetman* (highest military officer, leader) of the National State of Ukraine, or "The Hetmanat", which survived until December 1918.

Ten days later, Mogilânskiĭ was appointed deputy state secretary. From May until November he was present at the meetings of the cabinet and assisted Pavlo Skoropadskiĭ. Both Skoropadskiĭ and Mogilânskiĭ advocated for a "Russian orientation" in Ukrainian politics. Skoropadskiĭ saw himself as both Russian and Ukrainian: he was a descendant of the Ukrainian hetman of the eighteenth century, but spent all of his life serving in the imperial army. In addition, he and his family spoke Russian. While in office in Kiev, he supported the counter-revolutionary Volunteer Army, but opposed its commander Anton Denikin's unitarian Russian nationalism. As he explained in a letter to Mogilânskiĭ: "I believe that my Ukraine is stronger and more certain for [i.e. to contribute to] Russia's glory than the Malorossiîa that Denikin will create" (Ivantsova et al. 2014: 573). Mogilânskiĭ characterized Skoropadskiĭ as "a devoted nationalist Ukrainian who considers national feeling to be healthy, believes in the future of the national idea without being a separatist at all" — a characterisation that could be perfectly applied to Mogilânskiĭ's own political views (Ibid: 574).

It should be added, though, that this government was also emphatically anti-socialist and very sceptical in relation to so called "Ukrainization". Mogilânskiĭ claimed that the main supporters of this policy were well-to-do Ukrainian peasants — those who "elected"

Skoropadskiĭ and whose well-being was threatened by the pending "socialization" of the land (Ibid: 614). By the end of the hetman's rule there was a sharp opposition in the government between the Ukrainian nationalists and Russians. The hetman's failure to include the former into the government let to their open rebellion.

Skoropadskiĭ and Mogili͡anskiĭ's political programme failed with the defeat of Germany and the uprising of Ukrainian separatists and leftists led by Simon Petli͡ura. They seized power in Kiev on 14 December 1918. Skoropadskiĭ had to flee to Germany. A month before, he had sent Mogili͡anskiĭ to Paris as his representative and a potential representative of Ukraine at the Paris Peace Conference. While in the city, Mogili͡anskiĭ did not hide his "anti-separatist" position and saw his role as providing information about the situation in the country (Ibid: 635). Mogili͡anskiĭ recalled their last meeting in Kiev:

> I came into the study with a report: among the laws was one establishing the Kiev academy of sciences — I wanted this law to be signed in my presence. [...] I wanted to calm P. P. down: "There is not and cannot be any other way for Ukraine except in unity with Russia", I said. "Tell them that I am not a traitor", — were the last words P. P. Skoropadskiĭ told me. They were addressed to the French and to the Russian mission in Paris (Ibid: 569).

The years following Mogili͡anskiĭ's departure from Kiev were turbulent and full of political and literary activity. He organized a Ukrainian national committee in Paris, went to the Crimea to have talks with the general Pëtr N. Vrangel', edited the journal *La Jeune Ukraine* and, most importantly for our subject, wrote several long essays that summarized his ideas about Ukraine and its ethnography, history, political life, and future prospects. These writings pursued both political and educational purposes.

One of them, "The Memo about Ukrainian Question and the Perspectives Concerning Ukraine" (GARF R-5787-1-35) was a manifesto of the Parisian Ukrainian National Committee and contained a program for liberating Russia from the Bolsheviks. Mogili͡anskiĭ was highly disappointed by the Entente's failure to suppress the Bolsheviks,[4] as well

4 The Triple Entente was a military block that united Britain, France, and the Russian Empire in World War I. During the Civil War (1918–1922), Britain, France, and their allies occupied territories of the former Russian Empire and provided help to the counter-revolutionary White Movement.

as by the White Army's military fiasco and its nationalist ideology of a "united indivisible Russia". In response, he offered his recipe: restoring the order and solving the "Russian question" should start with Ukraine. The ethnographer used his understanding of Ukrainian psychological characteristics to argue that the "Ukrainian peasantry [...] have not accepted the socialization of land, proclaimed by the Central Rada, and by its deeply congenial individualism it will never accept socialism in any form" (GARF R-5787-1-35: 12). He also took aim at the left wing of the Ukrainian nationalist movement, considering the politics of Hrushevs'kiĭ, Petli͡ura, and others as unfortunate consequences of imperial ultra-centralization and not unlike the Russian revolutionary socialists. The main features of their politics, according to Mogili͡anskiĭ, were intransigence to Russia, Germanomania, "unrestrained demagogy", and the will to power by any means (Ibid: 15–16).

The results of Petli͡ura's rule were so devastating that Mogili͡anskiĭ strongly warned against any support for his government in exile. Instead, he called for a broad coalition of socialists and liberals under the aegis of his committee that would control the insurgent movement on the spot and would be supported by the Entente's armed forces. Mogili͡anskiĭ formulated the movement's political program in the following points:

> 1) The acceptance of the fact of the political revolution of February 1917;
>
> 2) The acceptance of the fact of the agrarian revolution and the transfer of land into the hands of peasants. In ideal, they [the National Committee and its allies] see Russia as a democratic federal republic where nations would be granted the right of cultural self-determination and free development of national life (Ibid: 19).

Mogili͡anskiĭ's other writings of the period elaborated on history rather than future. "Ukraine and Ukrainians" was the most ambitious work ever written by Mogili͡anskiĭ about the topic. The 45-page handwritten manuscript, written in Paris in 1921, presents an attempt to integrate ethnography, history, physical anthropology, and current politics into an inclusive characterisation of an "ethnic type":

> This word and concept [the Ukrainians] is a subject of hatred for Russian centralists who did not and do not want to accept the existence of this particular ethnic type which is characterized by exact and definite features; on the other hand, this notion is a symbol and credo of Ukrainian

> separatists who, against all evidence in support of close resemblance between Great Russians and Ukrainians, appeal to differences in anthropological features and try to create almost impassable gaps between them, both from anthropological and cultural points of view (GARF R-5787-1-34: 1).

As has been already shown, Mogilīanskiĭ disagreed with both extreme positions. He proceeded to give an overview of the history of the Russian plain to give an account of the making of two "types" — Great and Little Russians — as the result of their mixing with the Finns and the Turks, respectively. Mogilīanskiĭ referred to Volkov's conclusions as decisive evidence taken from the "modern science of anthropology with its exact methods of research" that proved the difference between Great and Little Russians and the existence of distinct homogeneous Ukrainian type (Ibid: 9–11). After an outline of the history of Ukraine from the earliest archaeological findings to the eighteenth century, Mogilīanskiĭ turned to language and literature as "the strongest characteristic of a people, aside from the anthropological type" (Ibid: 22). There he relied on Shakhmatov's and Korsh's conclusions about the independence of the Ukrainian language. As to the literature, he admitted that Ukrainian literature did not yet have works of "world significance", but attributed this to its young age.

Having considered the differences between Great and Little Russians that we discussed in the section dealing with his fieldwork, Mogilīanskiĭ returned to Volkov's conclusions:

> The Ukrainian people, on the whole its ethnic territory is characterized by a range of ethnographic features common to all its members, which do not leave any doubt about the fact that it constitutes one ethnographic whole that definitely stands out among other Slavic peoples (Ibid: 34–35).

He also subscribed to all of Volkov's other ethnographic conclusions about the comparative resilience, purity, and antiquity of Ukrainian culture, but emphatically stressed the point of Ukrainians' affinity with other eastern Slavs, the point that, in his opinion, should preclude them from appealing to Turkey or Germany for support and protection (Ibid: 36). Mogilīanskiĭ described the activity of Ukrainian "separatists" without any sympathy, portraying them as traitors who "presented themselves at the German headquarters right at the beginning of warfare, much earlier than Lenin and co., with the aim to contribute to the quickest and complete defeat of Russia and freeing Ukraine from the yoke of Moscow" (GARF R-5787-1-34: 37). In this text, written after the defeat of the Whites, Skoropadskiĭ, and Petli͡ura, Mogili͡anskiĭ had to admit that "the Ukrainian people were interested only in land. And this land — the ages old dream of popular masses in Russia — they could effectively and immediately get only from the Bolsheviks" (Ibid: 39). This, of course, did not make him reconciled with the latter, which he still considered as a totally destructive power. After the fall of the Bolsheviks that he still envisioned, he hoped for a "free and decentralized Russia" and denied the chances of Ukrainian separatism which, in his view, was "totally alien to the masses of the Ukrainian population" (Ibid: 45).

Ukrainian history was also discussed in Mogili͡anskiĭ's lectures on the geography of Russia. One can see that there he followed a rather standard narrative of early Russian history, dwelling on differences between the south and north that gradually evolved into the divergence between Great and Little Russia. The discrepancies between them lay on the level of the environment (forest versus steppe), historical encounters (subjugation of peaceful hunters versus defeat from the warlike nomads), and ethnic admixtures (Finns versus Turks). These variations created the distinct physical, social, and psychological types of Great and Little Russians (Mogili͡anskiĭ 1924: 93–108). However, Mogili͡anskiĭ's analysis did not conform to the Ukrainian nationalist narrative that saw the roots of the Ukrainian identity in Kievan Rus' or even earlier. What is more, in his account of the origins of eastern Slavic nationalities he seemed to follow Pogodin's theory of the desolation of Kiev's region after the Mongol invasion and the later colonization of this land from Galicia, which was notorious among Ukrainian nationalists:

> The centre of the formation of the Little Russian language and Little Russian *narodnost'* was Galicia and Volyn'. During the Tatar invasion a considerable share of the Slavic population of Southern Russia, as we know it, was exterminated and fled, partly to Chernigov's Poles'e and partly to the west to Volyn' and Galicia. There, in the west, appears a name for Southern-Western Russia — Little Russia. Beginning in the fifteenth century, a developed Little Russian *narodnost'* begins to pour itself into the zone of the Turk and Mongolian massacres of the southern steppe. The word "Ukraine" has been known already since the twelfth century and meant nothing else but the fringe, the borderlands of the Russian settlement (GARF R-5787-1-34: 108–09).

Mogilîanskiĭ's hopes for the formation of a democratic federalist Russian state after the fall of Bolsheviks were to remain unfulfilled, although the latter effectively used the idea of cultural self-determination for their purposes. The project of "freeing" Russia from the Bolsheviks, starting with Ukraine, which was the main object of the Ukrainian National Committee, did not come to fruition and Mogilîanskiĭ's relations with the committee ended dramatically. On 4 June 1922, the Russian-language Parisian newspaper, *Poslednie novosti* (The Latest News), published a set of correspondence between the committee's chairman, Sergeĭ Markotun, and the head of the government (Sovnarkom) and foreign minister of the Soviet Ukraine, Khristian Rakovskiĭ [Christian Rakovsky]. The letters indicated Markotun's willingness to cooperate with the Soviet authorities, which was confirmed by the agreement he signed with Rakovskiĭ during the Genoa Conference in May 1922. This correspondence was followed by a "Statement" by Mogilîanskiĭ, who accused Markotun of acquiescing to Soviet power, "a morally disreputable act aimed to harm the Russian and Ukrainian peoples", and resigned his membership of the committee. Mogilîanskiĭ pasted this publication in his diary with a comment: "National Ukrainian Committee is dead for me. Let it die for all" (GARF R-5787-1-12: 108–10).

There is no extended analysis of Mogilîanskiĭ's journalism and political activity in the 1920s. In this essay, we can only stress that this activity was guided by his ambivalent position as both a Ukrainian "patriot" and a supporter of the Russian-Ukrainian federation. He attacked Petlîura and Ukrainian nationalists, such as the first foreign minister of an independent Ukraine, Aleksandr Shul'gin, who, in Mogilîanskiĭ's words, "was with Petlîura against Skoropadskiĭ, and with an ambassador at the Paris Conference, Mr Sidorenko, hoaxed the political people of Europe. In a rather bookish pamphlet he tried to prove an anthropological basis of the impossibility of peaceful coexistence of the 'Moskals' and 'Ukrainians'" (GARF R-5787-1-11: 18).

From the opposite side Mogilîanskiĭ was confronted by Russian nationalists, as is evident from a letter written to him by another Shul'gin, Vasiliĭ Vital'evich, a monarchist and nationalist ideologist of the counterrevolutionary White movement. Shul'gin opposed the German occupation of Kiev and had to flee from the city when Skoropadskiĭ took control of it. After the final defeat of the white Volunteer Army he lived in a number of European countries and was active in journalism and émigré organizations. In a long letter, written in 1927, he reprimanded Mogilianskiĭ for using "Ukrainian terminology", which he considered the "main weapon" of the *samostiĭniki* (separatists), since an independent state was an inevitable consequence of the recognition of Ukrainians as a separate people or nation. Shul'gin, himself born in Kiev, wrote:

> We, the people of the South of Russia, identifying ourselves as not only Russian, but, so to say, double Russian, will not allow our Russian name to be taken away. We are Russian, and those in the North are Russian too, hence we are a united people not of 35 million, but of 100 million (GARF R-5787-1-160: 48).

Shul'gin called for strengthening and organizing people with Little Russian (Malorussian) identity: "Great Russians will never win a moral victory over Ukrainians, a moral victory over them can be only won by Little Russians. And to win physically, one must win a moral victory" (Ibid: 51).

In the middle of these ideological battles Mogilianskiĭ had to adapt to the life of an émigré. In 1923 he moved to Prague, the city that became one of the centres of Russian emigration (Figs. 3.12 and 3.13). Here he taught at the John Amos Comenius Pedagogical Institute, which trained teachers for a new post-Bolshevik Russia. Mogilianskiĭ was also active in other academic institutions in Prague: the Russian Free University, Russian Academic Group, the Pedagogical Bureau of the Russian School Abroad, and the Union of Russian Writers and Journalists of the Czech Republic. He lectured on geography, ethnography, anthropology, and other popular topics, took part in congresses, and published in newspapers and academic journals (Dmitriev 2002). While he was definitely part of the Russian émigré community, nothing is known about his contacts with Ukrainian circles, except for his vehement critique of S. Petliura and Ukrainian nationalists. Prague was also an important centre of the Eurasian movement with which Mogilianskiĭ's thinking was critically engaged in the 1920s.

Mogilianskiĭ's "Lectures on the Geography of Russia" (Mogilianskiĭ 1924), transcribed by a student of the Russian Pedagogical Institute and published in Prague, offer an important source for Mogilianskiĭ's teaching

Fig. 3.12 Nikolaĭ M. Mogilïanskiĭ near the hotel Graf in Prague, 1926 (GARF R-5787-1-16a-9v). © State Archive of the Russian Federation, Moscow

Fig. 3.13 Nikolaĭ M. Mogilïanskiĭ. Prague, 1926 (GARF R-5787-1-16a-11). © State Archive of the Russian Federation, Moscow

and thinking in exile. There can be little doubt that, although delivered during his Prague period, these lectures also relied on his previous teaching in St Petersburg. The course was a continuation of his "Basics of Physical Geography" lectures at the institute (Mogilîanskiĭ 1923), and it offered not only a survey of the region's physical geography, but a great deal of historical, anthropological, ethnographical, and economic information. Ratzel was mentioned on its first page as a thinker who developed the idea of the influence of a country's *Weltstellung* (position in the world) on its entire human geography (Mogilîanskiĭ 1924: 1). The introduction also illustrated Mogilîanskiĭ's awareness of Eurasianism, already evident in his citing of Nikolaĭ Trubet͡skoĭ in the anthropological lectures. He wrote:

> Regarding the development of culture, Russia, due to its geographical position, is an intermediate link between the Sino-Japanese cultural centre of eastern Asia and the Romano-German one of western Europe. Thus, fate itself posits for Russia the task of synthesizing cultural elements of the East and West (Ibid: 2).

In good Ratzelian fashion, similar to Koropchevskiĭ's *Political Geography*, Mogilîanskiĭ described the political development of the Russian Empire as being heavily preconditioned by the geography of the vast Russian plain. Still, unlike the Eurasianists, Mogilîanskiĭ pro-European sympathies are evident in the way he saw the Tatar conquest and the subsequent geographical and cultural isolation from western Europe as the major factors in Russia's backwardness and the superficiality of western civilization in her territory (Ibid: 4–5). Climate also contributed to unfavourable conditions: the cold in the north and droughts in the south made cultural activity precarious and made people rely on luck rather than "personal precaution". Long and idle winters were another cause of "physical and spiritual immobility" (Ibid: 30). Western culture was imposed on a small minority, the Russian elite, while the poor and ignorant masses were and continued to be separated from this elite by a "deep precipice".

Nevertheless, Mogilîanskiĭ was unequivocal in his evaluation of Russia's prospects:

> In the musty air of contemporaneity no progress is imaginable. The path is still the only one, the path of knowledge and culture, the European and not Asian, or Eurasian one (Ibid: 118–19).

Mogilı͡anskiĭ's critical engagement with Eurasianism had both personal and intellectual reasons. Many leading intellectuals of the Eurasian movement came from Ukraine, were interested in Ukrainian culture and identified themselves as Russians, Ukrainians, or "Ukrainians with Russian culture" depending on the context. Nevertheless, their project encountered what Sergeĭ Glebov has called "Eurasia's Ukrainian challenge":

> Drawing on identities and strategies of the so-called Ukrainians of Russian culture, the Eurasianist leaders also encountered the sustained and organized response of Ukrainian intellectuals, who challenged Eurasianist aspirations to construct a supranational identity for the postimperial space (Glebov 2017: 126).

While Mogilı͡anskiĭ shared Eurasianists' "Ukrainian challenge" and the aspiration to preserve the unity of the Russian post-imperial space, he envisioned it in liberal terms. Eurasian thinkers, by contrast, represented the generation of intellectuals, who discarded rationalism and liberalism in favour of "national mystique", based on "Russian nationalism and aristocratic conservatism, anti-Westernism and Orthodox religiosity, modernist debates and Christian theology" (Ibid: 41).

Mogilı͡anskiĭ's reaction to Eurasianism is also evident in his review of Pëtr Savit͡skiĭ's *Geographical Characteristics of Russia,* published in Prague (Savit͡skiĭ 1927). Mogilı͡anskiĭ and Savit͡skiĭ knew each other personally. Both were born in Chernigov. Savit͡skiĭ's father worked for a short period as the deputy minister of the interior in Skoropadskiĭ's government (Beisswenger 2009: 78). Savit͡skiĭ's work was a study in physical geography that aimed to prove the distinctiveness of Eurasia-Russia from Europe and Asia in purely physical geographical terms (the structure of climate zones, soils, flora, fauna etc.). Mogilı͡anskiĭ considered Savit͡skiĭ's work a serious scientific exercise and subscribed to some of his conclusions concerning geographical zoning and establishing a physical geographical border between Europe and Eurasia. Nevertheless, he did not agree with the idea of Eurasia as a purely geographical entity and argued that eastern Siberia did not conform to the Eurasian geographical pattern. More importantly, Mogilı͡anskiĭ came from an intellectual milieu that valued universal scientific laws, exemplified in the idea of evolution. He could not accept the Eurasianist worldview on a fundamental philosophical level:

> We must state from the start that we do not share Eurasianist's arguments, neither in their general form, nor in their particular attempts to prove the "peculiarities" of Russia in her cultural evolution. There are no identical individuals in the organic world [...] We will find even more individual "peculiarities" in elaborate social and anthropological complexes with their individual evolutions. Still, the laws of ontogenetic and phylogenetic development as discovered by modern biology remain common laws, and the laws of social, economical, and historical development for our motherland, which are not yet fully discovered by modern science, will also be common [laws] (Mogilîanskiĭ 1928: 243–44).

A comparison of this statement with those made by Mogilîanskiĭ in his "The Object and Tasks of Ethnography" reveals significant changes in his position. The tasks of this science, as he defined them in 1916, were "to study the development of intellectual and spiritual abilities of humankind, which proceeds in its own way in various groups or peoples of the Earth, depending on their racial characteristics, environment, and historical circumstances" (Mogilîanskiĭ 1916: 17). Apparently, the experiences of the Russian Civil War, emigration, and the critique of Eurasianism left their mark on Mogilîanskiĭ: he started to put more value on "European civilization" and became more sceptical about a *Sonderweg* (special path) for individual *etnos*es.

The Legacy of Volkov in the USSR and Ukraine

Mogilîanskiĭ died in exile, and his post-1917 writings remained for the most part unpublished and inaccessible to readers in the USSR. The legacies of Volkov's ideas were more lasting and more controversial. Volkov died on 29 June 1918 in Zhlobin, a small town in Belorussia, while he was on his way from St Petersburg to Kiev and to a realization of some of his life-long plans and aspirations. In 1916–1917 he had pressed for the opening of the department of anthropology at Kiev University. In March 1918, several months before his death, Volkov was elected the head of the department of geography and ethnography at the same university (Franko 2000a: 124–28). Volkov also hoped to take part in the creation of the Ukrainian Academy of Sciences, which was one of the aims of his move to Kiev. Three years before, in 1915, he bequeathed all his papers to an anthropological laboratory or "Ukrainian Anthropological Institute" to be created in Kiev (Kolesnikova, Chernovol, and Îanenko 2012: 9).

In March 1921, The F. K. Vovk Museum of Ethnology and Anthropology was established at the Ukrainian Academy of Sciences (soon the museum was renamed a "cabinet"). According to the plan drafted by its first director, Volkov's student Oleksandr Alesho, the museum consisted of three departments: anthropological, paleoanthropological, and ethnological. The first one was further divided into departments of general and racial anthropology, the latter devoted to "anthropological materials of individual races and peoples, especially peoples which live on the territory of Ukraine". The ethnological department consisted of three divisions: comparative ethnography, studying the evolution of human *byt* (culture, or everyday life); general ethnography, studying *byt* of Slavic peoples and peoples of the Black Sea region; and the ethnography of Ukraine, focusing on Ukrainians and other peoples of the country (Kolesnikova, Chernovol, and I͡anenko 2012: 20). Thus, the structure of the museum closely resembled the structure of an anthropological institute envisioned by Volkov and his idea of anthropology as science. The museum (cabinet) existed as an independent institution until 1933. After numerous restructurings during the Cultural Revolution period, it was finally incorporated into the newly established Institute of the History of Material Culture (since 1938, the Institute of Archaeology). All or most of the members of staff of the cabinet were repressed during the Stalinist purges and crackdown on the Ukrainian national intelligentsia in the mid-1930s.

The interpretation of Volkov's legacy and anthropological study of Ukrainians in the Soviet and post-Soviet Ukraine closely followed the ideological and political climate of the day. In 1954, the Institute of Ethnography (IE) in Moscow invited their colleagues from the Institute of History of Art, Folklore, and Ethnography in Kiev to write a chapter on Ukrainians for the volume *Eastern Slavs* in the series "The Peoples of the World". This idea eventually evolved into a plan for a two-volume edition, *The Ukrainians*, to be published in Kiev in Ukrainian (Guslistiĭ 1959). The institute launched the Ukrainian anthropological expedition, which between 1956 and 1959 measured 6,000 individuals on the "main territory of formation of the Ukrainian people". The head of this expedition, physical anthropologist Vasil' D. D͡iachenko (1924–1996), wrote the physical anthropological chapter of this book in which he criticized Volkov for "nationalistic tendencies" and deficient methodology (Guslistiĭ 1959: 50).

This deficiency, according to Dīachenko, was manifested in Volkov's definition of colour, which led to the exaggeration of the "darkness" of Ukrainians' eyes and hair. Brachycephaly also could not be interpreted as a feature of an "ancient Slavic type". Diachenko identified four anthropological types of the current Ukrainian population that shared their physical characteristics with neighbouring peoples, especially Russians and Belorussians. Features of the "Dinaric type", evident in part of the population of the Carpathian zone, to a certain extent connected Ukrainians to southern Slavs, but were not relevant for the whole nation (Ibid: 64–66).

The draft of the volume was presented at a meeting at the IE in Moscow in April 1959 and provoked quite an intense discussion that evoked the debates of the nineteenth century about the formation of the Ukrainian nation. Prominent Soviet ethnographer Sergeĭ A. Tokarev (1899–1985) critiqued the "bourgeois-nationalist" theory of Hrushevs'kiĭ concerning the existence of the Ukrainian people since the period preceding Kievan Rus'. The authors cited philologists who traced the origins of the Ukrainian language to this period, but did not consider the fact that, even in the nineteenth century, the population called themselves Russians (although, in Tokarev's view, they were already Ukrainians) (ARAN 142-1-1093: 47–49). Tokarev also complained that the analogues of Hrushevs'kiĭ's point of view that "the people exist from times immemorial" featured in numerous contemporary books on the history of the peoples of the Caucasus and central Asia (Ibid: 50).

Belorussian ethnographer Adam I. Zalesskiĭ [Zaleski] (1912–2002) and the director of the IE, Sergeĭ P. Tolstov, defended the correctness of the book's interpretation. Tolstov supported Guslistiĭ and Zalesskiĭ in their dating the roots of the formation of the Ukrainian nation to the fourteenth century. The ancient elements in the Ukrainian culture, in his view, united rather than divided three eastern Slavic nations, the successors of the single ancient Russian nationality (*drevnerusskaīa narodnost'*) (Ibid: 105). Physical anthropologists Maksim G. Levin and Georgiĭ F. Debet͡s lauded Dīachenko's efforts to counter Volkov's nationalistic writings, but expressed hopes that he would substantiate his theory with maps and tables of measurements, which he did in his later monograph *Anthropological Composition of the Ukrainian People* (Ibid: 26–27, 55; Dîachenko 1965). This discussion suggests that although the debates about primordialism and constructivism in the study of nationalism did not appear in press during the Soviet period, these issues were raised in internal discussions among scholars.

There is no need to review the whole literature on the ethnogenesis of Ukrainians here to note a tendency to look for deeper roots. In 1992, Dîachenko published a short article, "Not Only Brown Eyes, Black Brows: Anthropological Types on the Ethnic Territory of the Ukrainian People" in an unlikely forum for a scholarly article: the *Journal of the Supreme Council [Rada] of Ukraine* (Dîachenko 1992). In it, he apologized for the "superficial and tendentious" critique of "racist concepts of Ukrainian bourgeois nationalism" and acknowledged the outstanding role of Volkov in the development of Ukrainian anthropology.

Nevertheless, Dîachenko insisted on his disagreement with Volkov on the point of the colour of eyes among the majority of Ukrainians and their belonging to the "Dinaric (anthropological) complex". His statement was topped off with a scheme of periodization of Ukrainian ethnic history which started with the Indo-European proto-Slavic period at the end of the sixth through fourth millennia BC, thus proving one of the first statements of Dîachenko's text: "Centuries and millennia 'laboured' on our *etnos*" (Ibid).

The most authoritative assessment of Volkov's anthropology in contemporary Ukrainian scholarship comes from the distinguished physical anthropologist and ethnologist Sergeĭ Segeda. He concludes his afterword to the republication of Volkov's works:

> [...] it would be an exaggeration to claim that all points of the anthropological conception of Khv. Vovk stood the test of time. Thus, he simplified the causes of the appearance of mixed anthropological types on the Ukrainian territory, reducing them to admixtures of neighbouring peoples. The scientist was mistaken, crediting the ancestors of contemporary Slavic peoples with such features as brachycephaly. Khv. Vovk sometimes called anthropological features "ethnic", although there is no internal causal connection between such categories as "anthropological type" and "etnos". Nevertheless, the main ideas of Khv. Vovk's theory to a great extent stood the test of time (Segeda 2010: 134).

Conclusion

The idea of *etnos* as an "object of ethnography" arose at the intersection of several intellectual and political agendas. During his studies in St Petersburg and Paris, Mogili͡anskiĭ acquired the notion of peoples as subgroups within races, which was widespread in the European science of the second half of the nineteenth through the first third of the twentieth century. As Bruce Baum has shown, "racialized nationalism" was quite common during this period, as well as the idea of several European "races", as exemplified by Joseph Deniker's typology (Baum 2006: 118–61). Volkov, who had a formative influence on Mogili͡anskiĭ, created a model of anthropological and ethnographic description of an *etnos*, which the latter uncritically accepted.

The concept appeared at the moment of ethnography's institutionalization as a university discipline and legitimized its establishment. The debate between Volkov and Mogili͡anskiĭ, on the one side, and the evolutionists Shternberg and Iokhel'son, on the other, reflected divergent perspectives that divided nationally oriented scholars from the Russian Museum and cosmopolitan evolutionists from the MAĖ. The latter's rejection of the concept of *etnos* significantly affected its fate in the early Soviet academia.

Volkov and Mogili͡anskiĭ's ideas about *etnos* and ethnography were, of course, connected to their involvement in the Ukrainian nationalist project. The late nineteenth through the early twentieth century was a period of "nationalizing empires", when both peripheral and central nationalisms were ripening inside imperial states (Miller and Berger 2015). It is worth noting that this version of the Ukrainian project developed in the imperial capital within central scientific institutions, which must have affected its politics.

There is a controversy concerning Volkov's views on the future of Ukraine. Marina Mogilner considers him as a proponent of the "imperial anthropology of multi-nationality" and the federalization of the Russian Empire (Mogilner 2008: 294–95). The author of Volkov's Ukrainian-language biography, Oksana Franko, claims that as early as his Parisian period, Volkov had evolved from a moderate federalist and socialist into a staunch supporter of Ukrainian independence (Franko 2000a: 320–21). This uncertainty might be a result of the fact that the scholar died in 1918, when all the national projects of the former empire entered the stage of their real self-determination.

Mogilîanskiĭ, who outlived this period, remained a convinced federalist who held Mikhaĭlo Dragomanov's views as an example of the most tenable approach to the problem (GARF R-5787-1-34: 26–28). The distinctiveness of the Ukrainian "ethnic type" in his thinking was in harmony with the "tripartite" concept of the Russian people and did not require the status of a nation. Nevertheless, he also argued with Russian centralists, and his fieldwork conclusions by and large fit into clichés about the national characters of Great Russians and Ukrainians which had long existed in the "Ukrainophilic" circles (Leskinen 2012).

The variety of political positions is paralleled by the variety of applications the concept of *etnos* could have in Mogilîanskiĭ's writing. Thus, speaking about the period when cultural characteristics of peoples would diminish under the pressure of "European civilization", he listed the Chinese, the Negros, the American Yankees, the Malorussians, and the Georgians as the "peoples" who would preserve their "ethnic wholeness" (Mogilîanskiĭ 1916: 11). Apparently, these different identities did not conform to the strict definition of narod-*etnos*. Nevertheless, among Volkov's followers, *etnos* acquired an air of an objective conclusion of unbiased science, and Ukrainians were the people whose description became a model for future students of *etnos* to emulate.

Published References

Al. S. 1912. 'V Moskve' *Ukrainskaîa zhizn'* 1: 123–25.

Alekseeva, T. I. 1973. *Ėtnogenez vostochnykh slavîan po dannym antropologii* (Moskva: Izdatel'stvo MGU).

Anon. 1913a. '[Portret Dmitriîa Koropchevskogo]' *Ezhegodnik Russkogo antropologicheskogo obshchestva* 4: insert 3.

—. 1913b. '[Portret Ėduarda Petri]' *Ezhegodnik Russkogo antropologicheskogo obshchestva* 4: insert 2.

Antonovich, V. B. 1995. 'Tri nat͡sional'ni tipi narodni', in *Moîa spovid'* (Kiiv: Libid'), 90–100.

Anuchin, D. N. 1918. 'K antropologii ukraint͡sev *Russkiĭ antropologichsekiĭ zhurnal* 1–2: 48–60.

Baum, B. D. 2006. *The rise and fall of the Caucasian race: a political history of racial identity* (New York: New York University Press).

Beisswenger, M. 2009. *Petr Nikolaevich Savitskii (1895–1968) and the Invention of "Eurasia"* (PhD dissertation, University of Notre Dame).

Bilenkyi, S. 2012. *Romantic nationalism in Eastern Europe: Russian, Polish, and Ukrainian political imaginations* (Stanford: Stanford University Press).

Conklin, A. L. 2013. *In the museum of man: race, anthropology, and empire in France, 1850–1950* (Ithaca, NY: Cornell University Press).

Dîachenko, V. D. 1992. 'Ne til'ki karii ochi, chornii brovi... Antropologichni tipi ta etnichniĭ teritorii ukraïns'kogo narodu' *Zhurnal Verkhovnoï Radi Ukraïni "Viche"* 4: 114–22.

Dmitriev, S. V. 2002. 'Sud'by sotrudnikov ėtnograficheskogo otdela Russkogo Muzeîa: N. M. Mogilîanskiĭ', in *Muzei. Tradit͡sii. Ėtnichnost'*. XX–XXI vek: Materialy mezhdunarodnoĭ nauchnoĭ konferent͡sii, posvîashchennoĭ 100-letiîu Rossiĭskogo ėtnograficheskogo muzeîa, ed. by A. B. Ostrovskiĭ (Sankt-Peterburg-Kishinëv: Nestor-Historia), 151–55.

Franko, O. 2000a. *Fedir Vovk — vcheniĭ i gromads'kiĭ diîach* (Kiïv: Vidavnit͡stvo Evropeĭs'kogo universitetu).

Franko, O. 2000b. *Naukova ta suspil'no-politichna diial'nist' Fedora Kindratovicha Vovka* (Avtoreferat doktorskoĭ disseratsii, L'vivs'kiĭ nat͡sional'niĭ universitet imeni Ivana Franka).

Glebov, S. 2017. *From Empire to Eurasia: Politics, Scholarship, and Ideology in Russian Eurasianism, 1920s–1930s* (Northern Illinois University Press).

Grushevskiĭ, M. S. 1914. 'Razvitie ukrainskikh izucheniĭ v XIX v. i raskrytie v nikh osnovnykh voprosov ukrainovedeniîa', in *Ukrainskiĭ narod v ego proshlom i nastoîashchem*, ed. by F. K. Volkov, M. S. Grushevskiĭ, M. M. Kovalevskiĭ,

F. E. Korsh, A. E. Krimskiĭ, M. I. Tugan'-Baranovskiĭ, and A. A. Shakhmatov (Sankt-Peterburg: Tipografii͡a tovarishchestva "Obshchestvennai͡a pol'za"), 1–37.

Guslistiĭ, K. G., ed. 1959. *Ukraïnt͡si. Istoriko-etnografichna monografii͡a*. T. 1 (Kiïv: Vydavnit͡stvo AN URSR).

Hrushevs'kiĭ, M. 1904. *Istorii͡a Ukraïni-Rusi*. T. 1. (L'viv: Naukove Tovaristvo imeni Shevchenka).

Hrushevs'kiĭ, M. S. 1906. 'Zadachi ukrainskogo vestnika' *Ukrainskiĭ vestnik* 1: 3–7.

Ivanchenko, I. U. 1995. 'Vidatniĭ vcheniĭ i patriot Ukraïni', in Vovk, Khvedir, *Studii z ukrains'koï etnografiï ta antropologiï*, ed. by V. Kuz'menko, and N. Pribega (Kiïv: Mistet͡stvo), 3–6.

Ivant͡sova, O. K., E. V. Balushkina, N. V. Grigorchuk, E. I. Krivoruchko, and K. G. Li͡ashenko, eds. 2014. *Getman P. P. Skoropadskiĭ. Ukraina na perelome. 1918 god: sbornik dokumentov* (Moskva: Rosspen).

Kharuzin, N. N. 1901. *Ėtnografii͡a: lekt͡sii, chitannyi͡a v Imperatorskom moskovskom universitete* (Sankt-Peterburg: Gosudarstvennai͡a tipografii͡a).

Kolesnikova, V. A., I. V. Chernovol, and A. S. I͡anenko. 2012. *Muzeĭ (kabinet) Antropologiï ta Etnologiï imeni prof. Khv. Vovka* (Kiïv: Starodavniĭ Svit).

Koropchevskiĭ, D. A. 1901. *Vvedenie v politicheskui͡u geografii͡u* (Moskva: Tipografii͡a A. V. Vasil'eva i K.).

Koropchevskiĭ, D. A. 1905. 'Znachenie "geograficheskikh" provint͡siĭ v ėtnogeneticheskom prot͡sesse' *Ezhegodnik Russkogo Antropologicheskogo obshchestva* 1: 1–255.

Korotkiĭ, V., and V. Ul'i͡anovs'kiĭ. 1997. *Sin Ukraïni: Volodimir Bonifatiĭovich Antonovich* (Kiiv: Zapovit).

Korsh, F. E. 1929. 'Ukrainskiĭ narod i ukrainskiĭ i͡azyk' *Izvestii͡a Obshchestva slavi͡anskoĭ kul'tury* 1 (2): 24–40.

Kostomarov, N. 1861. 'Dve russkie narodnosti' *Osnova* 3: 33–80.

Leskinen, M. V. 2012. '"Malorossiĭskai͡a narodnost"' v rossiĭskoĭ nauke vtoroĭ poloviny XIX v. Problemy ėtnograficheskogo opisanii͡a', in *Russkie ob Ukraine i ukraint͡sakh*, ed. by E. I. Borisenok (Sankt-Peterburg: Aleteĭi͡a), 244–83.

Levin, M. G. e. 1960. *Ocherki po istorii antropologii v Rossii* (Moskva: Izd-vo Akademii nauk SSSR).

Li͡askoronskiĭ, V. G. 1908. 'V. B. Antonovich (nekrolog)' *Zhurnal Ministerstva Narodnogo Prosveshchenii͡a*, Novai͡a serii͡a 156: 51–75.

Miller, A. 2003. *The Ukrainian question: the Russian Empire and nationalism in the nineteenth century* (Budapest and New York: CEU Press).

Miller, A. I., and S. Berger, eds. 2015. *Nationalizing Empires* (Budapest: Central European University Press).

Mogil'ner, M. 2008. *Homo Imperii: Istoriı͡a fizicheskoĭ antropologii v Rossii* (konet͡s XIX – nachalo XX v.) (Moskva: Novoe literaturnoe obozrenie).

Mogilı͡anskiĭ, N. M. 1908. 'Ėtnografiı͡a i eë zadachi' *Ezhegodnik Russkogo antropologicheskogo obshchestva* 3: 1–14.

—. 1910. 'Poezdka v T͡sentral'nuı͡u Rossiı͡u dlı͡a sobiraniı͡a ėtnograficheskikh kollekt͡siĭ', in *Materialy po ėtnografii Rossii.*, ed. by F. K. Volkov (Sankt-Peterburg: izdanie ėtnograficheskogo otdela Russkogo muzeı͡a), 1–19.

—. 1911. 'Ėtnograficheskiĭ otdel Russkogo muzeı͡a Imperatora Aleksandra III' *Zhivaı͡a starina* 1: 473–98.

—. 1916. 'Predmet i zadachi ėtnografii' *Zhivaı͡a starina* 25: 1–22.

—. 1917. 'Ret͡senziı͡a na: Ukrainskiĭ narod v ego proshlom i nastoı͡ashchem' *Zhurnal Ministerstva narodnogo prosveshcheniı͡a* 68 (March–April): 130–38.

—. 1924. *Lekt͡sii po geografii Rossii* (Praga: Izdatel'skaı͡a komissiı͡a Russkogo pedagogicheskogo instituta imena I͡a. A. Komenskogo).

—. 1928. 'Novyĭ trud po geografii Rossii' *Versty* 3: 243–50.

—. 2014. 'Tragediı͡a Ukrainy', in *Getman P. P. Skoropadskiĭ. Ukraina na perelome. 1918 god,* ed. by O. K. Ivant͡sova, E. V. Balushkina, N. V. Grigorchuk, E. I. Krivoruchko, and K. G. Lı͡ashenko (Moskva: Rosspėn), 582–604.

Niderle, L. 1898. *Chelovechestvo v doistoricheskie vremena* (Sankt-Peterburg: Izdanie L. F. Panteleeva).

Ob otmene. 1905. *Ob otmene stesneniĭ malorusskogo pechatnogo slova* (Sankt-Peterburg: Tipografiı͡a Imperatorskoĭ Akademii Nauk).

Ocherk deı͡atel'nosti. 1910. 'Ocherk deı͡atel'nosti Ėtnograficheskogo otdela s 1902 po 1909 g.', in *Materialy po ėtnografii Rossii,* ed. by F. K. Volkov (Sankt-Peterburg: [n. pub.]), i–xvii.

Petri, Ė. I͡U. 1890. *Antropologiı͡a: Tom 1. Osnovy Antropologii* (Sankt-Peterburg: Kartograficheskoe zavedenie Il'ina).

Petri, Ė. I͡U. 1892. *Antropologicheskie kollekt͡sii i nablı͡udeniı͡a. Kratkaı͡a programma* (Sankt-Peterburg: Tipografiı͡a Imperatorskoĭ Akademii nauk).

Petri, Ė. I͡U. 1895. *Antropologiı͡a. Tom 2. Somaticheskaı͡a antropologiı͡a* (Sankt-Peterburg: Izdanie Kartograficheskogo zavedeniı͡a A. Il'ina).

Platonova, N. I. 2010. *Istoriı͡a arkheologicheskoĭ mysli v Rossii: vtoraı͡a polovina XIX – pervaı͡a tret' XX veka* (Sankt-Peterburg: Nestor-Istoriı͡a).

Plokhy, S. 2005. *Unmaking Imperial Russia: Mykhailo Hrushevsky and the Writing of Ukrainian History* (Toronto: University of Toronto Press).

Reshetov, A. M. 2002. 'N. M. Mogilı͡anskiĭ — vydaı͡ushchiĭsı͡a rossiĭskiĭ ėtnograf i muzeeved', in *Muzei. Tradit͡sii. Ėtnichnost'*. XX–XXI vek: Materialy mezhdunarodnoĭ nauchnoĭ konferent͡sii, posvı͡ashchennoĭ 100-letiı͡u Rossiĭskogo ėtnograficheskogo muzeı͡a, ed. by A.B. Ostrovskiĭ (Sankt-Peterburg: Nestor-Historia), 147–51.

Savit͡skiĭ, P. N. 1927. *Geograficheskie osobennosti Rossii. Ch. 1. Rastitel'nost' i pochvy* (Praga: Evraziĭskoe knigoizdatel'stvo).

Segeda, S. 2010. 'Antropologichna kont͡sept͡siı͡a Khv. Vovka v svitli suchasnikh naukovikh danikh', in Vovk, Khvedir, *Studiï z antropologiï Ukraïni* (Kiïv: Vidavnichiĭ dim Personal), 116–34.

Semenov-Tı͡an-Shanskiĭ, V. P. 1915. 'Vladimir Ivanovich Lamanskiĭ kak antropogeograf i politikogeograf' *Zhivaı͡a starina* 1–2: 9–20.

Semyonov, A., and J. Smith. 2017. 'Nationalism and Empire before and after 1917', *Studies in Ethnicity and Nationalism* 17 (3): 369–80.

Shakhmatov, A. A. 1899. *K voprosu ob obrazovanii russkikh narechiĭ i narodnosteĭ.* (Sankt-Peterburg: Tipografiı͡a V. S. Balashev" i K.).

Shirokogorov, S. M. 1923. *Ėtnos — issledovanie osnovnykh print͡sipov izmeneniı͡a ėtnicheskikh i ėtnograficheskikh ı͡avleniĭ* (Shanghai: Sibpress).

Taran, O. G. 2003. *Naukova spadshchina Fedora Vovka v galuzi antropologiï: spadkoemnist' tradit͡siĭ ta suchasne bachennı͡a* (Avtoreferat kandidatskoĭ disseratsii, Kiïvs'kiĭ nat͡sional'niĭ universitet imeni Tarasa Shevchenka).

Tikhonov, I. L. 2003. *Arkheologiı͡a v Sankt-Peterburgskom universitete* (Sankt-Peterburg: Izdatel'stvo Sankt-Peterburgskogo universiteta).

Tikhonov, I. L. 2012. 'Volkov v Sankt-Peterburge' *Arkheologiı͡a i davnı͡a istoriı͡a Ukraïni* 9 9: 302–9.

Volkov, F. K. 1906. 'Ukraint͡sy v antropologicheskom otnoshenii' *Ukrainskiĭ vestnik* 7: 418–26.

Volkov, F. K. 1915. 'Antropologiı͡a i eë universitetskoe prepodavanie' *Ezhegodnik Russkogo Antropologicheskogo obshchestva* 5. Tipografiı͡a Ė. Arngol'da: 99–107.

Volkov, F. K. 1916a. 'Antropologicheskie osobennosti ukrainskogo naroda', in *Ukrainskiĭ narod v ego proshlom i nastoı͡ashchem,* ed. by F. K. Volkov, M. S. Grushevskiĭ, M. M. Kovalevskiĭ, F. E. Korsh, A. E. Krymskiĭ, M. I. Tugan'-Baranovskiĭ, and A. A. Shakhmatov (Petrograd: Tip. tov-va "Obshchestvennaı͡a pol'za"), 427–54.

—. 1916b. 'Ėtnograficheskie osobennosti ukrainskogo naroda', in *Ukrainskiĭ narod v ego proshlom i nastoı͡ashchem,* ed. by F. K. Volkov, M. S. Grushevskiĭ, M. M. Kovalevskiĭ, F. E. Korsh, A. E. Krymskiĭ, M. I. Tugan'-Baranovskiĭ, and A. A. Shakhmatov (Petrograd: Tip. tov-va "Obshchestvennaı͡a pol'za"), 455–647.

Volkov, F. K., M. S. Grushevskiĭ, M. M. Kovalevskiĭ, F. E. Korsh, A. E. Krymskiĭ, M. I. Tugan-Baranovskiĭ, and A. A. Shakhmatov. 1914–1916. *Ukrainskiĭ narod v ego proshlom i nastoi͡ashchem* (Petrograd: tipografii͡a tovarichshestva "Obshchestvennai͡a pol'za").

Volkov, T. 1905. *Variations squelettiques du pied chez les primates et dans les races humaines* (Beaugency: Laffray fils et gendre).

Vovk, F. 1997. '"Pishu zh i͡a..., shchob i͡akomoga chastishe nagaduvati li͡udi͡am, shcho є na sviti Ukraïna" (upori͡adkuvali Vsevolod Naulko ta I͡Uliana Filipova)' *Rodovid* 15: 44–66.

Williams, E. A. 1985. 'Anthropological institutions in nineteenth-century France', *Isis* 76 (3): 331–48.

Zhurnal zasedanii͡a. 1916. 'Zhurnal zasedanii͡a Otdelenii͡a ėtnografii IRGO 4 marta 1916 goda' *Zhivai͡a starina* 2–3: 1–11.

Zukovsky, A. 1988. 'Kostomarov, Mikola', in *Encyclopedia of Ukraine*: Volume 2, ed. by V. Kubijovyč. (Toronto: University of Toronto Press), 629–631.

Archival References

AIVR — Archive of the Institute of Oriental Manuscripts, Saint-Petersburg

AIVR 28-1-197. Otdel'noe mnenie D. A. Klement͡sa o vyrabotke proekta razdelenii͡a ėtnograficheskogo muzei͡a Imperatora Aleksandra III. 31 folios.

AIVR 28-2-1. Pis'ma B. Adlera D. A. Klement͡su, 31 folios.

ARAN — Archive of the Russian Academy of Sciences

ARAN 142-1-1093. Stenogramma zasedanii͡a Uchenogo soveta Instituta ėtnografii po obsuzhdenii͡u toma "Ukraint͡sy," 13.04.1959. 121 folios.

GARF — State Archive of the Russian Federation, Moscow

GARF R-5787-1-11. Dnevnik M. N. Mogili͡anskogo. 1921. 153 folios.

GARF R-5787-1-12.Dnevnik M. N. Mogili͡anskogo, 1922. 182 folios.

GARF R-5787-1-13. Dnevnik M. N. Mogili͡anskogo, 1922., prodolzhenie. 141 folios.

GARF R-5787-1-17. "Za polveka", avtobiograficheskai͡a povest'. N. Mogili͡anskiĭ. 1921. 207 folios.

GARF R-5787-1-23. Osnovy antropologii, rukopis'. N. Mogilı͡anskiĭ. 1921. 305 folios.

GARF R-5787-1-34. Ukraina i ukrainfsy, ėtnologicheskiĭ i istoriko-kul'turnyĭ ocherk, rukopis'. N. Mogilı͡anskiĭ. 1921. 45 folios.

GARF R-5787-1-35. Zapiska po ukrainskomu voprosu i o blizhaĭshikh perspektivakh, svı͡azannykh s Ukrainoĭ, rukopis'. N. Mogilı͡anskiĭ. 1921. 22 folios.

GARF R-5787-1-38. Ukraina quasi una fantasia, rukopis'. N. Mogilı͡anskiĭ. No date. 4 folios.

GARF R-5787-1-93. Sistema antropologii, stat'ı͡a-rukopis'. N. Mogilı͡anskiĭ. 1928. 11 folios.

GARF R-5787-1-160. Pis'ma rodstvennikov, raznykh uchrezhdeniĭ i chastnykh lits͡. 1921–1932. 256 folios.

NAIA NANU — Scientific Archive of the Institute of Archaeology of the National Academy of Sciences of Ukraine

NAIA NANU 1/B-156. Pis'mo D. N. Anuchina F. K. Vovku, 11.11.1915. 2 folios.

NAIA NANU 1/B-158. Pis'mo D. N. Anuchina F. K. Vovku, 26.11.1915. 2 folios.

NAIA NANU 1/B-159. Pis'mo D. N. Anuchina F. K. Vovku, 27.10.1917. 2 folios.

OR RGB — Department of Manuscripts of the Russian State Library

OR RGB 10-20-135: 13-14. Pis'mo F. K. Volkova D. N. Anuchinu. 27.10.1897.2 folios.

OR RGB 10-20-136: 15-16. Pis'mo F. K. Volkova D. N. Anuchinu, 26.09.1898.2 folios.

OR RGB 10-20-138: 20. Pis'mo F. K. Volkova D. N. Anuchinu, 15.03.1911 2 folios.

OR RGB 10-20-139: 25–26. Pis'mo F. K. Volkova D. N. Anuchinu, 15.09.1912.2 folios.

OR RGB 10-20-142: 1–2, 29–31. Pis'mo F. K. Volkova D. N. Anuchinu, 30.10.1915. 2 folios.

REM — Photolibrary, Russian Ethnographic Museum, Saint Petersburg

REM 757-2. A view of the sloboda (a quarter of a village) "Bugor". Russians, Tula guberniı͡a. Photo by N. M. Mogilı͡anskiĭ 1902.

REM 758-12. A village. Russians, Kaluga guberni͡ia. Photo by N. M. Mogili͡anskiĭ, 1903.

REM 851-3. An izba, covered with reed. Ukrainians. Bessarabskai͡a guberni͡ia. Photo by N. M. Mogili͡anskiĭ, 1906.

REM 3747-43. "A khata". Ukrainians of Volynskai͡a guberni͡ia. Photo by F. K. Volkov, 1907.

REM 3747-64. "A street". Ukrainians of Volynskai͡a guberni͡ia. Photo by F. K. Volkov, 1907.

SPF ARAN — Saint Petersburg Branch of the Archive of the Russian Academy of Sciences

SPF ARAN 134-3-998. Pis'ma N. M. Mogili͡anskogo A. A. Shakhmatovu, 1910–1915. 8 folios.

SPF ARAN 1004-1-467:1. A photograph of Fëdor Volkov during his lessons with students in the Cabinet of Geography and Ethnography, Saint Petersburg University.

TsGIA SPb Central State Historical Archive of Saint Petersburg

TsGIA SPb 14-2-1390. Delo Universitetskogo soveta o dopushchenii magistra D. Koropchevskogo k chteni͡iu lekt͡siĭ kak privat-dot͡senta, 20.10.1899. 15 folios.

TsGIA SPb 14-1-8843. Delo o sluzhbe professora Petri. 159 folios.

TsGIA SPb 14-1-10085. Delo o dopushchenii k chteni͡iu lekt͡siĭ F. K. Volkova, 1907. 42 folios.

TsGIA SPb 14-3-26932. Universitetskoe delo studenta N. M. Mogili͡anskogo, nachatoe v 1889 g. 41 folios.

4. Mapping *Etnos*: The Geographic Imagination of Fëdor Volkov and his Students

Sergei S. Alymov and Svetlana V. Podrezova

The first formulation of the concept of *etnos* in the history of Russian ethnography has thus far been viewed as a somewhat isolated phenomenon — "a scientific insight, [that] apparently outpaced its time" (Soloveĭ 2001: 103). Nonetheless, Nikolaĭ M. Mogilīanskiĭ (1871–1933) , who first introduced the concept, was a representative of the "school" of Fëdor K. Volkov (1847–1918), which played a significant role in Russian science of the beginning of the twentieth century and had clear methodological and theoretical principles (Platonova 2010). In chapter 3, we discussed the context of Volkov and Mogilīanskiĭ's activities, including the Ukrainian national movement, museum construction, and ethnography's institutionalization as a university discipline (Alymov 2017). In this chapter, we would like to discuss one additional — but no less significant — context, namely the role of ethnographic and anthropological mapping (and of geographic imagination in a wider sense) in the formation of the concept of *etnos*. We aim to demonstrate how Volkov and his students were striving to use methods drawn from anthropology, ethnography, and cartography in order to establish scientific descriptions of "*etnos*es":

> The ἔθνος [*etnos*] concept — is a complex idea. It is a group of individuals united together as a single whole [*odno tseloe*] by [...] common physical

 https://doi.org/10.11647/OBP.0150.04

> (anthropological) characteristics; a common historical fate, and finally a common language — which is the foundation upon which, in turn, [an *etnos*] can build a common worldview [and] folk-psychology — in short, an entire spiritual culture (Mogilîanskiĭ 1916: 11).

The search for geographical correlations while mapping these characteristics was one of their main methodological instruments.

Volkov provided an example of work with such correlations in his 1916 publications discussing the findings of his anthropological and ethnographic researches. In his review of Volkov's work, Mogilîanskiĭ noted that an important characteristic of the article "Anthropological Features of Ukrainian People" is that "the somatic attributes are considered by him with regards to linguistic data" (Mogilîanskiĭ 1917: 133). Indeed, Volkov analysed anthropological indicators within three linguistic groups: northern (Polissya and Northern Polissya dialects), middle (Ukrainian and Galician dialects), and southern (Slobodsko-Ukrainian, Podol'skiĭ, upper-Strelian-Galician, and south Carpathian dialects) (Volkov 1916a: 432). He explained the anthropological differences between those groups as the results of "ethnic influences" upon the northern and middle groups, whereas the southern group "stayed purer" and preserved Slavonic traits to a larger extent (Volkov 1916a: 453). Conclusions and comparisons of that kind became typical for Volkov's students and colleagues. They tried to obtain material that covered a considerable geographic scope, used surveys as research methods, identified anthropological and cultural "types" within the territories under study, and came to conclusions concerning the origin of those "types", which were later labelled ethno-genetic conclusions.

Institutional conditions influenced the geographic orientation of those studies. Volkov and his students Mogilîanskiĭ, David A. Zolotarëv (1885–1935), Sergeĭ I. Rudenko (1885–1969) as well as Dimtriĭ K. Zelenin (1878–1954), Sergeĭ M. Shirokogorov [Sergei Shirokogoroff] (1887–1939) and others worked within the frameworks of the Commission for Making Ethnographic Maps of Russia (KSEK), established by the Imperial Russian Geographic Society (IRGO) in 1910. The work of this commission has been discussed by researchers (Hirsch 2005; Psîanchin 2004; Zolotarëv 1916b), but mostly with regards to the Commission for Studying the Tribal Composition of the Population of the USSR and of the Adjacent Countries (KIPS) which was established in 1917 based on the outcome of the KSEK (Cadiot 2007). Nevertheless, the existing literature does not fully engage with the methodological aspect of the Commission for Making Ethnographic Maps of Russia's work, resulting in a certain conflation of its work with the work of its successor, which was charged with the study of tribal composition. This article, however, pays close attention to the theoretical and methodological aspects of the commission's activity as well as to its influence on the work of its key participants. Three most vivid individual cases are chosen as examples: those of Zelenin, Zolotarëv, and Rudenko.

Map, Archive, Museum: The Sources and Methods of the Commission's Work

The commission followed and elaborated on the idea of a geographic approach to studying cultural phenomena and their correlations. In Russia, by the beginning of the 1900s, the geographical method had been already put to use with respect to linguistic and ethnographic material. Specifically, it had been employed in making a map of southern Russian dialects and regional accents (produced by the Southwestern Department of the Imperial Russian Geographical Society) and, later, for mapping dialects of the Russian language (undertaken by the Moscow Dialectological Commission of the University of Moscow). It was used in the expositional and collecting activities of the Ethnographic Department of the Russian Museum of Alexander III.

Such a large-scale undertaking as making ethnographic maps of Russia was based on well-established mechanisms of gathering data: the compilation of bibliographic references on current issues, the development of special surveys and questionnaires, the attraction of a wide range of correspondents, and drawing on what was by that time an already rich experience of ethnographic map-making in Russia.

Ethnographic Map-Making

In the second half of the nineteenth century, ethnographic map-making in the Imperial Russian Geographical Society was developing quite rapidly, as evidenced by such ambitious projects as the "Ethnographic Map of European Russia" by Pëtr I. Këppen [Peter von Köppen]

(1851), "Atlas of Populations of the Western Russian Region According to [Religious] Confessions" (1864), "Ethnographic Map of Slavonic Peoples" (1867), and the "Ethnographic Atlas of European Russia" by Aleksandr F. Rittikh [Alexander Rittich] (1875) (Seegel 2012). At that time, an "ethnographic map" referred to a geographic representation of the ethnic composition of the Russian Empire, or part thereof. Peoples were classified on the map primarily according to language, self-designation, and/or confession criteria. The so-called *revizii* [imperial census-like documents] were used as the main source for identifying populations' ethnicity, and as a result, researchers had to directly approach state and military agencies as well as religious institutions to get data to work with (Psi͡anchin 2004: 26–27) (NA RGO 1(1846)-1-8).

Sometimes cartographers were required to determine "the physical particulars of the type of tribe" along with languages and "way of life", but, as Steven Seegel showed in the case of the northwestern branch of the IRGO cartographer I͡Uliĭ Kuznet͡sov, it was extremely difficult "to find, discover, measure, and essentialize their [nationalities'] traits in true form" (Seegel 2012: 193). In the 1880s, however, Ėduard Petri attempted to critically revise the linguistic criterion as a major criterion in ethnic divisions of the population. At the end of 1887, he made a speech to the Department of Ethnography of the Russian Geographic Society and suggested that, when producing ethnographic maps, researchers should take into consideration "not some single attribute, but all known information, linguistic as well as somatic, ethnological, and psychological" (NA RGO 1(1888)-1-16: 35). In a certain way, the commission (KSEK) was following this idea and, for the first time, set itself the goal to produce, "not linguistic maps, ordinarily called in the past and still often referred to as ethnographic, but truly ethnographic maps, i.e. indicating the geographic spread of characteristic elements of folk ways of living" (Volkov 1914: 193).

Language: Creating a Dialectological Map

In 1872, the Southwestern Department of the Russian Geographic Society published the first exercise in linguistic geography in Russia: the "Map of Southern Russian Dialects and Accents", developed by Konstantin P. Mikhal'chuk on the basis of materials collected by Pavel P. Chubinskiĭ (1839–1884) and illustrating theses of his work "Dialects,

Sub-Dialects, and Parlances of Southern Russia with regards to Dialects of Galicia" (Mikhal'chuk 1872). Vladimir I. Lamanskiĭ (1833–1914), when he became chair of the Department of Ethnography of the IRGO for the second time in 1886, announced that a study of the geography of the Russian language would be one of the department's main goals; this involved compiling the "corpus of Russian dialectology" and a corresponding map (Veselovskiĭ 1915: 4).

This idea was further developed during the early 1900s by the Moscow Dialectological Commission (MDC), which operated within the University of Moscow and had Alekseĭ A. Shakhmatov (1864–1920) among its founders. In addition to a variety of objectives aimed at undertaking a systematic study of the various dialects of the Russian language and their classification, the commission suggested creating a geographic representation of those particularities (Durnovo, Sokolov, and Ushakov 1915: iii). The publication of the "Dialectological Map of the Russian Language in Europe" resulted from a collaboration between the MDC and the KSEK of the IRGO. At the end of March 1911, they reached an agreement concerning the map's publication. The authorship was assigned to the MDC, while the preparation of the map as such (the choice of the template, its refinement, marking data on the map, editing and proofreading) was entrusted to the KSEK of the IRGO (NA RGO 24-82: 29–30).

The participants of both commissions agreed that the map should be published quite quickly (MDC was aiming at summer 1911), be of middle scale (100 *verst* [1.07 km] per inch), and be of a general, schematic character, that is, "provide a picture of the main types of dialects" (Ibid: 39, 41–42, 62). Despite the long-term collaborative work of the commissions, the atlas was issued only in January 1915, "without its authors' awareness", revealing certain shortcomings and, also requiring "a great deal [...] of corrections and [making several] additions without consideration", that caused a negative reaction on the part of Dmitriĭ N. Ushakov (1873–1942), who was communicating with the IRGO commission on behalf of the MDC (Ibid: 26–28v, 31–32v).

The Language Department established in 1911 under the KSEK, planned to make a linguistic map of the whole of Russia that, while not pursuing some "particular subtleties", would point to "the existence of the main dialectical differences even between quite small language groups", paying special attention to regions with two languages (NA

RGO 24-82: 43). However, the work was limited to compiling the list of languages and dialects of the Russian Empire for further exploration of "their ethnographic and national foundations", and to identifying the persons willing to study them (Ibid: 44–45). Nevertheless, this idea served as the impetus in 1914 for beginning to prepare a tribal (linguistic) map of Siberia at the initiative of one member of the Language Department, Serafim K. Patkanov [Serovbe K. Patkanîan] (1860–1918) (Patkanov 1915).

Museum Activities as a Platform for the Commission's Work

Geographic imagination became the cornerstone of the activities of the Russian Museum of Alexander III. From its foundation in 1901, active research and collecting work in the museum combined the efforts of the leading ethnographic researchers and, initially, members of the Imperial Russian Geographical Society (Fig. 4.1). Lamanskiĭ viewed the aim of ethnographic museums as "the representation of the ethnographic diversity of the globe" (Sergeeva 1992: 4). He believed that the purpose of the Russian Museum's Ethnographic Department was to represent Russia within its imperial borders and the exhibition of its collections was to be organised according to the historic-geographic (or ethno-geographic) principle, that is, by cultural-ethnographic regions (Ibid: 5, 11).

In 1902, the museum compiled and published the general "Programme for Gathering of Ethnographic Objects" aimed at local amateurs and people knowledgeable about folk lifeways (Ėtnograficheskiĭ otdel Russkogo Muzeîa 1903: 6). Calling for the accurate certification of objects, the authors of the second edition of the programme pointed out: "In the ethnographic museum, the human beings, the people, who created this or that object are in the foreground" (Ibid: 12). It is well known that the author of this Ethnographic Department project, Lamanskiĭ, had a wide circle of correspondents — teachers, doctors, and social activists — with whom he communicated extensively. According to the reports, collections of objects gathered by local enthusiasts were coming to the museum even in the first years of its existence (Ibid: 13).

On the basis of the general programme, museum personnel developed their own guidelines concerning particular peoples. For instance, Alekseĭ A. Makarenko (1860–1942) prepared a handwritten programme especially for his trip to the Tungus on the river Katanga in 1907 (ARĖM 1-2-386: 121–22). The museum also designed and issued a detailed questionnaire that was to be mailed to amateur ethnographers for studying the Malorussians (NA RGO 1(1911)-1-32: 21v–26v). We found no indications of its authorship, but it is highly probable that it had been developed by Volkov, who had been taking part in the museum's activities almost since its foundation. Since 1904 he had been gathering collections of exhibits on behalf of the museum; from 1907 until 1918, for twelve years, he headed the museum's Department of Southwestern Russia and Foreign Countries (Cherunova 1992: 53). Volkov combined the aims of his own expeditions with the needs of the IRGO's KSEK and worked on the "identification of the geographic spread of ethnographic phenomena" (qtd. in Cherunova 1992: 56, 58).

Fig. 4.1 A group of the employees of the Ethnographic Department of the Russian Museum in Staraîa Ladoga. Sitting: Nikolaĭ M. Mogilîanskiĭ (far left). Standing: Fëdor K. Volkov (second from left), Aleksandr A. Miller (third from left). 1908–1910 (RĖM IM9-129-1). © Russian Ethnographic Museum, St Petersburg

Organization, Methods, and Results of the KSEK Commission's Work

The KSEK Commission was established as an outcome of discussions about the future and goals of Russian ethnography as a separate discipline that occurred at the twelfth Congress of Russian Naturalists and Doctors in Moscow in winter 1909–1910 (Bartol'd 1910) and adjacent meetings of the IRGO's Department of Ethnography (Fig. 4.2). This period of disciplinary formation coincided with a change in the leadership of the Russian Geographic Society: on 13 March, Sergeĭ F. Ol'denburg was elected chairman of the Department of Ethnography, replacing Lamanskiĭ (Sergeĭ K. Bulich was elected vice-chairman and Aleksandr N. Samoĭlovich became the secretary).

Key meetings were held on 30 April (chaired by Ol'denburg) and 10 May 1910 (chaired by Shakhmatov), at which, following debate, Volkov and Miller stressed the need for a systematic study of the peoples of Russia according to special programmes designed with regards to ethnographic categories. Ivan P. Poddubnyĭ added to this line of argument the idea of creating an ethnographic map of Russia. In response, Shakhmatov proposed organizing a commission to undertake the preliminary work needed to produce the ethnographic map (NA RGO 24-78: 56v–57) (Zolotarëv 1916b).

The goals and methods of work of the resulting KSEK were not defined immediately. Debate continued at the meetings of the commission held from the autumn of 1910 until the spring of 1911, and sometimes revealed ethnographers' opposing viewpoints on the immediate goals of the commission's research. The choice of the main criterion for map-making — should it be "peoples" (*narodnosti*) or "ethnographic subjects/topics" — prompted a heated discussion.

At several meetings, Zelenin argued in favour of preparing "separate maps for ethnic groups, with the aim of compiling one common map afterwards" (NA RGO 24-78: 64); that is, he advocated for the primacy of the ethnic map and a corresponding division of the commission into sub-commissions "according to nationalities" (*po narodnost͡iam*) (Ibid: 59v). At one of the meetings, Bulich, the meeting's chair, put Zelenin's proposal to make the "preliminary map of peoples" to a vote; it was defeated in a vote of two to fifteen. Volkov, in his turn, insisted on making maps of separate ethnographic attributes: "drawing the

Fig. 4.2 A group of Russian ethnographers, anthropologists, and orientalists, prior to 1917. First row (sitting): V. I. Iokhel'son, S. I. Rudenko, N. M. Mogilîanskiĭ, V. V. Bartol'd, the sixth from the left is F. K. Volkov. Standing in the second row, the fifth from the left is D. A. Zolotarëv. The bald man with closed eyes in the upper row is A. A. Miller, the tall man to the left of him is B. F. Adler. The second to the right from Miller is B. E. Petri (RĖM IM9-193). © Russian Ethnographic Museum, St Petersburg

boundaries of known types of buildings, clothing, agricultural tools and so on, according to ethnographic categories" (NA RGO 24-78: 64v). The general map would synthesise the individual maps developed by the thematic sub-commissions (Ibid: 65). The majority of Volkov's colleagues, including Shakhmatov and Ol'denburg, supported his idea.

At the heart of the debate about categories there were fundamental disagreements regarding the attributes that define the *narodnost'*. Some scholars viewed language as the major ethnic marker. Lev Shternberg suggested they also consider ethnonyms (self-designations), while the academician Nikolaĭ [Nicholas] Îa. Marr, on the contrary, emphasised the "shakiness of self-designation as an attribute" (Ibid: 59v).

Volkov's proposal broke with Russian ethnography's traditional prioritisation of *narodnost'* and its exclusively linguistic definition. Like the majority of the department's members, Volkov considered this notion to be "undetermined" and complicated (Mogilîanskiĭ, NA RGO 24-78: 59v), one that could only be "distinguished" by establishing the correlations between several attributes "linguistically, anthropologically, and ethnographically" (Volkov, NA RGO 24-78: 64v), that is, as a result of work of the KSEK (Volkov, NA RGO 24-78: 64v; Marr, NA RGO 24-78: 59v). In Volkov's opinion, the commission's main goal was to "establish the criteria for dividing the population into ethnographic groups and, in accordance with these criteria, to design programmes for studying language, clothing, food, etc." (NA RGO 24-78: 57v). Many members of the RGO approved of the proposal to organise sub-commissions dealing with separate ethnographic categories.

The identification of ethnographic categories to be represented in the map was quite challenging because, in addition to the conceptual considerations, it also required considering technical aspects of cartography. In Shakhmatov and Mogilīanskiĭ's opinion, it was essential "to avoid fractured tasks" and to limit the task to the most substantial attributes (Ibid: 65). Volkov, who had volunteered to compile a preliminary list of categories, discovered that some of them, such as "hunting", "fishing" ("the same forms here are often determined by the natural conditions of the zoological zones"), and "folk technology", "are hardly cartographically viable" (Ibid: 64v). He suggested beginning by examining (1) agriculture and animal husbandry, (2) modes of transportation, (3) food, (4) clothing and ornamentation, (5) built structures, (6) folk art, and (7) language and folklore. Beliefs, rituals, social concepts as well as folk knowledge and law should be mapped afterwards (15 Oct. 1910, NA RGO 24-78: 64v–65).

Initially Volkov did not put stress on the language among the other categories and did not rank them by their significance, supposing that the sub-commissions would work simultaneously (NA RGO 24-78: 65). However, other members of the commission, including Mogilīanskiĭ and Shakhmatov, prioritised the making of a detailed linguistic map that would provide the basis of comparisons with the other ethnographic criteria. Volkov agreed that the linguistic map could become the substratum for further work (Ibid: 60) and suggested that the other attributes be added to the maps with "already drawn linguistic borders" (Ibid: 65). Thus, at the very first meeting, the commission chose "language" as its central category and, as we will show below, consistently followed this line in the future. Another outcome of the discussions was the revision of the category of "agriculture and animal husbandry". The colleagues offered various options for combining this category with the others and chose the notion of "economic mode of life" (*khoziaĭstvennyĭ byt,* proposed by Shternberg) which embraced "agriculture", "food", "modes of transportation", and "crafts and utensils" (proposed by Miller).

It is worth mentioning that the list Volkov compiled did not include "anthropological features", although it was a significant category for him and his followers. Regarding anthropological map-making, Volkov noted some "practical difficulties", specifically, a lack of collected anthropological data and the high costs of gathering it. Mogilianskiĭ and Shakhmatov, however, suggested adding this category into the list (at number 8). Mogilianskiĭ, in particular, argued that, "after the dialectological borders, anthropological features have the next greatest significance". The proposal was approved by the members of the commission (NA RGO 24-78: 59).

As a result of the debates and the organizational activities of 1911, the commission was to include eight departments: (1) Department of Language, chaired by Shakhmatov with Andreĭ D. Rudnev as secretary; (2) Department of Anthropology, chaired by Volkov, with Rudenko as secretary; (3) Department of Housing and Building, chaired by Mogilianskiĭ, with Aleksandr K. Serzhputovskiĭ as secretary; (4) Department of Economic Life, chaired by Eduard A. Volter, later by Mogilianskiĭ, with Serzhputovskiĭ as secretary; (5) Department of Clothing and Decorations, chaired by Volkov, with Prince Diĭ Ė. Ukhtomskiĭ as secretary. The last three departments, (6) Department of Music, (7) Department of Folk Art, and (8) Department of Beliefs, failed to "organise themselves' and, unfortunately, did not work within the commission's framework (Zolotarëv 1916b: xix).

The mutability of ethnographic realities and, especially, of material culture would cause difficulties in the forthcoming research. Focusing exclusively on the "ethnographic" criteria that were "disappearing" and not accounting for the "new forms supplanting them" (Volkov; NA RGO 24-78: 65v), the commission stated that the maps would focus on "the present times", mapping current ethnographic characteristics and material culture, and, in some cases, be supplemented with "historical information in the form of special maps" that would consider the "vanished" characteristics (Zelenin, Mogilianskiĭ, NA RGO 24-78: 65v).

The KSEK was a separate structure under the Council of the IRGO and had its own budget comparable with that of the Department of Ethnography itself. The commission was usually headed by the chairman of the department: in the first years, it was Ol'denburg (with secretaries Aleksandr N. Samoĭlovich and Aleksandr A. Miller); at the end of 1912, he was replaced by Vsevolod F. Miller; from the end of 1913 until 1915, it was Shakhmatov (with secretaries, Aleksandr A. Miller and David A. Zolotarëv); then, in 1916, again Ol'denburg (with secretary Zolotarëv). The commission acted as the governing and unifying body for its departments. At general meetings, which in the pre-revolutionary period took place from one to four times a year, it discussed their plans, general issues, questionnaires, and trips, coordinated the activities of the departments and approved their proposals and budgets (Zolotarëv 1916b: xv). The main work, however, was done in the departments.

In 1913, on the initiative of the Siberian expert Alekseĭ A. Makarenko, an independent Siberian Sub-Commission was formed within the commission (NA RGO 24-78: 98) under the leadership of Shternberg (deputy chairman, Serafim K. Patkanov; secretary, Makarenko). The sub-commission's permanent bureau included the researchers and cartographers of Siberia: Lev [Leo] S. Bagrov, Vasiliĭ N. Vasiliev, Berngard Ė. Petri, Diĭ Ė. Ukhtomskiĭ, and Sergeĭ M. Shirokogorov (NA RGO 1(1912)-1-17: 78). At the end of 1914, the commission decided to single out two main divisions. "The First Division" (chairman, Volkov; secretary, Zolotarëv) continued to study the peoples of the European part of the empire and absorbed all the existing departments, which were transformed into sections. Another division (the former Siberian Sub-Commission) was renamed "The Second Division: Siberia and Central Asia", "due to the supposed expansion of its activities and their extension to Turkestan and the Stepnoĭ Kraĭ [Steppe Region]" (NA RGO 1(1912)-1-17: 78). In their first years, from 1911 until 1914, the departments were engaged in the preparation of questionnaires, the identification of the main categories that should be mapped, and the definition of the principles of mapping.

At one of the KSEK's first meetings (29 October 1910), Volkov proposed using the "questionnaires for South Russia", which were printed in large numbers by the Russian Museum of Alexander III. On 16 September 1911, 2,500 copies of the questionnaire (four boxes) were delivered to the IRGO (see the minutes of the meeting on 23 September 1911 [Otdelenie ėtnografii I.R.G.O. 1911: xxv]) and in the summer of 1912, they were sent to the field. This project used a unique format of the questionnaire, which made it convenient for further processing (see Fig.

4.3). In its left-hand part, there were a few questions grouped by topics (housing, clothing, agriculture, and food) and placed, in numbered order, in separate squares (the theme "housing" included nine sections, or micro-themes). The right-hand side, intended, apparently, for a short answer or summary, remained empty. It also contained the topic's title (for example, "Housing-1", "Agriculture-2", etc.) and a blank space for indicating the location of the survey. It was not recommended to write on the back of the sheet.

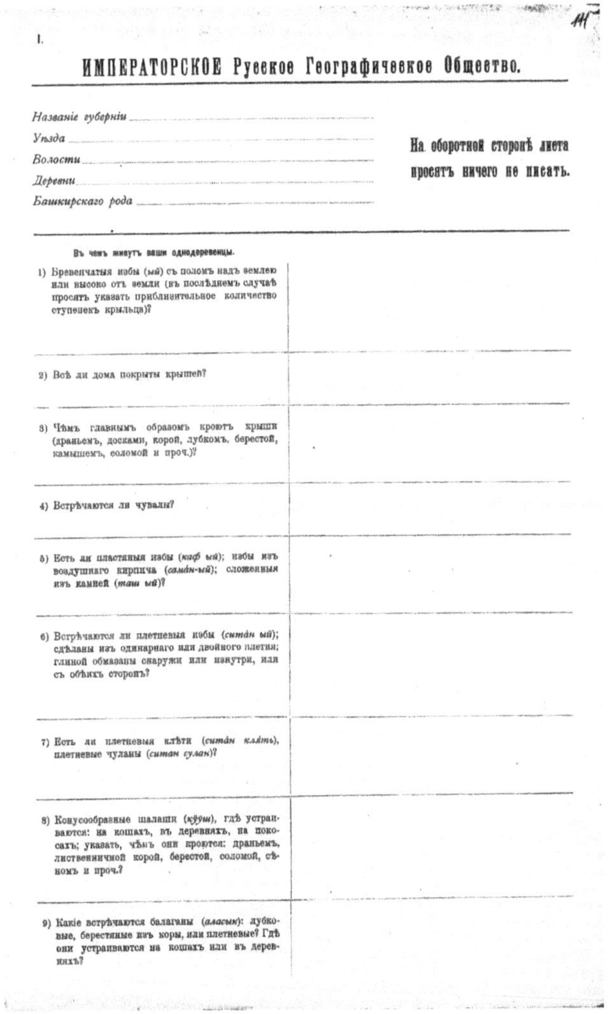

I.

ИМПЕРАТОРСКОЕ Русское Географическое Общество.

Названіе губерніи ……
Уѣзда ……
Волости ……
Деревни ……
Башкирскаго рода ……

На оборотной сторонѣ листа просятъ ничего не писать.

Въ чемъ живутъ ваши однодеревенцы.

1) Бревенчатыя избы (*ый*) съ поломъ надъ землею или высоко отъ земли (въ послѣднемъ случаѣ просятъ указать приблизительное количество ступенекъ крыльца)?

2) Всѣ ли дома покрыты крышей?

3) Чѣмъ главнымъ образомъ кроютъ крыши (драньемъ, досками, корой, лубкомъ, берестой, камышемъ, соломой и проч.)?

4) Встрѣчаются ли чувалы?

5) Есть ли пластяныя избы (*каф ый*); избы изъ воздушнаго кирпича (*самáн-ый*); сложенныя изъ камней (*таш ый*)?

6) Встрѣчаются ли плетневыя избы (*ситáн ый*); сдѣланы изъ одинарнаго или двойного плетня; глиной обмазаны снаружи или изнутри, или съ обѣихъ сторонъ?

7) Есть ли плетневыя клѣти (*ситáн клáть*), плетневые чуланы (*ситан сулан*)?

8) Конусообразные шалаши (*кўўш*), гдѣ устраиваются: на кошахъ, въ деревняхъ, на покосахъ; указать, чѣмъ они кроются: драньемъ, лиственничной корой, берестой, соломой, сѣномъ и проч.?

9) Какіе встрѣчаются балаганы (*аласык*): лубковые, берестяные изъ коры, или плетневые? Гдѣ они устраиваются на кошахъ или въ деревняхъ?

Fig. 4.3 Bashkir questionnaire, p. 1 (NA RGO 24-1-72-111). © Research Archive of the Russian Geographical Society, St Petersburg

The completed questionnaires were subsequently cut along the lines. This greatly facilitated processing of the data: the replies were literally stitched together, that is, they could be grouped according to the type of the information or geographically. By the end of 1912, the commission had received over 2,500 questionnaires with 587 "excellent answers", which were immediately "brought into the system" (NA RGO 24-78: 92).

Having completed their review of the existing literature and having concluded that "the already available literary material [...] is too inadequate and, most importantly, too casual", the departments began compiling questionnaires (Volkov 1914: 194).

Basing their work on the Russian Museum's research on the Malorussians, in 1911 Volkov prepared approximate schemes for collecting data on housing, clothing and decorations, and economic life, which were to "also serve as a canvas for developing questionnaires for each nationality [ethnic group] or a group of nationalities" (NA RGO 24-79: 2v–3v; NA RGO 24-81: 6–7, published in (Primernaia͡ skhema 1916). Public school teachers were considered to be the best correspondents, so the questionnaires needed to have an accessible and convenient form to complete, contain a small number of questions that would be "completely exhaustive [in terms of the] content of the future maps", while "clearly formulated" in such a way that "the answers to them could not be difficult [confusing]" for non-professional gatherers (Volkov 1914: 194). The commission hoped to receive help with dispatch of the questionnaires from the trustees of the educational districts, directors of the public schools, and the chairmen of the Zemstvo Boards (NA RGO 1(1911)-1-32: 58–59v, 75–75v, 79–79v).[1]

On 8 February 1913, the commission approved programmes for collecting data on the housing, clothing, and economic life of the Belorussians, Poles, and Bashkirs; in the summer, the questionnaires were printed and their dispatch began. During 1913, about 3,800 forms were sent out to the Belorussian Gubernia (925 copies), and to the Malorussian (1,802 copies) and Bashkir (990 copies) provinces (NA RGO 1(1911)-1-32: 90–91). The beginning of the war in 1914, however, made it difficult to mail questionnaires to and receive answers from the European part of Russia. Printed in the spring of 1914, the questionnaires "for the

1 Zemstvo (pl. *zemstva*) is an institution of local government set up in the course of the Great Reforms of Alexander II in 1864.

ethnographic study" of the Velikorussians (i.e. Great Russians) (10,000 copies) were put in envelopes, but their distribution was suspended "until [a] more favourable time" due to military operations (NA RGO 24-78: 113v, 116).[2] The large-scale dispatch of the Velikorussian questionnaires began only in the spring of 1916, and they were sent primarily to schools in the Moscow and Petrograd educational districts and to those of the central provinces (Ibid: 124-26, 128-29, 134).

Beginning in 1912, upon the receipt of the completed questionnaires, their analysis was carried out rather quickly. The responsibility for processing the materials regarding Malorossia was assigned to Volkov; Serzhputovskiĭ took care of the Belorussian data (Ibid: 102–02v); Rudenko handled the questionnaires on the Bashkirs. Towards the end of the war, in 1917–1918, the results of the Great Russian questionnaire were being analyzed under Zolotarëv's leadership. Indeed, the responses began to arrive in such great numbers that their processing required an increase in the number of staff and additional financing (Ibid: 132). The "summaries and the development [processing] of the questionnaires" resulted in detailed ethnographic descriptions of specific gubernias; these were deposited in the Archive of the IRGO (see NA RGO 24-105).

Simultaneously with the questionnaires' processing, the commission's sections discussed the principles of cartography and the compilation of preliminary maps. On 18 April 1914, the commission approved the "schemes worked out by the sections for mapping individual ethnographic and anthropological features" (Otchët 1915: vi). These features (see Table 4.1, NA RGO 24-78: 3) were originally developed with regards to the Ukrainian materials, and by that time were already well generalised, but they also served as reference points for the compilation of maps of other ethnic groups.

Drafting of the maps took place in stages as fresh materials came from processing (NA RGO 24-78: 104–05). The "breakdown" of the material on the maps was entrusted to specialists who were paid from the IRGO's coffers (Ibid: 102).

2 In March 1915, Volkov wrote to Anuchin about the distribution of the Velikorussian questionnaires and receipt of answers to the Belorussian ones: "Now [they] are receiving answers to the questionnaire on Belorussia and mailing the questionnaire sheets to Velikorussia" (OR RGB 10-20-138: 26).

Table 4.1. Ethnographic and anthropological features to be mapped by the KSEK's departments.

N.	Department	Name of the map	Main attributes, marked by the shades of the same color
1.	Department of Housing Map 1	_____	1) The material of built structures 2) The form of the roof
2.	Department of Housing Map 2	_____	1) The yard 2) The disposition of built structures
3.	Department of Economic Life	_____	The type of bread-like food
4.	Department of Clothing and Decorations Map 1	Female clothing	The shirt with or without a collar
5.	Department of Clothing and Decorations Map 2	Male clothing	The way of wearing the shirt: over the trousers, tucked into the trousers
6.	Department of Clothing and Decorations Map 3	Decorations	Material (wool, paper, etc.)
7.	Department of Anthropology Map 1	Map of the pigmentation of hair and eyes; broken by ethnic groups	Pigmentation of hair
8.	Department of Anthropology Map 2	Map of the height; broken down by ethnic groups	Height
9.	Department of Anthropology Map 3	Map of the head index; broken down by ethnic groups	Head index

The most consistent and coordinated work was conducted in the Department of Anthropology. The members of the department carried out regular expeditions according to Volkov's anthropometric programme, which was based on the principles of the French anthropological school (for the list of trips and their participants, see Zolotarёv 1916b: xviii). At Volkov's suggestion, the unpublished material of the Cabinet of Geography and Anthropology of St Petersburg University was also used in the maps' compilation. Following the example of the Moscow anthropologist Dmitriĭ N. Anuchin, who wrote a famous monograph about the height of the population of Russia based on the data about military recruits, the possibility of collecting data on physical height in the areas of "military presence" was also discussed (Ibid: 2). Volkov and his colleagues from the RGO admitted that "it is impossible to collect information on the categories of anthropological characteristics by means of a questionnaire", nor could "local people" — doctors, for example — be commissioned to do the measurements using the given instructions.

Finally, a review of the printed and manuscript materials on the measurements carried out by the department's staff during 1911–1912 (Volkov for the Ukrainians; Rudenko for the Bashkirs and the Urals Finns; Mogili͡anskiĭ and Zolotarёv for the Velikorussians; Chekanovskiĭ for the Poles, etc.) ultimately convinced the department's members to conduct a large-scale project on anthropometry in the field. In Volkov's opinion, only a few publications could be used in drawing the maps, and those only partially, while the rest "could not be taken into account" because they did not meet the Commission's requirements:

> due to the execution of the measurements not according to the generally accepted schemes but [according] to those invented by the authors themselves, and, moreover, often [following] quite imperfect instructions or without the proper differentiation of ethnic groups (NA RGO 24-83: 18).

In the first years, the trips took place in the form of expeditions composed of students and employees of the Russian Anthropological Society, the Anthropological Laboratory of St Petersburg University, and of the ethnographic department of the Russian Museum of Alexander III, with the permits issued by the commission (NA RGO 24-78: 83; see also the minutes of meeting on 29 Apr. 1911 [Otdelenie ėtnografii I.R.G.O. 1911: xix]; Volkov 1914: 194). Gradually, Volkov invited

Fig. 4.4 The Members of the Upper Volga expedition among peasants. The man taking measurements is most likely David A. Zolotarёv. I͡aroslavskai͡a gubernia, 1922–1925 (RĖM IM12-83). © Russian Ethnographic Museum, St Petersburg

his students — Rudenko and Zolotarёv (summer of 1911), Boris G. Kryzhanovskiĭ (1912), Sergeĭ A. Teploukhov (1915), etc. — to participate in the IRGO expeditions and then in the activities of the Department of Anthropology (Fig. 4.4). Many of them later became members of the society and made a serious contribution to the work of the commission. The majority of the measured people were men, but Zolotarёv also took measurements of women (see his report on the trip to Novgorodskai͡a and Tverskai͡a gubernii [provinces] in 1912: NA RGO 24-83: 12). This is how Rudenko described his method:

> 36 measurements were taken on each subject, 10 descriptive features were noted (the contours of the hand and foot were sketched out) (5 measurements), except for the information on the age, location, kin, [and territorial designations] *volost'*, *ti͡ub* and *aĭmak* (and so on) of each person measured; the places where the measurements were taken were immediately indicated on the map (NA RGO 24-83: 11) (Figure 4.5 and 4.6).

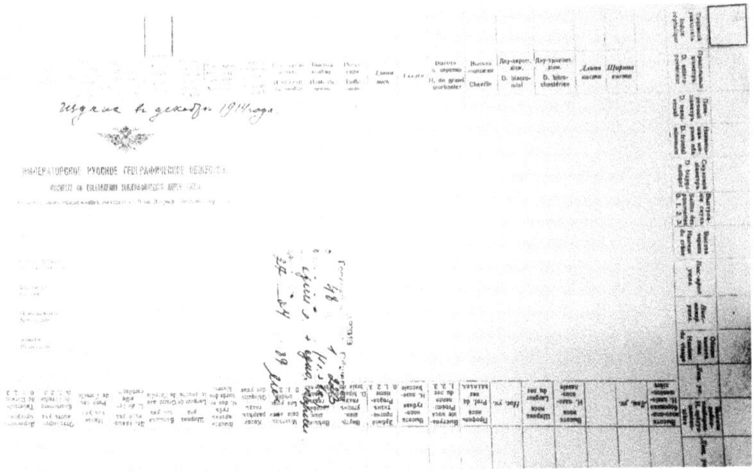

Fig. 4.5 A card for the record of anthropological measurements published by the IRGO in 1914 (NA RGO 48-1-223-1). © Research Archive of the Russian Geographical Society, St Petersburg

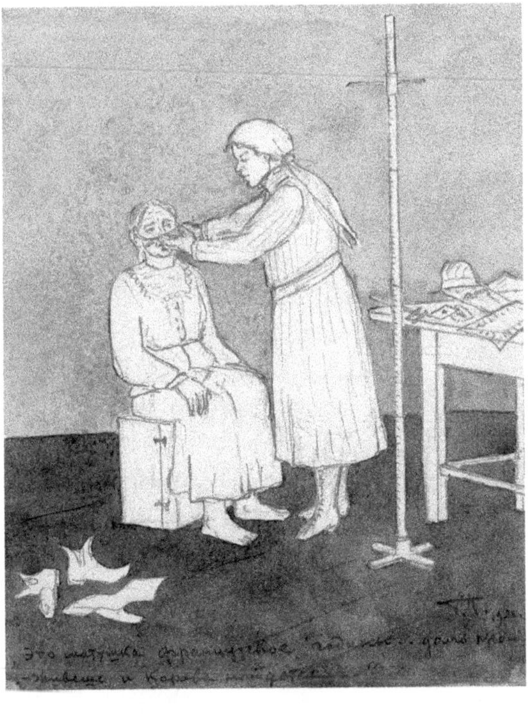

Fig. 4.6 A drawing by A. L. Kolobaev of Z. P. Malinovskaîa, taking measurements of a peasant woman during an expedition to the Rybinskaîa gubernia in 1922. The writing on the drawing reads: "It is a French fortunetelling, goody [...] you will live long, and your cow will be found" (RÈM IM14-1/19). © Russian Ethnographic Museum, St Petersburg

It was likely Volkov who suggested the idea of compiling several anthropological maps of particular characteristics, about which he wrote to Anuchin on 15 March 1911: "I wanted to consult with you also regarding those maps […] how to present them? I think that it would be necessary to make at least 3 maps: height, head index, and colour, rather than to combine everything into one [map]. What do you think?" (OR RGB 10-20-138: 20v). Initially, the department decided to make four maps according to four categories: (1) height, (2) head index, (3) hair colour, (4) eye colour, respectively (6 Apr. 1911, NA RGO 24-78: 83). However, at the beginning of 1914 the anthropologists decided to prepare three types of maps (combining the last two categories on one map, see Table 1), to break down the data by ethnic group, to consider a territorial unit (*uezd*) as the main unit, and to publish the maps as soon as they become ready — for a separate ethnic group or a district (10 Mar. 1914, NA RGO 24-83: 7).

In December 1911, at a meeting of the commission, Volkov presented the first anthropological map of Malorossia, prepared by him on the basis of the data collected by St Petersburg University's Anthropological Committee (NA RGO 24-78: 86v). By the end of 1913, Rudenko had compiled the maps of the height and head index of the Bashkirs (NA RGO 24-83: 6). At the end of 1914, the anthropological map of Malorossia was almost ready, with the exception of a few *uezds* (NA RGO 24-78: 104). However, due to the delayed production of the template of the map of southern Russia, Volkov's three Malorussian maps — covering (1) pigmentation, (2) height and some indicators characterizing body proportions, and (3) head and facial indexes — were completed only at the end of 1915 (Zolotarëv 1916b: xviii) and their publication with an explanatory note was postponed, initially, to 1916 (Otchët 1916: vii) and then to 1917 (NA RGO 24-78: 134).

By the end of 1915, the draft versions of the combined ethnographic maps of Malorossia were completed, but the department was forced to refrain from printing them "due to the exceptional timing [i.e. the war] and lack of funds" (Otchët 1915: vii). By the same time, Rudenko had processed all the collected material on the Bashkirs and had prepared the corresponding anthropological and ethnographic maps that had been scheduled for publication in 1916 (Otchët 1915: vii). However, because of the difficult financial situation caused by the war, the publication of these maps did not happen in that year. A number of the maps prepared by Volkov and Rudenko were included, on an enlarged scale, in their monographs to illustrate the most important theses of their research.

So, in 1916 Volkov published three anthropological maps (covering hair colours, height, and head indexes; see (Volkov et al. 1914-1916: 432, 440, 448) and one ethnographic map ("Geographical Distribution of Ukrainian Huts by Building Material"; see Ibid: 520. Fig. 4.7). In the same year, Rudenko supplemented the first volume of *The Bashkirs*, titled *The Physical Type of the Bashkirs* (1916), with three anthropological maps and a map of Bashkir *dachas*[3] and clan groups, while the monograph's second volume, published in 1925, was accompanied by three maps representing the geographical distribution of household elements among the Bashkirs and the final, combined, map.

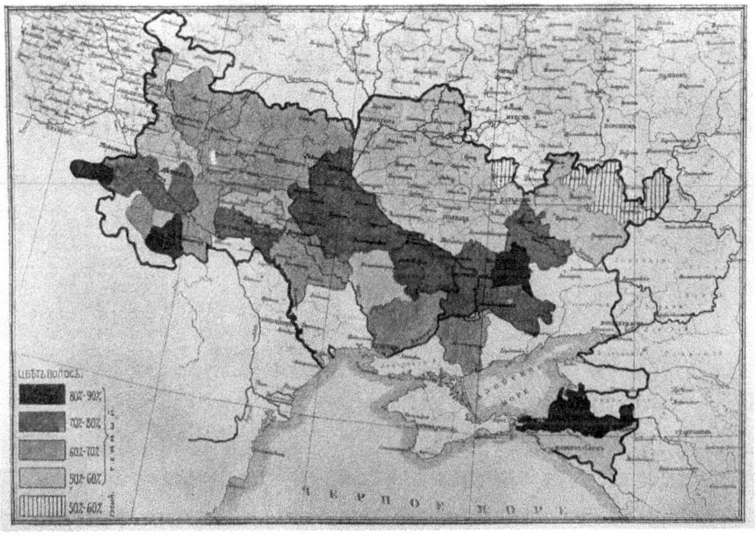

Fig. 4.7 "The Map of the Hair Colour of the Ukrainian Population" (Volkov 1916a: 432)

The commission could not fully realise its plans. The maps were not published; the collected data remained largely in the archives or in personal collections. Nevertheless, it served as a laboratory in which the methods of not only the future KIPS, but also those used by the researchers participating in its work were developed.

3 A landed property, held by the Bashkir nobility.

From Questionnaire to Monograph: A Model for Describing an *Etnos*

As detailed above, the compilation of questionnaires was recognised as an important part of the commission's work. Volkov's Malorussian research programme became the prototype for questionnaires and schemes developed for studying other peoples, including, the Belarusian (compiled by Serzhputovskiĭ under the leadership of Volkov), the Velikorussian (compiled by Zolotarëv, Zelenin, and Serzhputovskiĭ) and the Bashkir (Rudenko) questionnaires; "Schemes for the types of dwellings and buildings of Siberia" (compiled by Rudenko in 1914, NA RGO 24-78: 52, 53); and the survey form, "For Travellers", developed by the Siberian Subcommittee (1914, NA RGO 24-72: 14-46). The origins of these questionaires can be traced to Volkov's programme when we examine their general structure, formulations of their themes, the order of their questions, and their design. Because of its convenience, the form of Volkov's questionnaire was later used by the members of the Irkutsk-Zabaikalsk and Amur Sections headed by Shirokogorov for preparing their thematic — "tribal" — forms for the peoples of Siberia (NA RGO 24-72: 7-8, 9-11; AMAĖ RAN K1-8-1: 1).

Thus, the "Programme for Collecting Ethnographic Items" questionnaires developed by the Commission, as well as the well-known *Bibliographic Index* compiled by Zelenin for the needs of the KSEK (Zelenin 1913) relied on a single structure. This structure gave dwellings and/or clothing primary importance in describing the ethnographic features of an ethnic group, followed by sections devoted to the so-called *khozyaystvennyi byt* (economic and household life): folk technology, cultural products/ material culture, food, utensils, and forms of transportation. Two of the questionnaires — the Great Russian and Bashkir — deviated from this structure and closed with questions about clothes and decorations (Table 4.2). The same model formed the basis for the "Scheme of Ethnographic Characteristics Subject to the Clarification by Means of the Questionnaire and to the Application on Ethnographic Maps of Siberia" proposed by Makarenko on 4 December 1913 (NA RGO 1(1913)-1-23: 10–11).

However, in the published works a paradigm shift occurred with regards to the descriptive model, beginning with the "The Ukrainians" by Volkov (Volkov et al. 1914–1916) and followed by Rudenko's

Table 4.2: The structure of the Commission's questionnaire

The program for collecting ethnographic artifacts (issued by the Russian Museum)	Malorossian questionnaire (compiled by Volkov)	Velikorussian questionnaire (compiled by Zelenin, Zolotarev, Serzhputovsky) 1914	Belarussian questionnaire (compiled by Serzhputovsky), 1913	Bashkir questionnaire (compiled by Rudenko)
I. Settlements, buildings, dwelling and its utensils II. Clothing and decorations III. Household appliances IV. Food and beverages V. Activities, works and trades VI. Domestic household VII. Superstitions and fortune-telling VIII. Folk healing	1. Housing 2. Clothing 3. Agriculture 4. Food	1. Dwelling and buildings 2. Domestic household a. Folk technology (fire, processing of substances) b. Works and trades, agriculture, etc.) c. Food and beverages d. Methods of transportation 3. Clothing and decorations	A. Clothing B. Decorations C. Folk technology D. Works and trades (hunting, agriculture) E. Food F. Methods of transportation G. Buildings and dwelling	1. Dwelling ("Where the village mates live.") 2. "Activities, food, utensils, etc." 3. "What clothing men wear." "What clothing and decorations women wear." 4. "Are there musical instruments"

monograph, *The Bashkirs* (Rudenko 1925, 1916), the "Subject Index" on Siberia (Rudenko and Mark Azadovskiĭ: NA RGO 119-1-35) and, finally, Zelenin's *Russische (Ostslavische) Volkskunde* (Zelenin 1927). In these works the emphasis shifted to *economic activity*—the category underlying the traditional categories of means of subsistence. The other components of this system (folk technology, modes of transportation, housing, clothing, utensils, etc.) were conceptualised in connection with the most important kinds of activity: economic activity. Compare, for example, the structures of the abovementioned works with the questionnaires sent out by the commission and with the *Bibliographic Index* by Zelenin (Tables 4.2 and 4.3).

This model was later firmly entrenched in Soviet ethnography, as reflected in Kirill V. Chistov's representative evaluation of the *Compendium of Eastern Slavic Ethnography*:

> D. K. Zelenin well understood the socio-economic conditioning of the history of culture. He begins the study of traditional folk culture from agriculture, which was at the heart of the peasant economy of the Eastern Slavs, and [studies] agriculture from land use systems and tools (Chistov 1991: 441).

This idea of placing economics as the central activity is seen in the list of categories for ethnographic cartography proposed by Volkov in October 1910 (see above). In addition, beginning with Volkov, ethnographic monographs began to be accompanied by maps offering a geographical embodiment of scientific conclusions. The work of Zolotarëv, Zelenin, and Rudenko, reflects the influence of the idea of a comprehensive geographical approach that resulted from the commission's work.

David Alekseevich Zolotarëv (1885–1935)

David A. Zolotarëv was born in the city of Rybinsk to the family of a clergyman (Fig. 4.8). In 1904, he enrolled in Moscow University's Department of Natural Sciences, but he was expelled that same year for participating in student protests. In 1905, the young man continued his participation in the revolutionary movement, for which he was exiled to Siberia. His Siberian sentence was soon changed to deportation abroad, and in 1906 Zolotarëv arrived in Paris for a second time. On his first

Table 4.3: The structure of the published works of the Commission's participants

Zelenin, 1913 (Bibliographical Index)	Volkov, 1916b	Rudenko and Azadovsky, 1923 (Index on Siberia: the Bashkirs)	Rudenko, 1925 (Monograph on the Bashkirs)	Zelenin, 1991 (Monograph, 1927)
General division Dwelling Clothing Music Folk arts Economic and household life Utensils, cradle, weapons Methods of transportation Food and beverages Activities of various peoples: agriculture, irrigation, flax growing, animal husbandry, fishing, hunting, etc. Russians: - Utensils and weapons - Measures and weighting - Methods of transportation - Food - Activities, works and trades	Hunting Fishing Animal husbandry Agriculture Folk technology Methods of transportation Food Buildings Clothing Beliefs Rituals Folk lore	Hunting Fishing Animal husbandry Agriculture Folk technology Food Beverages Utensils Dwelling Clothing Decoration and tattoos Hair style Folk entertainment Arts Beliefs Superstition and sorcery Folk lore Family life Burials Greeting rituals Social relations Foreign relations	1. Brief literature overview 2. Hunting and fishing 3. Animal husbandry, aviculture, and bee-keeping 4. Agriculture 5. Food 6. Technology 7. Clothing 8. Dwelling and buildings 9. Methods and means of transportation 10. Family and kin 11. Social life and arts 12. Beliefs and elements of knowledge Conclusion	I. Agriculture II. Animal husbandry, fishing, and bee-keeping III. Food preparation IV. Work stock, harnessing, means of transportation V. Making of clothes and footwear VI. Clothing and footwear VII. Personal hygiene (from hair style to bathing and folk healing) VIII. Dwelling IX. Family life (from birth to commemoration [of the dead]) X. Social life XI. Calendar-related rituals XII. Folk beliefs

visit, in 1904, he had been a student of the Russian Higher School and became acquainted with Volkov. According to his brother, Alekseĭ A. Zolotarëv (1879–1950), these "two stays in Paris had left its mark on David's further scientific work: he remained a supporter and adherent of the French School in anthropology and the closest disciple and follower of Fëdor K. Volkov until the end of his days" (Zolotarëv 2016: 108).

Following his return from exile, from 1908–1912, David Zolotarëv studied in the Department of Physics and Mathematics at St Petersburg University under Volkov's direction. The rest of his scholarly life was connected with St Petersburg University, the Ethnographic Department of the Russian Museum, where he was in charge of the Russian-Finnish Ethnography Division, KIPS, and other scientific institutions (Shangina 1985). In 1930, Zolotarëv was arrested as part of a legal process (*delo kraevedov*) in which local historians were accused of counterrevolutionary activity; in 1932, he was released, but in the following year he was arrested again and died in a camp near the town of Mariinsk in Kuzbass.

Zolotarëv's early works are devoted to the physical anthropology of the Velikorussians and are based on his expeditions in the Arkhangelsk, Novgorod, and Tver provinces. His attempts to describe the generalised type of a "mixed" population and to distinguish the anthropological types from which the "mixed" one was formed can be considered the leitmotif of these works. Studying the western part of the Tver province, for example, the scientist tried to explain the anthropological characteristics of the population there in the light of linguistics and history. The types he singled out supposedly corresponded to Deniker's "Dinar race", the Chud', the Finns, and the Lapps (Zolotarëv 1912). In his work on the Velikorussians of the Sukhona and Northern Dvina Rivers, Zolotarëv interpreted his data in the light of the history of the colonization of the region. Pointing to the similarities between the Velikorussians and the Novgorodians, as well as the Balts and Scandinavians of the "northern race", he called for a "closer connection with the West" in the search for the origin of the population of the Russian North, rather than seeking the answer "primarily in the East" (Zolotarëv 1916a: 79).

Methods for distinguishing anthropological types were one of the key questions that excited Volkov's students. Zolotarëv published a critical review of the work of the Moscow anthropologist Efim M. Chepurkovskiĭ [Ethyme Tschepourkowsky] (1871–1950). In his work, Chepurkovskiĭ distinguished two types of the Velikorussian population:

Fig. 4.8 David Alekseevich Zolotarëv, 1929 (RĖM IM9-185). © Russian Ethnographic Museum, St Petersburg

the Valdaĭ type (broad-headed and fair-haired) and the Rîazan′ type (long-headed and dark-haired). He considered the former to be "the latest newcomer Slavs", and the latter to be descendants of the "ancient first settlers". Chepurkovskiĭ argued for abandoning the multiplicity of measurements examined by Zolotarëv, Rudenko, and Shirokogorov, and, instead, focusing on the main features and their geographical distribution. Zolotarëv, however, considered that Chepurkovskiĭ's material did not support his conclusions (Zolotarëv 1913). Rudenko was also "embarrassed" by Chepurkovskiĭ's work: "If Chepurkovskiĭ did not come to tangible results with the head index and colour [of hair]", he wrote to Anuchin, "then if he adds [to these] the height and at least the nasal index or the skull height, then, I know for sure, he will get such a chaos, which he, apparently, won't be able to sort out" (OR RGB 10-13-469: 3v).

Chepurkovskiĭ, meanwhile, continued his criticism of the works of Zolotarëv, Rudenko, and Shirokogorov, considering their method of distinguishing anthropological types to be based on "arithmetical misunderstandings" (Chepurkovskiĭ 1918; 1916: 140; 1924: 33, 45, 153). In Soviet anthropology, Chepurkovskiĭ's criticism was accepted as reasonable. Thus, Maksim G. Levin viewed the identification of the types based on the combination of the height, head index, and hair colour used by the Volkov school to be a method capable of producing a great variety of results (Levin 1960: 132).

Apparently, the polemics with Chepurkovskiĭ had a certain influence on Zolotarëv. Amongst Volkov's students, he stood out as the one who drew his conclusions with the utmost caution. His monograph, *The Karelians of the USSR*, summarizing his ten-year study of this group, was almost entirely devoted to detailing the data on anthropological measurements that he had collected, on the basis of which he made very cautious conclusions about the presence of elements of the northern, Baltic, Lappish, and other races among the Karelians' ancestors, as well as about the existence of two "variants" of the type: the Finnish-Karelian and the Russian-Karelian. Although the author argued that these variants were connected "with the uniqueness of the physical appearance reflecting both physical as well as mental and cultural-domestic features", there was no substantiation of this thesis in the monograph (Zolotarëv 1930: 110). Nevertheless, Zolotarëv's contribution to the development of the geographical conception of *etnos* was great. His influence is primarily seen in his organization of large-scale interdisciplinary field expeditions in the 1920s (such as the Verkhnevolzhskai͡a [Upper Volga], southeastern, and northwestern expeditions), during which dozens of Leningrad-based and local researchers collected linguistic, folklore, anthropological, and ethnographic materials within significant areas of European Russia (Shangina 1985: 79–81).

Dmitriĭ Konstantinovich Zelenin (1878–1954)

The biography of Dmitriĭ K. Zelenin, a classic figure in Russian ethnography, would be incomplete without relating his research to the programmatic work of the KSEK and the circle of Volkov's students. Zelenin came to ethnography, apparently, because of Mogili͡anskiĭ, who, recalling his travels along the Kama river, wrote in his memoirs: "Here I managed to find a valuable collaborator for the museum in the person of a teacher, Zelenin, who for several years had been gathering collections for the museum in the Viatskaia Guberniia [Viatka province], mainly among the Votyaks" (GARF P-5787-1-17: 110). In 1911, the KSEK instructed Zelenin to compile a general bibliographic index of ethnographic literature (NA RGO 24-78: 85v).

Earlier, on 11 February 1911, on his own initiative, Zelenin had drafted the "Project of Instructions to the Compiler of the [Bibliographic] Index" (NA RGO 24-78: 76–76v). Upon receiving the offer from Ol'denburg to compile the *Bibliographic Index,* Zelenin had actually been preparing it for several months and introduced it for publication in April 1913.[4] This index, prepared by the young scientist under the guidance of his teacher Shakhmatov (Zelenin 1913), reflected the commission's structure, met its needs, and included the following sections: (1) The General Section (including also ethnographic maps and lists of populated areas within individual gubernias); (2) Dwelling; (3) Clothes; (4) Music; (5) Folk Art; (6) Economic and Household Life (see Table 3).

Zelenin's second major work, "An Inventory of Manuscripts of the Scientific Archive of the IRGO", was also implicitly linked to the work of the commission. At its meetings, "the introduction of the archival material to a wider knowledge" was considered as a necessary stage of the preparatory work for mapmaking (NA RGO 24-78: 57v). The sorting and reviewing of the archive were included in the budget for 1911 (NA RGO 24-78: 68. See also the minutes of the meeting on 25 Feb. 1911 in Otdelenie ėtnografii I.R.G.O. 1911: 5). In the preface to the first issue of his *Inventory,* Zelenin wrote that he "came to the idea of making a detailed description of the manuscripts in the archive precisely because of my search for materials for studying the visible features of the Russian people's way of living" (Zelenin 1914: vii).

Apparently, it was during his work on the "Velikorussian Questionnaire" for the commission that he discovered that "a whole range of valuable manuscripts" in the IRGO's archives could provide

4 The *Bibliographical Index* was published in the first issue of the *Works of the Commission on Making Ethnographic Maps of Russia,* that is, it "marked the beginning of the publishing activity of the commission and was a necessary reference source in its work" (Zolotarëv 1916b: xv).

"important material for the study of the *geographical* distribution of different types of dwellings, utensils, etc." (Zelenin 1914: vii). Applying the geographical principle to the systematization of the archival sources, Zelenin tried to make his work useful for solving the commission's research tasks. This probably explains the limitations of Zelenin's *Inventory*, which focuses on the materials related to European Russia — the territory for which the "Velikorussian Questionnaire" was being developed at that time.

Simultaneously with his work in the commission, Zelenin wrote his master's thesis, "Velikorussian [Great Russian] Dialects with Inorganic and Intransitive Palatalization of Velar Consonants in Connection with the Flows of the Latest Velikorussian [Great Russian] Colonization", in which he revealed his interest in the notion of an ethnographic type or group — in this case, of the southern Russian *odnodvortsy*, whom he identified not only on the basis of dialectology, but also on the basis of the characteristics of clothing, food, and "mental constitution" (Saburova 1979: 17–18). In the opinion of Nikita I. Tolstoĭ and Svetlana M. Tolstaîa, in this work Zelinin had already substantiated his thesis about the ethnic and dialectal division of the eastern Slavs into four "branches" or peoples (Tolstoĭ and Tolstaîa 1979: 72–73).

This concept was theorised in detail in the book *Russian* (*East Slavic*) *Ethnography*, published in Germany in 1927. In the book's first pages, Zelenin stated that there are "sharp differences" between the northern and southern Great Russians and a significant ethnographic and dialectological proximity of the latter to the Belarusians. According to him, the two Russian ethnic groups "differ sharply from each other by the type of dwelling, clothing and other features of everyday life. This ethnographic distinctiveness that sets the southern Russian people apart from the northern Russian people will be examined in various chapters of this book" (Zelenin 1991: 29). Thus, a comprehensive approach to the definition of ethnic differences and to the identification of various peoples and ethnographic types in Zelenin's works was in line with the methodology of the commission.

Sergeĭ Ivanovich Rudenko (1885–1969)

Volkov's and the KSEK's methodology was developed to its fullest extent in the works of Volkov's most famous student: Sergeĭ Ivanovich Rudenko (Fig. 4.9). Rudenko was born in Kharkov in 1885 to the family of a nobleman and spent his early childhood in Transbaikalia (Zabaĭkal'e), where his father worked as an assistant to the chief administrator of the district (*okruzhnoĭ nachal'nik*). Later, the family moved to Perm', where Sergeĭ lived until he graduated from the gymnasium and was admitted to St Petersburg University. In the last years of his secondary schooling, the future researcher spent a great deal of time among the Bashkirs with his father, a former member of the Delimitation Committee of the Bashkir Lands, and "had an opportunity to learn their way of life in detail" (SPF ARAN 1004-1-199: 15). Rudenko considered himself to be of Ukrainian origin and wrote "Ukrainian" as his nationality in a 1924 questionnaire (Ibid: 5). Even while studying at the gymnasium, Rudenko was already collecting Bashkir items for the Ethnographic Division of the Russian Museum.

In 1904, Rudenko was admitted to the Department of Natural Sciences at St Petersburg University. His acquaintance with Volkov, who started teaching at the university in 1907, determined the direction of his scientific work and his specialization in geography and anthropology (Ibid: 16). By the time of his graduation, Rudenko was an experienced field anthropologist and museum worker. Staying at the department to prepare for a professorship, Rudenko spent a year (from summer 1913 to autumn 1914) on a foreign assignment, mostly devoted to attending classes at the Paris École d'anthropologie and working in Léonce Manouvrier's laboratory. However, in his letters to Anuchin, the young scholar stated that French anthropology "utterly did not satisfy" him and that most lectures in the École d'anthropologie were "something like the lectures at our public university" (OR RGB 10-13-469: 1).

In 1913, Rudenko became a member of the Paris Anthropological Society; in 1914 he became a member of the Taras Schevchenko Scientific Society. In 1915, he started teaching at the Department of Geography and Ethnography of St Petersburg University and became a secretary of the Russian Anthropological Society. As early as in 1911, Rudenko started actively contributing to the work of the KSEK.

Fig. 4.9 Sergeĭ Ivanovich Rudenko (RĖM IM9-131). © Russian Ethnographic Museum, St Petersburg

Rudenko's first major anthropological work was an article titled "Anthropological Study of the Inorodtsy in the North-West Siberia" — the result of his 1909 and 1910 expeditions commissioned by the Russian Museum. In addition to gathering ethnographic collections, the researcher had conducted measurements of the Ostiaks (Khanty), Voguls (Mansi), and Samoyeds according to Volkov and Manouvrier's scheme. Based on various measurements of 256 adult males, he identified generalised anthropological "types" within the studied groups. Then, by comparing these generalised "types", he arrived at the following conclusions about their relationship: "The anthropological types of the Samoyeds and Voguls are so different that their close relation is out of question", while the Voguls are "in a half-way position" between them that can be explained by the "mixing of the lower Ostyaks with Samoyeds". Referring to these physical anthropological comparisons, Rudenko also supported the hypothesis of the Samoyeds' Sayano-Altai origin and acknowledged the "isolated" position of the Ostyaks and Voguls, who "cannot be placed in the same tribal group on the basis of their physical features" (Rudenko 1914: 102–13).

Undoubtedly, it was his book, *The Bashkirs: An Ethnological Monograph,* that established Rudenko as one of the leading Russian anthropologists. It was published in two volumes: *The Physical Type of the Bashkirs* (1916) and *The Way of Life of the Bashkirs* (*Byt bashkir*) (1925). This book was written under the obvious influence of Volkov's methodology and reflected the model Volkov suggested in his writings on the "Ukrainian People in its Past and Present". Concurrently, in 1917 Rudenko defended the first part of his book as a dissertation at Moscow University to a committee chaired by Anuchin. The conflict between Anuchin and Volkov regarding the article of the latter provided a significant background for the work of the young researcher. Moreover, in a letter to Anuchin from 26 October 1915, Rudenko agreed with all Anuchin's criticisms of the "Anthropological Features of the Ukrainian People", offering only the haste and the brevity of the presentation as excuses to his teacher (OR RGB 10-13-472: 10).

A letter to Anuchin in December 1913 demonstrates Rudenko's concern about the debates on the identification of types that ran among Russian anthropologists. Rudenko confessed that the issue of whether one should "spend such an amount of labour, energy, and resources to measure such a mass of the Bashkirs" confused him, as did the work of Chepurkovskiĭ, who "came to no tangible results" by considering only two parameters: the [hair] colour and the head index. Rudenko formulated the purpose of *The Bashkirs* as follows:

> My goal was to establish the local types and match the regions (zones would be too much) of diffusion of the known ethnographic phenomena (or groups thereof) within these types; if along the way I come to any palpable results, I will feel satisfied (OR RGB 10-13-469: 3–4).

Therefore, the task of the geographical correlation of anthropological and ethnographical data promoted by Volkov was also central to Rudenko's monograph. Rudenko, in a letter to Anuchin, essentially repeated Volkov's description of the activities of the IRGO, whle describing his methodology:

> Besides, wherever the measurements were made, i.e. in 3/4 of the Bashkir clans, I conducted a survey concerning the types of dwellings, clothing, economic way of life (*khoziaistvennogo byta*), etc. Now 1100 copies of the questionnaire that I compiled has been distributed by the Geographical Society, with the help of the *zemstva,* over the entire

Bashkiria and, according to my knowledge, the responses are arriving in large numbers. Therefore, I can track the geographical distribution of all the most important ethnographic factors and compare ethnographic and the anthropological data (OR RGB 10-13-470: 5–6).

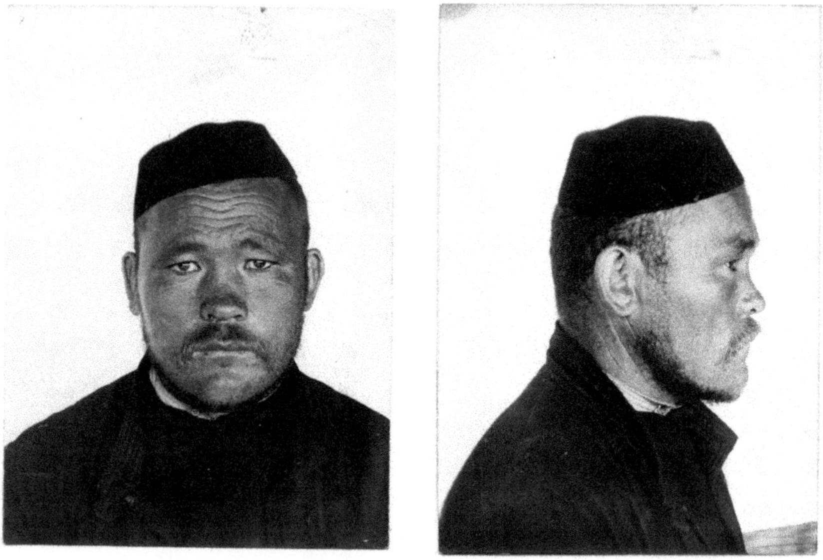

Fig. 4.10 A Bashkir from Orenburgskai͡a gubernii͡a, Troitskiĭ uezd. 1912. Photo by Sergeĭ I. Rudenko (RĖM 3935-15 a, b). © Russian Ethnographic Museum, St Petersburg

Rudenko could indeed feel quite satisfied because he was able to present solutions to all the postulated problems. In the first part of his monograph he attempted to describe the common physical-anthropological type of the Bashkirs, but acknowledged the large amplitude of the inter-type differences, which he argued indicated the presence of "several heterogeneous elements" of foreign ethnic groups that had been integrated into the Bashkirs (Rudenko 1916: 276). At the same time, Rudenko identified three basic types corresponding to three geographical settlement regions of the Bashkirs: (1) eastern, (2) southwestern, and (3) northwestern (Figs. 4.10–4.12). The monograph was accompanied by four maps that plotted: (1) Bashkir dachas and kinship groups, (2) pigmentation, (3) head index, and (4) a final map of the "division of the Bashkirs by the physical type", which showed the distribution of the three aforementioned basic types.

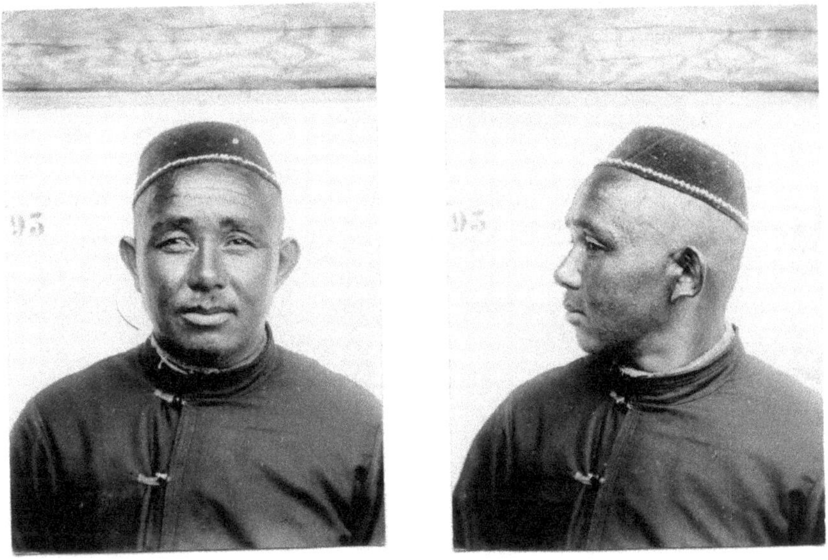

Fig. 4.11 A Bashkir from Orenburgskai͡a gubernii͡a, Cheli͡abinskiĭ uezd. 1912. Photo by Sergeĭ I. Rudenko (RĖM 3935-31 a, b). © Russian Ethnographic Museum, St Petersburg

Fig. 4.12 A family in a *kosh* (a mobile summer house of the Bashkirs). Orenburgskai͡a gubernii͡a, Cheli͡abinskiĭ uezd. 1912. Photo by Sergeĭ I. Rudenko (RĖM 3935-163a). © Russian Ethnographic Museum, St Petersburg

The second part of the monograph, *The Way of Life of the Bashkirs* (*Byt Bashkir*), was structured similarly to the article "Ethnographic Characteristics of the Ukrainian People" (Volkov 1916b). Like Volkov's work, Rudenko's monograph had twelve chapters and began with descriptions of hunting, animal husbandry, agriculture, and "technology". These were followed by chapters on food, dwelling, clothing, and transportation. Like Volkov's paper, Rudenko's work ended with a chapter on beliefs and the "elements of knowledge". Rudenko's only departure from his teacher's scheme was the presence of sections devoted to family, clan, and social life.

According to Rudenko, the "regional variations of the physical type" and the "variations of the way of life" (*variat͡sii bytovye*) demonstrated a significant correlation. The three regions identified in the monograph's first volume also had different cultural and domestic characteristics. The author's explanation was that "the physical mixing and the cultural interaction of the Bashkirs with the neighbouring peoples were apparently evolving side by side" (Rudenko 1925: 325). Rudenko strongly supported the theory of the Bashkirs' Turkish origin, since the most "enduring" (*stoĭkie*) elements of their culture (the cut of their clothing, social structure, and beliefs) belonged, according to him, to the "Turkish cultural world". The purest forms of these features were preserved by the Bashkirs of the eastern group, he contended, who retained many aspects of the nomadic cattle-breeding way of life. They revealed the connection of those Bashkirs with "their remote relatives — the Kazakh-Kyrgyz people", while the northern Bashkirs shared many elements with their neighbours — the Finns (Rudenko 1925: 320–25).

In conclusion, Rudenko expressed confidence that "roughly the same regions that we outlined, based on the study of the physical type and way of life of the Bashkirs, will be established through dialectological investigation" (Rudenko 1925: 327). Attached to the monograph were a map of the tribal composition of the Bashkir region compiled by the KIPS, two maps of the localization of cultural (*bytovye*) elements, and a map of the division of the Bashkirs into regions by cultural (*bytovye*) elements (Fig. 4.13).

The Bashkirs present an interesting case of the conceptualization of differences in the Russian Empire. According to Charles Steinwedel, there were three main stages of categorization. From the sixteenth to the mid-eighteenth century the Bashkirs were seen as a group of "tribes" and "clans", united by Islam, a common dialect, and a semi-nomadic lifestyle. In the late eighteenth century, the Bashkirs were recognized as an estate (*soslovii͡a*) of military landowners analogous to the Cossacks. Finally, by the late nineteenth-early twentieth century, they were described with increasing frequency as a *narodnost'* or *nat͡sional'nost'*. Steinwedel argues that this change reflects the tendency of the late Tsarist regime to promote "the organization of a polity based upon ethnic or national distinctions" (Steĭnvedel 2004; Steinwedel 2000: 80).

The historian and ethnologist Igor' V. Kuchumov argues that Rudenko's work played a key role in transforming the Bashkirs "from an estate into an *etnos*" (Kuchumov 2015: 161). In the process of creating a map of Bashkir ethnic territories, Rudenko reinterpreted Tsarist statistics, effectively transforming the Bashkirs from an "administrative" category into an ethnicity: "Having constructed the Bashkir territory, the *etnos* itself and "mapped it" [on to the territory], S. I. Rudenko thus for the first time institutionalized borders of the territory, which until this time had existed as an abstract and amorphous substance" (Ibid: 174). When the "Great Bashkirii͡a" was officially created by the decree of the VTsIK[5] on 14 June 1922, its territory "astonishingly resembled" the map published by Rudenko in 1916 (Ibid: 178).

At the First Turkological Congress in 1926, Rudenko gave a paper titled "The Current State and Next Tasks of the Ethnographical Studies of the Turkish Tribes", in which he presented an ambitious research programme and made a series of theoretical observations characteristic of the Volkov school. Starting from the premise that language functioned as the primary uniting factor for the Turks, he demonstrated that:

> the language, the culture, and the physical type live their own independent lives, without the seemingly natural links between the elements which we deem essential for every ethnic group (Rudenko 1926: 77).

Having noted that language is the "least resilient of the ethnical characteristics", Rudenko suggested concentrating on "the basic features of the Turkish physical type and the Turkish household". He claimed that it was possible to speak of a physical type that is characteristic for the Turks and which manifests itself most vividly in

5 All-Russia Central Executive Committee of the Russian Soviet Federal Socialist Republic — the highest legislative, administrative and revising body of the republic.

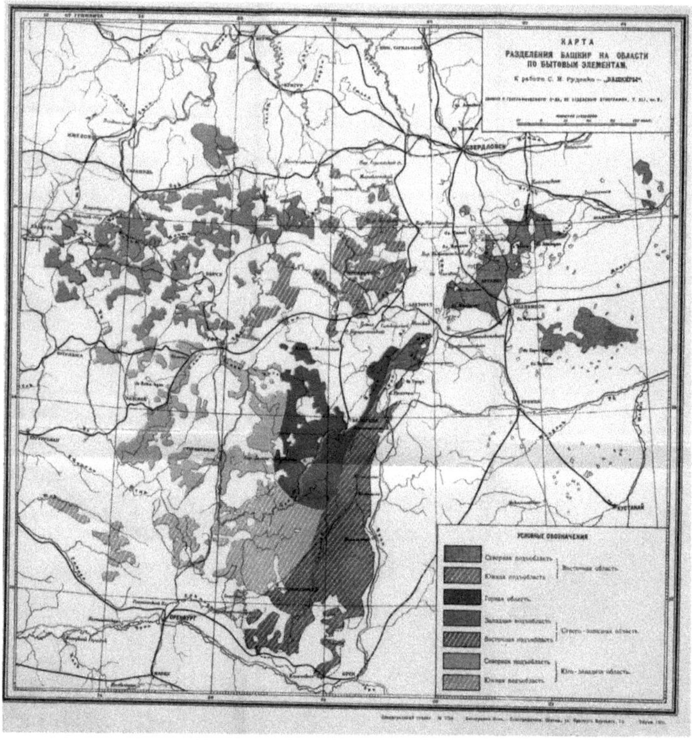

Fig. 4.13 Sergeĭ I. Rudenko's map of the division of the Bashkirs into regions by cultural (*bytovye*) elements (Rudenko 1925)

the Kazakh-Kyrgyzes. As the distance from this "center" increased, it was modified by the "metisation". He also described a generalised type of the "Turkish culture per se", with cultural features characteristic of nomadic cattle-breeders. Rudenko proposed to "determine the geographical distribution of the individual cultural (*bytovye*) elements and their combinations in the closed biological units that we call ethnic groups" (Rudenko 1926: 86). This study was to reveal the "provincial and regional groupings" that presumably coincided with the peculiarities of a physical type and dialects. His presentation ended with a reference to exact scientific methods and biological metaphors:

> In order to succeed in developing our knowledge about the biology of human societies, the life of ethnic groups, and the factors of their life activity, in order to clarify the evolution of the human culture, we must switch from dilettantism to precise scientific investigation (Ibid: 88).

Rudenko formulated his programme right before the Great Break[6] that, among other things, included an "ideological ban on any attempts to link the biological and the social" — a link described by the specially invented term "biologization" (Adams 1990: 184). It is well known that in Soviet ethnography Valerian B. Aptekar' spearheaded criticism of the terms "*etnos*" and "culture", defining them as a result of a "metaphysical hypothesising or biologization". He proclaimed these convictions at the pivotal Meeting of the Ethnographers of Leningrad and Moscow in 1929 (qtd. in Arzi͡utov, Alymov, and Anderson 2014: 21).

Rudenko was arrested in the summer of 1930 in Ufa, but there is no direct evidence that the repressions against Rudenko were related to his scientific views. The researcher was named in the so-called "academic case" against the All-People's Union for the Revival of Russia — an organization fabricated by the OGPU,[7] based on the testimony forced out of its "founder", the historian Sergeĭ F. Platonov. Rudenko was charged with the squandering of resources during his expeditions. According to the published materials of the "case", he denied these accusations throughout the investigation and pleaded guilty only to "shutting himself up within the confines of academism" (Reshetov 1998: 15–16; Tishkin 2004: 126). At the same time, in the scientific institutions where Rudenko had worked, his arrest led to an entire campaign to eliminate the *rudenkovshchina* (the Rudenko movement) and of uncovering the "class nature" of the Volkov school. The harsh ideological criticism of the "bourgeois heritage" hit many researchers, but in the epicenter of this campaign were Zelenin, Zolotarëv, and Rudenko.

The "Working-Through"

Soon after the momentous Meeting of Ethnographers in April 1929, in August 1929, a campaign was launched at the KIPS to review its tasks and structure that resulted in the reorganization of the KIPS into the IPIN (The Institute for the Study of the Peoples of the USSR).

6 The "Great Break" was the radical change in Soviet politics towards accelerated collectivization and industrialization in 1929.

7 OGPU (The Joint State Political Directorate) under the Council of People's Commissars of the USSR was the secret police of the Soviet Union from 1923 to 1934.

The initial events, which were held under the auspices of the audit of the Academy of Sciences apparatus, did not yet imply tangible consequences,[8] although they revealed certain disagreements within the KIPS. The board of the KIPS identified shortcomings in the work of some divisions (in particular, of the Siberian Division and of the KIPS itself that were described in the report of junior researchers Kapitolina V. Vi͡atkina, S. D. Churakova, and S. D. Rudneva to be insignificant and easily redeemable, while some of them were simply implausible (SPF ARAN 135-1-79: 9–9v). However, at the meeting of scientific workers on 15 August 1929 (Ibid: 7–8v) and at subsequent meetings of the Economic Bureau of the KIPS, more serious complaints were formulated: the unjustified expansion of the tasks of the KIPS, multiplicity of these tasks, inadequate to the funds and staff, overlapping of the KIPS's tasks with the tasks of other institutions, specifically, the Museum of Anthropology and Ethnography (MAĖ) and the Central Statistical Directorate, the "irrelevance" of certain projects to the plans of the KIPS, the absence of a general plan for the KIPS's "core" activity, as well as the autonomy of the divisions when "each department declared itself an independent republic with its own president" (Vi͡atkina, Ibid: 36).

According to the Resolution of the Commission for the Inspection of the KIPS and MAĖ, "a number of quite significant but derivative defects" (fifteen points) stemmed from two "cardinal shortcomings" of the KIPS — shortcomings of a political and methodological character (SPF ARAN 135-1-79: 102–09). The KIPS was charged with having a close relationship with the tsarist regime, with assisting the Provisional Goverment in resolving the "national question", as well as with the failure to "establish a connection with the needs of the proletarian state", resulting in the situation that "all the work on studying the ethnographic composition of our country, so necessary for carrying out national zoning and for finding solutions to a number of cultural and economic problems, flowed past the KIPS" (Ibid: 102). The "methodological guidelines" of the KIPS were found to be untenable, while the research work "was not sufficiently developed nor built on the basis of the Marxist methodology"

8 See the minutes of the general meeting of the workers of the KIPS at which the report of the Commission on the Audit of the Academy of Sciences Apparatus was discussed (SPF ARAN 135-1-79: 7–8v).

(Ibid: 102). All attempts of Ol′denburg, Zarubin, Zolotarëv,[9] Rudenko,[10] and others[11] to oppose the critics and to refute their allegations turned out to be useless and only intensified the snowballing accusations. As a result, "in connection with the ever-growing need of the USSR to study the national [ethnic] composition of the country and the impossibility of the KIPS, in its present form, to cope with this task", it was proposed to recognise the KIPS as unnecessary and to reorganise it (SPF ARAN 135-1-79: 104). The idea of the reorganization was also supported by the representatives of the "older generation", including, for example, Nikolaĭ I͡a. Marr, Vladimir G. Bogoraz [Waldemar Bogoras], Petr L. Mashtakov, and others (Ibid: 33, 46).

The causes of the KIPS's dismantling were not limited to these scientific and methodological issues. The manner in which the discussions of the commission's weaknesses took place shows that there were targeted actions to change its leadership that eventually turned into the open harassment of the senior researchers and established a new system of organization of scientific institutions. The main targets for this criticism were Ol′denburg (chairman of the KIPS), Rudenko (scientific secretary), and Zolotarëv (head of the European Department) who, according to the anthropologist Boris N. Vishnevskiĭ, had established "imperialism in science": they headed all the work, oppressed younger employees, and created barriers obstructing the attraction of new workers. In the spirit of the times, the verdict was delivered quite sharply: "A small group captured the command positions in a number of institutions — in the KIPS, in the University, in the Russian Museum, and in the I[nstitute] of

9 See remarks and arguments of Ol′denburg and Zolotarëv at the meeting on 15 August 1929 (SPF ARAN 135-1-79: 10–12v), at the meeting of the Economy Council (Ėkonomsoveshchanie) on 1 October 1929 (SPF ARAN 135-1-79: 32–34); and in the "Statement on the Report on the KIPS by D. A. Zolotarëv" (SPF ARAN 135-1-79: 14–14v).

10 On 1 October 1929, at the meeting of the Economy Council under the KIPS, the Archaeological Commission, and the Commission on Compiling the Reference Book [of the Peoples of Russia], Rudenko gave a speech about further goals and the structure of the KIPS (SPF ARAN 135-1-79: 35–35v). See also Rudenko's note to the Permanent Secretary of the Academy of Sciences of the USSR concerning an article in the newspaper *Vecherni͡ai͡a Moskva* (SPF ARAN 135-1-79: 97–97v).

11 See the "Comments to the Project of the Resolution of the Local Bureau on the KIPS" (SPF ARAN 135-1-79: 52–55) and a multiplicity of prepared reports about the activities of various departments of the KIPS and of other documents revealing the commission's connections with other organizations and its participation in different projects (SPF ARAN 135-1-79: 17, 22–26, 39–44v, 56–96).

Lesgaft — 'imperialism in science', [creating] a kind of 'anthropological and ethnographic trust'" (Ibid: 11).

The lack of proper guidance, "both from the academic secretary as well as from the majority of the departments' heads", was also mentioned in the Resolution (Ibid: 103). Ol'denburg, outraged by the distrust expressed to him and the KIPS, resigned from heading the KIPS on 1 October 1929 (Ibid: 34). Rudenko and Zolotarëv were expelled from their posts. The meetings of the early 1930s, according to academic Vasiliĭ V. Barthold, who became indignant at the on-going process, had "the nature of a trial of the activities of the KIPS and its European Department" to which Zolotarëv was invited "only for explanations" (Ibid: 148). In 1930, the KIPS was disbanded and — on the basis of the merger between the KIPS and the MAĖ — the Institute for the Study of Peoples of the USSR was established under the leadership of Nikolai I͡a. Marr.

Fig. 4.14 The Employees of the Ethnographic Department of the Russian Museum on the museum's stairs, c. 1920s. Rudenko is the second from the left in the first row, Zolotarëv is the forth in the third row (bald-headed) (RĖM IM9-7-1). © Russian Ethnographic Museum, St Petersburg

In May 1931, a series of meetings were held in the Russian Museum (Fig 4.14), where the pupils of Volkov "worked through" (*prorabatyvali*) their former colleagues. A report on the Volkov school was made by his

Fig. 4.15 Sergeĭ I. Rudenko and David A. Zolotarëv with members of the Upper Volga expedition in folk clothes. I͡aroslavskai͡a or Tverskai͡a gubernii, 1922–1925 (RĖM IM 12-92). © Russian Ethnographic Museum, St Petersburg

student Aleksandr A. Miller. He acknowledged its "progressiveness for its time", but pointed out the "biologism" of the teacher's views and his purpose to fulfil the "order of the bourgeoisie" (ARĖM 2-1-361: 13). Two of Volkov's students, archaeologists Mikhail P. Gri͡aznov and Sergeĭ A. Teploukhov, tried to withstand the critical attack, but their "formal" attitude towards Rudenko's works induced a storm (Khudi͡akov 1931).

The outcome of "working-through" the *rudenkovshchina* was a resolution in which Volkov and his student Rudenko were declared adherents of the "racial theory", and the latter was also accused of supporting the migration theory and Great Russian chauvinism. Rudenko's former colleagues blamed him for organising a group of like-minded individuals in the museum, in the KIPS, and in other institutions that opposed the entrenchment of Marxism and where anti-Soviet sentiments and the "caste closed-ness" reigned (ARĖM 2-1-361: 26–30) (V Metodbi͡uro 1932).

Soon, the accusation campaign spilled onto journal pages where Rudenko's legacy was characterised as nothing short of "the final scream of the dying class crushed by the iron heel of the proletarian dictatorship" (Bernshtam 1932: 27). According to Aleksandr N. Bernshtam, Rudenko "link[ed] the peculiarities of culture development with the immutable properties of various races" and, by correlating physical type with "cultural (*bytovye*) elements", supplanted the materialistic explanations of history with the "supersession of cultures". Further, he approached the problem of ethnogenesis with a "biologically constructed ethnogroup", deriving "ethnocreation from the physical properties of races" (Bernshtam 1932: 24).

Sergeĭ N. Bykovskiĭ emphasised Rudenko's tendency to explain all the changes in the Bashkirs' culture by their borrowing from other peoples, denying them the capacity for independent cultural creativity. When citing the above-mentioned speech by Rudenko at the Turkological Congress, Bykovskiĭ accused him of adhering to the idea of a unique Turkish culture that was either preserved in a pure form or "faded" under the influence of other cultures (Bykovskiĭ 1931: 7). Identification of the "geographical zones of diffusion of cultural elements among the Bashkirs" was interpreted by Bykovskiĭ as adherence to the theory of cultural circles (Ibid).

In 1932, a volume entitled *Ethnography at the Service to the Class Enemy* appeared, where the central role was given to the works of Zelenin, Zolotarëv, and Rudenko. The authors, Bykovskiĭ and Mikhail G. Khudi͡akov, assumed that those researchers had served both international imperialism as well as Russian great-power chauvinism. They all allegedly supported a "race theory", which was very broadly understood by the critics:

> Such are all ethnographic works where any analogy in the culture of two adjacent peoples is necessarily explained by borrowing. At the same time, the borrower is unavoidably the oppressed people and the inculcator of culture — the dominant nation in the country (Bykovskiĭ 1932: 8–9).

Bykovskiĭ presented the establishment of the KIPS as 'helping the government of a bourgeois imperialistic country in the implementation of its aggressive intentions' (Ibid: 10). The KIPS was criticised not only for "imperialism", but also for great-power chauvinism. According to Khudi͡akov, Rudenko's work was influenced by Alekseĭ A. Shakhmatov — a kadet[12] who maintained "great-power views on the unity of the Russian, Ukrainian, and the Belorussian nationalities" (Khudi͡akov

12 A member of the party of constitutional democrats (*kadety*).

1932: 68). He claimed that the KIPS members consistently adhered to this classification in their works until the end of the 1920s (Ibid).

The issues of methodology, ideology, and politics in the campaign against the "old school" ethnographers made for a volatile mix. Bykovskiĭ criticised Zolotarëv primarily for his studies of the Karels. According to Bykovskiĭ, Zolotarëv's identification of two "variants" of the Karels (the Russian-Karels and the Finn-Karels) ultimately aligned with the goals of the "old KIPS", i.e. to the division of the Karel people between the Russian and the Finnish imperialisms. For instance, the article "In the North-Western Karelia" justified the affiliation of the Ukhta region with Finland due to similarities in culture and language (Bykovskiĭ 1932: 13–17). By "tearing" the Karels into two groups, Zolotarëv presumably carried out the "kadet" national policy and attacked the self-awareness (identity) of this people as a whole (Bykovskiĭ 1930: 12).

Khudi͡akov, in his turn, accused Zelenin, Zolotarëv, and Rudenko of Russian great-power chauvinism, equating them to such right-wing conservatives as Timofeĭ D. Florinskiĭ or the racist Ivan A. Sikorskiĭ. Zelenin was declared chauvinist and the follower of Vladimir I. Lamanskiĭ, not only based on his early articles on "*inorodt͡sy*", but also his book, *East-Slavic Ethnography*. According to Khudi͡akov, references to "East Slavs" in Zelenin's language replaced the old chauvinistic union of the three peoples as Russians, and on the map accompanying the work, "Zelenin with a particular accuracy listed those formerly Hungarian comitats where the 'Russian language [was] widespread'". Zelenin's theory of the "four Russian ethnic groups" was viewed as chauvinistic because it equated the differences between the southern and northern Velikorussians [Great Russians] to that between the Belorussians and Ukrainians. This comparision led to the denial of the literary languages and the political independence of those peoples. The same direction, according to Khudi͡akov, was inherent in Zelenin's views on the "purity" of the Velikorussian [Great Russian] ethnic group free from the Finnish influences, which also induced a politicised critique by Sergeĭ P. Tolstov (Khudi͡akov 1932: 80–2).

The ideological criticism of the beginning of the 1930s singled out Zelenin, Zolotarëv, and Rudenko as the researchers sharing a common methodology and a hostile ideology. Khudi͡akov even wrote about a "group of S. I. Rudenko — D. A. Zolotarëv", who practically controlled Leningrad ethnography in the 1920s (Ibid: 69–72). In addition, the critique built upon the statement formulated by Valerian B. Aptekar' about the practical equivalence of the notions of race, *etnos*, and nationalism in the ethnographic discourse:

> It seems not an incident that this very *etnos* is nothing more than a projection of the bourgeois nationalism. And not incidentally, such modern terminology as "culture" or "cultural circle" or even "cultural complex" is nothing more than a replacement for the old and rather worn-out notion of "race"' (qtd. in Arzi͡utov, Alymov, and Anderson 2014: 196).

The alternative was a complete rejection of these terms, based on Marr's theory: "Neither tribal nor national [masses] exist. This conclusion of the Japhetic theory is indisputable. There exists no tribe, not a single people or a nation, which in their culture and language, in particular, would be a seamless whole (*edinoe t͡seloe*)" (Bykovskiĭ 1932: 21). That, Bykovskiĭ reasoned, made the studies of borrowings and of the geographical spreading of cultural phenomena meaningless, because an arbitrary choice of "ethnic characteristics" could enable one to "arbitrarily establish the boundaries of the ethnical or national regions in the interests of this or that imperialistic country" (Ibid).

Conclusion

In this article, we demonstrated that the circle of Volkov's students who first began to use the term *etnos* was closely connected with the activities of the Commission for Making Ethnographic Maps of Russia (KSEK) and relied on the ethno-geographical research methodology it developed. In 1917, the centre of gravity of the study of the ethnic composition of the population of Russia shifted from the KSEK to the Commission for Studying the Tribal Composition of the Border Regions of Russia, organised in early 1917 under the Academy of Sciences, and after the February Revolution, on 1 April 1917, transformed into the Commission for Studying Tribal Composition (KIPS). The work of the KSEK in those years was hampered by the scarcity of funding, the deaths of its founders (Volkov, Patkanov, Poddubnyĭ, Ukhtomskiĭ, Radlov), as well as a long absence of some members due to World War I and of others because of their involvement in the work of the KIPS (NA RGO 24-102: 14–15). The commission's activities were carried out at a modest scale and were reduced mainly to the processing of the Malorussian, Belorussian, and a large volume of the Velikorussian questionnaires and the continuation of the Second Division's bibliographic work.

The KIPS played an important role in the formation of the ethno-territorial division of the USSR in the 1920s and 1930s. By 1929, it had compiled a "List of Peoples of the USSR", and prepared and published ethnic maps of virtually all regions of the state and about twenty books on ethno-geographical issues (SPF ARAN 135-1-79: 14–14v). Nevertheless, in spite of the fact that it included the main figures of the RGO's[13] KSEK and that Volkov's, Zolotarëv's, and Rudenko's students became its key employees, the general methodology of the KIPS was remarkably different from the ideas of the KSEK. The initial intention of the KIPS closely correlated with the activities of the RGO commission: the identification and mapping of the regions where various peoples were settled had to be based on a set of characteristics and be produced "on the basis of the data of language and, in part, religion, cultural (*bytovykh*) characteristics, and objective self-identity or self-determination of individual peoples, as well as characteristics of their physical types (anthropological data)" (Ob uchrezhdenii 1917: 10). However, later the KIPS created ethnic maps based mainly on census materials (mostly the 1897 census) and other statistical sources (Psi͡anchin 2010: 12); that is, the KIPS returned to the idea of ethnic cartography and to the type of maps that were compiled in the last third of the nineteenth century, with some amendments.

Shortly before its dissolution, according to Rudenko, who became the academic secretary in late 1929, the KIPS hoped to continue the development of the KSEK's and the Volkov school's ideas and outlined a serious research plan that included the task of "working out and issuing a classification of the tribal composition of the population of the Union which should be based both on the self-determination of peoples and on linguistic, racial, and cultural (*kul'turno-bytovye*) attributes" (SPF ARAN 135-1-79: 35). However, under the new political and administrative conditions of the early 1930s, this project was not destined to be realised. At the same time, the discussions about the determinants of "nationality" that the KSEK had started led to the adoption by the KIPS

13 After the 1917 Revolution the Imperial Russian Geographical Society (IRGO) ceased to be "Imperial".

of "self-determination", or self-identification, as the main criterion of "nationality" and of a two-step procedure for defining ethnic identity that had been laid down in the 1926 census (Hirsch 2005: 112; Sokolovskiĭ 2001: 157–84).

Methodologically, the work of the KSEK bears a certain resemblance to the "systemic structuralism" of Pëtr Savitskiĭ and Roman Jakobson. As Sergei Glebov has shown, in the 1920–1930s Eurasianist thinkers identified a specific "Russian science", whose method of finding regularities and geographical correlations of various phenomena implied "a systemic exploration of interrelationships between different forms of organic and nonorganic nature on the given territory, including humans and their societies" (Glebov 2017: 158). Both scholars attempted to define the unity of Eurasia by mapping geological, geographical, and linguistic characteristics of that space. This method, as Glebov explains, "consisted in comparing data from various disciplines and followed Savitskiĭ's attempt to put Russian dialects on the map side by side with the lines marking major climatic and orographic changes"(Glebov 2017: 163).

The idea of the geographical correlation of the physical-anthropological, ethnographic, and language characteristics has been most vividly realised in Rudenko's work. Apparently it was not a coincidence that, in the middle of the 1920s, he urged the staff of the Russian Museum to use the notion of *etnos* as central to the museum's work (Hirsch 2005: 196). The emphasis placed in Rudenko's concept on the "objective" cultural and physical-anthropological characteristics of *etnos* went against the "constructivist" national politics of the Bolsheviks, which led to the later accusations of biologisation and racism.

It was not until 1950 that Rudenko was able to return to his reflections on *etnos*. In his sketch "*Etnos* and Culture", written in response to Stalin's works on linguistics, he defined *etnos* as a people [*narod*] or a group [*narodnost'*] demonstrating all the characteristics of a nation and differing from the latter by the "presence of the commonality of the somatic origin of its members, which is not a requirement for a nation" (SPF ARAN 1004-1-40: 1). In 1966, during a discussion at the RGO, he repeated his thesis that "each *etnos* is distinguished by a specific physical type of its member specimens", as well as by the commonality of language and culture determined by the 'landscape conditions, which it inhabits' (SPF ARAN 1004-1-118: 8).

It is, nevertheless, significant that Rudenko never applied the term *etnos* to the group he studied most of his life: the Bashkirs. In 1955, a new expanded edition of his monograph was published under the title *The Bashkirs: Essays in History and Ethnography*. In a newly written chapter on the "questions of ethnogenesis" of Bashkirs, Rudenko, following Stalin, placed his emphasis on language as the determining factor in Bashkir identity. He dated the origin of the Bashkirs as a "united group of tribes" to the beginning of the first millennium AD — the period of the "formation of the Bashkir language" (Rudenko 2006 [1955]: 298, 304). He saw the issue of a "specific physical type", presumably unifying the *etnos*, as highly ambiguous. In a single paragraph, Rudenko stated that "a single type, characterictic to all Bashkirs, is out of question" since they formed out of various Caucasian and Mongoloid tribes, but added that "the intermarriage between Bashkir tribes on a relatively limited territory [...] facilitated the formation of their relatively unified physical type" (Rudenko 2006 [1955]: 282). In spite of all the diversity of lifestyles of Bashkirs that he documented and their "complicated historical past", numerous ethnic contacts "neither radically changed their physical type, their language, nor culture (*byt*)" (Rudenko 2006 [1955]: 304).

Rudenko's Bashkirs appeared to be both stable and malleable, culturally unified and diverse, physically specific, yet not racially predetermined — that is, a collective that does not fit too well into Rudenko's own clear and crisp definitions of *etnos*. Therefore, Rudenko — a "student of Volkov and the teacher of Gumilëv" (Taran 2003) — was able to build a bridge of continuity between the first generation of *etnos* theoreticians and their followers in the 1960s, bequeathing to them the dilemmas that have been characteristic to *etnos* thinking from its beginning.

Published References

Adams, M. B. 1990. *The Wellborn Science: Eugenics in Germany, France, Brazil, and Russia* (New York: Oxford University Press).

Alymov, S. S. 2017. 'Ukrainskie korni teorii ėtnosa', *Ėtnograficheskoe obozrenie* 5: 67–84.

Arzi͡utov, D. V., S. S. Alymov, and D. D. Anderson. 2014. *Ot klassikov k marksizmu: soveshchanie ėtnografov Moskvy i Leningrada (5–11 aprel͡i͡a 1929 g.)*. Serii͡a "Kunstkamera — Arkhiv" 7 (St Peterburg: MAĖ RAN).

Bartol'd, V. V. 1910. 'XII s"ezd russkikh estestvoispytateleĭ i vracheĭ v Moskve', *Zhivai͡a starina* 1–2: 176–87.

Bernshtam, A. N. 1932. 'Idealizm v ėtnografii (Rudenko i rudenkovshchina)', *Soobshchenii͡a* GAIMK. 1932, 1–2: 22–27.

Bykovskiĭ, S. N. 1930. 'Ob ocherednykh zadachakh po izuchenii͡u karel', *Karelo-Murmanskiĭ kraĭ* 6: 10–12.

—. 1931. 'Ėtnografii͡a na sluzhbe klassovogo vraga', *Sovetskai͡a ėtnografii͡a* 3–4: 3–13.

—. 1932. 'Ėtnografii͡a na sluzhbe mezhdunarodnogo imperializma', in *Ėtnografii͡a na sluzhbe klassovogo vraga* (Leningrad: Sot͡sėkgiz-GAIMK), 5–21.

Cadiot, J. 2007. *Le laboratoire impérial. Russie-URSS, 1860–1940* (Paris: CNRS).

Chepurkovskiĭ, E. M. 1916. 'Ret͡senzii͡a na: Ezhegodnik Russkogo antropologicheskogo obshchestva', *Russkiĭ antropologicheskiĭ zhurnal* 1–2: 139–46.

—. 1918. 'Ret͡senzii͡a na: Sbornik MAĖ. 1916', *Russkiĭ antropologicheskiĭ zhurnal* 3 (1–2): 75–76.

—. 1924. *Ocherki po obshcheĭ antropologii*. Trudy Dal'nevostochnogo gosudarstvennogo universiteta (Vladivostok: Tipografii͡a Dal'nevostochnogo gos. un-ta).

Cherunova, N. K. 1992. 'F. K. Volkov i ego rabota po komplektovanii͡u kollekt͡siĭ ėtnograficheskogo otdela Russkogo muzei͡a', in *Iz istorii formirovanii͡a ėtnograficheskikh kollekt͡siĭ v muzei͡akh Rossii (XIX–XX vv.): sbornik nauchnykh trudov*, ed. by I. I. Shangina, O. V. Karpova and V. P. Ivanova (St Peterburg: GĖM), 52–61.

Chistov, K. V. 1991. 'Vostochnoslavi͡anskai͡a ėtnografii͡a D. K. Zelinina', in *Vostochnoslavi͡anskai͡a ėtnografii͡a*, ed. by K. V. Chistov (Moscow: Nauka), 427–51.

Durnovo, N. N., N. N. Sokolov, and D. N. Ushakov. 1915. *Opyt dialektologicheskoĭ karty russkogo i͡azyka v Europe s prilozheniem ocherka russkoĭ dialektologii* (Moscow: Sinodal'nai͡a tipografii͡a).

Ėtnograficheskiĭ otdel Russkogo Muzeīa. 1903. *Programma dlīa sobiranīia ėtnograficheskikh predmetov.2-e izd.* (St Peterburg: Tipografiīa T-va Nardonaīa Pol'za).

Glebov, S. 2017. *From Empire to Eurasia: Politics, Scholarship, and Ideology in Russian Eurasianism, 1920s–1930s* (DeKalb, IL: Northern Illinois University Press).

Hirsch, F. 2005. *Empire of Nations: Ethnographic Knowledge and the Making of the Soviet Union* (Ithaca, NY: Cornell University Press).

Khudīakov, M. G. 1931. 'Kriticheskaīa prorabotka rudenkovshchiny', *Sovetskaīa ėtnografiīa* 1–2: 167–69.

—. 1932. 'Velikoderzhavnyĭ shovinizm v russkoĭ ėtnografii', in *Ėtnografiīa na sluzhbe u klassovogo vraga* (Leningrad: Sot͡sėkgiz-GAIMK), 23–100.

Kuchumov, I. V. 2015. 'S. I. Rudenko i vozniknovenie granit͡s Bashkirskoĭ respubliki', in *Ot plemeni k ėtnosu*, ed. by A. V. Psīanchin (St Peterburg: Svoe izdatel'stvo), 160–79.

Levin, M. G. 1960. *Ocherki po istorii antropologii v Rossii* (Moscow: izdatel'stvo Akademii nauk SSSR).

Mikhal'chuk, K. P. 1872. 'Narechiīa, podnarechiīa i govory īuzhnoĭ Rossii v svīazi s narechiīami Galichiny', in *Trudy ėtnografichesko-statisticheskoĭ ėkspedit͡sii v Zapadno-Russkiĭ kraĭ*, ed. by P. P. Chubinskiĭ (St Peterburg: Imperatorskoe Russkoe Geograficheskoe Obshchestvo), 453–512.

Mogilīanskiĭ, N. M. 1916. 'Predmet i zadachi ėtnografii', *Zhivaīa starina* 25: 1–22.

—. 1917. 'Ret͡senziīa na: Ukrainskiĭ narod v ego proshlom i nastoīashchem', *Zhurnal Ministerstva narodnogo prosveshcheniīa* 68 (March–April): 130–38.

Ob uchrezhdenii. 1917. *Ob uchrezhdenii Komissii po izucheniīu plemennogo sostava naseleniīa Rossii* (Petrograd: Tip. Rossiĭskoĭ Ak. nauk).

Otchët. 1915. 'Otchët o deīatel'nosti Otdeleniīa ėtnografii i sostoīashchikh pri nem komissiĭ za 1914 god', *Zhivaīa starina* 1–2: i–vii.

—. 1916. 'Otchët o deīatel'nosti Otdeleniīa ėtnografii i sostoīashchikh pri nem komissiĭ za 1915 god', *Zhivaīa starina* 1: i–x.

Otdelenie ėtnografii I.R.G.O. 1911. 'Zhurnaly zasedaniĭ Otdeleniīa ėtnografii I.R.G.O.', *Zhivaīa starina* 1: i–l.

Patkanov, S. K. 1915. 'Proekt sostavleniīa plemennoĭ karty Rossii', *Zhivaīa starina* 14 3: 217–44.

Platonova, N. I. 2010. *Istoriīa arkheologicheskoĭ mysli v Rossii: vtoraīa polovina XIX–pervaīa tret' XX veka* (St Peterburg: Nestor-Istoriīa).

Primernaīa skhema. 1916. 'Primernaīa skhema dlīa sostavleniīa oprosnykh listov', *Zhivaīa starina* 1: xxi–xxiv.

Psi͡anchin, A. V. 2004. *Ocherki istorii ėtnicheskoĭ kartografii v Rossii XVIII–XIX vv.* (Moscow: T͡SITMO).

—. 2010. *Komissii͡a po izuchenii͡u plemennogo sostava naselenii͡a: ot ėtnokartografii k perepisi naselenii͡a* (Ufa: Gilem).

Reshetov, A. M. 1998. 'S. I. Rudenko — antropolog, ėtnograf, arkheolog', in *S. I. Rudenko i bashkiry*, ed. by R. M. I͡Usupova and M. V. Murzabulatova (Ufa: Gilem), 5–25.

Rudenko, S. I. 1914. 'Antropologicheskoe issledovanie inorodt͡sev Severo-Zapadnoĭ Sibiri', *Zapiski Imperatorskoĭ Akademii nauk po fiziko-matematicheskomu otdelenii͡u* 33 3: 102–13.

—. 1916. *Bashkiry: Opyt ėtnologicheskoĭ monografii. Chast' 1: Fizicheskiĭ tip bashkir.* Zapiski Russkogo geograficheskogo obshchestva po otdelenii͡u ėtnografii 43 1 (Petrograd: Tipografii͡a I͡Akor').

—. 1925. *Bashkiry. Opyt ėtnologicheskoĭ monografii. Chast' 2: Byt bashkir.* Zapiski Russkogo geograficheskogo obshchestva po otdelenii͡u ėtnografii 43 2 (Leningrad: Gosudarstvennai͡a tipografii͡a imeni I. Fedorova).

—. 1926. 'Sovremennoe sostoi͡anie i blizhaĭshie zadachi ėtnograficheskogo izuchenii͡a turet͡skikh plemen', in *Pervyĭ Vsesoi͡uznyĭ ti͡urkologicheskiĭ s"ezd* (Stenograficheskiĭ Otchët) (Baku: Obshchestvo obsledovanii͡a i izuchenii͡a Azerbaĭdzhana), 77–88.

—. 1955. *Bashkiry. Istoriko-ėtnograficheskie ocherki* (Moscow: Izdatel'stvo Akademii nauk SSSR).

—. 2006 [1955]. Bashkiry. Istoriko-ėtnograficheskie ocherki (Ufa: Kitap).

Saburova, L. M. 1979. 'D. K. Zelenin-Ėtnograf', in *Problemy slavi͡anskoĭ ėtnografii: k 100-letii͡u so dni͡a rozhdenii͡a D. K. Zelenina: sbornik stateĭ*, ed. by A. K. Baĭburin and K. V. Chistov (Leningrad: Nauka), 9–43.

Seegel, S. 2012. *Mapping Europe's Borderlands: Russian Cartography in the Age of Empire* (Chicago, IL: University of Chicago Press).

Sergeeva, G. I. 1992. 'V. I. Lamanskiĭ i organizat͡sii͡a ėtnograficheskogo otdela Russkogo muzei͡a', in *Iz istorii formirovanii͡a ėtnograficheskikh kollekt͡siĭ v muzei͡akh Rossii (XIX–XX vv.): sbornik nauchnykh trudov*, ed. by I. I. Shangina (St Peterburg: GĖM), 3–13.

Shangina, I. I. 1985. 'D. A. Zolotarëv (k 100-letii͡u so dni͡a rozhdenii͡a)', *Sovetskai͡a ėtnografii͡a* 6: 76–84.

Sokolovskiĭ, S. V. 2001. *Obrazy drugikh v rossiiskikh nauke, politike i prave* (Moscow: Put').

Soloveĭ, T. D. 2001. '"Korennoĭ perelom" v otechestvennoĭ ėtnografii (diskussii͡a o predmete ėtnologicheskoi nauki kontsa 1920-kh–nachala 1930-kh gg.)', *Ėtnograficheskoe obozrenie* 3: 101–20.

Steĭnvedel, C. 2004. 'Plemi͡a, soslovie ili nat͡sional'nost'? ', in *Novai͡a imperskai͡a istorii͡a postsovetskogo prostranstva*, ed. by I. V. Gerasimov, S. V. Glebov, A. P. Kaplunovskiĭ, and M. B. Mogil'ner (Kazan': T͡Sentr issledovaniĭ nat͡sionalizma i imperii), 473–500.

Steinwedel, C. 2000. 'To Make a Difference: The Category of Ethnicity in Late Imperial Russian Politics, 1861–1917', in *Russian Modernity: Politics, Knowledge, Practices*, ed. by D. L. Hoffmann and Y. Kotsonis (Basingstoke: Palgrave), 67–86.

Taran, O. G. 2003. *Naukova spadshchina Fedora Vovka v galuzi antropologiï: spadkoemnist' tradit͡siĭ ta suchasne bachenni͡a* (unpublished doctoral dissertation, Taras Shevchenko Kiev National University).

Tishkin, A. A. 2004. *Zhiznennyi put', tvorchestvo, nauchnoe nasledie Sergeia Ivanovicha Rudenko i deiatel'nost' ego kolleg: sbornik nauchnykh statei* (Barnaul: Izd-vo Altaiskogo universiteta).

Tolstoĭ, N. I. and D. K. Tolstai͡a. 1979. 'D. K. Zelenin-Dialektolog', in *Problemy slavi͡anskoĭ ėtnografii: k 100-letii͡u so dni͡a rozhdenii͡a D. K. Zelenina: sbornik stateĭ*, ed. by A. K. Baĭburin and K. V. Chistov (Leningrad: Nauka), 70–92.

V Metodbi͡uro. 1932. 'V Metodbi͡uro Ėtnograficheskogo otdela Russkogo muzeia (kriticheskaia prorabotka rudenkovshchiny)' *Sovetskai͡a ėtnografia* 1: 117–18.

Veselovskiĭ, N. I. 1915. 'Dei͡atel'nost' V. I. Lamanskogo v Imperatorskom Russkom geograficheskom obshchestve', *Zhivai͡a starina* 1–2: 1–8.

Volkov, F. K. 1914. 'Anketnye voprosy Komissii po sostavlenii͡u ėtnograficheskikh kart Rossii, sostoi͡ashcheĭ pri Otdelenii ėtnografii Imperatorskogo Russkogo geograficheskogo obshchestva', *Zhivai͡a starina* 1–2: 193–94.

—. 1916a. 'Antropologicheskie osobennosti ukrainskogo naroda', in *Ukrainskiĭ narod v ego proshlom i nastoi͡ashchem*, ed. by F. K. Volkov, M. S. Grushevskiĭ, M. M. Kovalevskiĭ, F. E. Korsh, A. E. Krymskiĭ, M. I. Tugan'-Baranovskiĭ and A. A. Shakhmatov (Petrograd: Tip. tov-va "Obshchestvennai͡a pol'za"), 427–54.

—. 1916b. 'Ėtnograficheskie osobennosti ukrainskogo naroda', in *Ukrainskiĭ narod v ego proshlom i nastoi͡ashchem*, ed. by F. K. Volkov, M. S. Grushevskiĭ, M. M. Kovalevskiĭ, F. E. Korsh, A. E. Krymskiĭ, M. I. Tugan'-Baranovskiĭ, and A. A. Shakhmatov (Petrograd: Tip. tov-va "Obshchestvennai͡a pol'za"), 455–647.

—. M. S. Grushevskiĭ, N. Kovalevskiĭ, F. E. Korsh, A. E. Krymskiĭ, M. I. Tugan-Baranovskiĭ, and A. A. Shakhmatov. 1914–16. *Ukrainskiĭ narod v ego proshlom i nastoi͡ashchem* (Petrograd: tipografii͡a tovarichshestva "Obshchestvennai͡a pol'za").

Zelenin, D. K. 1913. *Bibliograficheskiĭ ukazatel' russkoĭ ėtnograficheskoĭ literatury o vneshnem byte narodov Rossii. 1700–1910 gg.: Zhilishche. Odezhda. Muzyka. Iskusstvo. Khozi͡aĭstvennyĭ byt* (St Peterburg: Tip. A. V. Orlova).

—. 1914. Opisanie rukopiseĭ Uchenogo arkhiva Imp. Russkogo geograficheskogo obshchestva (Petrograd: Tip. A. V. Orlova).

—. 1927. *Russische (Ostslavische) Volkskunde* (Berlin: de Gruyter).

—. 1991. *Vostochnoslavi͡anskai͡a ėtnografii͡a* (Moscow: Nauka).

Zolotarëv, A. A. 2016. *Campo Santo moeĭ pami͡ati* (St Peterburg: Rostok).

Zolotarëv, D. A. 1912. 'Antropologicheskoe issledovanie velikorusskogo naselenii͡a Ostashkovskogo i Rzhevskogo uezdov Tverskoĭ gubernii', *Ezhegodnik Russkogo antropologicheskogo obshchestva* 4: 9–66.

—. 1913. 'Ret͡senzii͡a na: Chepurkovskiĭ E. M. Geograficheskoe raspredelenie form golovy i t͡svetnosti krest'i͡anskogo naselenii͡a preimushchestvenno Velikorossii v svi͡azi s kolonizat͡sieĭ eë slavi͡anami', *Ezhegodnik Russkogo antropologicheskogo obshchestva* 4: 173–84.

—. 1916a. 'Antropologicheskie dannye o velikorusakh poberezh'i͡a rek Sukhony i Severnoĭ Dviny', *Ezhegodnik Russkogo antropologicheskogo obshchestva* 6: 49–82.

—. 1916b. 'Obzor dei͡atel'nosti postoi͡annoĭ komissii po sostavlenii͡u ėtnograficheskikh kart Rossii pri Imperatorskom Russkom geograficheskom obshchestve (15 okt. 1910–15 okt. 1915 goda)', *Zhivai͡a starina* 1: xi–xxi.

—. 1930. *Karely SSSR* (Leningrad: Izdatel'stvo AN SSSR).

Archival References

AMAĖ RAN: Archive of Peter the Great Museum of Anthropology and Ethnography, Russian Academy of Sciences, St Petersburg

AMAĖ RAN K1-8-1: 1. "I[mperatorskoe] R[usskoi͡e] Geogr[aficheskoi͡e] Obshche[st]vo. Komissii͡a po sostavlenii͡u ėtnograficheskikh kart Rossii. II Otdel — Amurskai͡a sekt͡sii͡a. Oprosnyĭ listok № 1".

ARĖM: Archive of the Russian Ethnographic Museum, St Petersburg

ARĖM 2-1-361. Protokoly i materialy po diskussii o roli S. I. Rudenko v ėtnografii, 22 May 1931–29 Jan. 1932. 67 folios.

ARĖM 1-2-386: 121–22. Makarenko, Alekseĭ A."Podgotovlennai͡a programma dli͡a sobiranii͡a ėtnograficheskikh predmetov sredi tunguzov po r. Katanga (Sr. Tunguzka)". Prilozhenie k dokladnoĭ zapiske, 13 Jan. 1907.

NA RGO: Scientific Archive of the Russian Geographical Society, St Petersburg

NA RGO 1(1846)-1-8. "Ob izdanii ėtnograficheskoĭ karty Rossii 1846–1847 goda". 141 folios.

NA RGO 1(1888)-1-16: 35–46. "Godovoĭ Otchët Otdelenii͡a Ėtnografii [za 1887 god]".

NA RGO 1(1911)-1-32: 22v–26v. Malorossiĭskai͡a programma.

NA RGO 1(1911)-1-32: 58–58v; 59–59v. Obrazt͡sy obrashchenii͡a popechiteleĭ uchebnogo okruga.

NA RGO 1(1911)-1-32: 75–75v. T͡sirkuli͡arnoe pis'mo direktoram narodnykh uchilishch Vilenskogo uchebnogo okruga.

NA RGO 1(1911)-1-32: 79–79v. Soprovoditel'noe pis'mo N. D. Artamonova Predsedateli͡u Zemskoĭ upravy, 10 Aug. 1913.

NA RGO 1(1911)-1-32: 90–91. "Spravka" o sostoi͡anii rassylki anket, 27 Sep. 1913.

NA RGO 1(1912)-1-17: 78, 79, 82, 83. "Dei͡atel'nost' II-go Otdela Komissii [po sostavlenii͡u ėtnograficheskikh kart Rossii za 1913–14".

NA RGO 1(1913)-1-23: 10–11. Makarenko, Alekseĭ A. "Skhema ėtnograficheskikh priznakov, podlezhashchikh anketnomu vyi͡asnenii͡u i nanesenii͡u na ėtnograficheskie karty Sibiri". Predlozhena. 4 Dec. 1913.

NA RGO 24-72: 7–8. "Sekt͡sii͡a Irkutsko-Zabaĭkal'skai͡a. Oprosnyĭ listok № 1".

NA RGO 24-72: 9–11. "Sekt͡sii͡a Irkutsko-Zabaĭkal'skai͡a. Oprosnyĭ listok № 2".

NA RGO 24-72: 14–46. "Oprosnyĭ listok Sibirskoĭ Podkomissii pri Otdelenii ėtnografii IRGO" ("Dli͡a puteshestvennikov").

NA RGO 24-78: 3. (first pagination) Postanovlenii͡a otdelov o tipakh kart [18 Apr. 1914].

NA RGO 24-78: 53. (first pagination) "Skhema o tipakh zhilishch i postroek podlezhashchikh nanesenii͡u na karty Sibiri i Sredneĭ Azii. Sostavil S. I. Rudenko" [13 Feb. 1915].

NA RGO 24-78: 52. (second pagination) "Skhema k sostavlenii͡u programm o tipakh zhilishch nadlezhashchikh nanesenii͡u na karty Sibiri i Sredneĭ Azii. Predlozhena S. I. Rudenko" [13 Feb. 1915].

NA RGO 24-78: 56–58v. "Zhurnal zasedanii͡a Vremennoĭ komissii pri Otdelenii Ėtnografii I.R.G.O. po obsuzhdenii͡u predlozheniĭ, vnesennykh v zasedanie otdelenii͡a 30/04/1910", 10 May 1910.

NA RGO 24-78: 59–62v, 64–66, 68, 70v–71, 82–87, 92–93v, 102–02v, 104–05, 115–18, 124–26: Protokoly zasedanii͡a Komissii po sostavlenii͡u Ėtnograficheskikh kart Rossii, 29 Oct. 1910–16 Mar. 1916.

NA RGO 24-78: 76–76v. Zelenin, Dmitriĭ K. "Proekt instrukt͡sii sostaviteli͡u 'Bibliograficheskogo ukazateli͡a ėtnograficheskoĭ literatury o naselenii Rossiĭskoĭ Imperii', sostavli͡aemogo dli͡a naneseniĭaa na karty razlichnykh ėtnograficheskikh kategoriĭ".

NA RGO 24-78: 98. "Zai͡avlenie D[eĭstvitel'nogo] ch[lena] I.R.G.O. A. A. Makarenko", 8 Feb. 1913.

NA RGO 24-78: 113–14, 127–29, 132–34 Protokoly zasedaniĭ͡y I-go otdela Komissii po sostavleni͡u ėtnograficheskikh kart Rossii, 29 Apr. 1915–2 Oct. 1917.

NA RGO 24-79: 2–4. "Zasedanie Otdela po zhilishchu i postroĭkam, 3 May 1911".

NA RGO 24-81: 6–7. Protokol zasedanii͡a Otdela "Odezhda i ukrasheni͡a" Komissii po sostavleni͡u ėtnograficheskoĭ karty Rossiĭskoĭ imperii, 18 Apr. 1911.

NA RGO 24-82: 26–28v. Pis'mo D. N. Ushakova S. F. Ol'denburgu, 16 June 1915.

NA RGO 24-82: 29–30. "Uslovii͡a, na kotorykh Moskovskai͡a Dialektologicheskai͡a komissii͡a predostavli͡aet Imperskomu Russkomu Geograficheskomu Obshchestvu izdat' i eë dialektologichesku͡iu kartu russkogo i͡azyka", [30 Mar. 1911] (attachment to the letter from D. N. Ushakov to S. F. Ol'denburg, 16 June 1915).

NA RGO 24-82: 31–32v. Ushakov, Dmitriĭ N. "Spisok ukazaniĭ, ne prini͡atykh vo vnimanie pri izgotovlenii poslednego originala (chernogo kontura) karty", 12 June 1915.

NA RGO 24-82: 39–39v. [Ushakov, Dmitriĭ N.] "Ob"i͡asnitel'nai͡a zapiska k Dialektologicheskoĭ karte russkogo i͡azyka", [1911].

NA RGO 24-82: 41–45. [Rudnev, Andreĭ D.] Protokol 1-go zasedanii͡a Otdela i͡azyka Komissii po sostavleni͡u Ėtnograficheskoĭ karty Rossii, 26 Mar. 1911.

NA RGO 24-82: 62–63. Pis'mo D. N. Ushakova S. F. Ol'denburgu, 2 May 1911.

NA RGO 24-83: 5–8. Zolotarëv, David A. Protokoly zasedanii͡a Antropologicheskogo Otdela Komissii po sostavleni͡u ėtnograficheskikh kart Rossii, 21 Nov. 1913–10 Mar. 1914.

NA RGO 24-83: 10–11. Rudenko, Sergeĭ A. "Otchët po komandirovke v Priural'e dli͡a proizvodstva antropologicheskikh izmereniĭ bashkir", 12 Sep. 1913.

NA RGO 24-83: 12–14. Otchët o poezdke D. A. Zolotarëva v Novgorodsku͡iu gub. letom 1912.

NA RGO 24-83: 17–18. Volkov, Fëdor K. "O dei͡atel'nosti antropologicheskoĭ komissii po sostavleni͡u ėtnograficheskikh kart", [after 17 Oct. 1911].

NA RGO 24-102. Makarenko, Alekseĭ A. "Svedenii͡a o dei͡atel'nosti II-go Otdela (Sibiri i D[al'nego] Vostoka) Komissii po sostavleni͡u ėtnograficheskoĭ karty Rossii pri Russkom Geograficheskom obshchestve", [after 1917]. 20 folios.

NA RGO 24-105. "Svodki i razrabotki anket. Zapiski k ėtnograficheskim kartam". 15 copybooks (unknown number of folios).

NA RGO 119-1-35. Rudenko, Sergeĭ A., Mark K. Azadovskiĭ. Sistematicheskiĭ ėtnograficheskiĭ ukazatel' k trudam puteshestvennikov po Sibiri", [1923]. 294 folios.

GARF: State Archive of the Russian Federation, Moscow

GARF P.-5787-1-17: 110. Mogili͡anskiĭ, Nikolaĭ M. "Za polveka", avtobiograficheskai͡a povest', 1921, 207 folios.

OR RGB: Department of Manuscripts of the Russian State Library, Moscow

OR RGB 10-13-469: 1–4v. Pis'mo S. I. Rudenko D. N. Anuchinu. Parizh, 26 Dec. 1913.

OR RGB 10-13-470: 5–7v. Pis'mo S. I. Rudenko D. N. Anuchinu. Parizh, 16 Nov. 1913.

OR RGB 10-13-472: 10–11. Pis'mo S. I. Rudenko D. N. Anuchinu, 26 Oct. 1915

OR RGB 10-20-138: 19–20v. Pis'mo F. K. Volkova D. N. Anuchinu, 15 Mar. 1911

OR RGB 10-20-138: 25–26v. Pis'mo F. K. Volkova D. N. Anuchinu, 1 Mar. 1915

SPF ARAN: St Petersburg Branch of the Archive of the Russian Academy of Sciences

SPF ARAN 135-1-79: 7–8v. Protokol obshchego sobranii͡a rabotnikov KIPS, 14 Aug. 1929.

SPF ARAN 135-1-79: 9–9v. Zai͡avlenie Sotrudnikov Sibirskogo Otdela KIPS: K. V. Vi͡atkinoĭ, S. D. Churakovoĭ i S. D. Rudnevoĭ v Komissii͡u po proverke apparata Akademii Nauk, [1929].

SPF ARAN 135-1-79: 10–12v. "Protokol № 6 Soveshchanii͡a nauchnykh rabotnikov Akademii Nauk SSSR", 15 Aug. 1929.

SPF ARAN 135-1-79: 14–14v. "Izlozhenie doklada o KIPS D. A. Zolotarëva", 16 Aug. 1929.

SPF ARAN 135-1-79: 17. Marr, Nikolaĭ I͡A. Dokladnai͡a zapiska Nepremennomu sekretari͡u AN [S. F. Ol'denburgu], 5 Sep. 1929.

SPF ARAN 135-1-79: 22. Otchët o rabote Kavkazskogo otdela KIPS [1929].

SPF ARAN 135-1-79: 23. Otchët o rabote Turkestanskogo otdela KIPS [1929].

SPF ARAN 135-1-79: 24–25. Otchët o rabote Sibirskogo otdela KIPS za 1929.

SPF ARAN 135-1-79: 26. Otchët o rabote gruppy statistov po sostavleniîu [illegible] i ėtnograficheskikh kart SSSR [1929].

SPF ARAN 135-1-79: 32–34. "Protokol № 1 Zasedaniîa Ėkonomsoveshchaniîa pri KIPS, Arkheologicheskoĭ Komissii, Komissii po sostavleniîu spravochnika N.R.", 1 Oct. 1929.

SPF ARAN 135-1-79: 35–35v. Prilozhenie № 1 [Doklad S. I. Rudenko] k Protokolu № 1 Zasedaniîa Ėkonomsoveshchaniîa pri KIPS, Arkheologicheskoĭ Komissii, Komissii po sostavleniîu spravochnika N.R., 1 Oct. 1929.

SPF ARAN 135-1-79: 36–36v. Prilozhenie № 2 "Polozheniîa, vyskazannye Vîatkinoĭ" k Protokolu № 1 Zasedaniîa Ėkonomsoveshchaniîa pri KIPS, Arkheologicheskoĭ Komissii, Komissii po sostavleniîu spravochnika N.R., 1 Oct. 1929.

SPF ARAN 135-1-79: 39–39v. Tematicheskiĭ plan rabot KIPS na 1929–30, 11 Oct. 1929.

SPF ARAN 135-1-79: 40–41v. Perechen' shtatnykh sotrudnikov KIPSa s perechisleniem vypolnennykh rabot, no date.

SPF ARAN 135-1-79: 42. "Kartograficheskiĭ Otdel", 18 Nov. 1929.

SPF ARAN 135-1-79: 43. Kartograficheskiĭ otdel KIPSa: sostav, predlozheniîa po rabote, 18 Nov. 1929.

SPF ARAN 135-1-79: 44–44v. Kartograficheskiĭ Otdel Akademii nauk: sostav, predlozheniîa po rabote, 18 Nov. 1929.

SPF ARAN 135-1-79: 46. "Zasedanie Prezidiuma i rukovoditeleĭ otdelov KIPS", 2 Dec. 1929.

SPF ARAN 135-1-79: 52–55. "Zamechaniîa na proekt rezolîut͡sii Lokal'nogo Bîuro po KIPSu", no date.

SPF ARAN 135-1-79: 56–96. Dokumenty, Otchëty, spiski rabot otdelov KIPS.

SPF ARAN 135-1-79: 97–97v. Dokladnaîa zapiska Uchenogo sekretarîa S. I. Rudenko Nepremennomu sekretarîu Akademii Nauk SSSR [S. F. Ol'denburgu] [after 24 Oct. 1929].

SPF ARAN 135-1-79: 102–09. "Rezolîut͡siîa po voprosu o sovremennom sostoîanii i neobkhodimykh meropriîatiîakh po reorganizat͡sii KIPS i MAĖ Akademii Nauk SSSR" [9 Dec. 1929].

SPF ARAN 135-1-79: 148–48v. Pis'mo Akad. V. V. Bartol'da v Prezidium IPIN, 22 Feb. 1930.

SPF ARAN 1004-1-40. Rudenko, Sergeĭ I. "Ėtnos i kul'tura". Zametka, stat'îa i materialy k neĭ [after 1950]. 3 folios.

SPF ARAN 1004-1-118: 8–14. Rudenko, Sergeĭ I. "Ėtnos i ėtnogenez (po povodu diskussii v Otdelenii ėtnografii VGO)". Stat'îa [before 1966].

SPF ARAN 1004-1-199. Rudenko, Sergeĭ I. Avtobiografii, ankety, 1918–1965. 20 l.

5. Notes from His "Snail's Shell": Shirokogoroff's Fieldwork and the Groundwork for *Etnos* Thinking

David G. Anderson

Sergei M. Shirokogoroff was a prolific, and enigmatic, ethnographer of eastern Eurasia, whose writings evoked strong reactions among his students and colleagues both during his life, and after. Although sometimes, and in some places, he is hailed as one of anthropology's founding figures — especially in China (Liú 2007; Fèi 1994; Guldin 1994) — his work was for decades ignored or undervalued in his Russian homeland. Despite this disdain, Shirokogoroff's passion for specifying a bio-spatial theory of how identities evolve, known as *etnos* theory, nevertheless became a core pillar of late-Soviet ethnography, and also had some influence on the Chinese version of the term known as *mínzú*. Despite this posthumous and sometimes anonymous recognition in Eurasia, he had hoped to make a name for himself in Europe. To this end he poured his energy into an extraordinary circle of correspondence and published an entire shelf of often self-funded English-language brochures and books. It would be fair to say that Shirokogoroff is rarely associated today in English language anthropology with his fascination with the "growth and decline of

 https://doi.org/10.11647/OBP.0150.05

etnoses". Instead, he is known predominately as an ethnographer of shamanism and as an authority on Evenki-Tungus peoples.

Because of his complicated transnational life trajectory, and difficult character, there has been little understanding of how Shirokogoroff's ideas and fieldwork fit together. Indeed trying to assemble a reasonable biography of the man has been hindered by the fact that he taught and researched at eight different universities or academic societies between 1912 and 1939 in Russia and China, at times when these nations were transforming themselves through revolution and/or resistance to foreign occupation (Anderson and Arzyutov forthcoming). While many observers appreciate his attention to detail and the broad range of interests in his fieldwork, they all chaff against the fact that his notes and letters are often chaotic or are broken up between a large number of institutions around the globe.

This chapter represents a first attempt to try to ground Shirokogoroff's theoretical thinking on the biosocial and bio-spatial identity he called *etnos* in the day-to-day activities of his fieldwork using recently discovered archival materials. The chapter puts its emphasis on Shirokogoroff's first Siberian fieldwork in the region to the east of Lake Baikal known as Zabaĭkal'e (literally, "beyond Baikal"). The 1912 and 1913 expeditions to the region were jointly planned, documented, and written-up with his wife Elizaveta [née Robinson], who it has now emerged played a pivotal role in his research (Fig. 5.1). In his later publications, and in correspondence, Shirokogoroff would credit their joint fieldwork with having a profound effect on his thinking both about what he would later describe as the "Tungus hypothesis" [the Tungus mentalité], and on what he overwhelmingly came to describe as "his" *etnos* theory. Given the long-lasting impact of Shirokogoroff's writing on Eurasian styles of doing anthropology, it is important to unravel this first Siberian fieldwork. This chapter for the first time brings together the scattered photographs, diaries, manuscripts, letters, and other artefacts generated by this first expedition. A full account of the archival material is presented in an appendix. A preliminary version of this chapter was published in Russian (Anderson 2017).

In studying the Zabaĭkal fieldwork of this ethnographic couple, I will place special emphasis upon what is today experienced as a chaotic bundle of documentary techniques ranging from invasive anthropometry, to classical philology, to the study of material culture,

Fig. 5.1 Elizaveta Shirokogoroff posing in the forests around Tyksyr, 1912 (EVR)

and finally the incorporation of cellular and mathematical metaphors to structure the data. The central argument of the paper is that the very first ethnographic encounter of the couple with the Evenkis and Orochens of eastern Siberia destabilised Shirokogoroff's expectations of the structure of culture, and led him on a life-long search to measure "cultured-ness" [*kul'turnost'*] within amalgams of constantly shifting populations on the frontiers of Russia and China. This changing political landscape encouraged him to develop a hyper-positivist approach of measuring and documenting physiognomic and phonetic stabilities, and collecting representative artefacts, that transcended the chaos of political change.

This attention to stability-within-change, I will argue, led to the ironic yet ultimately successful imprinting of this theory as a hallmark quality of late twentieth century Eurasian states. Certain anomalies in the texts suggest that the field project might have also developed into an exploration of performative identities creating an exotic tension in Shirokogoroff's writing between an almost racialist biology and a relativistic and culturalist ethnographic account. In trying to balance these contradictory intentions, I contextualize the production of *etnos* thinking as a personal journey wherein Shirokogoroff's increasing alienation from intellectual circles in Petrograd bolstered his confidence and authority as an arbitrator of ethnic boundaries in eastern Eurasia.

Etnos Theory… Unwound

Near the end of his life, Shirokogoroff confessed to his lifelong friend, the linguist Władysław Kotwicz (1872–1944), that he "began to formulate the heart of my *etnos* theory in 1912". He wrote these words in February 1932 in Beiping [Běijīng] at the beginning of a very dark period for northeast Asia. By the time that he had posted his letter, Harbin had fallen to the Japanese Imperial Army, and by 18 February the state of Manchukuo had been imposed over much of northeastern China. Shirokogoroff's mind in this letter, however, was focussed on past affronts he suffered in Petrograd more than two decades earlier. He was writing to complain that he had not been sent the most recent volume on Tungus linguistics (Bogoraz 1931), which, in a style that is uniquely his own, led him to recall his disenchantment with his mentors at the Museum of Anthropology and Ethnography. This rather bitter train of thought led him to explain the somewhat accidental way that he became a field ethnographer, and how that experience gave him a drive to systematise everything he read and everyone he met:

> In 1912 I had several — two or three — discussions on theoretical topics with Shternberg. After, I came to the conclusion that we would never understand each other. […] V. V. [Radlov] insisted that I study some group of languages and that I do some fieldwork [to further study them]. He has raised this question several times. My objection was that I could not see myself as a "fieldworker" and would not even know how to start to study a language. V. V. decisively declared that I could do this, and I accepted his judgement, since I trusted him. Nonetheless I refused the financial support that V. V. offered for the first expedition. From the moment of taking this decision I had to meet often with Shternberg, since as V. V. explained to me, Shternberg was responsible for the technical organization [of the expedition] and he advised me not to argue with him. […] However, as soon as Shternberg came into "contact" with me he began to "explain" things to me. […] I had no other choice but to keep silent (*molchat'*). I first began to formulate the heart of my *etnos* theory in 1912 partly from analysing literature on a large number of peoples, partly after my experiences with living groups of people in Zabaĭkal'e,

> and of course partly as a result of my desire to find laws and regularities (*zakonomernosti*). As I did this I became more and more isolated. I withdrew into my snail's shell (*ushel v ulitku*) only continuing to discuss mainly linguistic topics with V. V. (BPANvK 4600-7: 55)

Shirokogoroff's metaphor of a slowly unwinding snail intriguingly captures how his thinking either recoiled from the intellectual environment around him, or somewhat surreptitiously crawled around it. He confesses that the snail-like trajectory of his thinking was provoked by his fieldwork, and the productive contradiction that that experience created with the received thinking around him in St Petersburg. To link Shirokogoroff's snail metaphor to his first fieldwork we have to first understand what he understood as the "heart" of his *etnos* theory.

As discussed in the introduction to this volume, it is not easy to summarize the early versions of *etnos* theory. This lightly evolutionist and primordialist worldview was pervasive at the end of the nineteenth century in France, Germany and Russia. The theory itself underwent its own involution from an early classificatory definition stressing a "crystallised" identity, single-language use, and a bundle of unique customs to a later version stressing "processes" and "equilibria" (Shirokogoroff 1935). However, Shirokogoroff himself gives us a clue as to the heart of the theory in a footnote first published within a rare Chinese-language journal (Shirokogoroff 1930; 1931; 1970).

This is the only place, published or not, where Shirokogoroff situates his theory mainly against *fin de siècle* French thinking on *ethnie*. To contrast his vision to those of Ferdinand de Saussure, Arnold van Gennup, and the prehistorian Félix Regnault, he stresses three elements: that (1) the *etnos* is first and foremost a "biological unit of man" (Shirokogoroff 1930: 11); that (2) it holds something that we might now describe as its environmental fitness (what Shirokogoroff calls "strength") (Ibid: 12); and (3) that this bio-spatial unit struggles to obtain an equilibrium against other neighbouring *etnoses* (Ibid: 16–18). In this text, Shirokogoroff places a great emphasis on the last point — that an *etnos* can only exist if it is in a state of equilibrium. As proof of the attractiveness of his theory, he cites a miscellaneous pantheon of theorists from Franz Boas to Alfred Lotka who at the time also showed an interest in various forms of equilibria — thereby claiming that his unique invention was "in the air" (Ibid: 16–17n1).

Shirokogoroff's intense interest in technological skills, corporally borne — existing in a state of unsteady competition with neighbouring groups — can be linked to an early sense of shock and disorientation in his first Siberian fieldwork of 1912. In revisiting this journey, I will try to contextualize what Shirokogoroff understood as his "ethnical equilibrium" by documenting his contribution to anthropometrics, his cataloguing of what I will call "adaptive technologies" and what he saw as the problem of assimilation.

The Mystery of the Missing Tunguses: the 1912 Zabaĭkal Expedition

The 1912 expedition of Sergei and Elizaveta Shirokogoroff was formally sponsored by the Petrograd-based "Russian Committee for the Study of Central and Eastern Asia in its Historical, Archaeological, Linguistic, and Ethnographic Aspects". This was an early interdisciplinary agency founded by Sergeĭ Ol'denburg in 1903 that brought together scholars from across a variety of institutions to focus on what we might call today "area studies" (Ol'denburg 1903; Kisli͡akov 2013). The committee organized sets of field studies between 1903–1919 among Buri͡ats and Tunguses (Evenkis) in Zabaĭkail'e. According to Shirokogoroff, the key goal of the research was a systematic programme for "minute investigations and the collecting of linguistical and ethnographic material concerning Tungus groups" (Shirokogoroff 1923b: 514).

The focus on Zabaĭkal'e was important for two reasons. First, in Petrograd, it seems there were linguists "anxious" for a detailed dataset on Tungus languages in order to better compile their overview of Siberian, Chinese, and Mongolian languages. Second, it was feared that rapid agricultural development and resettlement here would lead to the disappearance of the Tungus tribes, and with them this important insight into the origins of eastern Asian cultures. Thus a need for comprehensiveness, and what we would call today urgent ethnography, led Radlov to send the young couple to step off their train at the railway station of Urul'ga on 7 June 1912 — the place where Matthias Alexander Castren had started his pioneering study of Tungus dialects during his expedition of 1841–1844 (Castren 1856). The couple, therefore, rather than striking out into the frontier were following a well-documented and well-trodden route (Fig. 5.2).

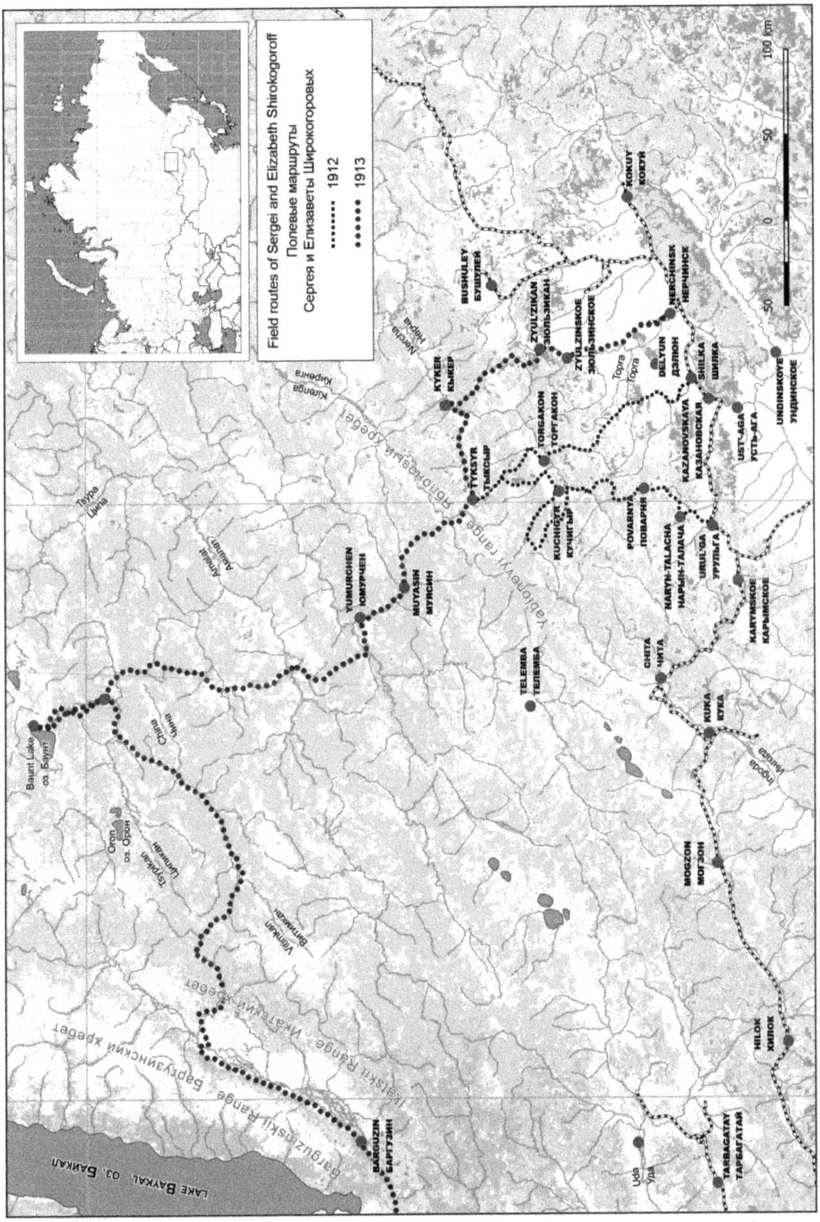

Fig. 5.2 Topographical Map of Zabaĭkal'e illustrating the routes of the two field expeditions of Sergei and Elizaveta Shirokogoroff in 1912 and 1913. Map by Alessandro Pasquini

A defining moment in this first fieldwork seems to have been their disappointment in not finding the same articulate Tunguses whom Castren had met. In a letter to Lev Shternberg, Shirokogoroff confesses:

> We had hoped to find the Tungus language here, but all the Tunguses speak Buri͡at (or likely [Buri͡at-]slang). Those transcriptions which we were able to make show that if the Tungus language is present, it is present in only a very small amount. [...] I have to admit, from the bottom of my heart, that I felt somewhat disoriented. I don't know if I should accept this as a language or not. If they speak a broken Buri͡at, then what would be the reason to study this slang? The Tunguses say that earlier they all spoke Orochen, and that before they could not speak "Tungus" — that is Buri͡at. I decided that while we are living among the Tunguses I will record their misc. words. That's my conclusion. However when we reach the Orochens I will record them as well (SPF RAN 282-2-319: 2–2v).

In order to properly understand Shirokogoroff's disorientation it is important to unpack the hierarchy of identity terms used in this region of Eurasia. As viewed from Petrograd, the region was neatly divided between the broad language families of the Mongolic-speaking Buri͡ats and two distinct groups of Tunguses speaking dialects thought to be related to Manchurian. This ethnolinguistic classification overlapped with government taxation units, each calibrated to the "level of culture" of each people. Therefore, the "settled" Mongolic-speaking Buri͡ats would pay fur tax at the highest rate, the "nomadic" (*kochevye*) Manchu-speaking Tunguses would pay their taxes at a median rate, and the "wandering" (*brodi͡achie*) Tunguses paid their fur tribute at the lowest rate.

The Shirokogoroffs found that the official picture had either changed, or was never detailed enough. Locally, residents distinguished between reindeer-herding Orochens, who were often described as being "wild", and horse-pastoralists — "who once spoke Orochen" — whom they labelled locally as "Tunguses". For a linguistically-oriented fieldworker, it must have been a shock to digest the fact that a clearly Mongolian speech pattern, albeit creolized, was labelled locally as "Tungus".[1]

1 In my own field research in the same region in 1989 and 2004 (Anderson 1991; 2006) I encountered the same hearsay terminology in the village of Kyker. It was common to describe reindeer herders carrying the official nationality "Evenki" as Orochens. Individuals of mixed Orochen-Russian descent, who would be registered

The interplay in Shirokogoroff's mind of pure categories, which did not really exist, and creole categories, which were vibrantly-lived everywhere, would become a central obsession in his thinking. What he would later call his drive "to find laws and regularities" would lead him to treat the linguistic categories as epiphenomenal and to search for regularities in physical form and adaptation.

The couple adapted to their situation in a number of ways. Sergei abandoned his linguistic work and quickly implemented a programme of anthropometric measurement, combined with a detailed household survey, and a set of formal drawings and photographic portraits to accentuate the anthropometry. The main data-set from this part of the fieldwork was a complete set of anthropometric measurements of 91 individuals in Urul'ga, of which the core measurements were of 65 Tungus men and fifteen Tungus women all of which had "pure" Tungus parentage (Shirokogorov and Shirokogorova 1914: 132).

The couple, then, changed their fieldwork itinerary to try to also patch up their linguistic programme. They chose to move from the steppes around Urul'ga northwards into the mountainous taiga to a tributary of the Nercha river called the Akima with the goal of finding a group of Orochens who, as it were, did not yet speak Tungus (Fig. 5.2). They found a settled community of Orochens called Tyksyr consisting of several built log structures in a meadow adjacent to the taiga which served as a hub for other reindeer-herding Orochens. They were to live in this community for an entire month. According to their joint fieldwork report, they collected a vocabulary of 1,800 words, 130 phrases, and five short texts (Shirokogorov and Shirokogorova 1914: 135).[2] We also know from Elizaveta's diary that a programme of anthropometric measurement and anthropometric photography was implemented at Tyksyr, with Elizaveta's participation, and perhaps even led by her (Fig. 5.3). These

as Russians, would describe themselves as Tunguses. This local way of speaking shocked some of my Russian colleagues, as it did Shirokogoroff almost eighty years earlier. They thought our hosts were confused and tried to convine them that they were Evenkis.

2 According to their published report, the vocabulary lists were prepared for publication immediately after the fieldwork but were never published. A recently discovered manuscript dictionary in AMAĖ, dated 1912–1913 but without a classmark (see Appendix), likely corresponds to this document. It is likely that parts of this manuscipt were published by Elizaveta after Sergei's death in a rare Japanese edition (Shirokogoroff 1953, 1944).

measurements, oddly, were never published and were later described by Sergei as being "incomplete". The couple also prospected for and opened several Orochen graves in order to retrieve the skulls of the deceased (Fig. 5.4). Perhaps the most significant part of the Tyksyr collections was a set of artefacts demonstrating aspects of Orochen material cultural. These are a set of small sewn items and a collection of bows and arrows (MAĖ collection No 2003). These items would play an important role in Shirokogoroff's later thinking about Orochen adaptive technology.

Fig. 5.3 Orochen Gorbun as a subject of anthropometric photography in the village of Tyksyr. "Gorbun" is a nickname for "hunchback". Photo by Sergei Shirokogoroff (MAĖ 2002-54). © Peter the Great Museum of Anthropology and Ethnography, Russian Academy of Sciences, St Petersburg

It remains unclear if the anthropometric programme, which the Shirokogoroffs suddenly pulled out of their saddlebags, was originally part of Shternberg's plan for the fieldwork. It seems rather unlikely that this was a last-minute improvisation. On leaving St Petersburg, Sergei had taken care to pack with him his Swiss-made anthropometer

Fig. 5.4 An Orochen above-ground burial, likely for a child, near the settlement of Tyksyr. Elizaveta Shirokogoroff recorded the following in her diary: "2 August. We woke up early due to my ill health. We opened three graves: a child's grave, a woman's and a man's. [...] The child's body was naked. He only had a small cup beside him. All of the bodies had decomposed. We then made tea for the women of the camp, and let them listen to the phonograph" (SPF ARAN 849-5-803: 29). Photo by Sergei Shirokogoroff (MAĖ 2002–12). © Peter the Great Museum of Anthropology and Ethnography, Russian Academy of Sciences, St Petersburg

(a set of calibrated rods holding a set of clamps used for measuring the body), and two callipers (used for measuring the skull and hands) — suggesting that he had always planned to follow his own programme of measurement (Shirokogoroff 1923a: 1). We also know that he signed out his equipment from the common storeroom of equipment that Ol'denburg and Shternberg kept for the Russian Committee for the Study of Central and Eastern Asia (SPF ARAN 148-1-22: 68). Perhaps his intention to perform an anthropometric study was one reason why he refused the funding offered by Radlov and preferred to self-finance the expedition himself.

It also remains unclear how Shirokogoroff actually received his anthropometric training. The anthropometry of Paul Broca would certainly have formed a large part of the courses that Sergei audited at l'École d'anthropologie in Paris. We further know that Sergei may have audited two courses in St Petersburg taught by Fëdor Volkov on ethnography and human anatomy (TsGIA SPb 14-3-59098: 29v). However, more likely than not, Sergei was improvising in this fieldwork since it seems he had no direct experience carrying out these measurements in the past.

What is clear is that the anthropometric measurements of the Zabaĭkal Tunguses and Orochens would exercise a lasting effect on Sergei's thinking and writing. They would be the topic of his first unpublished manuscript entitled *The Nomadic Tunguses: Anthropological Studies* (SPF ARAN 849-6-806), which he wrote in between the first and the second Zabaĭkal expeditions. Further, we know that by 20 September 1917, Sergei Shirokogoroff would be co-opted into the role of Head of Department of Physical Anthropology in the Museum of Anthropology and Ethnography by recommending himself not by his training "but by his enthusiasm" (SPF ARAN 4-4-672: 1). His first academic publication was a methodological essay on how to properly measure Eurasian peoples (wherein he advertised the existence of his then unpublished anthropological measurements from Zabaĭkal'e) (Shirokogorov 1919: 25,41). The measurements that the couple first made would be analysed and published only in 1923 in a wide-ranging volume entitled *The Anthropology of Northern China* comparing a number of peoples across eastern Eurasia (Shirokogoroff 1923a). This publication shortly followed the Russian-language debut of his *etnos* theory first in pamphlet form and then in book form (Shirokogorov 1923, 1922).

From the surviving field materials, it would seem that the anthropometric work was not easy to do. In his published work, Sergei mentions that he was forced to omit certain anthropometric body measurements in order to minimize the discomfort of his informants (Shirokogoroff 1923a: 2; Shirokogorov 1919: 18). In her diary, Elizaveta notes that many of the Tunguses living closer to the railway were skittish of the anthropometric work, and would have to be convinced:

> 3 July [1912]
>
> We arrived at 2 o'clock in Delĭun. Our neighbours came by and we talked.
>
> Sergei went out visiting the ĭurts, but he was only able to complete his survey in 8 ĭurts.

> Everyone treats us with mistrust and with the fear that their life would later get worse [if they participated]. Many are even afraid to be photographed. They even do not ask to be photographed.
>
> Sergei has to endure many squabbles. He patiently explained why the measurements were necessary. In Del͡iun the Tunguses are more skittish than in other places. This seems to be due to their proximity to civilisation (SPF ARAN 849-5-803: 12-12v).

To allay the Tunguses' fears, Elizaveta made creative use of the phonograph she and her husband carried with them. Almost every evening was spent replaying the songs recorded on that day, or playing music that the couple brought with them. In their jointly published field report, the couple report that having a phonograph is highly recommended for any fieldwork:

> Based on our own experience with using phonographic recordings, we came to the conclusion that a phonograph, even of an older design, is very useful and necessary for fieldwork especially for the study of motifs. Playing-back our already-recorded motifs and stores made such a wonderful impression on the Orochens and Tunguses. The stories that they themselves recorded were understandable, and comic stories made them lively and provoked them to laugh. I [sic] would like to note that not all Orochens enjoyed European music but some found it so pleasing that they listened to the same cylinder three or four times. The first part of Beethoven's IV symphony [Symphony no. 4 in b-flat major opis 60] was particularly popular (Shirokogorov and Shirokogorova 1914: 136).

In their day-to-day work, a phonograph concert was often a first step to organizing the anthropometric work:

> 19 [July 1912] We were famished upon returning home and we immediately started to prepare food and we shared it with <unclear> the Elder and *Kandidat*. The latter was extremely happy and smiled to himself. Our moods were very high. We took a few photographs and wound-up the phonograph. One of the boys out of excitement sung four wonderful cylinders. Sergei decided to start his anthropometric measurements.
>
> He measured two without any resistance. However when he called for the Elder's nephew it immediately triggered an unexpected resistance. The Elder categorically stated he would not give up his nephew since things would only get worse for him if did. [He cried out,] "Leave me the boy! I beg you, please leave him" with a fearful, threatening intonation. He was extremely distraught at that time. He would not listen to anyone,

> and all of the time interrupted and stated his position. He did not seem to have any effect on the bystanders and I think that in a little while we can go back to the anthropometry (SPF ARAN 849-5-803: 19v-20).

From what we can deduct from the archive, the anthropometric work always had a similar routine. Typically men, women, and children — or preferably entire families — would be posed in front of the same standard backdrop — typically a log building. If individual portraits were taken they were done frontal and profile. Extrapolating from the Shirokogoroffs' publications, calipers were used to measure the length and breadth of the head, the forehead and important feature such as the ocular and nasal cavities. The anthropometer was used to measure the body height and the length of the forearms and thighs. The device was mounted on a plank evidently preventing Sergei from measuring the leg bones. Twenty-three absolute measurements were taken in what was said to be an international programme approved in Geneva in 1912 (Shirokogoroff 1923a: 1–3).

An interesting photographic artefact of this fieldwork is the smiling portrait of one young Tungus (Fig. 5.5). At first glance it seems a typical anthropometric photograph, with the subject holding up a sign declaring himself to be of mixed descent. His somewhat puzzled expression stands in a sullen contrast to the label, making it an evocative photograph. However, from consulting Elizaveta's diary, we learn that Mélange was not a category but a nickname that the couple gave to one of their most important informants in the village. Mélange helped them organize meetings, helped with translations, and in general facilitated their fieldwork. The photograph, therefore, seems somewhat more like a souvenir (despite the anthropometric notations below the title). This playful use of the concept of mixed descent seemed to foreshadow the creative way that Shirokogoroff would soon write about the subject.

Upon returning to St Petersburg, the first intellectual product of the fieldwork was devoted to a short unpublished essay on physical anthropology focussing exclusively on the mysterious nomadic Tunguses (SPF ARAN 849-6-806: 239, 242, 244–56) along with a second, perhaps linked, fragment describing their geographic location (SPF ARAN 849-6-806: 72, 100–24v). The anthropological essay consists of sets of absolute skull and body measurements, and

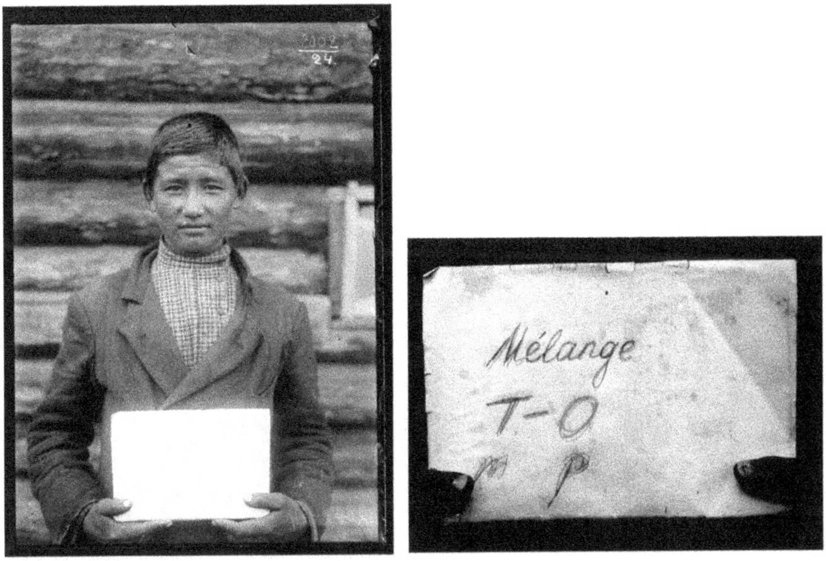

Fig. 5.5 A portrait of the local Tungus guide "Mélange". The sign he is holding is in Elizaveta's handwriting. The notations likely mean Tungus-Orochen. This would be consistent with other handwritten notes. The bottom line is more mysterious but could refer to parentage — such as "mère — père". This would be the only surviving photograph classified in this manner (MAĖ 2002–24). © Peter the Great Museum of Anthropology and Ethnography, Russian Academy of Sciences, St Petersburg

coefficients derived therefrom, enlivened by a set of ten drawings and photographs (which are missing from the archive). From his initial measurements of the above mentioned 91 individuals, Shirokogoroff distinguished two different groups by the length of their heads, their body height, and the length of their arms — which he labelled type A and type B (Fig. 5.6). He associated the long-headed type B with the horse pastoralist Tunguses — especially those living at Naryn-Talacha (Fig. 5.7). He also associated this type with the Buri͡at population. He associated his short-headed type A with the cattle pastoralist Tunguses at Torgakon (Fig. 5.8). He notes that there were signs of another unidentified type — likely that associated with the reindeer herding Orochens — which Shirokogoroff would hint at in many publications but never specify.

ТАБЛИЦА.

Признаки	Типъ. А.	Типъ В.
Ростъ	Низкiй	Высокiй
Фор. ~~Уха~~ Головы	Длинн~~оголовый~~ая	Коротк~~оголовый~~ая
Форма лица	Узко~~лицый~~е	Широко~~лицый~~е
Высота головы	Высокая	Низкая
Относ. ширина нижн. челюсти	Широкая	Узкая
Форма носа	Широкiй	Узкiй
Форма лба	Высокiй	низкiй
Ширина лба	Узкiй	Широкiй
Абс. ширина нижн. челюсти	Узкая	Широкая
Относит. высота головы (къ росту)	Высокая	Низкая
Длина головы	Короткая	Длинная
Отн. длина руки	Короткая	Длинная
Отн. дл. предплечья съ кистью	Короткая	Длинная

Fig. 5.6 Table of anthropometric qualities distinguishing type A and type B (SPF ARAN 849-6-806 249). © St Petersburg Filial of the Archive of the Russian Academy of Sciences

Fig. 5.7 "Type Beta": two unidentified Buriat men posing at the steppe at Naryn Talacha (MAÉ 2002–64). © Peter the Great Museum of Anthropology and Ethnography, Russian Academy of Sciences, St Petersburg

Fig. 5.8 "Type Alpha": Tungus Afanasiĭ with his wife and another unidentified relative posing at their home in Torgakon (MAĖ 2002–81). © Peter the Great Museum of Anthropology and Ethnography, Russian Academy of Sciences, St Petersburg

The conclusion to this unpublished manuscript outlines an ambitious pan-hemispheric research programme based on his analysis of these 91 individuals. By consulting sets of anthropometric photographs made by other fieldworkers, he identified similar long-headed types among Soĭots (SPF ARAN 849-6-806: 253), Eniseĭ Osti͡aks [Kets] (Ibid: 254), the Northern Tunguses documented by Ivan I. Maĭnov (1901) (Ibid: 255), and even North American indigenous peoples (Ibid: 256). Here he for the first time makes references to the need to critically evaluate "ethnic groups" (*ėtnicheskie gruppy*) by making a call to liberate the local peoples of Siberia and eastern Asia from belonging to a "Mongoloid race" (Ibid: 254).

From this first fieldwork, and from a relatively small sample of measurements, Sergei penned his first insight that anthropometric typologies could be used to break down the dominant system of ethnolinguistic classification. There seems to be a direct link of this ambitious programme to his disenchantment with the linguistic categories he found on the ground during his first fieldwork.

It is remarkable how stable Shirokogoroff's first field typology became. In 1923, in *The Anthropology of Northern China* (Shirokogoroff 1923a), he would republish the same measurements of the same 91 individuals he met at Urul'ga in a comparative dataset with the measurements taken from Chinese, Manchus and Koreans. In this work the Buri͡ats and Nomadic Tunguses became type-Delta, while the reindeer herding Orochens were distinguished as type-Gamma (Fig. 5.9). He later used the fact that Gamma-type features were distributed all across China as a proof of the southern origin of the Tungus tribes and his hypothesis that they were a "guiding [*rukovodi͡ashchiĭ*] *etnos*" of Asia (Shirokogoroff 1925: 134; 1923b: 618; 1926: 177 n4).

Fig. 5.9 "Type Gamma". This photograph from Tyksyr was published in Czaplicka's classic work *Aboriginal Siberia* (Czaplicka 1914: plate 11). The original negative, reproduced here, is in MAĖ 2002–42. Shirokogoroff published a correction to her attributions of his photograph in a self-published brochure where he identifies the man as a "Nerchinsk Tungus representing type Gamma" (Shirokogoroff 1932: 47 n39). © Peter the Great Museum of Anthropology and Ethnography, Russian Academy of Sciences, St Petersburg

It would seem that Shirokogoroff's first unpublished treatise on physical anthropology was written in a flush of enthusiasm and remained a point of reference throughout his life. He had intended to publish it, but the couple left for Chita almost immediately on 10 May 1913 for their second expedition, and with the exception of short return visit in 1917, never again returned to St Petersburg. The typescript on physical anthropology was constantly cited by Shirokogoroff as if it had been published and consultable, and in some cases, with the fear and conviction that it had already been widely pirated. Very much later he would confide to his friend Kotwicz his worries that Shternberg coveted the manuscript as a "museum reference" (BPANvK 4600 t.7 folio 55v).

It is curious that in these 1913 texts one also finds a politicised distaste for how the Orochens are treated and a liberal concern over the "dying-out" of this nationality. This is somewhat ironic given his sharp criticism of Shternberg for his paternalistic politics (see chapter 6). This section differs little from that of other Russian liberal writers of the turn of the last century:

> Recently, Russian traders play a large role, if not the main role in the lives of Orochens. They call the traders "friends" (*druz'i͡a*). These friends literally rob these unlucky wild people (*dikareĭ*). Their system of fleecing the Orochens is very simple. The trader gives an Orochen on credit cloth, dishes, gunpowder, flour, etc., and the Orochen is obliged to repay the debt either in December, when the squirrel season is over, or by Ivanov Day [23 June], when the reindeer velvet horn season is finished. At this time the nearby Russian settlements organize a market, and the Orochens all gather there. Since there are no other buyers other than the traders who had advanced credits, the traders set the prices on the fur or horns, etc. The Orochens are forced to accept the offer of their "friends" at the prices that are convenient for the trader. [...] Gradually out of the decline and death of their reindeer, the Orochens are becoming fewer and soon will die out completely, as many other Siberian peoples have died out (SPF ARAN 849-6-806: 110–11).

It would seem that his first shock at encountering a highly creolized group at Urul'ga, that was neither Mongol nor Tungus, took hold of Shirokogoroff's imagination. To his credit, what he first experienced as an enigmatic creolism — a population lacking a single clear language but yet displaying a strong cultural "equilibrium" — did not lead him to turn his back on the community and discard his measurements as polluted. Instead, according to his reminiscences in 1930, it drove him to form an early idea of how "growth and decline" [assimilation] could lead to a newly sustainable cultural form:

> Early work on the problem of population and correlation of cultural and other phenomena characteristic of the *etnos* in 1912 led me to the idea of binding this relationship into [a] simple formula [...] It may here be noted that the idea of such a relationship was formulated during my first travelling in Siberia when I saw a series of ethnical groups showing the same kind of equilibrium, but existing under different conditions. The field observations of other groups during following expeditions (1913–1918) has strengthened the impression of the reality of such a relationship, which was naturally supported by well-known facts from historic records, and by observations of other travellers (Shirokogoroff 1930: 16 n1).

Typically for Shirokogoroff, and frustratingly for his readers, it is never quite clear what he imagined as the "same kind of equilibrium". The formula he cites parodies anthropometric calculations to demonstrate that a robust sustainable cultural type — the *etnos* — can come about through the balance of technological advances, population expansion, climate — all of which are confined by the competitive pressure of neighbouring "ethnical units" (Shirokogoroff 1930: 34–35). It remains unclear how anyone could ever assign numbers to these elements in the same way that one could measure a skull — and Shirokogoroff nowhere provides an example of his equation in action. The only detailed examples he gives are random cultural or historical examples, such as the rise and fall of the popularity of the *dormeuse* horse carriage in France (Ibid: 30–33) or how the Manchu plough and Manchu millet mill facilitated Manchu territorial expansion (Shirokogoroff 1924b: 135–38). As will be discussed in the next section, a similar techno-cultural trigger in Tungus civilisation was the shaman's costume — a veritable toolbox of metallic instruments used to regulate relationships with the land-spirits.

The common denominator in these three examples was how a single determining material artefact could facilitate the expansion of an ethno-cultural group over space. What remains unique in this anthropometric-fueled ecological anthropology was that he did not reduce adaptation to physical form. The mixture of anthropological types among the pastoralist Tungus was proof that their robust livelihood attracted and assimilated bodies from surrounding groups. What he saw in the adaptation of the bodies of the "older" type Gamma-form was an equally robust adaptation that was forced to confine itself in the mountainous regions "away from civilization" for ecological reasons. Through his interest in adaptation and the selective use of new technologies, including new languages, Shirokogoroff's snail had crawled some distance away from the authority of ethnolinguistic typologies.

A Curious Guest at the Wedding: The 1913 Zabaĭkal Expedition

Fig. 5.10 Sergei Shirokogoroff at home. St Petersburg. Before 1917 (EVR)

The Shirokogoroffs did not rest much in St Petersburg (Fig. 5.10). Aside from drafting at least three manuscripts over the winter of 1912–1913, they lobbied for, and accepted, funding for a return expedition to Zabaĭkal'e. They departed St Petersburg on 10 May 1913 and would remain in the field until the frosty deep autumn of 20 September 1913. The Shirokogoroffs re-focused the work of the second expedition on the reindeer-herding Orochens living in the Northerly taiga regions of what is today Zabaĭkal'skiĭ Kraĭ and Buri͡atii͡a. With superior financing, the couple was able to purchase a team of horses and hire guides — whom Shirokogoroff, perhaps ironically, evaluated anthropometrically:

> I decided to change the guide/translator. But aside from him I had hired yet another Russian-anthropoid for the loading of horses, the care of the horses, etc. This expense will mean we will overspend our anticipated [budget] but there was nothing to be done. One man cannot look after 6 horses. I bought the horses at a price not over what we had budgeted (SPF ARAN 282-2-319: 3v).

They began their work this time along the Nercha river tributaries and rather ambitiously covered the entire territory of Zabaĭkal'e returning via Lake Baikal (Fig. 5.1). According to their report they covered 1,500 *versty* [1,600 km] on horseback (Shirokogorov and Shirokogorova 1914).

This expedition is not well represented in the archives (see Appendix 1). We do know from their published report that they compiled further word lists and texts documenting the Nerchinsk and Baunt Orochen dialects, that they measured another 111 individuals (mostly men), and collected an equally rich library of 100 photographic plates, twenty wax cylinder recordings, drawings, and artefacts (Shirokogorov and Shirokogorova 1914) — although most of these have not been found. A rich collection of shamanic artefacts from this region, however, does still exist in the museum (MAĖ collection No 2216). Aside from the published reports, the richest source we have on this expedition are a series of letters that he shared with Shternberg from the field, and a comprehensive untitled unpublished manuscript which Shirokogoroff would later cite in English as *The Ethnography of the Orochen of Transbaikalia.*

The letters that Shirokogoroff sent from the field were confident and operational. He provided Shternberg with updates on the quantities of anthropometric measurements they managed to make and often made requests for money to purchase artefacts for the museum. An intriguing part of the correspondence, which is partly reflected in the published reports, is the fieldwork method of amassing ethnographic and anthropometric data by participating in regional weddings. As Sergei would recount to Shternberg in one letter:

> As you can see, I did make it in the end to the Bargunzin taiga. This came about due to a great degree of luck. After one Orochen wedding we travelled with the Orochens further westwards to another wedding. After the second wedding, we travelled with the Orochens to a third.

> These wedding-excursions were very successful. Many people gathered together and it was possible to choose the appropriate [informants] for our work. At the weddings it was possible to even find the shaman with whom I think I have struck up a friendship. I ran into one elder at one wedding, and at the third another was supposed to attend. Both of them I believe will be able to give us linguistic data - stories. I have been able make a lot of ethnographic observations. There are some differences between the Barguzin [Orochens} and the Nercha [Orochens]. They also differ linguistically, although by a small degree. Because of the large weddings we were able to measure 47 people. I intend to measure the same amount at the third. In a word, we will have anthropological data. Up until now we have travelled 600 *verst* on horseback (SPF ARAN 282-2-319: 5–5v).

The correspondence gives a clear impression of the routinization of a mobile laboratory where the Shirokogoroffs would take advantage of these festive assemblies of kin to photograph, measure skulls, and document folklore. It's possible that the festive group and family portraits that the couple likely took during these weddings might have been designed also to function as surreptitious anthropometric photographs (Fig. 5.11).

Fig. 5.11 A "formal reception" but perhaps a wedding photograph taken during the 1912 expedition in the village of Naryn Talacha, in June. The Shirokogoroffs are sitting in the middle of the photograph in white clothing (Fragment MAĖ 2002–66). © Peter the Great Museum of Anthropology and Ethnography, Russian Academy of Sciences, St Petersburg

This wedding-centred fieldwork seemed to have had a second far more interesting impact on the Shirokogoroffs' thinking. The surviving manuscripts suggest that the attention of the couple seems to have shifted away from an interest in anthropometry to classic topics of social organization and kinship. This is deeply reflected in Sergei's long manuscript on Orochen ethnography. At 189 folios, it is by far his most complex reflection on the reindeer herding Orochens. It moves paragraph by paragraph to summarize economic activities, kinship, material culture, and belief in much the objective fashion as one would expect to find in a late nineteenth-century text. It reads very well for the ethnological standards of the time.

Moreover, the Orochens in this text are *recognizable* — the text speaks dryly but truthfully to a way of life which to some extent is still present in the northern regions of Zabaĭkal'skiĭ Kraĭ. In some sense, this focused ethnography reads more convincingly than the assorted snapshots of Orochen life which would later be cut and pasted into composite works such as the *Social Organization* and the *Psychomental Complex.* This manuscript would never be published, and given the haphazard way it was deposited in the archive, was likely never properly read by anyone (see Appendix 1).

The original intention of the Shirokogoroffs was to publish the text upon their return from their 1916–1917 Manchurian fieldwork, but a series of events prevented this. First, for reasons beyond their control, the couple made a hasty decision to leave Russia in the events leading up to the second Russian revolution — which separated them from their archive of drawings and manuscripts (see chapter 6). Further, it seems that Sergei's thinking had continued to unwind since the fieldwork. Writing the foreword to his *Social Organization* in Shanghai in 1929, he dreamt of writing a manuscript exclusively about material culture based on the Zabaĭkal fieldwork should he ever regain access to these collections. Further, he explained how his thoughts on Tungus identity had changed after his 1916–1917 fieldwork with the Manchus. He saw the Manchu complex (Shirokogoroff 1924b) as a pale reflection of a more general Tungus adaptation which was best illustrated by the Orochens with whom they once lived. The unpublished manuscript on the Orochens, therefore, is very useful as a snapshot of his thinking about social identity, and how it might have unwound in a different direction instead of the one neat spiral pathway that gave birth to his mature *etnos* theory in 1933.

There are two striking qualities of this enormous manuscript, which may come as a surprise to those familiar with Shirokogoroff's later English-language work. The first is a somewhat disorienting shift in the way he identifies his subject of study — the term Tungus is almost entirely absent in this text. The second is the heavy emphasis on the classification and description of artefacts, clothing, weapons, and tools, which seems to be the result of his ongoing interest in adaptive technology.

Shirokogoroff tended to frame his study in terms of the administrative and tax divisions which divided Tungus and Orochen groups geographically. However, this text has the quality of an investigative report, which probes the inaccuracies of Tsarist administrative classifications. Breaking with his earlier texts, from the first paragraphs he distinguished the reindeer-herding Orochens from the pastoralist Tungus, applying the the term Tungus — which today is usually associated with reindeer herders — exclusively to horse pastoralist populations:

> Officially, the Orochons are divided into 6 groups: Baunt, Angara, Podelmor, 2 groups of Nercha, and finally the Olekma Orochen. The first three groups are called Tunguses and the latter three — Orochens. I am accepting only the second name and will apply it all Zabaĭkal Tungus reindeer herders (folio 18).
>
> [The name Orochen] is derived from *orón* — reindeer, and it means "of the deer". In contrast one can hear *múrcher, murche'sal,* which are derived from *muri'in* — horse, or perhaps one might translate as "of the horse" (SPF ARAN 849-6-806: 19).

The slippery nomenclature used by Shirokogoroff for these regional groups can be linked to his first shock over the inconsistency between the hearsay categories in the Tungus villages and the authorized identifiers in Tsarist tax registers. In this manuscript, he chose to divorce the "real" reindeer-herding Orochens from the Tungus label, relegating the Tungus to the mixed, creolized steppe communities to the south. This pragmatic classification, which cleaves close to local ways of speaking, would not emerge in the published work of the couple. In the jointly published field report (1914), the couple would place their emphasis on Buriats and Tunguses (and the different types of pure or impure groups in between) with a fleeting reference to reindeer-herding Orochens. In a later publication of the couple's future fieldwork in

Manchuria, Elizaveta would flip the classification by making Orochen the master category for all of the groups — horse pastoralist and/or reindeer pastoralist — that are today distinguished as separate Evenki and Orochen nationalities (Shirokogorova 1919). In his overview of all his fieldwork (Shirokogoroff 1923b), and then in each of his famous publications, Sergei would revert to grouping all the Zabaĭkal indigenes together as Tunguses.

On the one hand, there is nothing terribly surprising about these shifts in ethnographic terminology. Ethnographers wield an extraordinary power to define the boundaries of groups and to offer expert advice on which groups are pure and which are mixed. However, given that Shirokogoroff's later theory was defined by its ability to peer inside this process, one is tempted to hold him to a higher standard. The casualness with which Shirokogoroff himself assigned and reassigned identities suggests that at least to some degree the equilibrium-formation process of the *etnos* was as much in the eye of the beholder than an objective reality on the ground.

On the other hand, the use of local hearsay classifications in direct contradiction to formal administrative and linguistic orthodoxy points to an early instance of Shirogoroff's use of what we today would describe as performative identities. By citing the roots of local expressions, Shirokogoroff employs an evaluative framework within which "real" Orochens are the ones travelling with reindeer, while *murcher* travel with horses. The fact that ethnic names might be keyed to how people move on the landscape is a type of pragmatic classification. This is one example of how his somewhat unwieldy, mathematical system of identity might have unwound in a different direction towards a culturalist or relativistic understanding of identity. It is directly related to his ecological or "equilibric" vision of distinguishing reindeer pastoralists from horse pastoralists.

A similar argument can be made of Shirogoroff's discussion of clan identity and kinship discourse — much of which was also never carried over into the published, English language works. The discussion of clan names begins in a section on "clan groups" (SPF ARAN 849-6-806: 25v-26v). The concept of a group is described as a finer designation than the regional/dialect groups thought to exist among Barguzin or Angara Orochens. From the first paragraph, Shirokogoroff notes that the three officially designated clans "absolutely do not correspond to reality"

(Ibid: 25v). In order to untangle the real from the unreal, Shirokogoroff organizes his fieldnotes into a table showing the presence and absence of exogamy between named clans (Ibid: 29). In his analysis, Shirokogoroff places a special emphasis on the suffix *-gir*, which is often placed at the end of many Evenki clan names, as a special marker to distinguish ancient clans (Ibid). The conclusion of his comparison is a second table which breaks down the three officially recognized administrative clans into two parallel sets of local clan names as recognized by the Orochens themselves (Fig. 5.12).

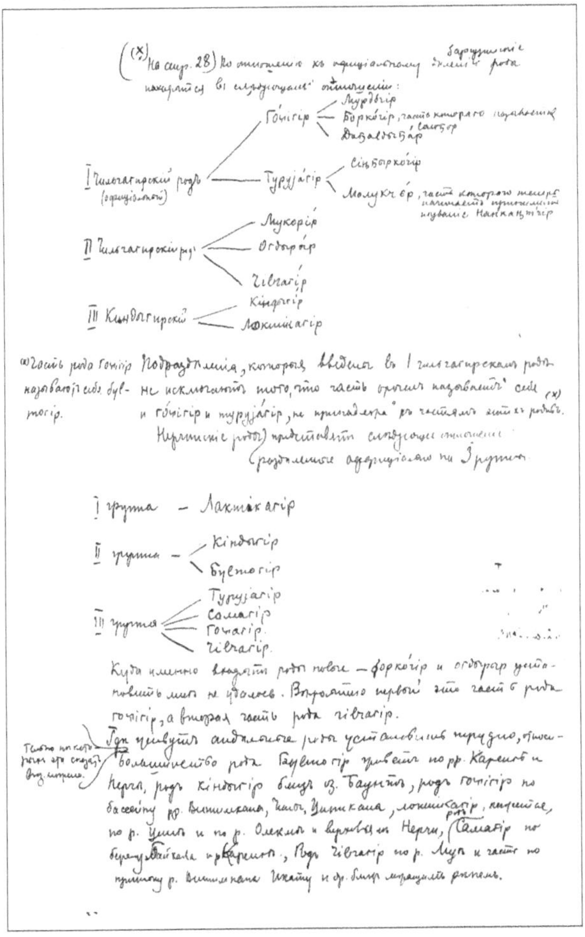
(x) На стр. 28) По отношению къ официальному делению рода находятся въ следующемъ отношении:

I Чильчагирский родъ (официальный) — Гочiгiр — Мурдыгiр, Боркогiр, Дабалдыбар; — Турујагiр — Сiнборкогiр, Молукчогiр

II Чильчагирский родъ — Лукорiр, Огдорпр, Чiвчагiр

III Киндыгирский — Кiндогiр, Локшикагiр

I группа — Лакшикагiр

II группа — Кiндогiр, Буемогiр

III группа — Турујагiр, Самагiр, Гочагiр, Чiвчагiр

Куда именно входятъ роды новые — Боркогiр и Огдорпр установить мне не удалось. Вероятно первые это часть рода Гочiгiр, а вторая часть рода Чiвчагiр.

Fig. 5.12 A handwritten table demonstrating how official Tsarist administrative units break up into living clan groupings (SPF ARAN 849-6-806: 29v). © St Petersburg Filial of the Archive of the Russian Academy of Sciences

Unfortunately, this particular discussion on clans does not branch out into a pragmatic or performative examination of marriage strategy and alliance. Missing in the manuscript are illustrations of clan fission or fusion in practice. The manuscript presents an authoritative summary of how each clan "fits". This is somewhat disappointing knowing, as we do, that the couple participated in a large number of weddings, and presumably witnessed the joking, and the inevitable skirmishes that would have occurred during these events. They do provide, however some intriguing hints of who Orochens consider to be a good match:

> The Orochens say that marriages with Tungus women are not desirable since the Tungus women will run away from their husbands. I can see that this would be possible since these women are used to living all of the time in warm dwellings in the steppes. Life in the taiga — in the tents — with all of the difficulties of constant travel on reindeer, and the care of the reindeer, would make it difficult to get used to these new conditions. For a Tungus woman, a marriage with an Orochen would be considered a *mésalliance* [sic]. The Tunguses, in their turn, look down upon the Orochens since "Orochens do not own permanent dwellings and wander the forests like animals". The Tunguses adopted this attitude to the Orochens likely from the Buri͡ats (folio 33).

On the whole, in this early manuscript there is a strong ambiguity in Shirokogoroff's ethnography about the solidity of group boundaries. On the one hand, he confidently dissolves existing governmental administrative divisions with evidence of the mismatch between exogamy and alliance practice and pre-existing designations. Further, he is sensitive to local racial hierarchies and performative aspects of identity management. However, on the other hand, he asserts the authority of the urban ethnographer to declare correct ethnic applications (although here his own designations vacillate back and forth).

The second strong, and sometimes surprising quality of Shirokogoroff's writing after the second expedition is its emphasis on material culture in almost every chapter. The Orochen manuscript is divided into four numbered chapters roughly arranged by topic: Geography, Subsistence Strategy, Social Relationships, and Belief. While at first glance each bundle of topics sound like a classic ethnological overview, each chapter is built around descriptions of objects. Thus, a description of hunting strategy is not complete without a three-page typology of arrows (folios 43–44). Or, a description of worldview is framed by a description of clothing the Orochen shaman would wear with all of its metallic icons (folios 66–68, 219–35). On the one hand, this is perhaps not surprising. The young Shirokogoroff was trained as a museum cataloguer and an avid collector of statistics about things. His typology of arrows would likely have informed late nineteenth century ethnological debates about cultural evolution. His description of a shaman's dress would undoubtedly be used to contextualize the artefacts already on display in the museum. The fact that every two-sentence description also had an Orochen word attached to it undoubtedly reflects his first research goal as a collector of word lists.

However reading between the lines, the sometimes numbing descriptions of material culture can also be read with his eye for "growth and decline" and "ethnical equilibria". Thus in the midst of a discussion of hunting technique, we are given a relatively long section on household belongings (*utvar'*), ranging from tea kettles to reindeer harnesses. Shirokogoroff's attention to materiality would be on par with a contemporary ethnoarchaeologist. He would distinguish the materials within an object as a way of establishing inter-regional or inter-*etnos* contacts. On the other hand, he would be quick to evaluate the pragmatic qualities of the acquired objects contextualizing how they fit into the "equilibrium" of a certain subsistence strategy — for example, that of a highly mobile hunting camp. Thus, the objects of daily use on the one hand draw Orochens into regular communication with their neighbours, yet within a curious limit that defines their lifestyle:

> [...] they take from the I͡Akuts most of the daily items they need like the tools needed for working with skins, and previously, spears and machetes (*pal'my*). They obtain copper items from the Buri͡ats: pots, pipes, and similar items. Today the household items of the Russians are pushing out the I͡Akut and Buri͡at items. Copper pots are being replaced by teapots and enamel dishes. Wooden plates are being replaced with ceramic plates.
>
> The most necessary household goods for the Orochens are a pot, kettle, dishes, tables, a set of birch-bark containers, sacks of various sizes made of skins, hooks for setting above the fire, spoons, pliers, large and small knives, a spear, a saw, and an axe. The richer [Orochens], that is the ones with more people in their family have more items, but their quantity is always limited. Orochens do not like unnecessary items and they abandon them when travelling (Folio 130).

A similar line of argument characterizes his description of shamanic equipment. Shirokogoroff states that he received his information from ten different shamans, the majority of whom were women. According to what he was told shamans divide themselves into those performing with elk-styled costumes and those performing with "duck-" [more likely, loon] styled costumes. Only one shaman in the region performed as an elk (Fig. 5.13). The dearth of shamanic elks was associated by the Orochens themselves with the decline in the good fortunes of the Zabaĭkal Orochens (Folio 58). The growth and decline of the Orochen lifestyle is thus roughly reflected in their costumes. This idea is crudely thought out in the manuscript.

Fig. 5.13 Detailed photograph of a Tungus "elk" shaman and his costume taken at Naryn-Talacha around 7 June 1912. The photograph emphasises the metallic elements to the costume including the circular mirror *tolchi* (MAĖ 2002–58). © Peter the Great Museum of Anthropology and Ethnography, Russian Academy of Sciences, St Petersburg

Here Shirokogoroff carries on a rhetorical argument with his Orochen shaman informants across several folios about meaning behind the quantity and character of the iron artefacts sewn onto a shamanic costume. He notes with cautious irony that the "duck" shamans claim that the rare and hard-to-find metallic objects should ideally not be sewn onto their costumes:

> On one [duck] tunic one might find only the bones of [a set of] wings, and on another there might be different bones — the backbone or the shoulder blades, etc. It can be the case that there would not be one metallic object on either the tunic or the entire costume. According to the shamans, a real duck-costume should not have any metallic objects [...] the metallic objects could interfere during the shaman's flight — they might make the shaman too heavy. This explanation is unlikely to be true [...] (folios 224–25).

Shirokogoroff goes on to argue with the consistency of this argument demonstrating that various types of metallic objects, or even "elk" objects can be found on other air-bound costumes (folios 222–26). From other parts of this manuscript it seems clear that the small society of local shamans was struggling to keep up with their clan duties and ritual performances in this quickly changing environment. Much like those squirrel hunters suffering the exploitative terms of trade of their "friends", the shamans seemed to have adapted their performances and their equipment to their available materials. It is in somewhat argumentative passages like this that one can find glimpses of the more pragmatic descriptions Shirokogoroff would write later of the various types of spirits and the clever ways that shamans engage with them. Shirokogoroff concludes his overview of shamanic apparati with a touching insight into the difficult if not exploitative life of a shaman:

> It is without a doubt that each performance extracts much energy and strength from a shaman. After a session, and I have witnessed three large performances and at least ten smaller ones, the shaman is literally exhausted, even if he had not drank [alcohol] or smoked. [...] I twice observed that the [female] shamans shed tears during the performance at particularly pathetic moments. At the end of the performance all male and female shamans were covered in a cold sweat (folios 58–59).

While grounded in the objective style of a nineteenth-century ethnological manuscript, Shirokogoroff's first ethnological treatise describes how various aspects of Orochen society remains in equilibrium or risks being torn apart. In this way, the text frames the goals of the second expedition to document a population described by the state as either Tungus or Orochen, who at their heart formed a single *etnos*. The core of this *etnos* was an anthrometrically distinct people, with a hunting equilibrium defined by their modest use of adaptive technologies. At the same time, one can see glimpses of a thoughtful, pragmatically engaged people who — through ritual and clan organizaiton — creatively adapted to an exploitative colonial situation.

Conclusion: "Equilibria", "Valence", and the Snail Metaphor

Sergei Shirokogoroff would go on to build on his intuition that the heavily assimilated, and poverty-striken Zabaĭkal Orochens and Tunguses nevertheless displayed a unique "ethnical equilibrium". In contrast to the declining Manchus, he represented the Tunguses and Orochens of his very first fieldwork as people with a high cultural consistency despite their vulnerability to external forces. He noted that they would prefer to retreat to the most inaccessible alpine taiga to continue to hunt and herd reindeer than be incorporated into the expanding Mongolic milieu around them. His painstaking physical anthropological work was intended to illustrate the continuity of physcial types within the groups in spite of linguistic and cultural assimilation. From his first fieldwork he developed the counter-intuitive idea that a demographically sparse, hunting culture could define the ethnic landscape of half of a continent.

As he wrote up his material first within White-controlled Vladivostok, and then in China, he began to design the increasingly convoluted equations which still puzzle some readers today. Sergei would come to represent the "ethnical equilibrium as the coefficient ω [small omega]. This coefficient could be calculated by estimating the density of the population and relating it to a numeric figure for territory to a numerical value of culture. Critically, to make the equation work, a highly trained expert was needed to put a number to "cultured-ness" (Shirokogoroff 1924a: 11). The strength of a people's "ethnical equilibrium" would further be influenced by the vibrancy of its neighbours (Fig. 5.14a). Here, Shirokogoroff tried to model the way that one cultural group could influence, or be incorporated into a neighbouring group.

change of one of two of the other elements, the impulses and their effects will be equal. Thus if

$$\pm i_{ST} = \omega \frac{\Delta q}{q} \quad \text{and} \quad \pm i_{Sq} = \omega \frac{\Delta T}{T}, \quad \text{where} \quad i_{ST} = i_{Sq},$$

so $$\omega \frac{\Delta q}{q} = \omega \frac{\Delta T}{T}, \quad \text{whence} \quad \Delta q = q \frac{\Delta T}{T}$$

on the supposition that the culture remains the same.

By the same reasoning we may thus formulate,—

$$\Delta T = T \frac{\Delta S}{S} \quad \text{the population being the same;} \quad \Delta S = S \frac{\Delta T}{T}$$

the population being the same. I cannot go into the very interesting details as to the effects of the same impulses on

Fig. 5.14a The ethnical equilibrium as represented in *The Psychomental Complex of the Tungus* (Shirokogoroff 1935: 15). The original formulae were published in a less-compact form in the pamphlet *Ethnical Unit and Milieu* (Shirokogoroff 1924a)

In his early work, using this formula, Shirokogoroff portrayed a model of the strength of demography and technology over space. The result was a concept that to contemporary readers seems to combine the anthropogeography of Ratzel, with a concern over performed ethnic boundaries anticipating those of Frederik Barth. Shirokogoroff noted that certain cultures had a higher "valence" (*valentnost'*) or what we can understand as a "capacity to incorporate neighbouring cultures" (Fig. 5.14b). This process — what we might today call an "ability to assimilate" — nevertheless could also weaken the internal cultural consistency of the expanding culture.

Furthermore, as the ethnos may be pressed by several ethnoses which vary their q, S and T, then the sum of impulses will be,—

$$\Sigma i = \left(\omega \frac{T_1}{\Delta T_1} + \omega \frac{T_2}{\Delta T_2} + \cdots + \omega \frac{T_n}{\Delta T_n}\right) + \left(\omega \frac{S_1}{\Delta S_1} + \omega \frac{S_2}{\Delta S_2} + \cdots + \omega \frac{S_m}{\Delta S_m}\right) + \left(\omega \frac{q_1}{\Delta q_1} + \omega \frac{q_2}{\Delta q_2} + \cdots + \omega \frac{q_p}{\Delta q_p}\right) = \sum_1^n i_{sq} + \sum_1^m i_{Tq} + \sum_1^p i_{sT}.$$

To this pressure the ethnos opposes its power of resistance and this will be a correction to its ethnical power, so that the *actual ethnical power* will be $\varepsilon = \frac{q^2}{\omega} . \Sigma i$.

Fig. 5.14b The "actual interethnical value" [valence] as represented in *Ethnical Unit and Milieu* (Shirokogoroff 1924a: 15)

The expanding culture thereby might find itself in "disequilibrium" if it did not compensate for its growth with some fantastic technological innovation — like the Manchu plough, the French *dormeuse*, or the Tungus shaman's dress. Failing that, it would risk being thrown into decline and subsequent incorporation into some other group. Shirokogoroff called the pressure between ethnic groups an "interethnical valience", which he represented with the constant ε [small epsilon] (Shirokogoroff 1924a: 23–24). Frustratingly, he rather poorly translated his ambitious model into English. He dubbed it the "actual interethnical value". This clunky translation likely confused many of his English-language readers perhaps leading some reviewers to describe his theories as "mystical".

Shirokogoroff's involuted equations are likely recognized, but not taken seriously, by most specialists today. Their elevated pretensions to mathematical precision confuse humanities-oriented scholars who today read his work for the themes of symbolism and cosmology. However, Shirokogoroff also took some trouble to represent his ideas visually (Fig. 5.15). In his work on the *Psychomental Complex* (Shirokogoroff 1935), a portion of which was pre-published and circulated as a pamphlet (Shirokogoroff 1934), he represented interethnical valience in a series of colourful spirals and representations of cells. In spite of his pretentions to positivistic accuracy, he intended that the diagrams be read intuiutively. The illustrator and future historian Boris Romanovskiĭ, who was interviewed by our colleague Don Tumanisonis in Vancouver, describes the process by which Shirokogoroff guided his pen to produce these puzzling drawings:

> Diagrams showing the movements of ethnic groups were prepared by me in this way: Shirokogoroff would carefully explain to me how the ethnic groups intermixed; in which direction and what numbers of one ethnic group would move, and how far. Also, how after contact, the "invaded" group would also re-act and in turn "invade the invaders". After I prepared the diagram to the best of my ability, I would give it to him for approval. Later, when I began to understand what was required, less and less corrections were needed (Letter to Donald Tumasonis, 20 Apr. 1979).

On the one hand, one is immediately drawn to the military metaphors in this account — but we might discount this as an elaboration of the informant who spent his life in a region that was constantly under invasion — and not necessarily that of Shirokogoroff. Graphically, the images seem to evoke a medical text such as those Shirokogoroff may have encountered as a young man growing up within a community of pharmacists, physicians, and biologists in the then Russian city of I͡Ur′ev (Tartu).

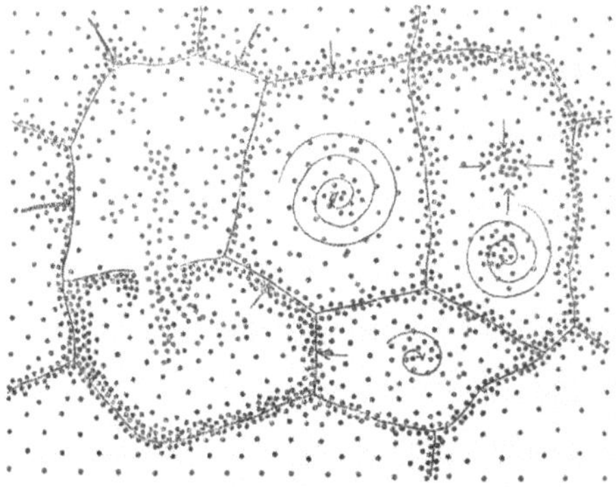

Table IV

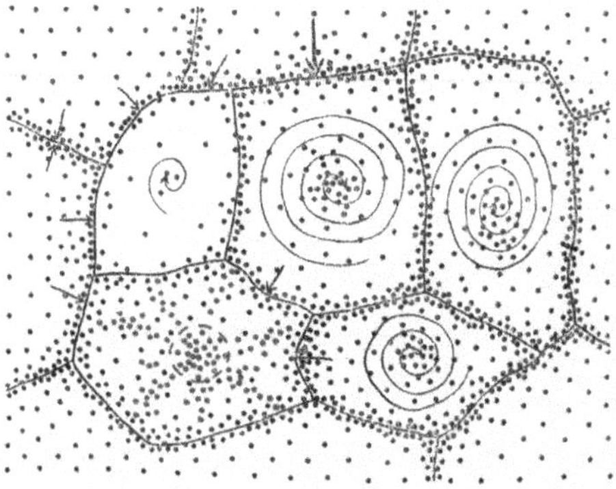

Table VI

Fig. 5.15 Table IV and VI from *The Psychomental Complex of the Tungus* overtly illustrating the "parasitizing" of an ethnical unit but graphicaly illustrating the spiral motif (Shirokogoroff 1935: 36)

It is perhaps useful to draw attention to the spirals within the cells — or what we might call the snail-metaphor — an image which haunted him. The spirals structure these diagrams in the same way that Shirokogoroff once confessed that his own line of thought was like that of a snail first protecting itself, and then unravelling. This snail-like unravelling of Shirkogoroff's *etnos* thinking seems a good description of his fraught professional life. Clearly in his letter to Kotwicz, he describes withdrawing into his shell because of the pressure of competition with colleagues whom he did not trust. Inflexible, and unwilling to change, he, like a wild Tungus, chose to strike out first for the White-held republic in Vladivostok, and then to the farthest frontier of China, where he could develop his ideas in isolation. Perhaps his cellular model of interethnic pressure, expansion, and diffusion is a model writ-large of the insecurities and professional choices that he himself made, just as his ethnographic description of the freedom-loving Tunguses is a model of the life he yearned to build.

Whatever the origins of his intuitions, his work on defining stable ethnic markers within the contested landscapes of eastern Eurasia never provided him with the firm professional base that he sought. He moved from institution to institution, from the north to the south, in a series of short-term contracts living at the behest first of a nationalizing academy in Canton, and then within the Fu Ren University within Japanese-occupied Beiping. In Canton, he tried and failed to start a physical anthropological field laboratory to support an *etnos*-defined measurement programme for the nationalist government (Anderson and Arzyutov forthcoming). Within Japanese-controlled Manchukuo, he tried to be an intellectual pillar for a modernizing imperialist administration that wished to govern Manchuria through a network of politically orchestrated ethno-confessional units (Duara 2004; Shimizu 1999). After his death, his widow and lifetime field partner Elizaveta tried and failed to find a publishing house in Japan for his *magnum opus* — the document that Shirokogoroff described "his big *etnos* [manuscript]" (Inoue 1991).

Despite these failed and perhaps overly ambitious political overtures, Shirokogoroff's interest in defining long-term, measurable, and stable ethnic units did make an important impression on the work of his students (see chapter 6). The brightest example of his legacy in ethnic ratification can be seen in the work of Fèi Xiàotōng who became the leading ideologist of ethnic policy under the People's Republic. For example, one of the leading theorists of Chinese cultural anthropology today reads Shirokogoroff's influence in Fèi's concept of "unity in diversity":

> Fei Xiaotong noted [...] that credit for his own "unity of diversity" theory should be given to Shirokogoroff, that he himself had "roughly drew an

> outline or a simple sketch-map of a succession of changes from the point of view of the historical *fenhe* (separations and mergers) of *minzu* within China's borders, but had not gone deeply into Shirokogoroff's ethnos theory to point out how or why the various ethnic entities had separated or merged during that history of separations and mergers." After rereading Shirokogoroff's writings, Fei Xiaotong felt that [he] had failed to grasp the concept of cohesive and centrifugal forces that had always been active among ethnic people. [...] There are indeed some connections between Fei Xiaotong's unity of diversity and Shirokogoroff's ethnos theories. However, by casually describing unity of diversity as a "simple sketch map," Fei Xiaotong de-emphasized his own originality. In doing so, he wished to draw support from Shirokogoroff's ethnos theory to show that sociological elements should be introduced in the overall issue of ethnic studies and to elicit a reconsideration of *minzu* research by means of a concept of ethnos somewhat akin to ethnological concept of culture (Wang 2010: 62–63).

As discussed in the introduction to this volume, the fascination for identifying and explaining the long-term stability of identity groups is what distinguishes modern Eurasian *etnos* theory from the north Atlantic discourse of ethnicity. This fascination with ethnographic persistence can be read back into into the phonograph-mediated fieldnotes of the Shirokogoroffs' first fieldwork. Their Zabaïkal fieldwork clearly reflects the questions and the training that the couple brought with them from Paris and Petrograd. The surviving unpublished texts and letters reflect the intense interest in material culture and linguistics that remains a hallmark of Russian ethnology.

The texts also reveal an awareness of social disruption, of exploitation — of "disintegration" — but perhaps not yet a mechanism to explain it. The modern element of the texts is the conviction that there was nevertheless some yet-unnamed ethnic consciousness persisting in the region despite the creolization of the language and the adoption of foreign material objects. Had the Shirokogoroffs lived in a different time or place, perhaps their keen interest in material culture, or in Tungus psychology, would have led them to build a theory of enskillment and practice instead of a mathematically-driven account of cultural diffusion. Instead, their concern to identify ethnic persistence in spite of adversity stands as a testimony to the unstable settings and unstable alliances in which they built their own lives.

Appendix 1: Archeography

The archival record of the two Zabaĭkal expeditions is detailed but nonetheless fragmentary. The two expeditions are well described in two difficult-to-access publications (Shirokogorov and Shirokogorova 1914; Shirokogoroff 1923b). The first, a jointly authored field report, is itself mirrored by two manuscript versions in the St Petersburg archives; one for each year. The manuscript version of the 1912 expedition corresponds to the reverse side of folios: SPF ARAN 849-6-80: 41v, 42v, 44v, 45v, 95v-98v although it cannot be read in that order. The manuscript report of the 1913 expedition can be found on the reverse sides of SPF ARAN 849-6-80: 43v, 51v-55v, 74v-87v, 89v, 91v and again cannot be read in that order. This second report is missing at least four folios.

By far the most interesting source for the first expedition (1 June 1912 to 10 August 1912) is Elizaveta's field diary which documents their one-month stay on the Akima river primarily in the Orochen settlement of Tyksyr (SPF ARAN 849-5-803). It can be linked to a set of 116 glass-plate photographs documenting primarily Tyksyr but also the steppe Tungus communities that they visited earlier (MAĖ collection no. 2002). The 1912 expedition is further documented by a single surviving letter that Sergei wrote to Lev Shternberg from the field (SPF ARAN 282-2-319: 1–2v).

The wax cylinder recordings made by Elizaveta, originally deposited with the Academy of Sciences, now sit in the Archive of the Institute of Russian Literature (Pushkin House). The institute holds an accession record describing 28 recordings from the 1912 expedition and nineteen recordings from the second expedition (FA IRL RAN Papka 61). A preliminary review of their holdings revealed an uncatalogued collection of 86 wax cylinder recordings associated with the Shirokogoroffs of which a minimum of 25 cylinders can be associated with the 1912 expedition and to some extent matched to Elizaveta's diary (PD FB 1010-1033, 3299). The jointly published field report documents that 72 photographs and fourteen wax cylinder recordings were made among the nomadic Tunguses and fifty photographs and fifteen wax cylinder recordings in the Orochen settlement of Tyksyr (Shirokogorov and Shirokogorova 1914: 132, 135). The accession record of MAĖ RAN 2003 record seven artefacts accessioned by the museum from Tyksyr. Further, the MAĖ RAN holds a set of skull and hair samples that the couple removed from Orochen graves around Tyksyr (MAĖ 1996, MAĖ 5244).

An important record of the first Zabaĭkal expedition are two unpublished and untitled manuscripts each written immediately after each expedition. They give a deep insight into how the thinking of the two fieldworkers developed year by year. The first is a short, lively written handwritten overview of the geography and the ethnography of eastern Asia with a focus on the nomadic Tungus and Orochens of Zabaĭkal'e. It is filed at SPF ARAN 849-6-806: 72–72v, 100–15v, 119–19v, 121–24v — but the pages cannot be read in that order. The second is an incomplete and untitled typescript which seems to correspond to what the Shirokogoroffs later cited as a ready-to-publish manuscript entitled "Anthropological Notes on the Nomadic Tunguses of Zabaĭkal'skai͡a oblast', Chita uezd" (1914: 136). The folio references for the text SPF ARAN 849-6-80: 239, 242, 244–56 and follow in that order. The first page is missing. It is possible that the two manuscripts represent one work, with the ethnographic part being the foreword to the anthropometric tables.

The second expedition (14 May 1913 to 17 September 1913) is not as well documented. The best primary source is a set of letters that Sergei regularly sent to Shternberg giving updates on their work (SPF ARAN 282-2-319: 3–9 and SPF ARAN 142-1(1918)-65: 188–92v). There were approximately 100 photographs, 100 drawings, and twenty wax cylinder recordings from the second expedition, but these have not been identified (Shirokogorov and Shirokogorova 1914: 143–44). There are some unattributed wax cylinders in the Institute of Russian Literature, which may refer to the second expedition, and an accession record does exist for this collection (FA IRL RAN: Papka 61: 11–12).

In MAĖ there are accession records for a fur covering (MAĖ collection No 2067) and a large collection of 131 shamanic objects, clothing and tools (MAĖ collection no. 2216) both gathered in Barguzin uezd. Sergei would later write that he had intended to publish a work on the material culture of the Orochen based on these collections, but was prevent from doing so by lack of access to the items (Shirokogoroff 1933). There is also one manuscript dictionary, entitled *An Orochen-Russian Dictionary* (collected between 1912–1913 — not compiled from the [folklore] texts) which is currently held in the Department of Siberian Ethnography, MAĖ without a classmark. It would seem that the former

Head of Department, Chuner Taksami, was endeavouring to publish the dictionary. The manuscript has his name stamped on it.

The results of the second expedition are best represented in a long untitled manuscript on Orochen ethnography. The history of this manuscript is hard to understand. The copy I am quoting from in this chapter is a handwritten — and painstakingly hand-edited — copy, chaotically collated, in SPF ARAN 849-6-806. The manuscript likely corresponds to a substantial work on Orochen ethnography which Shirokogoroff often referred to but cited with wildly different titles:

The Ethnography of the Reindeer Tungus of the Transbaikal (Shirokogoroff 1923b: 517; 1923a: i)

The Ethnography of the Orochen of Transbaikalia (Shirokogoroff 1929: vii)

Ėtnograficheskiĭ ocherk tungusov Zabaĭkal'skoĭ oblasti (D. 1940: 31)

The text is scattered across 189 folios in folder SPF ARAN 849-6-806 between folios 1 and folio 210 in very little order. Their coherence is essentially broken by the texts of the two above-mentioned manuscript field reports, which are printed on the verso sides of the same folios. It would seem that four folios are missing. According to Shirokogoroff there existed a corrected typescript copy of the same, which has not been found, and a third copy which he had with him in emigration (Shirokogoroff 1929: vii). Key paragraphs of this manuscript found their way verbatim (albeit in English translation) into his two main publications on Tunguses (Shirokogoroff 1935, 1929). There are three handwritten dates in the text: 26 January 1914 at the end of chapter 2 (folio 138), 20 March 1914 at the end of chapter 3 (folio 210), and 2 April 1914 at the end of the last unfinished chapter 4 (folio 71).

All three of these unpublished and untitled manuscripts have been untangled, and reprinted with editorial footnotes in Arzi͡utov and Anderson (forthcoming).

Published References

Anderson, D. Dzh [G]. 2017. 'Zapiski 'ushedsheĭ v sebi͡a ulitki': Zabaĭkal'skie ėkspedit͡sii S. M. Shirokogorova i formirovanie osnov ėtnos-myshlenii͡a', *Ėtnograficheskoe obozrenie* 5: 104–22.

Anderson, D. G. 1991. 'Turning Hunters into Herders: A Critical Examination of Soviet Development Policy among the Evenki of Southeastern Siberia', *Arctic* 44 (1): 12–22, https://doi.org/10.14430/arctic1513.

—. 2006. 'Dwellings, Storage and Summer Site Structure among Siberian Orochen Evenkis: Hunter-Gatherer Vernacular Architecture under Post-Socialist Conditions', *Norwegian Archaeological Review* 39 (1): 1–26, https://doi.org/10.1080/00293650600703894.

—. and D. Arzyutov. Forthcoming. 'The Etnos Archipelago: Sergeĭ M. Shirokogoroff and the Life History of a Controversial Anthropological Concept', *Current Anthropology*.

Arzi͡utov, D. V. and D. G. Anderson. Forthcoming. *Puteshestvie cherez man'chzhurskiĭ les k antropologicheskim kont͡sept͡sii͡am: ėtnoistorii͡a Sergei͡a i Elizavety Shirokogorovykh* (Moscow: Indrik).

Bogoraz, V. G. 1931. *Tungusskiĭ sbornik*. vyp 1 (Leningrad: Izd-vo AN SSSR).

Castren, M. A. 1856. *Grundzüge einen Tungusichen Sprachlehre nebst kurzem worterverzeichnis* (St Peterburg: Kaiserlichen Akademie der Wissenschaften).

Czaplicka, M. A. 1914. *Aboriginal Siberia: A Study in Social Anthropology* (Oxford: Clarendon).

D. 1940. 'Pami͡ati russkogo uchenogo', *Kitaĭskiĭ blagovestnik* Nov.: 33–39.

Duara, P. 2004. *Sovereignty and Authenticity: Manchukuo and the East Asian Modern* (Oxford: Rowman).

Fèi Xiàotōng. 1994. 'Cóng shǐ lù guó lǎoshī xué tǐzhí rénlèi xué', *Běijīng dàxué xuébào: Zhéxué shèhuì kēxué bǎn* 5: 13–22.

Guldin, G. E. 1994. *The Saga of Anthropology in China: From Malinowski to Moscow to Mao* (London: Sharpe).

Inoue, K. 1991. 'Introductory Notes to Sergei Shirkogorofff's Tungus Literary Language', *Asian Folklore Studies* 50: 35–9.

Kisli͡akov, V. N. 2013. 'Russkiĭ Komitet dli͡a izuchenii͡a Sredneĭ i Vostochnoĭ Azii (RKSVA) i kollekt͡sii po Vostochnoĭ Azii MAĖ RAN', in *Ki͡unerovskiĭ sbornik: materialy vostochnoaziatskikh i i͡ugo-vostochnoaziatskikh issledovaniĭ: ėtnografii͡a, fol'klor, iskusstvo, istorii͡a, arkheologii͡a, muzeevedenie, 2011–2012*, ed. by I͡U. K. Chistov and M. A. Rubt͡sova (St Peterburg: MAĖ RAN), 114–31.

Liú Xiǎoyún. 2007. 'Shǐ lù guó duì zhōngguó zǎoqí rénlèi xué de yǐngxiǎng', *Zhōngnán mínzú dàxué xuébào: Rénwén shèhuì kēxué bǎn* 27 (3): 10–14.

Maĭnov, I. I. 1901. 'Dva tipa tungusov', *Russkiĭ antropologicheskiĭ zhurnal* 6 2: 1–13.

Ol'denburg, S. F. 1903. 'Russkiĭ komitet dli͡a izuchenii͡a Sredneĭ i Vostochnoĭ Azii', *Zhurnal Ministerstva narodnogo prosveshchenii͡a* 9: 44–47.

Shimizu, A. 1999. 'Colonialism and the Development of Modern Anthropology in Japan', in *Anthropology and Colonialism in Asia and Oceania*, ed. by J. van Bremen and A. Shimizu (Richmond: Curzon), 115–71.

Shirokogoroff, S. M. 1923a. *Anthropology of Northern China* (Shanghai: Commercial Press).

—. 1923b. 'Ethnological investigations in Siberia, Mongolia, and Northern China Part 2', *The China Journal of Science and Arts* (*Shanghai*) 1 (6): 611–21.

—. 1924a. *Ethnical Unit and Milieu: A Summary of the Ethnos* (Shanghai: E. Evans).

—. 1924b. *Social Organization of the Manchus: A Study of Manchu Clan Organization* (Shanghai: Commercial Press).

—. 1925. *Anthropology of Eastern China and Kwangtung Province* (Shanghai: Commercial Press).

—. 1926. 'Northern Tungus Migrations in the Far East (Goldi and their Ethnical Affinities)', *Journal of the North China Branch of the Royal Asiatic Society* 57: 123–83.

—. 1929. *Social Organization of the Northern Tungus* (Shanghai: Commercial Press).

—. 1930. 'Ethnological and Linguistic Aspects of the Ural-Altaic Hypothesis', *Qinghua Xuebao* 6 (3): 199–396.

—. 1931. *Ethnological and Linguistic Aspects of the Ural-Altaic Hypothesis* (Peiping: Commercial Press).

—. 1932. *Letter to Professor Dr D. H. Kulp, 30 July 1932* (Peiping: [no. pub.]).

—. 1933. *Social Organization of the Northern Tungus* (Shanghai: Commercial Press).

—. 1934. *Ethnos: An Outline of Theory* (Peiping: [Catholic University Press] Qinghua University).

—. 1935. *The Psychomental Complex of the Tungus* (London: Kegan Paul).

—. 1944. *A Tungus Dictionary: Tungus-Russian and Russian-Tungus Photogravured from the Manuscripts* (Tokyo: Minzokugaru Kyokai).

—. 1953. *A Tungus Dictionary: Tungus-Russian and Russian-Tungus, Photogravured from the Manuscripts* (Tokyo: Minzokugaku Kyōkai).

—. 1970. *Ethnological and Linguistical Aspects of the Ural-Altaic Hypothesis* (Oosterhout: Anthropological Publications).

Shirokogorov, S. M. 1919. 'O metodakh razrabotki antropologicheskikh materialov', *Uchenye zapiski istoriko-filogicheskogo fakul'teta v Vladivostoke* 1 (2): 3–20.

—. 1922. *Mesto ėtnografii sredi nauk i klassifikat͡sii͡a ėtnosov* (Vladivostok: izd "Svobodnai͡a Rossii͡a").

—. 1923. *Ėtnos — issledovanie osnovnykh print͡sipov izmenenii͡a ėtnicheskikh i ėtnograficheskikh i͡avleniĭ* (Shanghai: Sibpress).

—. and E. N. Shirokogorova. 1914. 'Otchët o poezdkakh k tungusam i orochonam Zabaĭkal'skoĭ oblasti v 1912 i 1913 gg.', *Izvestii͡a Russkogo komiteta dli͡a izuchenii͡a Sredneĭ i Vostochnoĭ Azii* 3: 129–46.

Shirokogorova, E. N. 1919. 'Severo-Zapadnai͡a Man'chzhurii͡a (geograficheskiĭ ocherk po dannym marshrutnykh nabli͡udeniĭ)', *Uchenye zapiski istoriko-filologicheskogo fakul'teta v Vladivostoke* 1: 109–46.

Wang Mingming. 2010. 'The Intermediate Circle', *Chinese Sociology & Anthropology* 42 (4): 62–77, https://doi.org/10.2753/CSA0009-4625420404.

Archival References

BN PAU i PAN: Scientific Library of the Polish Academy of Skills and the Polish Academy of Sciences, Kraków

BPANvK 4600 t. 7 folio 54–57. Pis'mo S. M. Shirokogorova V. L. Kotvichu, 6 Feb. 1933.

FA IRL RAN: The Phonograph Archive of the Institute of Russian Literature (Pushkin House) of Russian Academy of Sciences, St Petersburg

FA IRL RAN PD FB 1010-1033, 3299. Fonograficheskie valiki Sergei͡a i Elizavety Shirokogorovykh. Zabaĭkal'e, Chitinskai͡a oblast', 1912.

FA IRL RAN PD FB 3255-3298. Fonograficheskie valiki Sergei͡a i Elizavety Shirokogorovykh. Manchuria, Heilongzhang region, 1915–1917.

FA IRL RAN PD FB 3590-3606 Fonograficheskie valiki Sergei͡a i Elizavety Shirokogorovykh. Shamanskie pesni. [No date].

FA IRL RAN: Papka 61: 6–10v. Ruskopisnyĭ Fond. Opis' Fn2. Ot S. M. Shirokogorova i E. N. Shirokogorovoĭ. Sibir'. Zabaĭkal'skai͡a oblast'. Chitinski uezd. Kochevye tungusy (Khamnagan), Buri͡aty, Orocheny po komandirovke 1912 goda (Maĭ-Senti͡abr'), 30 Nov. 1913, 28 items.

FA IRL RAN: Papka 61: 11–12. Ruskopisnyĭ Fond. Opis' Fn4. Ot S. M. Shirokogorova i E. N. Shirokogorovoĭ. Sibir'. Zabaĭkal'skai͡a oblast'. Nerchinskiĭ i Barguzinskiĭ uezd. Orocheny po komandirovke 1913 goda (Maĭ-Senti͡abr'), 30 Mar. 1915, 19 items.

EVR: Elena V. Robinson's Personal Archive, St Petersburg

Photographic collection

MAĖ: [Numbered Collections of] Peter the Great Museum of Anthropology and Ethnography, Russian Academy of Sciences, St Petersburg

MAĖ 2002. Stekli͡annye negativy Sergei͡a i Elizavety Shirokogorovykh, Zabaĭkal'skoĭ oblasti, Chitinskogo uezda Okti͡abr' 1912, 179 x 129", glass plates. 116 plates.

MAĖ 2003. Predmety obihoda Tyksyr Zi͡ul'zinskoĭ volosti, Chitinskogo uezda Zabaĭkal'skoĭ oblasti 1912 Okti͡abr', 13 items.

MAĖ 1996. Cherepa Orochon Chitinskokogo uezda Zi͡ulzinskoĭ volosti, 1913, 3 items.

MAĖ 5244. Obrazt͡sy volos muzhchiny. Orocheny. Pogrebenie v verkh. r. Akimy (pritok Nerchi) v Zi͡ul'zinskoĭ volosti Chitinskogo uezda 1912 [iz cherepa 1996-2].

MAĖ 2067. Mekhovoĭ kover. Orocheny Zabaĭkal'skoĭ oblasti Barguzinskogo uezda, 22 Nov. 1913, 1 item.

MAĖ 2216. Veshchi kul'ta, odezhda, orudii͡a. Orocheny Zabaĭkal'skoĭ oblasti Barguzinskogo uezda, 1913, 131 items.

SPF ARAN: St Petersburg Filial of the Archive of the Russian Academy of Sciences

SPF ARAN 4-4-672. Delo kant͡seli͡arii pravlenii͡a Imperatorskoĭ Akademii Nauk ob opredelenii S. M. Shirokogorova na gosudarstvennui͡u sluzhbu na dolzhnost' mladshego antropologa Muzei͡a Antropologii i Ėtnografii Ak. Nauk 1917.

SPF ARAN 142-1(1918)-65: 188–92v. Pis'mo S. M. Shirogorova L. I͡A. Shternbergu, 25 May 1913.

SPF ARAN 148-1-22: 68. Veshchi prinadlezhashchie Russkomu Komitetu, vzi͡atye v ėkspedii.

SPF ARAN 282-2-319: 1–2v. Pis'mo S. M. Shirogorova L. I͡A. Shternbergu, 11 Jun. 1912.

SPF ARAN 282-2-319: 3–4v. Pis'mo S. M. Shirogorova L. I͡A. Shternbergu, 12 Jun. 1913

SPF ARAN 282-2-319: 5–7v. Pis'mo S. M. Shirogorova L. I͡A. Shternbergu, 4 Jul. 1913.

SPF ARAN 282-2-319: 8–9. Pis'mo S. M. Shirogorova L. I͡A. Shternbergu, 31 Jul. 1913

SPF ARAN 849-5-803: 1–37v. Shirokogorova, Elizaveta N. Polevoĭ dnevnik, 1912.

SPF ARAN 849-6-806: 41v, 42v, 44v, 45v, 95v–98v. Otchët o poezdke k tungusam i orochenam Zabaĭkal'skoĭ oblasti S. M. i E. N. Shirokogorovykh v 1912 g.

SPF ARAN 849-6-806: 72–72v, 100–15v, 119–19v, 121–24v. Shirokogorov, Sergeĭ M. [vmeste s E. N. Shirokogorovoĭ?]. Untitled Manuscript [Ėtnograficheskiĭ ocherk o tungusakh i orochenakh, 1912–1913].

SPF ARAN 849-6-806: 239, 242, 244–56. Shirokogorov, Sergeĭ M. [vmeste s E. N. Shirokogorovoĭ?]. Untitled Typescript [Kochevye tungusy. Zabaĭkal'skoĭ oblasti. Chitinskogo uezda. Antropologicheskiĭ ocherk, 1912–1913].

SPF ARAN 849-6-806: 43v, 51v–55v, 74v–87v, 89v–91v, 93v–94v, 99v. Otchët o poezdke k orochenam Zabaĭkal'skoĭ oblasti S. M. i E. N. Shirokogorovykh v 1913 g.

SPF ARAN 849-6-806: 1–45, 47–71, 73–91, 93–99, 126, 129–38, 140, 142–50, 151–86, 206–38 Shirokogorov, Sergeĭ M. [vmeste s E. N. Shirokogorovoĭ?] [Ėtnografii͡a Orochenov Zabaĭkal'i͡a 1914].

TsGIA SPb: Central State Historical Archive of St Petersburg

TsGIA SPb 14-3-59098. Delo Sergei͡a Mikhaĭlovicha Shirokogorova [41 folios], 1911–1914.

6. Order out of Chaos: Anthropology and Politics of Sergei M. Shirokogoroff

Dmitry V. Arzyutov

> Vanîushin fell out of [Merkulov's] car [...]: in the past two days he had been drinking hard in the company of a new member of the government — Serge Shirokogoroff. An ethnographer and biologist, Shirokogoroff had his own vision of the ends and beginnings of human evolution and had the gift of telling his stories in such a way that one couldn't refrain from drinking. According to his logic, no matter what one did there was no way to avoid the onset of the beastliness in the world (Semënov 1994 [1966]: 316–17).

Through this unexpected passage from the popular Soviet-era spy thriller series featuring Max Otto von Stierlitz, one of the central authors of Russian *etnos* theory entered Soviet popular culture. The patriotic and duplicitous theme of these novels, which featured a Soviet agent embedded in the heart of the Nazi war machine, in a sense parallels the intellectual career of Sergei M. Shirokogoroff. While known in Europe and North America primarily as a scholarly student of shamanism, Shirokogoroff also lived a second life: he was a political actor, as well as a pamphleteer, both collaborating with and protesting against the Merkulov brothers' short-lived breakaway administration within the provisional government of Priamur'e (1921–1922), and before that, one of several anti-Bolshevik governments in the Russian Far East

 https://doi.org/10.11647/OBP.0150.06

(1918–1920) (Lîakhov 2013; Stephan 1978). Later in his career, living in Japanese-occupied Manchukuo, he collaborated with scholars working under the Japanese imperial regime and took a one-year sabbatical to work with ethnographers working within Nazi Germany.

In this chapter, I draw a panoramic picture that connects Shirokogoroff's dissenting political work to his theoretical work on *etnos*. I will show how, throughout his intellectual life and especially during the political chaos engendered by the collapse of the Russian Empire, Shirokogoroff developed his theory in the context of public debates with the Bolshevik and socialist movements in the Russian Far East, and later deployed it as a political tool aimed against Soviet power when he lived in China. His political publications are a lens though which we can understand the history of *etnos* theory as one reflecting the political chaos in Russia and Eurasia at the start of the twentieth century.

Ethnographer, Politician, Shaman

Shirokogoroff's cameo role in Îulian Semënov's 1966 novel *No Password Required* placed him close to the heart of the Merkulov administration and identified him as a person intimately connected to the political landscape of the Russian Far East (Fig. 6.1). Semënov used his artistic license to dramatize our hero and in places muddied the facts. It is true that for a short time in 1921 and 1922, Shirokogoroff served as a secretary to the local Parliamentary Assembly (*Narodnoe Sobranie*) following the coup launched by the Merkulov brothers (SPF ARAN 142-1(1924)-4: 11). Earlier, in 1918, Shirokogoroff's political life also put him in the company of a different short-lived anti-Bolshevik administration as the head of the Diplomatic Chancellery of the Provisional Priamur'e Government in Vladivostok (MRC SF 45-3-9; 45-4-1).

The depth of Shirokogoroff's engagement with these two anti-Soviet administrations, and his interest in regional politics is generally not well known, and is not discussed or even mentioned in any of his existing published biographies. According to his own account, these positions provided him a good opportunity to "observe the mechanisms of the [political process] while at the same time reading lectures on ethnography" (BN PAU i PAN 4600-6: 5). In another report, he states that he served the Merkulov parliament only until

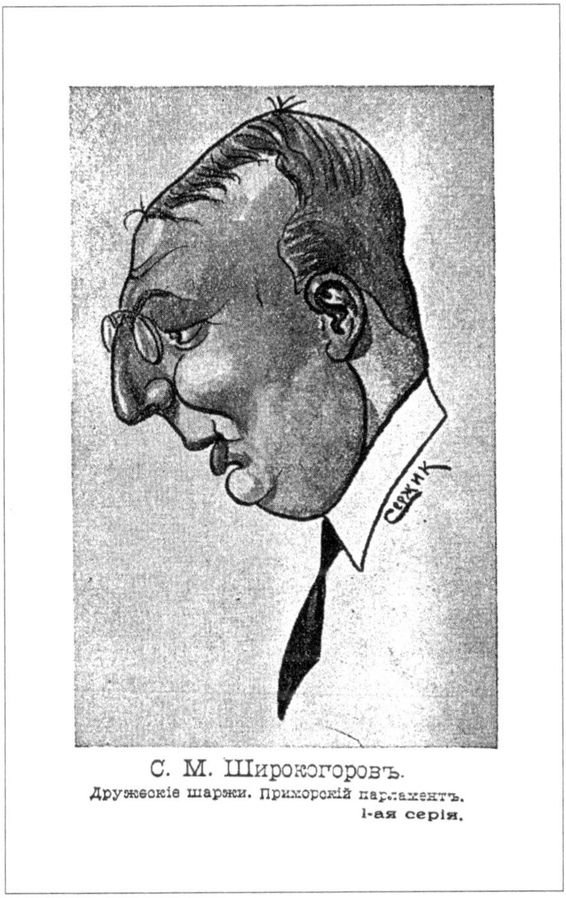

Fig. 6.1 Sergei Shirokogoroff ("Serzhik") as a member of the Primorskiĭ parliament (MRC: unnumbered). © Museum of Russian Culture, San Francisco, California

such time as "it was disbanded by still another government in a series of administrations" (SPF ARAN 142-1(1924)-4: 12v). Shirokogoroff's dispassionate evaluation of the galloping change around him captures the flavour of the period that Jonathan Smele describes as "the compound compendium of overlapping wars and conflicts in a disintegrating *imperium*" which he christens, in the plural, as the Russian Civil Wars (Smele 2015b: 7). Shirokogoroff himself hinted at the importance of this period of his life to his ethnographic work and offered a no less colourful portrait of himself in one of his last letters to Lev Shternberg, written in 22 December 1922. This passage connects rather well to the theme of subterfuge and intrigue that the novelist Semënov highlighted:

> I was able to use only a small part of my observations and conclusions for my *Ėtnos* [1923]. When I was forced to leave the Tunguses and the Manchus to one side, as well as the other nice peoples, and found myself in the company of all kinds of Europeans, including some Russians, I involuntarily developed a habit of studying them as an "ethnographer". This created a psychologically very curious situation — a feeling of complete isolation from all and sundry, and a monstrous, never until then experienced, desire to "observe". I've always felt and still feel an observer in public and could only be myself sitting behind my desk. It was roughly the same feeling as the one I had in the capacity of a shaman's assistant, or a Manchu jury member whose business was to elect a new shaman.
>
> Particularly often this *quid pro quo* happened when I served as the People's Assembly secretary in Vladivostok. Because no one apart from [my wife,] Eliz[aveta] Nik[olaevna,] could know of my interest in these observations, I had to be a true shaman, find the right approaches, etc. (SPF ARAN 282-2-319: 26–26v).

This extract offers at least one clue to the origin of Shirokogoroff's version of *etnos* theory. It suggests that the theory owes its conception to both the political instability in Vladivostok and Shirokogoroff's own conservative and (sometimes) vehemently anti-Bolshevik political beliefs. This passage allows us to expand our view of his "field" to include not only his pioneering fieldwork in Zabaĭkal'e (see chapter 5), but also to include the way that he honed his observational skills in the seething political environment in eastern Eurasia.

A key notion in both contexts is his concept of an "equilibrium" (*ravnovesie*), which he sought to apply to Tungus ethnography within the context of the deep political crisis in his own country. Much later, first when he was living in the capital of nationalist China in Canton [Guǎngzhōu] and then in Beiping [Běijīng] during the Japanese occupation, he would attempt to apply his theories of "ethnical equilibriums" to the major political movements unsettling Europe at the dawn of World War II. His extensive correspondence with ethnographers within Nazi Germany and with Nazi-sympathizers within England, is also not well known. In this correspondence, *etnos* theory emerges as an imaginary sociological and anthropological ideal where order exists through the overlapping of an ideal past and an ideal future, eclipsing the present, which is dismissed as chaos. In order to trace the theme of "order through chaos" I propose to review Shirokogoroff's personal and ethnographic biography with an eye to the political movements he allied himself with in his youth and at the height of his career.

Vol'sk and I͡Ur'ev: Political Life in the Provinces

Sergei Mikhailovich Shirokogoroff was born in Suzdal' to the family of the pharmacist Mikhail Ivanovich (1862/63–?) and Aleksandra I͡Ul'evna Shirokogorov in 1887. At some point, the family moved to Vol'sk, where Sergei's father served as a member of the Vol'sk town council from 1907 to 1916. This provincial Russian town played an important role in Russian revolutionary politics in the days preceding the first Russian revolution. Aleksandr Fedorovich Kerenskiĭ, whose business as a lawyer often brought him to Vol'sk, was elected to the State Duma from a constituency in Vol'sk. In the Duma, he led the Trudoviki faction of the Socialist Revolutionary Party and was a prominent official in a number of posts in the provisional government (Kerensky 1965). This moderate socialist party was later overthrown by the Bolshevik faction during the second Russian revolution.

According to contemporary descendants of the Shirokogorov family, Natal'i͡a and Vladimir Shirokogorov, Kerenskiĭ was a frequent guest in the Shirokogorov's home (pers. comm., 25 Jan. 2017), perhaps indicating that Sergei's family was involved in the political life of a provincial town and to some extent sympathetic to socialist ideals. It was said that Kerenskiĭ was also courting Sergei's cousin, Evgenii͡a. In addition, it is also known that Sergei's father was at the centre of events during the 1905 revolution. Natal'i͡a Shirokogorova noted that the Shirokogoroff pharmacy was used as a safe house by the revolutionaries. She further noted that, during a demonstration on 20 October 1905, Mikhail Ivanovich was heavily beaten by the members of the monarchist and nationalist movement known as "The Black Hundreds" (*Chernosotent͡sy*), after which he had to spend over a month in hospital (pers. comm.).

Fig. 6.2 Sergei Shirokogoroff and Elizaveta Robinson, 1906 (EVR)

The Shirokogoroff family also maintained close ties with the city of ÎUr'ev (now known as Tartu, Estonia). This was the home of Sergei's uncle, Ivan Ivanovich Shirokogorov (1869–1946), who was an outstanding and internationally renowned anatomist and pathologist and University Professor of Anatomical Pathology (EAA 384.1.3443; EAA 402.1.29600; EAA 402.3.1864). Ivan's brothers Vladimir (1885–?) and Mikhaĭl (1892–?) also studied law and history at ÎUr'ev University (EAA 402.1.29599; EAA 402.1.29601; EAA 402.1.29602). Sergei visited the city, and later moved there in 1903 to complete his primary education at the Hugo Treffner Gymnasium (TsGIA SPb 14-3-59098: 3–3v). In ÎUr'ev, he met the woman who would become his wife: Elizaveta [Elizabeth] Robinson (1884–1943) (Fig. 6.2). According to Elena V. Robinson, both Sergei and Elizaveta travelled to Paris to continue their studies in 1906 or 1907 (pers. comm., May-June 2016). It is likely that their study placement at the Sorbonne was organized through Ivan Shirokogorov's international connections, as he himself would be seconded to the Pasteur Institute in 1908 (Chirokogorov 1909).

While Sergei and Elizaveta were pursuing their studies in Paris, Sergei's brother Vladimir, then an undergraduate student at ÎUr'ev

University, became embroiled in student protest movements, which caused a lot of embarrassment to his uncle Ivan. Ivan Shirokogorov was forced to write numerous letters of support and explanation to the university leadership in a vain attempt to save his nephew's career. In the end, Vladimir was not allowed to finish his university education (EAA 402.1.29599; GARF 102 D-7-207(1910)-2877). While these dramas were unfolding in I͡Ur'ev, Sergei and Elizaveta were developing their own contacts and alliances in Paris, not to mention formalizing their relationship with their marriage in 1908 at the Nevskiĭ cathedral in Paris (TumA 243).

Fig. 6.3 Sergei Shirokogoroff with Elizaveta's family, June 1911 (EVR). First row, right to left: Sergeĭ M. Shirokogoroff, Elizaveta (Lili͡a) Nikolaevna Robinson, Nadezhda Fëdorovna Robinson (Elizaveta's mother), Nikolaĭ Fedorovich Gamburger (Elizaveta's maternal uncle). Second row, left to right: the wife of Nikolaĭ F. Gamburger, Mikhail Nikolaevich Smirnov (Marii͡a N. Robinson's husband), Marii͡a (Mura) Nikolaevna Robinson

Sergei's correspondence from this period, intercepted and filed by the Russian secret police, gives us our first clues as to his political identity.

Paris: on the "Degeneration" of Political Parties

It is difficult to say what made Sergei and Elizaveta go to Paris (Fig. 6.4). We might assume that their parents wanted to give their children a good education while protecting them from the instability already developing in Russia. It is curious that, despite being free from the political distractions that scuttled his cousin's career, Sergei never completed a university degree. His education was limited to his attendance at the Paris University's Faculté des Lettres from 1907 to 1910, where he audited courses (*lecteur des lettres*) (TsGIA SPb 14-3-59098; RGIA DV P-289-2-1573: 27). He also attended some lectures at L'École d'anthropologie de Paris and at L'École pratique des hautes études, likely in an unofficial capacity.

Fig. 6.4 Elizaveta Robinson in Paris (EVR)

Sergei's polymathic interest in various courses in politics and physical anthropology is probably not that unusual for an era before the professionalization of anthropology. However, it is important to correct the record since some Russian historians credit him with taking a *docteur des lettres* at the Sorbonne (Reshetov 2001: 8). Later, in Vladivostok and China, Shirokogoroff himself used his French training to provide the justification for his title of professor.

While living in Paris on the Boulevard Saint-Germain, Sergei often and regularly wrote home to Russia. He wrote one letter on 10 January 1910 to Lev (Shlema-Leiba) Efimovich (Khaimovich) Berkovich (1863–1911), his former neighbour in Vol'sk and the former leader of a so-called Marxist group. This letter was intercepted by the secret police on 2 March 1910 and presumably did not reach its addressee, but instead found its way to the Hoover Institution Archives in Stanford:

> I live quite far from the Russian colony. Do not go anywhere. However, sometimes I am told curious things. I'll tell you what I know. *The process of our* [Russian] *parties' degeneration is, of course, in full swing*. And everyone is degenerating in their own way. This, to my mind, is the most interesting aspect of it all. [...] All their activity in the meanwhile is reduced to desperate squabbles on entirely personal grounds. And if you add to all this the fact that all of them are busy with "settling down", concentrate on their petty businesses, prepare for careers as lawyers, administrators, judiciary and others, policemen, provocateurs, medical doctors, authors, etc. as best they can — no holds barred. This is what degeneration really means. What will be left over? Apparently, the "students" without the "teachers". And we'll start telling the tale from the beginning, only, in all probability, in a different manner. A mood of depression everywhere and there's nothing to help it. Russian history, apparently, went through a certain stage and now neither the "students", nor the "teachers" can quite recover from the experience (HILA 26001/141, emphasis added).

From a historical point of view, this passage reflects a bitter disappointment to political hopes of the Russian society after the upheavals of 1905–1907. This fragment about the degeneration of political parties is, in my opinion, important for the understanding of what Shirokogoroff would write several years later in his self-published political brochures, proclaiming that parties cannot form a foundation of the state or the nation. In his academic or educational texts he preferred to employ the "scientific" term *etnos*, reserving "nation" and "state" solely for his political writing. However, I would argue that the meanings are more or less the same.

In this period Sergei became infatuated with comparative ethnology, which he pursued through intensive reading in the Paris National Library. Some years later he would recollect in a letter to his friend Władysław Kotwicz, a Russian-Polish linguist:

> Having arrived in Petersburg with an already significant theoretical knowledge base, I immediately felt the difference in methodology of what could be called "philosophy", and even the research interests and competence. After all, by that time I had already been studying these disciplines for over five years [...] [One] very large and meticulous work I was completing in my first year in Petersburg was on the application of statistical analysis methods to the problems of the forms of social organization and conditions [for the development] of technical culture, as well as the relationship with the primary environment. I worked with almost over two thousand peoples, predominantly from Africa, India, and America, the literature on which was mostly available to me in the National Library in Paris. (I must say that I wasn't much interested in Siberia at the time). I discarded the idea of that type of correlation after I finished that work; however there was a certain positive result: I became familiar with a number of peoples, literature, methodology, and the formulation of problems (BN PAU i PAN 4600-7: 55, 6 Feb. 1933).

His "statistical" interest in comparative examples would find its way into his published works on ethnology, as well as the political brochures that he would publish during his association with the Merkulov administration. Some of his reading notes taken from Paris libraries survive to this day (SPF ARAN 849-5-805). Written primarily in French and Russian, they show a wide reading of works in theoretical ethnology ranging from Marcel Mauss to Edward Tylor (Ibid: 204–05v), as well as curiosity about a variety of cultures, economies and political systems across the globe.

We also may presume that, as a student, Shirokogoroff witnessed some of the discussions taking place in Paris about how to distinguish ethnological research from sociological or (physical) anthropological research. For example, Georges Papillault (1908) — who likely was one of Shirokogoroff's lecturers — published an overview of ethnology's place among all the sciences that looks similar, if not identical, to an overview that Shirokogoroff himself would publish in Vladivostok (Shirokogorov 1922a). Papillault's overview also recommended the use of the term "etnos" to denote the study of peoples (*peuples*) who, irrespective of racial differences, presented themselves as one community (Papillault 1908: 127). Although there is no direct evidence of an intellectual link between Papillault's lecturers in Paris, and Shirokogoroff's career in Petrograd, Vladivostok, and Beiping, it is a remarkable coincidence that the debate over the definition of ethnology as a discipline, and the methods needed to define an *etnos*, would come to dominate his political and ethnographic writing upon his return to Russia.

Between Petrograd and the Far East

After his return from Paris, Sergei Shirokogoroff began a second programme of studies in the Faculty of Physics and Mathematics at St Petersburg University. Interestingly, he never completed this programme either. His curriculum records, however, show that he took a wide range of courses from chemistry to ethnology. For the purposes of this book, it is significant that the pioneer physical anthropologist Fëdor Volkov probably was one of his lecturers, or at least Shirokogoroff had to attend his courses without official registration (TsGIA SPb 14-3-59098). Parallel to his studies, he took a position as a cataloguer in the Museum of Anthropology and Ethnology. There he fell under the influence of Vasiliĭ V. Radlov, and Lev I͡A. Shternberg, who encouraged him to take up the Tungus language for his future studies (see chapter 5). From his later correspondence and memoirs we may guess that Shirokogoroff was dissatisfied with Shternberg's liberal views, which were the result of Shternberg's own political evolution from a member of the terrorist group *Narodnai͡a voli͡a* to a liberal journalist and thinker (Kan 2009). Beyond this, some of his evaluations of Shternberg were properly anti-Semitic. Shirokogoroff himself wrote in a letter to Władysław Kotwicz:

> That is what interested me in 1911 when I met Shternberg. [...] He was an evolutionist of the provincial-revolutionary school, a comparativist of Frazer's type who was his ideal, and with whom I felt sick, a sentimental judophile (believe me, this was a true complex[1]!), an idealist seeking

1 In using the term *complex* Shirokogoroff made the reference to his own forthcoming work on the psychomental complex (1935) where he coined this term as a combination of spiritual, biological, social, and material characteristics of human communities and societies.

> improvement of the "non-Russians" situation in Siberia by means of embracing them into [the ranks of] "progressive humanity", and other things which only interested me in my senior high school years (BN PAU i PAN 4600-7: 55, 6 Feb. 1933).

From this letter, it would appear that Shirokogoroff positioned himself as an opponent of evolutionism and any discussions of progress. His early writings on the "growth and decline" of *etnoses* seem to imply a collage of small communities changing, expanding or being incorporated into neighbouring groups without a central line of development.

As David G. Anderson documents in chapter 5, Shirokogoroff would date his first intuitions on *etnos* theory to both his 1912 fieldwork with the Tunguses and Orochens and, partly, to his earlier comparative "statistical" library reading in Paris. However, one could add that his interest in politics was also intertwined with this first fieldwork. His first unpublished ethnographic manuscript on Orochens can be read as an analysis of their political situation in terms of their relationship to the Russian state and their internal clan structure. His letters make clear that the fieldwork itself forced him to decipher the political situation in every particular *ulus* (district). This fact was not lost on public authorities, who were suspicious of his research. During their third period of fieldwork among the Orochens of Manchuria, Shirokogoroff wrote to Shternberg that he and Elizaveta were perceived by the Chinese as "secret bearers of Russian political influence" (see, for example, SPF ARAN 142-1(1918)-68: 140–44v, 4 Aug. 1916). The Shirokogoroffs themselves sometimes requested the support of local military detachments. According to one account, their team looked much like a military expedition, outfitted with horses, uniformed and armed Cossacks, and directed by Shirokogoroff in a gallant leather jacket (Gurevich 1940; see also MRC 3-2-31-6: 357).

During his fieldwork in Manchuria, Sergei documented political protests. In Sakhali͡an he took photos of a Chinese protest picket and wrote about it in his diary (photos MAĖ 2639-465-470; TumA 1915/16: 1). In May 1917, while on their way to China for their final Manchurian fieldwork, the Shirokogoroffs were detained and arrested in Rukhlovo station (now Skovorodino in Amurskai͡a oblast′) under suspicion of being German agents. This incident had a profound impact on Sergei, who wrote about the arrest several times both in letters and in publications. Shirokogoroff would add more detail and more drama with each telling of the story. The first person to whom he wrote, from Hăilāěr, was Shternberg:

> The reason for the arrest was, of course, police abuse [of power], which has today become a common thing, in line with the [illegible] understanding of political freedom and the fear of spies who allegedly infested the country and painted themselves in [illegible] the colours of the Romanovs' regime supporters. First we were told that we were [illegible] the Germans. Later, that we were the "acolytes of the old regime", then again that S. Shirokogoroff died in 1915, and it was a German who travelled under his name, and then even that Mrs Shirokogoroff died too, and her place was taken by an Austrian spy. It all looked like a bad joke to me. It was just short of rough justice (SPF ARAN 282-2-319: 21–22v, 13 May 1917).

Later Shirokogoroff would add a biblical tint to the story, presenting himself as a wise man surrounded by chaotic and quite naïve people who were like "lost sheep". Such an updated version of the story he retold in his open and published letter to his colleague Daniel Kulp:

> I was arrested together with my wife and a Tungus when travelling, with all my paraphernalia of an ethnological expedition, along the Amur Railway. I was suspected (chiefly physiognomically) of having been a "reactionary". The local Committee of Social Safety (it consisted of twelve members, evidently in an unconscious imitation of Twelve Disciples, gathered among the local "liberal intelligentsia" so much now appreciated abroad) in its general meetings discussed my case, sometimes in my presence. Among other interesting situations, I now want to quote one which happened on the tenth day, or so, of their labour on my case. The president at my trial told me for reconciliation, —
>
> "When you produce us evidence of your real loyalty to us, we will recognize you as good as we are. "I lifted up my eyes to the ceiling and recited:
>
> "God, I thank thee that I am not as other men are." [Luke 18:1]
>
> The president, who evidently was familiar with the Testament, vividly asked me:
>
> "Why?"
>
> "Because, — I replied — I do not want to go together with you into the jail".
>
> As ethnographer, I must confess that my prediction was wrong. In so far as I could gather, most of these unfortunate people physically perished from the hands of both "whites" and "reds" (Shirokogoroff 1932: 33).

The Shirokogoroffs were rescued thanks to the timely actions of an old friend from Vol'sk. The then-minister of justice of the Provisional Government in Petrograd, Aleksandr F. Kerenskiĭ, sent the following cable:

> Dukhnovo station,[2] East Siberia.
>
> Attn. of the Public Security Committee.
>
> I insist on immediate release of a researcher Shirokogoroff well known to me personally who was commissioned by the Academy of Sciences to do scientific research on its behalf. I request to be personally informed of the forthcoming orders to this effect.
>
> Minister of Justice Kerenskiĭ (GARF 124-55-338: 2, 30 Apr. 1917).

In all his descriptions of the arrest, Sergei never placed his captors in a political landscape of the Far East. We do not know exactly who they were. The only thing I might presume, they definitely did not sympathise with the monarchy.

The archival records suggest that the Shirokogoroffs' arrest became a turning point in Sergei's life. Before the incident, there is no mention in the correspondence of any thought of leaving Russia nor abandoning his duties at the museum. On the contrary, the field correspondence reads more like a programme for further repeated anthropological, linguistic and museum research. I suppose the arrest itself put him into the awkward position of looking like a sympathiser of the "old regime". The life history of his family suggests the opposite. Nevertheless, his reflections on his arrest — together with the disintegrating political events which surrounded him — encouraged Sergei to choose a more conservative political agenda. From a position of being strictly against political parties of any kind, he seems to have moved to a strong belief in the power of pure science to reveal the internal motions of an *etnos/narod* (people).

Following their release, the Shirokogoroffs continued on to Petrograd and then to Elizaveta's family retreat in the far south in Ekaterinodar (Krasnodar). During their stay there, the couple tried to make a difficult decision on whether or not remain in Petrograd, or to avoid the building political instability by emigrating to the east or to the west. The correspondence contained in the archives sheds light on

2 This is a misprint in the original. The Shirokogoroffs were arrested in Rukhlovo station. See above.

Sergei's political thinking. In August 1917, Sergei wrote a series of letters to Radlov asking his opinion as to what to do. He also met Shternberg at the nearby resort town of Essentuki and discussed with him their future plans (SPF ARAN 282-2-319: 23–24v). These weeks were a real test for the Shirokogoroffs. In a letter to Radlov, dated 1 August 1917 [OS], Shirokogoroff wrote rather candidly:

> we are still living with as little knowledge about our immediate next steps, as before. I and Lev I͡Akovlevich [Shternberg] have agreed to decide what to do depending on the general political situation. To my mind, there are no clear indications of any certainty yet, and I keep mentally oscillating between [choosing] Petersburg and the Far East (SPF ARAN 142-1(1918)-72: 17).

Shternberg was of two minds. His liberal politics led him to believe that the February Revolution was a special moment in history and exhorted Shirokogoroff to remain in Russia. Radlov, took the opposite position: he urged that the couple travel abroad instead (BN PAU i PAN 4600-7: 54–57). A month later, in a telegram dated 13 September 1917 [OS], Shirokogoroff demanded that Shternberg make at least some decision about his fate:

> [YOUR] DELAYED DECISION ON THE SITUATION MIGHT HAVE UNFAVOURABLE CONSEQUENSES PLEASE INFORM OF [YOUR] ADVICE SOON SHIROKOGOROFF (SPF ARAN 142-1(1918)-71: 44).

Shternberg played a special role in Shirokogoroff's life. He was Shirokogoroff's supervisor, the designer of his first fieldwork (see chapter 5) as well as his close colleague. Undoubtedly, Shirokogoroff thought that the older man had his finger on the pulse of the unfolding revolutionary events in the capital. Unfortunately, we do not know what Shternberg's reply was. I can only speculate that Shternberg, like Radlov, would recommend that Shirokogoroff leave Petrograd. Perhaps he simply did not reply. In any event, upon their return to Petrograd the Shirokogoroffs made a round of all their acquaintances and, apparently, made a decision to go "East".

Prior to their departure on 16 October 1917 [OS] Shirokogoroff paid a visit to the well-known geochemist, philosopher, and close friend of Elizaveta and Sergei's family, Vasiliĭ I. Vernadskiĭ. The latter's diary contains a very brief note thereof: "An anthropologist S. Shirokogoroff visited. A ticket to Peiping" (Vernadskiĭ 1994: 21). A week later, on 23 October 1917 [OS], Shirokogoroff visited Władysław Kotwicz, only two days before the Bolsheviks stormed the Winter Palace (BN PAU i PAN 4600-6: 5).

By May 1918, the Shirokogoroffs were already in Beiping, but they were still unsure of where to go next. On 17 May 1918, Sergei wrote to Shternberg:

> In Manchuria and part of Mongolia, as you know, groups opposed to the Bolsheviks were formed, and this adds significant instability to the general situation. Of course, one cannot even think of [undertaking] any research in the area of conflict. From my contacts with the local people in the Ussuri land we gathered that it would have been possible to work there, and intended to depart in early April, but the occupation of Vladivostok and the subsequent migrations of the people destroyed that plan (SPF ARAN 142-1(1918)-72: 22).

Shirokogoroff's opinion of the revolution, as seen from this extract, was rather ambiguous. Despite his later anti-Bolshevik sentiments, at this period of time he places the blame on the opponents of the Bolsheviks for creating instability in the region.

The details of the couple's life during the height of the civil wars from May 1918 to June 1920 remain murky and unclear. Scraps of commentary in various published documents hint at the fact that Shirokogoroff began to develop an expressly anti-Bolshevik view while striking up a close relationship with General Dmitriĭ Khorvat (Horvath) (1858–1937). General Khorvat, who at the time of the October Revolution directed the Russian-owned Chinese Eastern Railway in Manchuria, refused to accept Soviet power. In late 1917, he formed the Far Eastern Committee for the Defence of the Fatherland based in Harbin, which served as a counter-revolutionary government in the Russian sphere of influence in Manchuria. From 1918–1920 Khorvat became the Supreme Plenipotentiary of the Provisional Siberian government headed by Admiral Kolchak (Smele 2015a: 571). It would seem that Khorvat encouraged Shirokogoroff to work for the White administration in the Russian Far East. Shirokogoroff was hired as a staff member in the Diplomatic Office of the Provisional Government of the Far East (MRC 45-3-9), and in December 1918 he was appointed the head of that office (MRC 45-4-1).

At about the same time, he joined the Far East Committee located in Vladivostok and Harbin. There he put his name to a welcoming address to Admiral Kolchak upon his visit to Vladivostok (not later than 25 November 1918):

> We, members of the Far East Committee located in Vladivostok, sincerely welcome your taking this high and responsible position. We see in this act an accomplishment of the *idea of autocracy which alone can put Russia back on the road to its former glory and power,* the idea which had been driving all our efforts. From the bottom of our hearts we wish you every success in this hard work to the benefit and glory of our beloved Motherland. Shirokogorov, Zaĭtsev, Usakovskiĭ, Ratushenko, Bukhman (Zhuravlev 2012: 42, emphasis added.).

Shirokogoroff's relationship with Admiral Kolchak likely also interwove politics and ethnography. The admiral, who had a background in polar exploration, most likely invited Shirokogoroff to his capital in Omsk in June 1919 to help organize a Siberian Studies Institute (1919–1920/1921) (Fominykh 2008). This institute would have brought together many of Shirokogoroff's old acquaintances from St Petersburg and, in particular, his former co-workers from the Commission on Cartography (e.g. Sergeĭ I. Rudenko, who was at that time in Tomsk).

Kolchak intended for Shirokogoroff to establish a Far Eastern branch of the institute. In the institute's proposed structure we may see also the influence of the "regionalists" (*oblastniki*), (Koval͡iashkina 2005) whose ambitions were, as is known, not just the separation of Siberia, but also the attribution to this territory of a special social, cultural, and political meaning. It is interesting that the course which Shirokogoroff himself would later teach in the Far East University was also on Siberian studies. Further, as noted by historians of the Civil War, Vladivostok at the time seemed like a good place to live: the city was buoyed by burgeoning international trade (Smith 1975: 5), and was seen to offer intellectual and economic opportunity.

The Kolchak government fell in 1919 and Vladivostok came under the influence of the pro-Soviet Far Eastern Republic (April 1920–November 1922). This regime then became subject to yet another coup launched by the Merkulov brothers, who created the provisional government of Priamur'e (1921–1922). During this time Shirokogoroff served as a secretary of the local parliament, lectured in ethnography at the Far

Eastern University, and, according to his own account, honed his skills as an "observer" of political processes.

While firmly based within the Russian Far East up until the end of 1922, Shirokogoroff was still uncertain about where to base his career. He wrote to Franz Boas asking for work in the United States. Boas advised him to remain where he was and "to acknowledge the elementary force which is carrying along the social development of Russia and to make the best of it, trying to develop on the given basis a happier future" (APS Boas Collection 82: 1, Boas to Shirokogoroff, 13 July 1920). Throughout this period, he also remained the Head of Department of the [Physical] Anthropological Division of the Museum of Anthropology and Ethnography. He continued to file regular annual reports to the museum on his activities. In a letter to his life-long friend Kotwicz, he described his life in Vladivostok in this period as a "business trip without end" (*bessrochnaīā komandirovka*) (BN PAU i PAN 4600-6: 5), suggesting that in at least one part of his mind he still rooted himself in Petrograd's intellectual environment.

It would seem that the feeling was mutual. As late as 28 February 1923, Shternberg invited Shirokogoroff to return to the museum and join the Department of the Evolution of Culture (SPF ARAN 142-1(1923)-3: 13–14). There was a material link to Petrograd as well. It seems that in their rush to leave Petrograd on the eve of the October Revolution, most of the Shirokogoroffs' field materials remained in the city. In future letters, Sergei would chafe at the loss of the materials abandoned in the "committee's closet"[3] (SPF ARAN 282-2-319: 24–24v). In this important period of his life, where he had to choose between Petrograd and the Russian Far East, Shirokogoroff would publish his first works on *etnos* theory *and* his first political pamphlets simultaneously. The region's seething instability seemed to feed into his need to theorize and systematize. It was during this period that the theoretical interplay between politics and ethnography was at its height.

3 Most likely what he had in mind was one of the closets of the RGS Commission for Making the Ethnographic Maps of Russia. Those manuscripts would later find their way to the archives of Dmitriĭ K. Zelenin, probably because Shirokogoroff and Zelenin worked together on the commission.

Shirokogoroff in Vladivostok: A Lecturer and a Politician

According to his official biographies, and the introductions to his publications, Shirokogoroff began working at a newly established private Department of History and Philology in Vladivostok in 1918.[4] He and his other colleagues were central figures in the establishment of the Far Eastern University in 1920 on the foundation of the Oriental Institute (*Vostochnyĭ Institut*) in Vladivostok. In January 1922 Shirokogoroff moved to the Department of Ethnography in the Oriental Faculty (RGIA DV P-289-2-1573: 26–26v). Initially the University was under control of one of the local governments, Primor'e Zemstvo Government (*Primorskaia͡ oblastnaia͡ zemskaia͡ uprava*) and later of the Far Eastern Republic.

Shirokogoroff's contribution to the study of Siberian ethnography at the Far Eastern University is well known. It is here that he was first appointed as an adjunct lecturer/professor (*privat-dot͡sent*) of ethnography on the strength of his association with the Sorbonne in Paris (RGIA DV P-289-2-1573). He published his widely cited book, entitled *Ėtnos*, in 1923. Although published in Shanghai, this work was based on the course of lectures that he gave at the university in 1921–1922 (Shirokogorov 1923). Building on a very brief note that he worked in a Russian publishing house in Shanghai (SPF ARAN 142-1(1924)-4: 12), we might assume that *Ėtnos* was likely published in a publishing house called Sibpress that Shirokogoroff either owned or managed. Further, the first of his signature studies were all published during Shirokogoroff's Vladivostok period. These included his first work on Tungus shamanism (Shirokogorov 1919b), the published field report of his and Elizaveta's Manchurian fieldwork (Shirokogorova 1919), and Sergei's programme for re-organising all Siberian physical anthropological research (Shirokogorov 1919a).

Despite these successes it would seem that Shirokogoroff's academic work did not bring him any income or, as he put it himself, pleasure, unlike his involvement in local political struggles:

4 Initially this department was independent and became part of the Far Eastern University in 1920.

> I had to […] lecture at [Far Eastern] University. The latter was especially unpleasant since I had to do my unloved job putting to use my lovely knowledge. [They] paid [me] wretchedly and lately very poorly (Shirokogoroff to Shternberg, SPF ARAN 282-2-319: 27v, 4 Dec. 1922).

He also found intellectual life in Vladivostok during that period rather dull:

> The energy of all [the scholars in Vladivostok] was spent on finding ways to get paid by various governments, — between 1917 and 1922 alone there were 8 of them!! Seems to be a record? — defending their interests and other similar trivial affairs (Ibid: 26v).

He adapted to his situation by trying to hone his ethnographic skills within the rapidly changing political context. In one of his annual reports to the Museum of Anthropology and Ethnography in Petrograd, Shirokogoroff described himself to his museum superiors as a politician who ethnographically observed the life of the "civilized peoples". He felt that during times "of political instability the ethnographic characteristics of the peoples and their individual groups became a lot more visible" (SPF ARAN 142-1(1924)-4: 11). The international environment of the city of that time likely encouraged Shirokogoroff to view his thoughts as universal. We may also conclude that Shirokogoroff was perhaps one of the first ethnographers to study the Russian Revolution and the Civil War. He lived on the outskirts of a disintegrating empire and observed all these events with his own eyes. Here he travelled a parallel road to his would-be mentor Shternberg, who also wrote an ethnographic account of the revolution but from the point of view of living at the centre of the collapsing empire (Shternberg 2009).

Between his lectures on Siberian studies and *Ėtnos*, in March and May of 1921, Shirokogoroff was actively involved with the "Non-Socialist Movement" (NSM) an umbrella group of anti-Bolshevik organisations in the Far East. His activity even inspired the journalist Vsevolod Ivanov (Posadskov 2015) to mention "Shirokogoroff's flannel suit" in passing in a satirical poem about the People's Assembly (Anon. 1921).[5] It was during this period of time that Shirokogoroff most likely collaborated

5 Apparently, Ivanov was a prototype for the character of Van͡iushin from Semёnov's novel *No Password Required* with which I started my article.

with the Merkulov brothers. Canfield Smith sums up the political debates within non-socialistic movements in the following way:

> The right wing of the nonsocialists, to whom the term "nonsocialist" was most generally applied, was hostile to the socialists of all parties. Politically they ranged from dedicated monarchists to conservative republicans, and they had nothing philosophically common with the socialists. They were not as committed to democratic methods as the other nonsocialists and moderate socialists, as their subsequent actions indicated. Like the Communists, they believed the goal justified the means. They could plan a coup with no regrets, and they could take a much more favourable view towards the Japanese because, as long as the Japanese were present, they could enjoy political and economic rights (Smith 1975: 84–5).

Although it remains a little unclear exactly which "wing" Shirokgoroff represented, there are some clues in a series of little-known brochures he published on behalf of the NSM. These brochures, all published in the same year, paint a picture of a man with many hats: a politician, a teacher, and an ethnographer. In one brochure, "The Goals of the NSM", he develops the idea of the "bankruptcy of political parties" by concluding that "parties will never be able to rule a state, no matter how good their programs and their members could be" (Shirokogorov 1922c: 5). At the end of his pamphlet, he offered up two solutions to the raging chaos: either a parliamentary monarchy with a constitution, as in Great Britain, or a monarchy supported by institutions of local self-government (*zemstvo*). These brochures move on to elaborate his somewhat unorthodox concept of a "national movement", while another self-published brochure promoted his idea of a self-regulating *etnos* (Shirokogorov 1922a).

It should be noted that Shirokogoroff's political brochures outlined a non-standard definition of the nation. He describes a vision of an "all-state [*obshchegosudarstvennyĭ*] or national movement uniting the entire population [of those] not belonging to any political party" (Shirokogorov 1922d: 6). Here he believed that this nation of people rejecting political parties would be represented by a type of non-socialist parliament:

> Those elected by the people, who are currently working together [in a coalition] of different organizations, have already recognized their national misfortune. They have taken upon themselves the heavy weight

> of public service. They, the representatives of the population themselves, who are in fact part of the population, have come to a national awareness. They have escaped the clutches of the political parties. They are a real people [*podlinnyĭ narod*] (Shirokogorov 1922d: 13).

In a second pamphlet, "Have We Made a Mistake?" Shirokogorov develops a principle of popular rule (*narodopravstvo*) that he associated with the work of the People's Assembly of which he had been a part (Shirokogorov 1922c: 4, 5). Shirokogorov saw the "people" being animated by a popular "will" (*voli͡a*) which manifested itself within a broad "national" movement (Shirokogorov 1922d: 6). It might be possible to read into his interest in reading and representing the "popular will" a kind of Rousseauian "general will" with its sometimes authoritarian connotations (N. Knight, pers. comm., 11 Jun. 2018). Shirokogoroff's model of representing the "popular will" through an assembly is mirrored in his early writing on Tungus shamanism, where he represents the "elected shaman" as a kind of diplomat who negotiates between people and spirits (Shirokogorov 1919b). He most likely was alluding to this work when he wrote to Shternberg describing his role in the People's Assembly as that of a shaman.

Although it is difficult to read much into the pamphlets, the tone of which is primarily critical of the Bolshevik coup, there is a strong hint that his "real" people are a self-organizing coalition much like his *etnos* was a self-regulating group identity:

> The wishes of the population themselves, the healthy instinct of the people themselves that comes to a state of mental equilibrium is the basis of this [non-socialistic] movement. This new movement is a national movement which has discarded political parties and is shaped in an absolutely different way (Shirokogoroff 1922c: 13).

The same year, he published yet another booklet on Russia's international position that seems to be a summary of his critical reflections on the annotations that he made on Karl Marx and other philosophers when he studied in the National Library in Paris. In this pamphlet, there were only three countries on his geopolitical map: Germany, the United States and Russia. Here he reiterated his view that political parties are malign entities, stating that the "division into parties in Russia is based, mostly, on psychology and the level of education of the people, rather than on the dominance of a certain idea as a purely logical concept" (Shirokogorov 1922b: 32). Elsewhere in his booklet he spoke about yet another threat: the appearance of a "people-less internationalism" (*beznarodnyĭ internat͡sionalizm*) (Ibid: 23). He understood Russia's fate in this regard as a rather simple development:

> Imperial Power under the effect of new trends, and the changes in the economic and political structure of the state, had degraded into a party organization. That was the state Russia was in when the war started. And even though the rise of national sentiment in 1914 had seemingly smoothed out the differences, the people's cold relations with the government stayed unchanged and all the warmness of the national feeling was transferred onto the army (Ibid: 33; See also Shirokogorov 1922c: 13).

As an opponent of political parties and the idea of classes Shirokogoroff put forward the notion of "the people" as a social unit and the main driving force of social life. Sometimes he elaborated on this picture with the concept of races, which were degenerating, parasitical, or new (Shirokogorov 1922b: 50). These ideas seem to shadow his ideas of assimilation (or as he called it later "amalgamation"), which had puzzled him during his first ethnographic fieldwork in Siberia (see chapter 5).

His enthusiasm for the NSM, and the People's Assembly, however, did not last long. By the autumn of 1921 a new conflict had erupted. Ivanov publicly criticized the NSM's leadership — which included Shirokogoroff among others — by saying: "Your Council has become a *sovdep*,[6] a source of devastation and collapse, an assembly of some actions and speeches driven exclusively by your petty egos" (qtd. in Posadskov 2015: 47). The exact reason for this conflict remains unknown, but it clearly incited harsh sentiments. In the archives of the Museum of Russian Culture in San Francisco there are several leaflets from that time (Fig. 6.5), one of which was probably related to the events described by Ivanov.

6 An abbreviation for the Soviet of Deputies, which carries the pejorative meaning of an amoral and formal adherence to party politics.

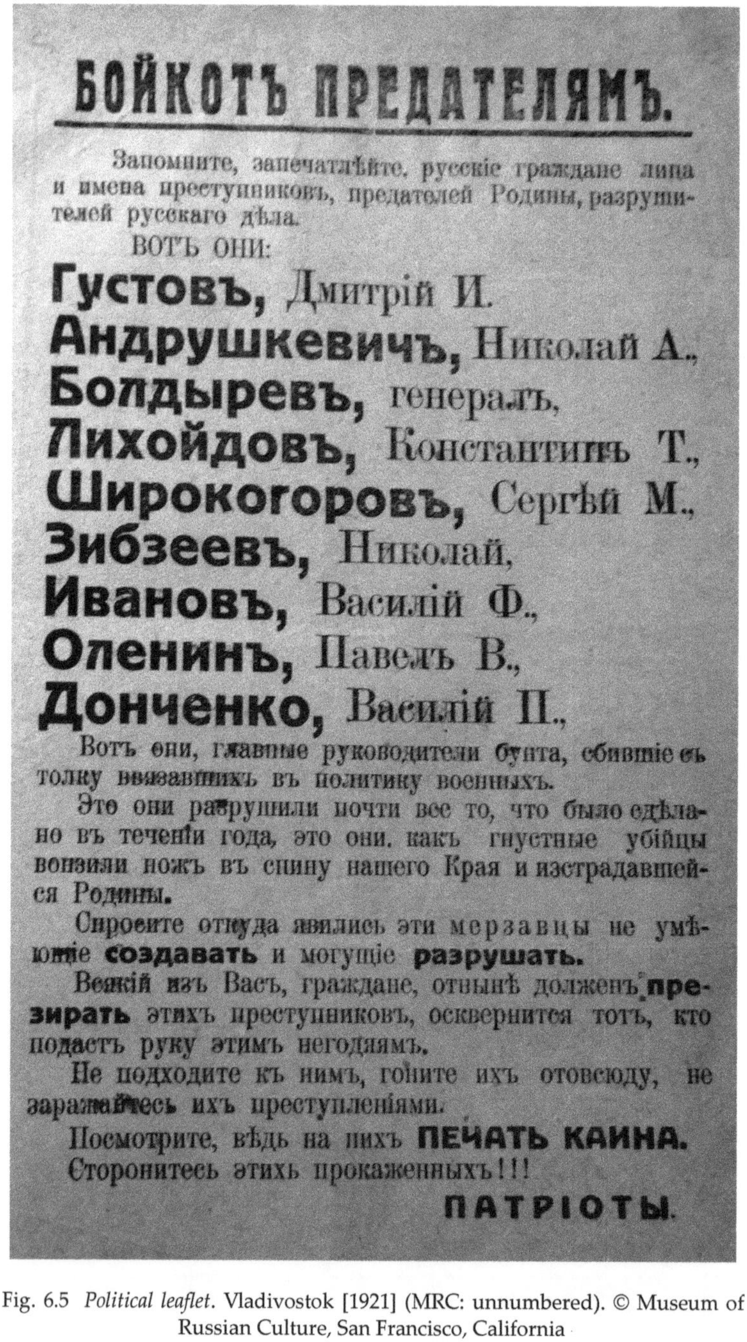

БОЙКОТЪ ПРЕДАТЕЛЯМЪ.

Запомните, запечатлѣйте, русскіе граждане лица и имена преступниковъ, предателей Родины, разрушителей русскаго дѣла.

ВОТЪ ОНИ:

Густовъ, Дмитрій И.
Андрушкевичъ, Николай А.,
Болдыревъ, генералъ,
Лихойдовъ, Константинъ Т.,
Широкогоровъ, Сергѣй М.,
Зибзеевъ, Николай,
Ивановъ, Василій Ф.,
Оленинъ, Павелъ В.,
Донченко, Василій П.,

Вотъ они, главные руководители бунта, сбившіе съ толку ввязавшихся въ политику военныхъ.

Это они разрушили почти все то, что было сдѣлано въ теченіи года, это они, какъ гнусные убійцы вонзили ножъ въ спину нашего Края и изстрадавшейся Родины.

Спросите откуда явились эти мерзавцы не умѣющіе **создавать** и могущіе **разрушать.**

Всякій изъ Васъ, граждане, отнынѣ долженъ **презирать** этихъ преступниковъ, осквернится тотъ, кто подастъ руку этимъ негодяямъ.

Не подходите къ нимъ, гоните ихъ отовсюду, не заражайтесь ихъ преступленіями.

Посмотрите, вѣдь на нихъ **ПЕЧАТЬ КАИНА.**

Сторонитесь этихъ прокаженныхъ!!!

ПАТРІОТЫ.

Fig. 6.5 *Political leaflet*. Vladivostok [1921] (MRC: unnumbered). © Museum of Russian Culture, San Francisco, California

The leaflet reads:

> Boycott the traitors.
>
> Remember, impress, Russian citizens, the faces and names of these criminals, the traitors to the Motherland, the destroyers of the Russian cause.
>
> HERE THEY ARE:
>
> …
>
> [5] Shirokogorov, Sergei M.
>
> …
>
> Here they are the main leaders of the riot, who confused the military engaged in politics.
>
> They themselves destroyed almost everything that has been accomplished during the year. They themselves are the vilest killers who stabbed a knife in the back of our Land [*Kraĭ*] and the suffering Motherland.
>
> One may ask where did these *bastards* come from, who cannot *create* and can *destroy*.
>
> Every one of you, citizens, should henceforth *despise* these criminals. Anyone who assists these scoundrels will be defiled.
>
> Do not approach them, turn them out everywhere, do not become infected with their crimes.
>
> Look, they have the MARK OF CAIN on them, after all.
>
> Stay away from these lepers!
>
> PATRIOTS.

The intensity of the anger that this incident generated led to Shirokogoroff being fired from the university on 26 October 1922 (RGIA DV P-289-2-1573: 16–16v, 18v). In fear of the political persecution they might suffer, he and his wife were forced to leave Vladivostok for Shanghai.

The Chinese Years: In the Shadow of Imperial Japan and Nazi Germany

The political instability in Vladivostok, and Shirokogoroff's own unsuccessful political debut, seems to have driven the couple to leave Russia. They travelled first to Japan,[7] before setting on China as a place where they might enjoy some stability. They ended up living in China, and its various shifting nationalist and Japanese-occupied fragments, for the rest of their lives — even if that may not have been their original intention. Largely, they traded one unstable political context for another. This move would have a great influence on Shirokogoroff's work and career. In this equally shifting political landscape he would compose all of the published works for which he is best known. Substantively, he shifted his research to communities within China; he also switched from using Russian to English as his main language of publication (BN PAU i PAN 4600-6: 11v).

Shirokogoroff's tether to St Petersburg was broken in 1923 when he was dismissed from his position as head of the Department of Physical Anthropology at the museum. However, while based in China he continued to expand his network. He started active collaborations with foreigners such as the sociologist Daniel Kulp, who studied the Chinese peasantry (Shirokogoroff 1932), and the medical doctor Vivia B. Appleton, with whom he conducted anthropometric measurements on Chinese children (Appleton 1976; Shirokogoroff and Appleton 1924). He also reached out to scholars around the globe through correspondence. We have found more than 100 letters that represent this period of his life between 1923 and 1939. In these letters he often presents himself as a key person who could provide foreign scholars access to the Chinese field.

In China he was constantly "migrating" from university to university on a number of short-term contracts. His failure to secure a permanent position might be put down to his personality, which many contemporaries remember as being acerbic and antagonistic, or it might be put down to the instability of the times. He began his Chinese career by giving lectures informally, or by contract, for a range of scholarly

7 The choice of the country was most probably based on his personal involvement in the diplomatic relations between Kolchak, Khorvat, the Merkulovs and the Japanese.

associations in Shanghai between 1922 and 1926. During that period of time, he translated and published a summary of his *etnos* theory in *Ethnical Unit and Millieu* (Shirokogoroff 1924), which was printed in booklet form by Edward Evans and Sons, a popular publishing house in Shanghai at that time (Chen 2013). While in Shanghai he completed a number of works on Tungus shamanism, physical anthropology, kinship studies, and even some memoirs about his heroic Zabaĭkal and Manchurian expeditions. By 1924–1925 he had become involved in Chinese academic life through his anthropometric fieldwork in eastern China and Kwangtung Province.

Thereafter Shirokogoroff worked in the south at the core of the new nationalist institutions formed after the first Chinese revolution. He worked for short periods at the University of Amoy (Xiàmén) (1926–1928), the Institute of History and Philology at Sun Yat Sen University in Canton (Guǎngzhōu) (1927–1930), as well as the renowned Academia Sinica (1928–1930). Often his appointments overlapped. His tenure at Academia Sinica was arguably the pinnacle of his career. It was there that he attempted to set up an anthropometric laboratory designed to work in the service of the new nationalist government to help define the contours of the Chinese nation (Anderson and Arzyutov forthcoming).

Here he set out upon, but did not complete, a challenging field expedition to the Yi (Lolo) nationality in Yunnan. This failed fieldwork eventually led to controversy, which ended with him being fired from the Academia Sinica on the grounds that foreign scholars could not adequately function within and understand the Chinese situation (Liú Xiǎoyún 2007b; Krı͡ukov 2007). However, he left a lasting contribution to Chinese science in Canton through the training of a young fieldworker, Yáng Chéngzhì, who would go on to become one of the foremost Chinese specialists on the Yi people and a key figure in the development of Chinese anthropology (Guldin 1994: 50–55; Liú Xiǎoyún 2007a).

Although Shirokogoroff angered people he also had good friends. His patrons managed to find him a position in Beiping at the Tsing Hua University where he worked from 1930 to 1937. An interesting short memoir by Frances Hsu captures the testy, international setting of Beiping during this period:

> Western scholars also brought their Chinese co-workers and students actively into European academic quarrels. During many months between

> 1935 and 1936 Professor Radcliffe-Brown resided in Yenching University. Father Wilhelm Schmidt entrenched himself behind the castle-like structures of the Catholic University of Peking, while Professor S. M. Shirokogoroff was on the faculty of Tsing Hua University, but these men could not be persuaded to see each other. Radcliffe-Brown lectured to one group of students on "Synchronic and Diachronic Study of Chinese Villages", Schmidt impressed on a different group of students the basic ideas of 'primary and secondary cultures' as well as his theory of "All Father" or one universal god, while Shirokogoroff pounded up and down the platform before a third group on his theory of Ethnos or the "Psycho-mental Complex" of a racial group (Hsu 1944: 13–14).

It would be in nationalist Beiping where he completed what came to be his defining work: *The Psychomental Complex of the Tungus* (Shirokogoroff 1935). He also trained another young student, Fèi Xiàotōng (1910–2005), who would later become the central figure in the development of nationality studies in the People's Republic. The young Fèi, with his first wife, published their own field observations from Guangxi wherein he concluded that the Yaos were crafting their own identities through the reflexive and biosocial "ethnical unit" that Shirokogoroff propounded (Leibold 2007: 132; Fèi 1999: 468–69). Late in his life, Fèi would credit Shirokogoroff for providing a key inspiration in his search for "unity in diversity" (Wang 2010; Fèi 1994) (see also chapter 5) (see Fig. 6.6).

Shirokogoroff was fired from Tsing Hua for participating in a students' demonstration that may have been related to the Japanese occupation of the city (TumA 109). It is significant that the Shirokogoroffs chose not to evacuate from Beiping after the Japanese occupation in 1937. Instead, Sergei found a job at the Catholic FuJen University (1937–1939). Controversially, during this period he intensified his links with Japanese scholars, who were keen to use ethnography, and in particular ethnographic descriptions of religious confessions, to aid in designing institutions for occupied Manchuria (Duara 2004). This led him to curtail his correspondence with Chinese colleagues to the south in nationalist China.

While living in Beiping, Shirokogoroff even fell out of contact with his Russian relatives. He wrote his last letter to his uncle Ivan Ivanovich Shirokogorov in 1932 (SPF ARAN 820-3-879) when he sent him his newly published brochure, *Ethnological and Linguistic Aspects of the Ural-Altaic Hypothesis* (Shirokogoroff 1931).

Fig. 6.6 Sergei Shirokogoroff working with one of his students, China (EVR)

Sergei Shirokogoroff died in 1939 during the occupation and was buried in the Russian cemetery around the Uspenskaia͡ Church (TumA 183), now part of the Russian embassy complex in Běijīng. After his death, his widow Elizaveta turned to Japan as a place where Sergei's manuscripts might be published. She tried, and failed, to publish Sergei's now lost two-volume book-length manuscript on *etnos* theory, but did manage to publish under his name a Tungus dictionary that she herself transcribed and wrote by hand (Shirokogoroff 1944).

While in Canton and Beiping, Shirokogoroff started an active, not to say aggressive, promotion of his ideas, circulating self-published brochures and seeking to ingratiate himself with like-minded people in various corners of the world. Not all of his correspondents shared his ideas and nor were they ready to communicate with him, but some of them promoted his ideas in Great Britain and Europe. One of the "principal defenders" of Shirokogoroff's ideas in London in the mid-1920s was Arthur Keith (BN PAU i PAN 4600-6: 65–66). Shirokogoroff valued Keith's opinion highly, in spite of the fact that Keith never cited him in his book, entitled *Ethnos; or, the Problem of Race Considered from a New Point of View* (Keith 1931) (BN PAU i PAN 4600-7: 32–32v).

But international contacts helped Shirokogoroff made his own career in China. For example, in 1927, as part of his last-ditch effort to keep his job, Shirokogoroff cited his collaboration with Keith to the president of the Academia Sinica as evidence of his international reputation (SPF ARAN 820-3-880: 40–43; BN PAU i PAN 4600-6: 64–66; AS Yuan 46–26). Suffering from a lack of understanding from the majority of his Russian colleagues (Chepurkovskiĭ 1938: 7–9), Keith's interest encouraged Shirokogoroff to further promote his concepts, including *etnos* and the psychomental complex.

It is difficult to gauge Shirokogoroff's reaction to the disintegrating political situation in China. Only a few letters hinted at his ongoing reflections on the October revolution and political chaos. In general, in this period of his life he did not intervene in Chinese domestic politics, but wrote to his confidants and even made public speeches, in Russian, about political affairs in the Soviet Union. His day-to-day scientific work remained in English. Thus, in one of his first letters from China, addressed to Kotwicz on 14 August 1924, Shirokogoroff wrote:

> The name I'd like to give to all this [the revolution] is ethnic disintegration, and it's even hard to imagine how deeply it has affected the world (BN PAU i PAN 4600/6: 9–9v).

Another startling example is an article on Tungus linguistics, which was first published many decades after his death (Shirokogoroff and Inoue 1991 [1939]), wherein he made scathing criticisms of how Soviet policies had been affecting Tungus Evenki people.

The most intriguing moment in Shirokogoroff's intellectual and political biography is the sabbatical year he spent in Nazi-controlled Germany (1935–1936). Although we still know very little about his contacts there or what he was working on at the time, we have reconstructed some scattered episodes that shed light on his political and anthropological reflections. Donald Tumasonis kindly shared with us some of the letters in which Karl H. Menges, the German linguist, recollected his meeting with Shirokogoroff in Germany. In one of the letters (3 March 1987) Menges wrote that during their meeting in Berlin in the spring of 1936, Shirokogoroff shared with him his desire to leave

China. Menges, on his part, rather bluntly told him that Germany was far from the best place to move to, primarily because of the "new state religion" (i.e. Nazism), and recommended that he go to the United States instead.

Ivan I. Gapanovich, a fellow Russian émigré living with him in Beiping, paints a picture of a Shirokogoroff as a German patriot:

> Political opponents jokingly called Shirokogoroff Breitberg, but there were some grounds for this nickname. His Russian name sounds as if it were translated from German and he studied at I͡Ur'ev University,[8] where the German influence was strong. Further, in his appearance and manners there also was something German. He did not disapprove of Hitler and said that the latter did well for Germany, but found that Hitler himself was a rather ignorant person, and his race theory unsound. However, I do not have any facts confirming that he was a "German". Maybe [he was] second generation [German] (TumA 183).

What was Shirokogoroff's intention in visiting Germany during this difficult time? Was he hoping to move there? It is impossible to answer these questions. His German sabbatical gave him an opportunity to meet some of his correspondents in person and to promote his *etnos* theory. During his German trip Shirokogoroff came into contact with another British scholar — perhaps one of the most controversial British anthropologists, George H. L. F. Pitt Rivers (1890–1966), infamous for his promotion of racial eugenics and his interest in the Nazi regime (Hart 2015). On 14 November 1935 Shirokogoroff sent him a letter from Berlin, writing the following:

> All these years I was following the development of your important work in connection with the "population problem" and your shifting *to the practical problem of ethnogenics.*
>
> [...] In so far as I can see from what you have published within recent years, a *practical application of our knowledge of the population problem occupies you more than anything else.* I am also interested in this aspect of the problem, but even now it is questionable, at least for myself, when we were "practically acting" and when we bring up a theoretical justification of our "acting", whether we are merely "functioning" in a certain ethnical body, or we are really consciously "directing" the process? (Chu.Cam PIRI 22/3, emphasis added).

8 This claim that Shirokogoroff studied at I͡Ur'ev University seems to be incorrect.

Even this short excerpt from his letter shows some desire on Shirokogoroff's part to apply his theoretical ideas to practical ends.

After the Shirokogoroffs' return to China, Sergei began promoting his work with renewed energy. He published in French and German translations of his earlier articles on *etnos* theory, originally written between 1919 and 1923 (Shirokogoroff 1937, 1936). While Pitt Rivers was citing Shirokogoroff's name in an attempt to build a eugenics programme within the International Union for the Scientific Study of Populations (Chu.Cam PIRI 11/2), in one of his last public speeches Shirokogoroff spoke to the importance of being able to translate one's ideas into practice:

> *but it is not enough to come up with an idea, to devise an ideal system* — it is necessary to bring it in action, only then will it come to life (Shirokogorov 1938a: xvi, emphasis added).

That speech was made on the occasion of the 325th anniversary of the House of Romanov (Shirokogorov 1938a, 1938b). It was held in the so-called "Russian House" in Beiping — a centre of Russian expatriate life in the Chinese capital. This speech may be considered Shirokogoroff's last major political address and political publication (Speshnev 2004: 125–43). It is important to note that at that time Shirokogoroff was a member of the Beiping group of the Russian anti-communist committee (Fig. 6.7), which was headquartered in Tientsin (Tiānjīn), but also had branches in Beiping, Kalgan (Zhāngjiākǒu), Qingdao, and Cheefoo (Yāntái). This organization was a successor to the Russian nationalistic organizations in China, including the so-called Russian national community (Khisamutdinov 1999). At a time when the Soviet politicians supported anti-Japanese propaganda, the Russian emigrants in China sympathized with the "new order" in Asia and persisted in their commitment to the fight against Bolshevism, sometimes confusing them with the anti-American propaganda.[9]

Shirokogoroff spoke of his vision of history as a merger of power and the people into a single whole, an entity that should be responsible for all political actions. It is the people (or *etnos* in his anthropological

9 Among other people of "The Beiping anti-communist committee" in Figure 6.7, there is General Sergeĭ N. Rozanov (1869–1937), who was a right-hand man of Admiral Kolchak in Vladivostok. As Canfield Smith writes, his militaristic regime in Vladivostok was actively supported by the Japanese (Smith 1975: 12).

Fig. 6.7 The Beiping anti-communist committee. Shirokogoroff sits second from the right. From Ivan I. Serebrennikov's collection (HILA 1A/5: 40). © Hoover Institution Library and Archives, Stanford University, California

texts) that for him represented a vital force, and at the very end of his Russian House speech he spoke about the "individuality of the peoples", which he saw as having been stable inside the Romanov's empire, primarily owing to the system of hereditary transfer of power. Ironically, it represented his imaginative returning to his Vladivostok years and his personal desire to establish an ideal order composed of *etnoses* and nations, hopefully dispelling the political chaos around him.

Order out of Chaos

Having made a decision to go to Vladivostok instead of staying in revolutionary Petrograd, Shirokogoroff became part of the unstable far eastern political landscape. The actual absence of any borders, as well as of the state itself, turned the Far East into a peculiar space produced by the flows of people, armies, and ships from many countries. It is well-known that the Japanese, the Chinese, the American, and the Russian forces were all involved in local politics in various degrees, turning the territory into not a "slightly complicated door", as the French anthropologist Grégory Delaplace (2013) put it referring to the contemporary Russian-Chinese-Mongolian border, but rather into a wide-open door without any locks or keys.

Vladivostok and Blagoveshchensk were the centres of gravity for many intellectuals from the European part of Russia. On the one hand, since the beginning of the nineteenth century, that territory had been historically part of the system of the forced relocation of Russian intellectuals. However, many of these people stayed in the area, where they married and had children. This created what to an outsider appeared to be a vivid intellectual life on the outskirts of the empire. On the other hand, the political chaos of the 1920s forced people to look for freedom, and then, after they found it for some time, they went back in their minds to the restoration of the monarchy and the re-establishment of the new/old political order.

In that sense, Shirokogoroff is a good example of such an intellectual, one who converted his "provincialism" into an ideological weapon in both his academic research and politics. His *etnos* and the diagrams he sketched on his university blackboard illustrating the structure of ethnology, along with his slogans of "non-partied national movement" and "real people", which he uttered at political meetings, created a type of equilibrium in his thought. This stability reflected the way he himself balanced between different political forces in the region. Thus, as I pointed out above, he worked both for the Far East University, which collaborated with the Soviet-supporting Far Eastern Republic, and at the People's Assembly, which was radically anti-Socialist. In China, Shirokogoroff developed his anti-Soviet political agenda further, putting himself on the right wing of the local political landscape. His sense of isolation combined with his unrealised dream to work in a major scientific centre probably made him less sensitive to the dramatic political changes in countries outside his rather small world.

In this particular context, Shirokogoroff's desire to fulfil his academic plans and political ideas blossomed. At that time, he was already the author of many books and was just finishing his *magnum opus*, "Big *Ėtnos*" (or *Ethnology* in two volumes). His works and name were known to many researchers internationally, but it would seem he was more of a pen pal for them than a colleague. His still-poorly-understood visit to Nazi Germany, and the active correspondence he began there with racialists like Pitt Rivers, suggest that he would have liked to have seen his ideas like *etnos* and psychomental complex implemented politically. He felt that the ideas he developed at the margins of empire should now be employed at the centre.

The stories of Shirokogoroff and those of many other intellectuals of that time reflect the lives of those who lived at the borders of empire as much as they represent alternative concepts of popular rule or ethnicity. They are the works of emigrants who, in their thinking, tried to find the imagined centre of the imperial political landscape via the categories of nationality and ethnicity (see chapters 2, 3 and 4). The geographic and intellectual localization of the theory made its biography interesting not only for the history of anthropological thought, but also for the understanding of political instability as a condition for the development of social theories. Placed right in the middle of the chaotic present and sharing the strong anti-tsarist feelings, the early Soviet ethnographers "made up lists of nationalities for all three censuses using their own experience for *the creation of order from chaos and for the creation of a new order of definitions*" (Hirsch 1997: 251, emphasis added). This wording was strangely reminiscent of the discussions in the Russian Geographical Society's Commission for Making Ethnographic Maps of Russia of which the central figure of this article — Sergei Mikhailovich Shirokogoroff — was also an active participant. It is quite amazing that, some time after, his ideas (and not only his) were incorporated as quite acceptable by Soviet ethnography — contrary to all the logic of history.

Published References

Anderson, D. G., and D. Arzyutov. Forthcoming. 'The Etnos Archipelago: Sergeĭ M. Shirokogoroff and the Life History of a Controversial Anthropological Concept', *Current Anthropology*.

Anon. 1921. *Vecherni͡ai͡a gazeta* 14 Sep. 1921.

Appleton, V. B. 1976. *A Doctor's Letters from China Fifty Years Ago* (Honolulu, HI: [no pub.]).

Chen, L. 2013. 'The Switched-On City', *Global Times*, 30 Jan. 2013.

Chepurkovskiĭ, E. M. 1938. *Na zadvorkakh i okolo dvort͡sov. Ėpizody iz zhizni i mysli trekh russkikh studentov, izlozhennye poslednim iz nikh* (Tianjin: A. I. Serebri͡annikov i K.).

Chirokogorov, I. I. 1909. *Rapport sur une mission scientifique à Paris (à l'Institut Pasteur)* (Iuriev: [no pub.]).

Delaplace, G. 2013. 'A Slightly Complicated Door: The Ethnography and Conceptualisation of North Asian Borders', in *Frontier Encounters: Knowledge and Practice at the Russian, Chinese and Mongolian Border*, ed. by F. Billé, G. Delaplace, and C. Humphrey (Cambridge: Open Book Publishers), 1–18, https://www.openbookpublishers.com/product/139; https://doi.org/10.11647/OBP.0026

Duara, P. 2004. *Sovereignty and Authenticity: Manchukuo and the East Asian Modern* (Oxford: Rowman & Littlefield).

Fèi Xiàotōng. 1994. 'Cóng shǐ lù guó lǎoshī xué tǐzhí rénlèi xué', *Běijīng dàxué xuébào: Zhéxué shèhuì kēxué bǎn* (5): 13–22.

Fominykh, S. F., ed. 2008. *Zhurnaly zasedaniĭ soveta Instituta issledovanii͡a Sibiri* (13 noi͡abri͡a 1919 g. — 16 senti͡abri͡a 1920 g.) (Tomsk: Izdatel'stvo TGU).

Guldin, G. E. 1994. *The Saga of Anthropology in China: From Malinowski to Moscow to Mao* (London: Sharpe).

Gurevich, B. B. 1940. 'Svetloĭ pami͡ati prof. S. M. Shirokogorova', *Zari͡a* 19 Nov. 1940: 4.

Hart, B. W. 2015. *George Pitt-Rivers and the Nazis* (London: Bloomsbury).

Hirsch, F. 1997. 'The Soviet Union as a Work in Progress: Ethnographers and the Category of Nationality in the 1926, 1937, and 1939 Censuses', *Slavic Review* 56 (2): 251–78.

Hsu, F. L. 1944. 'Sociological research in China', *Quarterly Bulletin of Chinese Bibliography* (ser. 2) 4 (1–4): 12–26.

Kan, S. 2009. *Lev Shternberg: Anthropologist, Russian Socialist, Jewish Activist* (Lincoln, NE: University of Nebraska Press).

Keith, S. A. 1931. *Ethnos, or the Problem of Race Considered From a New Point of View* (London: Kegan Paul).

Kerensky, A. F. 1965. *The Kerensky Memoirs: Russia and History's Turning Point* (London: Cassell).

Khisamutdinov, A. A. 1999. 'Russkie v Kitae. Ti͡an't͡szin'ska͡ia vetv' ėmigrat͡sii' *Problemy dal'nego Vostoka* 2: 118–22.

Kovali͡ashkina, E. P. 2005. *Inorodcheskiĭ vopros v Sibiri: kont͡sept͡sii gosudarstvennoĭ politiki i oblastnicheska͡ia mysl'* (Tomsk: Izdatel'stvo Tomskogo universiteta).

Kri͡ukov, M. V. 2007. 'S. M. Shirokogorov i I͡Un'nan'ska͡ia ėkspedit͡sii͡a 1928 g.', in *Problemy obshcheĭ i regional'noĭ ėtnografii (k 75-leti͡iu A. M. Reshetova): Sbornik stateĭ*, ed. by E. V. Ivanova (St Peterburg: MAĖ RAN), 93–109.

Li͡akhov, D. A. 2013. *Nebol'shevistskie modeli politicheskogo ustroĭstva Dal'nego Vostoka Rossii (dekabr' 1919 g.–okti͡abr' 1922 g.)* (unpublished doctoral dissertation, Far Eastern State University, Vladivostok).

Liú Xiǎoyún. 2007a. 'Shǐ lù guó duì zhōngguó zǎoqí rénlèi xué de yǐngxiǎng', *Zhōngnán mínzú dàxué xuébào: Rénwén shèhuì kēxué bǎn* 27 (3): 10–14.

—. 2007b. 'Zhī háng liǎng xiāng nán: Shǐ lù guó yúnnán diàochá shìjiàn tànxī', Xuéshù tànsuǒ 4: 112–17.

Papillault, G. 1908. 'L'anthropologie est-elle une science unique?', *Revue de l'ecole d'anthropologie* 18 (April): 117–32.

Posadskov, A. L. 2015. 'Pisatel' V. N. Ivanov vo glave izdatel'skogo dela vremennogo Priamurskogo pravitel'stva (1921–1922 gg.)', *Gumanitarnye nauki v Sibiri* 3: 44–9.

Reshetov, A. M. 2001. 'Peterburgskiĭ period zhizni i dei͡atel'nosti S. M. Shirokogorova', in *Izbrannye raboty i materialy. Kniga 1*, ed. by A. M. Kuzentsov (Vladivostok: Izd. DV univ.), 6–31.

Semënov, I. S. 1994 [1966]. 'Parol' ne nuzhen', in *Sobranie Sochineniĭ*, by I. S. Semënov (Moscow: KUBK-a), 289–590.

Shirokogoroff, S. M. 1924. *Ethnical Unit and Milieu: A Summary of the Ethnos* (Shanghai: E. Evans and Sons).

—. 1931. *Ethnological and Linguistic Aspects of the Ural-Altaic Hypothesis* (Peiping: Commercial Press).

—. 1932. *Letter to Professor Dr D. H. Kulp, 30 July 1932* (Peiping: [no pub.]).

—. 1935. *Psychomental Complex of the Tungus* (London: Kegan Paul).

—. 1936. 'La Théorie de l'Ethnos et sa place dans le système des sciences anthropologiques', *L'Ethnographie. Nouv. Ser.* 32: 85–115.

—. 1937. 'Ethnographie und Ethnologie', *Archiv für Anthropologie* 52: 1–7.

—. 1944. *A Tungus Dictionary: Tungus-Russian and Russian-Tungus Photogravured from the Manuscripts* (Tokyo: Minzokugaru Kyokai).

Shirokogoroff, S. M. and V. B. Appleton. 1924. 'Growth of Chinese', *China Medical Journal* 38 (5): 400–13.

Shirokogoroff, S. M. and K. Inoue. 1991 [1939]. 'Tungus Literary Language', *Asian Folklore Studies* 50: 35–66.

Shirokogorov, S. M. 1919a. 'O metodakh razrabotki antropologicheskikh materialov', *Uchenye zapiski istoriko-filologicheskogo fakul'teta v Vladivostoke* 1 (2): 3–20.

—. 1919b. 'Opyt issledovanii͡a osnov shamanstva u tungusov', *Uchenye zapiski istoriko-filologicheskogo fakul'teta v Vladivostoke* 1: 47–108.

—. 1922a. *Mesto ėtnografii sredi nauk i klassifikat͡sii͡a ėtnosov* (Vladivostok: izd "Svobodnai͡a Rossii͡a").

—. 1922b. *Mezhdunardnoe polozhenie Rossii* (Vladivostok: Iosif Korot).

—. 1922c. *Sdelali li my oshibki na pervom nesot͡sialisticheskom s"ezde*? (Vladivostok: Iosif Korot).

—. 1922d. *Zadachi Nesot͡sialisticheskogo dvizhenii͡a: doklad prochitannyi na otkrytom zasedanii Soveta S"ezda Predstavitelei nesotsialisticheskogo naseleniia Dal'nego Vostoka 26 marta 1922 goda* (Vladivostok: Tip. Voennoĭ akademii).

—. 1923. *Ėtnos — issledovanie osnovnykh print͡sipov izmenenii͡a ėtnicheskikh i ėtnograficheskikh i͡avleniĭ* (Shanghai: Sibpress).

—. 1938a. 'Znachenie dinastii Romanovykh dli͡a Rossii (nachalo)', *Kitaĭskiĭ blagovestnik* 36 (9): 17–19.

—. 1938b. 'Znachenie dinastii Romanovykh dli͡a Rossii (okonchanie)', *Kitaĭskiĭ blagovestnik* 36 (10–11): 15–23.

Shirokogorova, E. N. 1919. 'Severo-Zapadnai͡a Man'chzhurii͡a (geograficheskiĭ ocherk po dannym marshrutnykh nabli͡udeniĭ)', *Uchenye zapiski istoriko-filologicheskogo fakul'teta v Vladivostoke* 1: 109–46.

Shternberg, L. I. A. 2009. 'Anthropological Suggestions and Perspectives During the Revolutionary Years In Russia', *Ab Imperio* 1: 271–77.

Smele, J. D. 2015a. 'Khoravat, Dmitrii Leondinovich', in *Historical Dictionary of the Russian Civil Wars, 1916–1926*, ed. by J. D. Smele (London: Rowman & Littlefield), 571–72.

—. 2015b. *The "Russian" Civil Wars, 1916–1926: Ten Years that Shook the World* (Oxford: Oxford University Press).

Smith, C. F. 1975. *Vladivostok under Red and White Rule: Revolution and Counterrevolution in the Russian Far East, 1920–1922* (Seattle, WA: University of Washington Press).

Speshnev, N. A. 2004. *Pekin-strana moego detstva. Kitaĭskai͡a rapsodii͡a. Zapiski sinkhronnogo perevodchika* (St Peterburg: Bel'veder).

Stephan, J. J. 1978. *The Russian Fascists: Tragedy and Farce in Exile, 1925–1945* (New York: Harper & Row).

Vernadskiĭ, V. I. 1994. *Dnevniki 1917–1921 (oktîabr′ 1917–îanvar′ 1920)* (Kiev: Naukova dumka).

Wang Mingming. 2010. 'The Intermediate Circle', *Chinese Sociology & Anthropology* 42 (4): 62–77, https://doi.org/10.2753/CSA0009-4625420404.

Zhuravlev, V. V., ed. 2012. *Privetstvennye poslanii͡a Verkhovnomu Praviteli͡u i Verkhovnomu glavnokomandui͡ushchemu admiralu A. V. Kolchaku.* Noi͡abr′ 1918–noi͡abr′ 1919 g. (St Peterburg: European University in St Petersburg Press).

Archival References

APS: American Philosophical Society, Philadelphia, Pennsylvania

APS Boas Collection, Box 82. A letter from F. Boas to S. M. Shirokogoroff, 13 Jul. 1920. Manuscript. 1 folio.

AS: Academia Sinica, Taipei

AS Yuan 46-26. A letter from S. M. Shirokogoroff to Y. P. Tsai, 15 Jul. 1930.

BN PAU i PAN: Scientific Library of the Polish Academy of Skills and the Polish Academy of Sciences, Kraków

BN PAU i PAN 4600-6: 4–8. Pis′mo S. M. Shirokogorova V. L. Kotvichu, 28 Apr. 1924. Manuscript. 4 folios.

BN PAU i PAN 4600-6: 9–13. Pis′mo S. M. Shirokogorova V. L. Kotvichu, 24 Aug. 1924. Manuscript. 5 folios.

BN PAU i PAN 4600-6: 65–66. Pis′mo S. M. Shirokogorova V. L. Kotvichu, 2 Oct. 1927. Manuscript. 2 folios.

BN PAU i PAN 4600-7: 32–32v. Pis′mo S. M. Shirokogorova V. L. Kotvichu, 24 Apr. 1931. Manuscript. 1 folio.

BN PAU i PAN 4600-7: 54–57. Pis′mo S. M. Shirokogorova V. L. Kotvichu, 6 Feb 1933. Manuscript. 4 folios.

BN PAU i PAN 4600-7: 67–69v. Pis′mo S. M. Shirokogorova V. L. Kotvichu, 5 Aug. 1935. Manuscript. 3 folios.

BN PAU i PAN 4600-7: 70–70v. Pis′mo S. M. Shirokogorova V. L. Kotvichu, 28 Nov. 1935. Manuscript. 1 folios.

Chu.Cam: Archive of Churchill College, Cambridge

Chu.Cam PIRI 22/3. A letter from S. M. Shirokogoroff to G. Pitt Rivers, 14 Nov. 1935. Typeset. 2 folios.

Chu.Cam PIRI 11/2. Pitt Rivers, G. Science of Population. Interim Report on Scientific Organization and Classification. [Undated]. 6 folios.

EAA: Estonian Historical Archive, Tartu

EAA 384.1.3443. Lichnoe delo I. I. Shirokogorova, 2 Jun. 1915–11 Jun. 1916. 46 folios.

EAA 402.1.29599. Lichnoe delo V. M. Shirokogorova. 1906. 57 folios.

EAA 402.1.29600. Lichnoe delo I. I. Shirokogorova, 1 June 1907–28 May 1917. 105 folios.

EAA 402.1.29601. Lichnoe delo M. M. Shirokogorova, 1912. 47 folios.

EAA 402.1.29602. Lichnoe delo M. M. Shirokogorova, 1913. 6 folios.

EAA 402.3.1864. Lichnoe delo I. I. Shirokogorova, 1 Jun. 1907–20 Mar. 1917. 7 folios.

EVR: Elena V. Robinson's Personal Archive, St Petersburg

Photographic collection

GARF: State Archive of the Russian Federation, Moscow

GARF 102 D-7-207(1910)-2877: 12–13. Kopii͡a pis'ma I. I. Shirokogorova V. M. Shirokogorovu, 30 Aug. 1910. Typescript. 2 folios

GARF 124-55-338: 2. Pis'mo A. F. Kerenskogo Komitetu obshchestvennoĭ bezopasnosti, 30 Mar. 1917. Typescript. 1 folio.

GARF 393-86-639. Lichnoe delo V. M. Shirokogorova, 26 Aug. 1923–20 May 1924. 33 folios.

HILA: Hoover Institution Library and Archives, Stanford University, California

HILA 26001-141. Pis'mo S. M. Shirokogorova L. E. Berkovichu, 21 Jan. 1910. 1 folio.

HILA 1A-5 [1938–1939]. Serebrennikov Collection. Dnevnik I. I. Serebrennikova.

HILA 1A-5 [1938–1939]. Serebrennikov Collection. Photographs.

MAĖ: [Numbered Collections of] Peter the Great Museum of Anthropology and Ethnography (Kunstkamera), Russian Academy of Sciences, St Petersburg

MAĖ 2639-465–470. Fotografii kitaĭskikh piketov, 1915–1916. Photo prints. 102x40 mm.

MRC: Museum of Russian Culture, San Francisco, California

MRC 3-2-31-6. Lifanovskiĭ, A. A. Opisanie plavaniīa po r. Arguni v 1915 g. Typescript. 43 folios.

MRC 45-3-9. Ofitsial'nye dokumenty generala Khorvata. Prikaz Vremennogo pravitelīa No 43 (Vladivostok, 18 Oct. 1918)... po Diplomaticheskoĭ kantselīarii o naznachenii S. M. Shirokogorova chinovnikom osobykh porucheniĭ V klassa s 9 iīulīa 1918 g. 1 folio.

MRC 45-4-1. Kantselīariīa generala Khorvata. Otchëty i finansovye dokumenty.

MRC Photographic and leaflet collection.

NA RGO: Scientific Archive of the Russian Geographical Society, St Petersburg

NA RGO 24-1-78. Protokoly № 1–4 II Otdela [Komissii] sostavleniīa ėtnograficheskikh kart Sibiri i Sredneĭ Azii i dr[ugie] materialy [dated 1910–1924]. 124 folios.

NA RGO 109-1-15. L. ĪA. Shternberg, F. K. Volkov, N. M. Mogilīanskiĭ. Zapiska ob ėtnografii i antropologii [undated]. 13 folios.

RGIA DV: Russian State Historical Archive of the Far East, Vladivostok

RGIA DV P-289-2-1573: 11–11v. Pis'mo dotsenta Dal'nevostochnogo gosudarstvennogo universiteta A. M. Mervarta dekanu Vostochnogo fakul'teta s otzyvom o S. M. Shirokogorove. 19 Jan. 1922. 1 folio.

RGIA DV P-289-2-1573: 16–16v. Pis'mo S. M. Shirokogorova rektoru Dal'nevostochnogo universiteta. 15 Dec. 1922. 1 folio.

RGIA DV P-289-2-1573: 17–18v. Pis'mo S. M. Shirokogorova dekanu Vostochnogo fakul'teta. 14 Nov. 1922. 2 Folios.

RGIA DV P-289-2-1573: 26-26v. Postanovlenie sobraniīa Vostochnogo fakul'teta o priznanii S. M. Shirokogorova privat-dotsentom s porucheniem chteniīa lektsiĭ. 25 Jan. 1922. 1 folio.

RGIA DV P-289-2-1573: 27–28. Biograficheskai͡a spravka, spisok ėkspedit͡siĭ, komandirovok i trudov S. M. Shirokogorova. 1922. 2 folios.

SPF ARAN: St Petersburg Filial of the Archive of the Russian Academy of Sciences

SPF ARAN 142-1(1918)-68: 140–144v. Pis'mo S. M. Shirokogorova L. I͡A. Shternbergu, 4 Aug. 1916. Manuscript. 5 folios.

SPF ARAN 142-1(1918)-71: 44. Pis'mo S. M. Shirokogorova L. I͡A. Shternbergu, 13 Sep. 1917. Typeset. 1 folio.

SPF ARAN 142-1(1918)-72: 17–17v. Pis'mo S. M. Shirokogorova V. V. Radlovu, 1 Aug. 1917. Manuscript. 1 folio.

SPF ARAN 142-1(1918)-72: 22–23. Pis'mo S. M. Shirokogorova L. I͡A. Shternbergu, 17 May 1918. Manuscript. 2 folios.

SPF ARAN 142-1(1922)-4: 195–96. Otchët S. M. Shirokogorova v Rossiĭskui͡u Akademii͡u Nauk, 26 Oct. 1922. Typeset. 2 folios.

SPF ARAN 142-1(1923)-3: 13. Pis'mo L. I͡A. Shternberga S. M. Shirokogorovu, 28 Feb. 1923. Manuscript. 1 folio.

SPF ARAN 142-1(1924)-4: 11–12v. Otchët S. M. Shirokogorova v Rossiĭskui͡u Akademii͡u Nauk, 26 Jan. 1923. Typeset. 2 folios.

SPF ARAN 282-2-319: 21–22v. Pis'mo S. M. Shirokogorova L. I͡A. Shternbergu, 11 May 1917. Manuscript. 2 folios.

SPF ARAN 282-2-319: 23–24v. Pis'mo S. M. Shirokogorova L. I͡A. Shternbergu, 28 Aug. 1917. Manuscript. 2 folios.

SPF ARAN 282-2-319: 25–27v. Pis'mo S. M. Shirokogorova L. I͡A. Shternbergu, 04 Dec. 1922. Manuscript. 3 folios.

SPF ARAN 820-3-879: 1–1v. Pis'mo I. I. Shirokogorova V. M. Alekseevu, 03 Mar. 1941. Manuscript. 1 folio.

SPF ARAN 820-3-880: 40–43. Pis'mo S. M. Shirokogorova V. M. Alekseevu, 9 Apr. 1931. Manuscript. 7 folios.

SPF ARAN 849-5-805: 1–269v. S. M. and E. N. Shirokogorovy. Konspekty lekt͡siĭ. Vypiski iz literatury. In Russian and French. 1906–1911.

TsGIA SPb: Central State Historical Archive of St Petersburg

TsGIA SPb 14-3-59098. Lichnoe delo S. M. Shirokogorova. 1911. 41 folios

TumA: Donald Tumanisonis's Personal Archive, Horten, Norway

TumA 109. Incoming Correspondence Letter 109. Letter from Ivan I. Gapanovich to Donald Tumanisonis, 1 May 1979.

TumA 183. Incoming Correspondence Letter 183. Letter from Ivan I. Gapanovich to Donald Tumanisonis, 8 Jun. 1980.

TumA 243. Incoming Correspondence Letter 243. Letter from the Archpriest of the St. Aleksandr Nevsky Cathedral in Paris to Donald Tumanisonis, 8 Jan 1981.

TumA 1915/16. Photocopied Field Diary of Sergei Shirokogoroff, 1915–1916.

7. Chasing Shadows: Sharing Photographs from Former Northwest Manchuria

Jocelyne Dudding[1]

In 2014 a new social trajectory was set in place for two photographic collections made by two couples who photographed and researched the region formally known as Northwest Manchuria at the start of the twentieth century. Working with digital copies of these images, I was privileged to share them with the descendants of those originally portrayed. Gě Jùn Gǔ, the Headman of Ewenki Camp 1, scanned the files and recognised a photograph of his family (Figs. 7.1a and 7.1b). His face displayed a keen interest in the imagery, but he also revealed a deeper

1 I am most grateful to Mrs Erdongua, Bái Yín, Āntè Bù, Mèng Huìjīn, Naragaowa and the many other community members who welcomed us in Inner Mongolia and shared their knowledge and stories. Sincere thanks also to Mèng Sōnglín, head of the Mongolian Ethnic Origin Project and Daur and Orochon descendant; Bái Jīnsēn, director, Hūlúnbèiěr Museum of Nationalities; Hāda, curator, Hūlúnbèiěr Museum of Nationalities; Nasan Bayar, head of the School of Anthropology, and Bǎohuà, associate professor, at the Inner Mongolia University. All of them had a personal role, as well as academic and political agency, in supporting the project that enabled the sharing of photos with stakeholders who would not otherwise have been able to access them. My gratitude to my co-partners in this digitisation project and their related institutes for their generosity and dedication. Finally, I wish to thank John Lindgren, who in 1992 donated his parents' photographs to the MAA and continues to contribute knowledge and stories that bring the images and their makers to life. In 2017, Stein Mamen donated his grandfather's remaining photographic and manuscript collection to the Museum of Cultural History, Oslo, so the story is set to continue.

https://doi.org/10.11647/OBP.0150.07

sense of excitement. "We had heard of a woman [Ethel Lindgren] coming here many years ago and taking photos", I remember him explaining, "but we didn't know where [the photos] were or what they would show us. We have been hunting for them and now you bring them to us".[2]

Fig. 7.1a "Look, those are the bridles of my clan — this picture must be of my family". Gě Jùn Gǔ and herders of Ewenki Camp 1. Photo by Jocelyne Dudding, Áolǔgǔ yā, 16 April 2014

Fig. 7.1b "Petr Ivanovich's daughter and daughter-in-law riding reindeer to look for lost deer. Holding long sticks = Tiawun used for mounting the deer". Photo by Ethel Lindgren, Ulugit River, 24 June 1932 (MAA P.78208.LIN). © Museum of Archaeology and Anthropology, Cambridge

2 Translations from Russian and the analysis of Shirokogoroff's unpublished manuscripts were done by David G. Anderson.

My arrival carrying copies of this set of photographs brought a pleasing and unexpected end to a search for family photographs. It also started a new process of the herders and their families looking at, enjoying, and investigating their own histories as represented by earlier explorers. For the small team of academics, curators, and film crews — who gathered together from Cambridge, Hohhot [Kökeqota], and Hǎilāěr [Hailar] — to accompany us on that day to the snow forests north of Áolǔgǔyā, Hūlúnbèiěr, it was their first opportunity to see the magic and power of gifting photographs.

This account really begins with the story of two couples who worked and travelled in Manchuria in the early twentieth century. Sergei and Elizaveta Shirokogoroff conducted anthropometric fieldwork on both the Siberian and Chinese sides of the Amur River between 1912 and 1917. Their collections are primarily held at the Peter the Great Museum, St Petersburg (MAĖ). Ethel Lindgren and Oscar Mamen travelled along many of the same trails in Northwest Manchuria between 1928 and 1932, and much of their work and collections correspond closely with the Shirokogoroffs'. Lindgren and Mamen's northwestern Manchurian collections are now cared for at the Museum of Archaeology and Anthropology, University of Cambridge (MAA). The photographs and collections of these two couples had been rarely seen. Their biographies, and hence, their motives and practices in creating and using their photographs were little known. This chapter represents an attempt to contextualize these images.

The chapter is based on the work of a group of university-based scholars and curators in Cambridge and St Petersburg who rediscovered, researched, and digitised the field photographs and papers of these two anthropological couples.[3] Our work was to share these images with their originating communities in Inner Mongolia.

3 This work began as part of an International Research Network funded by the Leverhulme Trust (IN-2012-138). Through this project, a subset of both photographic collections documenting Ewenki and Oroqen were digitised and prepared for display and sharing with local communities. At a later stage of the project, two partners of our research network, Uradyn Bulag of MIASU, University of Cambridge, and Nasan Bayar of Inner Mongolia University, sought additional funding from the Mongolian Ethnic Origin Project to digitise and return to their sites of creation all of the images contained in the extensive Lindgren-Mamen collections. Several members of the Leverhulme Project conducted fieldwork at Ewenki settlements at Áolǔgǔyā and Gēnhé; Oroqen communities at Ālǐhé; and Yīmǐn River; with Daur in Nántún (formerly Omul Ail); Russian Cossack descendants at

The chapter explores the ways in which the acts of locating, digitising, printing, and displaying those images, created a forum for talking about people's lives. The chapter documents the questions that these images helped to resolve in the minds of the descendants of the people who traditionally herded reindeer or hunted in the region. However, it also documents the shadows created by these images and the new uncertainties these digital collections have created. In the process of chasing these shadows, the chapter addresses the ongoing questions of identity, visual representation, and alternative histories, particularly in the context of sometimes rigid frameworks of state-controlled *etnos-mínzú* identity, among Ewenkis and Oroqens.[4]

One of photography's inventors, Henry Fox Talbot, in 1839 described his process as "partaking of the character of the marvellous, providing almost as much as any fact which physical investigation has yet brought to our knowledge" in the "Art of fixing a Shadow" (Talbot 1839: section 4). He continued with startlingly evocative language:

> The most transitory of things, a shadow, the emblem of all that is fleeting and momentary, may be fettered by the spells of our "natural magic," and may be fixed for ever in the position which it seemed only destined for a single instant to occupy (Ibid: 5).

By happenstance, Talbot's language captures much of the wonder and curiosity of the Ewenki herders looking at the images of their ancestors, 100 years previously riding in a similar environment and perhaps camping in similar glades as they. It is this preservation of an event that seems magical within a society that exists in a constant eruption of political change and development. These photographs are more than just an image or interpretation of the past; as Susan

---

Éěrgǔnà [Argun]; Buriat, Mongol and Barga groups around Gānzhūěr sūmù; and academic and minority migrant communities in Hǎilāěr and Hohhot.

4 Orthography and naming is a significant issue when discussing this transborder region where there are representatives of each nationality or *mínzú* living in the Russian Federation, the People's Republic of China, and sometimes, Mongolia. Although it has become standard to describe the name of the Tungus-speaking people эвенки as *Evenki* in Latin script, within the China studies literature, *Ewenki* is standard. Different generations used different naming conventions. The Shirokogoroffs named most Tungus-speaking peoples in northwestern China as Orochens, while Lindgren and Mamen distinguished between Ewenkis and Oroqens. In China, the term Ewenki also includes the sub-groups Solon, Daur, and Khamnigans, so unless otherwise specified, the use of the term "Ewenki" refers to "Reindeer Ewenki".

Sontag notes, they are a direct trace stencilled off what was real (Sontag 1978: 120). In these historically remote areas, incredibly few local people owned or had access to a camera, and missionary or colonial postings to these regions — frequently a principle source of photographic archives — were uncommon. The use of the camera by the Shirokogoroffs and by Lindgren and Mamen thereby produced some of the earliest known imagery of Ewenkis and Oroqens. It is for such reasons that the visual archives of early twentieth-century travellers cared for by museums are so highly valued by people living today.

The Field Photography of Sergei and Elizaveta Shirokogoroff

Sergei Shirokogoroff and his wife Elizaveta conducted three expeditions to Siberia and Northwest Manchuria between 1912 and 1917 (see Fig. 5.2). Their first tour was self-funded, and the later expeditions were made on behalf of the Russian Academy of Science and partly the Russian Committee for Central and Eastern Asia Studies. Their expeditions in 1912 and 1913 were to Zabaĭkal'skaÍa oblast' (Fig. 7.2), and each lasted for approximately four or five months (see chapter 5). Their 1915–1916 expedition went from Gan to the Amur River valleys (Fig. 7.3). The expedition continued westward overland, assembling equally significant collections among the Amur Oroqens and then in Daur and Manchu territories along the Amur River. This expedition built on the experience of their two previous expeditions and arguably lasted for the rest of their lives as they found themselves living as émigrés in China.

Sergei Shirokogoroff and Elizaveta Robinson were born into families of provincial intelligentsia in late imperial Russia. They received their primary education in what is now Estonia, where they first met. They married in Paris at a young age while Elizaveta studied law and Sergei audited a number of lecture courses at the École d'anthropologie, and also at a number of other institutions in Paris (see chapter 6). As discussed in some detail in other chapters in this book, neither were initially drawn to Manchuria or east Asia or to fieldwork, but they were sent on their first expedition on the recommendation of their supervisors. That fieldwork would change their lives. Working together at a time when anthropology was a discipline in formation, they combined what today seems to be a chaotic ensemble of research techniques: exhaustively

Fig. 7.2 "Ceremonial welcoming of guests" with Elizaveta and Sergei Shirokogoroff at the centre. Photographer unknown, Akima River, tributary of the Nercha River, October 1912 (MAÈ 2002-66). © Peter the Great Museum of Anthropology and Ethnography, Russian Academy of Sciences, St Petersburg

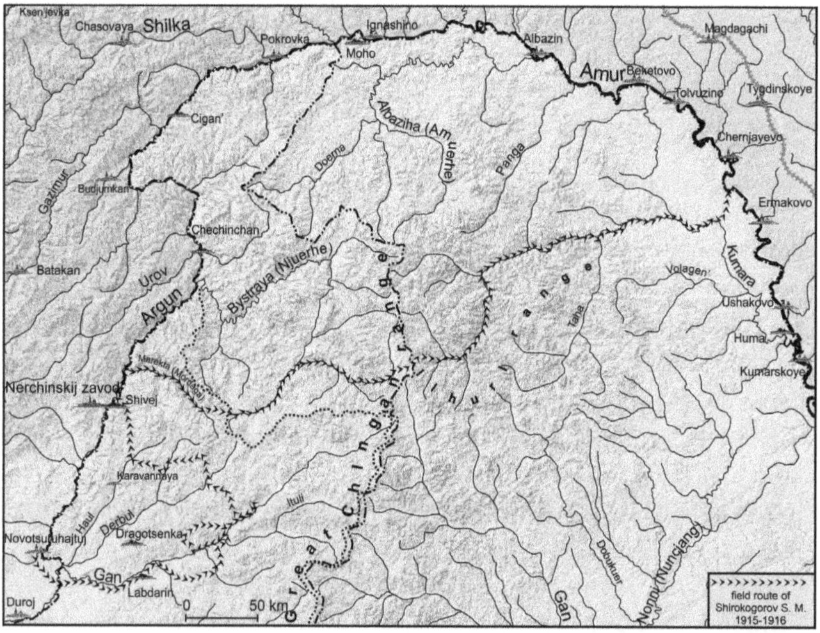

Fig. 7.3 Shirokogoroffs' expedition routes in Siberia and former Northwest Manchuria, 1915–1916. Map by Alekseĭ G. Akulov

documenting folklore, creating dictionaries, measuring heads, noting and transcribing music, and collecting artefacts.

Although photography was not a new technique in 1912, the camera was rarely seen in this region. Accessing photographic materials and laboratories for printing was difficult. The first camera that the Shirokogoroffs took to the field with them was a 5 x 7 inch glass plate camera with a wide angle and standard lens, loaned to them by the Russian Geographical Society. This camera was recommended by the British Association for the Advancement of Science and also, they note, by the École d'anthropologie de Paris (citing 1898: 109) for the visual recording of anthropometric types (British Association 1909: 51).[5] A specific requirement was portraits of individual's head and shoulders of "the left side of the face in exact profile" and "in strictly full-face", but it was noted that with the 5 x 7 inch negative the prerequisite full-length portraits could also be enlarged to produce a suitable quality head and shoulders portrait (British Association 1909: 50–1) (Figs. 7.4a and 7.4b). An additional instruction notes: "Very interesting series are afforded by whole families" (Ibid: 49) (Fig. 7.5).

Figs. 7.4a and 7.4b. "An Orochen man (Bagadarin) (F.)" and "An Orochen man (translator Pavel) (Pr.)". Photo by Elizaveta and Sergei Shirokogoroff, Akima River, tributary of the Nercha River, October 1912 (MAĖ 2002-44 and 2002-37). © Peter the Great Museum of Anthropology and Ethnography, Russian Academy of Sciences, St Petersburg

5 The RAI in *Notes and Queries* also recommended the British equivalent half-plate camera (Marreco and Myres 1912).

Fig. 7.5 "Old man Antyrov with his wife and daughter at their yurt". Photo by Elizaveta and Sergei Shirokogoroff, Akima River, tributary of the Nercha River, October 1912 (MAĖ 2002-70). © Peter the Great Museum of Anthropology and Ethnography, Russian Academy of Sciences, St Petersburg

It is clear from the resulting photographs of their 1912 expedition that the Shirokogoroffs perceived the camera as a scientific instrument to be used for documenting physical types. Apart from three posed photographs of women preparing skins and portraits of families against the backdrop of their homes, there is little visual documentation of material culture or social contexts. There is only one landscape view, which might have been intended to "document factors that would affect peoples' evolution" (British Association 1909: 47; Shirokogoroff 1925: 10). The selection of subjects may have been a conscious decision or a limitation of their photographic equipment. The 5 x 7 inch plate camera was cumbersome and required the use of a tripod during exposure, resulting in often formal and static photographs. The necessary glass plates were difficult to transport because of their weight and fragility — with an expected twenty per cent loss due to breakages — and with the difficulty of obtaining additional plates in the field, the Shirokogoroffs would have had to justify and ration every exposure. The heavy, fragile technology also limited the ability of the couple to share photographs. There is only one mention of Sergei gifting a photograph of himself to an Oroqen friend who had given him several gifts (SPF ARAN 849-5-803: 3v).

Although the photographic collections were accessioned under Sergei's name, it is clear that Elizaveta was equally, if not more, active as Sergei in the making and printing of photographs. Her field diary for the 1912 expedition makes several references to her taking pictures (SPF ARAN 849-5-803, 5v; 19v; 21v; and 24).

During the later expedition in Manchuria, the couple used a twin lens stereo camera that produced two offset images of the same scene that, when viewed together in a dedicated viewer, created a three-dimensional impression of depth and solidity. Yet it is unclear why the Shirokogoroffs moved to the stereoscope format. Geographical societies and Francis Galton had historically promoted the stereo camera for land surveying, particularly for monuments and buildings (Livingstone and Withers 2005: 20). If the Shirokogoroffs were engaged in land surveying or cartography, this choice of equipment would make sense. Indeed, within the Shirokogoroff collection there are two images that include a surveyor's pole in the frame (Fig. 7.6) (MAĖ 2638-55a and b). These had previously been read as evidence of the Shirokogoroffs being engaged in surveying work. However, on closer inspection, the pole is fixed in the ground and marked with *di͡uĭmy* (inches) to measure levels, most likely water depth during floods or the depth of accumulated snow.[6]

Fig. 7.6 "Orochen equestrians". Identified as "Administrative heads among the Orochen population" in 2638-78. Photo by Elizaveta or Sergei Shirokogoroff, Radde, Upper Amur basin, 1915–1916 (MAĖ 2638-55b). © Peter the Great Museum of Anthropology and Ethnography, Russian Academy of Sciences, St Petersburg

6 One of the men in Figure 7.6 appears next to a government building in a later photograph, perhaps indicating that hydrological measurements might have been one of his duties (MAĖ 2638-77).

Some early anthropologists also considered the stereo camera as a tool of authenticity that provided a spatial physical presence of peoples who were "dying out" (Matiasek 2016: 193). Yet despite efforts by David Brewster, the developer of the stereoscope (Livingstone and Withers 2005: 209), to promote the camera, it was seldom recommended for anthropological work. In addition, the smaller-sized negative of the stereo camera the Shirokogoroffs used produced portraits that were deemed "of comparative little value" (British Association 1909: 50).[7] However, if showing photographs in the field, as Elizaveta potentially did (SPF ARAN 849-5-803, 3), the stereoscope could be considered a magical format. Not only could individuals see their own or friend's likeness, but they also could be seen three-dimensionally — an early form of virtual reality.

Based on the 45 x 107 mm format of the negative, the camera used was probably a Richard verascope, which was smaller, lighter and more flexible for fieldwork. And with a 1/60 shutter speed and a magazine that stocked twelve negatives that were simply changed by turning the camera upside down, instant snapshot photography suddenly became possible (Henriot and Yeh 2012: 65). The verascope certainly changed the styles, genres, and number of photographs the Shirokogoroffs took during their latter two expeditions. During their 1915 expedition — the images from which form the photographic series MAĖ no. 2500 — one gets the sense they were experimenting with a new "toy". Gone were the head and shoulders portraits against a blank backdrop. Instead there were informal "snapshot" portraits of individuals taken as opportunities arose. Landscapes and studies of houses and settlements now appear more frequently (Fig. 7.7). We also find images of the anthropologist in the field (MAĖ 2500-6), the anthropologist on the trail (MAĖ 2500-36), and the more personal holiday snap (MAĖ 2500-8) (Fig. 7.8).

7 BAAS's criterion for cameras used in anthropometric work was that "the portraits should be on such a scale that the distance between the top of the head and the bottom of the chin shall in no case be less than 1 ¼ inch (30 mm.)" (British Association 1909: 50). The verascope as used by the Shirokogoroffs produced headshots no larger than 15mm.

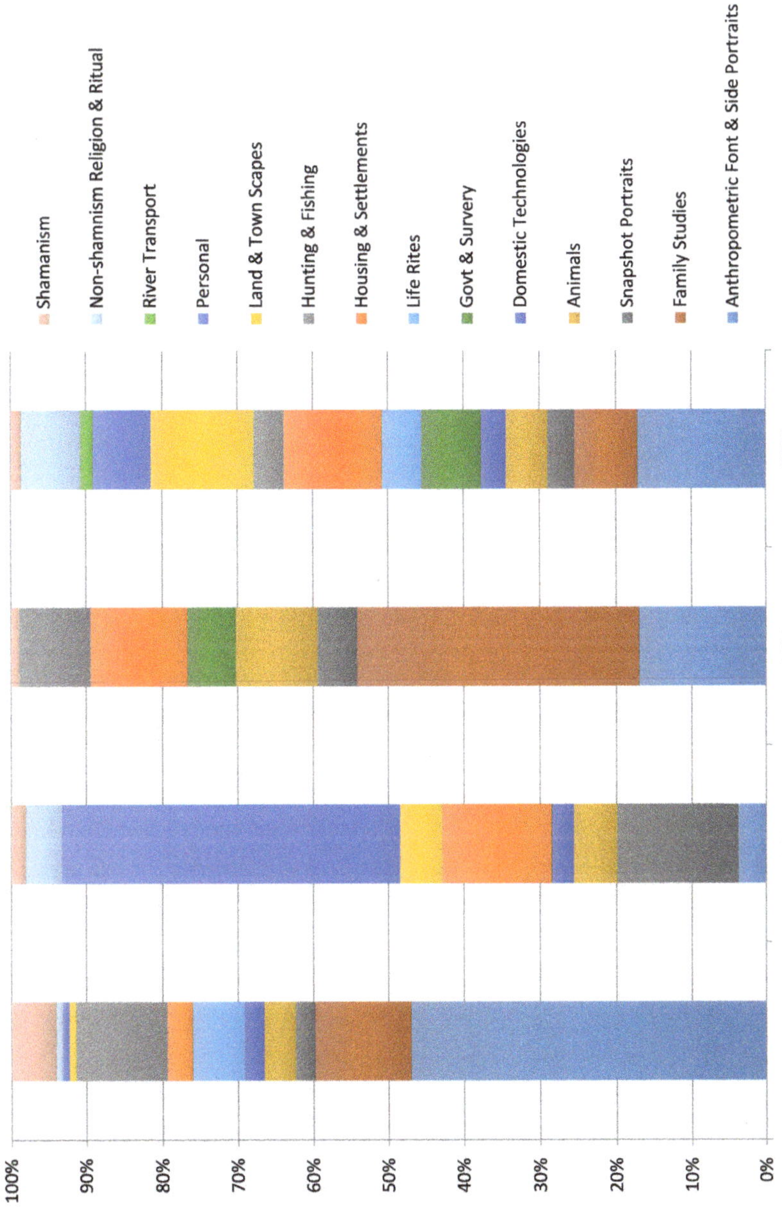

Fig. 7.7 The genres of photography undertaken by Elizaveta and Sergei Shirokogoroff, 1912–1917 (see also Arzîutov 2017), graph by Jocelyne Dudding

Fig. 7.8 "Man (?) with two dogs outside a tent". Elizaveta with the camp dogs and their tents in the background. Photo by Sergei Shirokogoroff, Priamurskiĭ Kraĭ, 2015 (MAĖ 2500-8). © Peter the Great Museum of Anthropology and Ethnography, Russian Academy of Sciences, St Petersburg

During the 1915–1916 and 1917 expeditions the Shirokogoroffs returned to taking anthropological portraits, although possibly still through chance encounters such as when Oroqen and military troops visited their camp (e.g. MAĖ 2639-342 - 2639-377 and MAĖ 2639-435 - 2639-457 respectively). Families appear posing in front of their houses (e.g. MAĖ 2638-15 - 2638-18), and thus the images could be used to illustrate social as well as material culture. This reformatting of anthropological portraits also may have been a reaction to the difficulties Elizaveta noted of photographing and measuring individuals in 1912 (SPF ARAN 849-5-803: 12v, 20), but it also illustrates Sergei's early interest in family characteristics and kinship systems and properties, which resulted in a series of manuscripts and several published books (Arzi͡utov 2017).

An anomaly in the Shirokogoroffs' archive is the relative lack of a visual presence of shamans and shamanism. Since Sergei came to be known after his death as an expert on shamanism, this absence is curious and frustrating. For today's Oroqens and Ewenkis, many of whom have lived through the Cultural Revolution, glimpses of religious practices before they were banned are important. In the surviving photographic archive, Shirokogoroff documented eight shamans dressed in their full regalia and two portraits of a shaman in everyday wear (Fig. 7.9). This links quite well to Shirokogoroff's interest in clothing and interpretation of regalia as "equipment", as discussed in chapter 5. Along these lines, there are also two photographs of a shaman's spirit-apron misleadingly captioned as "Utensils" (MAĖ 2500-87 - 2500-088). There is also one photograph of "Birches stuck in the ground, with rags and rabbit skins attached", which is likely a shamanistic site (MAĖ 2002-9). Finally, there is a series labelled "Oforo (Kalun-Shan'). A sacrifice" (MAĖ 2639-568 - 2639-571) that appears to show meat being prepared and guests attending but not of the ritual performance. None of these material or social aspects are mentioned in Sergei's epic *Psychomental Complex of the Tungus* (1935) nor are there any written accounts of performances in Elizaveta's 1912 field diary. It would seem that for them shamanic ritual generated objects rather than relationships.

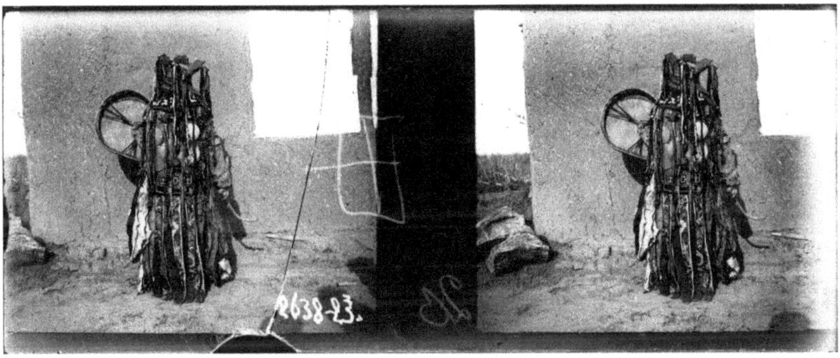

Fig. 7.9 "A female shaman (in traditional dress with her drum)". Photo by Elizaveta Shirokogoroff, Orochen compound, Upper Amur basin, 1915–1916 (MAĖ 2638-23). © Peter the Great Museum of Anthropology and Ethnography, Russian Academy of Sciences, St Petersburg

A disadvantage of the verascope camera was that it used a thinner glass plate, meaning its lightness for transportation and use was offset by a much higher breakage rate. For example, it's almost certain that the Shirokogoroffs made a frontal and probably a side portrait of the female shaman depicted in Fig. 7.9, yet only the photograph of the back of her costume ever reached MAĖ. The Shirokogoroffs also had difficulties with soft focusing, poor exposures, light leakage, and chemical staining during developing or printing.[8] Elizaveta records developing her own negatives (SPF ARAN 849-5-803, 24), and during their 1915–1917 expeditions they were printing images in the field using printing-out

8 The series of plates in MAĖ with the classmark 2002, taken on the 5 x 7" camera has nineteen damaged and/or poorly taken negatives. The verascope series with classmark MAĖ 2500 has 44 damaged negatives, series MAĖ 2638 has sixteen, and series MAĖ 2639 has 127.

paper.[9] This adds to the lack of quality of the Shirokogoroffs' photographs, which often makes their images difficult to read. Unfortunately, with so many of the portraits having undistinguishable features, it made them of limited interest for today's viewers looking for family resemblances.

The Shirokogoroff photographic archive is poorly documented. It would seem that the couple themselves undertook their portraiture for extremely formal or typological purposes, without any thought to delving into the individual's personal biography. Elizaveta notes in her 1912 field diary that the photographs were taken to support anthropometric measurements, and that census cards were also completed on each family (SPF ARAN 849-5-803: 3, 5, 10v, 12v, 13, 19v, and 20). The census cards, which may have held the attributions, have not been found. The photographs from the 1912–1913 expeditions were attributed by Sergei Shirokogoroff himself and generally were classified by region, year, and ethnic group, with few if any detail concerning the individuals in each photograph.

The much more extensive archive from the 1917 expedition often lacks even this basic information, which probably was due to the fact that the couple posted their undeveloped glass plates to St Petersburg for processing (TumA 1915/16: 95). Although they returned to St Petersburg briefly in 1917, it is likely that they never even saw the printed results. It is further likely that museum workers who did not know the context of the expedition documented the collection. In addition, the museum's classmarks do not reflect the photographs' chronological order. This lack of documentation meant that when contemporary Ewenki searched the databases for connections, the Shirokogoroffs' photographs were frequently overlooked.

As typologies, the Shirokogoroffs' photographs were rather more successful. It is significant that the 1915–1916 expedition was planned to investigate what we can recognize today as ethnogenetic curiosity. Sergei described the Tungus of eastern Mongolia and Northwest Manchuria as living in a "transitory belt" and interested himself in the study of "degrees of assimilation and even of amalgamation" with neighbouring groups (Shirokogoroff 1923a: 518, 520). His conclusions — perhaps in some unknown way illustrated by his anthropometric photographs and

9 Gelatin-chloride paper that is contact-printed with a negative using the sun as a light source.

collections of material culture — were that the southern Tungus groups were "leading ethnoses". He argued that they heavily influenced both Manchu and Chinese cultures, the latter of which he controversially described "as an amalgam" (Shirokogoroff 1923b: 619, 621).

Fig. 7.10 "Transbaĭkal Orochon woman (Collection of the Peter the Great Museum of Anthropology and Ethnography)". Reproduced in Czaplicka 1914: plate 13. Originally entitled "Woman (front)" (MAĖ 2002-39). © Peter the Great Museum of Anthropology and Ethnography, Russian Academy of Sciences, St Petersburg

Copies of the Shirokogoroff's photographs found their way into the hands of collectors and many images were published in a host of Soviet-era publications, often without attribution to the photographer (Anderson and Arzyutov 2016: 205 n18) (Fig. 7.10). The results of the 1915–1916 Manchurian expedition were cited in many of the English-language scientific publications published under Sergei's authorship, although often not in a way that allows easy interpretation of the photographic archive. Sergei published one English-language account of the 1912 and 1913 fieldwork in a scientific journal that is now difficult to find

(Shirokogoroff 1923a, 1923b). Elizaveta wrote and published in Russian a detailed account of their journey with a heavy emphasis on a description of the watersheds and roads used to access the area (Shirokogorova 1919). Elizaveta also published her analysis of the songs and music that she recorded during their fieldwork (Shirokogorova 1936).

This interesting latter aspect of their first expedition, and perhaps also of their Manchurian fieldwork, was an early attempt at sharing museum phonographic collections. The couple took with them a phonograph and printed copies of unidentified types of music, which they played for local Oroqens and Ewenkis, to great interest. In return, they also recorded local songs. As Elizaveta explained in a much later publication:

> The Museum of Anthropology and Ethnography in Petrograd in 1911–12 opened a Department of Musical Phonograms [...] Every researcher was given a phonograph and wax cylinders in order to record original versions of folk music among the peoples of Siberia and Asia. In the United States [at the Smithsonian Institution] this movement has already created its own literature on the study of folk music (Shirokogorova 1936: 283).

In her handwritten field diary, it was clear that the playing of the phonogram, and the recording of music, often functioned as a social ice-breaker, and thereby made individuals more comfortable with Elizaveta undertaking measurements and the photographing of physical types:

> 22 June. [...] A lot of people came to join our company. The women agreed to be measured. The phonograph made a great impression on everyone. I let them listen to the entire collection (SPF ARAN 849-5-803: 3).
>
> 15 [July] [...] In the evening, we opened the phonograph. It was with great difficulty we managed to get someone to sing something. On the one hand, they wanted to, but they got shy. They wanted to sing. It proved necessary to isolate Serëzha [Sergei] [to get them to sing]. Their songs are not long and very monotonous. They sang, laughing (Ibid: 16v-17).

However crackly and faint these wax cylinder recordings are, when played back in 2015–2016 they instantly appealed to all groups alike. Even when the songs were not recognised, or were not from the same cultural group, listening to the old songs linked people across the centuries. Invariably the listener would reply in song, to which many would then add their voices (Fig. 7.11).

Fig. 7.11 Mrs Erdongua listening to and then singing the lullaby recorded by Elizaveta Shirokogoroff in 1912. Photo by Bǎohuà, 2 April 2015. Wax cylinder, Institute of Russian Literature (Pushkin House) (FV 3276)

The Field Photography of Ethel Lindgren and Oscar Mamen

Ethel Lindgren, a Cambridge social psychology graduate, and Oscar Mamen, the Norwegian explorer and trader (and later, her husband), conducted social anthropological research from their base in Hǎilāěr, Hūlúnbèiěr province, between 1929 and 1932. Lindgren's most well-known work is from her and Mamen's three short expeditions northwards to stay with Reindeer Ewenkis in summer 1929, winter 1931, and spring 1932. On each of these trips they also spent a number of weeks with the Russian Cossack communities along the Argun [É'ěrgǔnà] River. The routes of these expeditions often overlapped with the earlier paths of the Shirokogoroffs (Fig. 7.12). During their time in Hūlúnbèiěr, Lindgren and Mamen amassed a staggering visual archive of 8,813 photographs covering all minorities in the area including Reindeer Ewenkis.[10] The collection is not only notable for the high quality and pleasing artistic composition of its images, but that it provides some of the earliest known photographs of the diverse peoples and landscapes of the region

10 This figure represents the number of unique images in their collections and consists of 5,778 negatives, 2,816 prints without an original negative currently located, and 219 drawings.

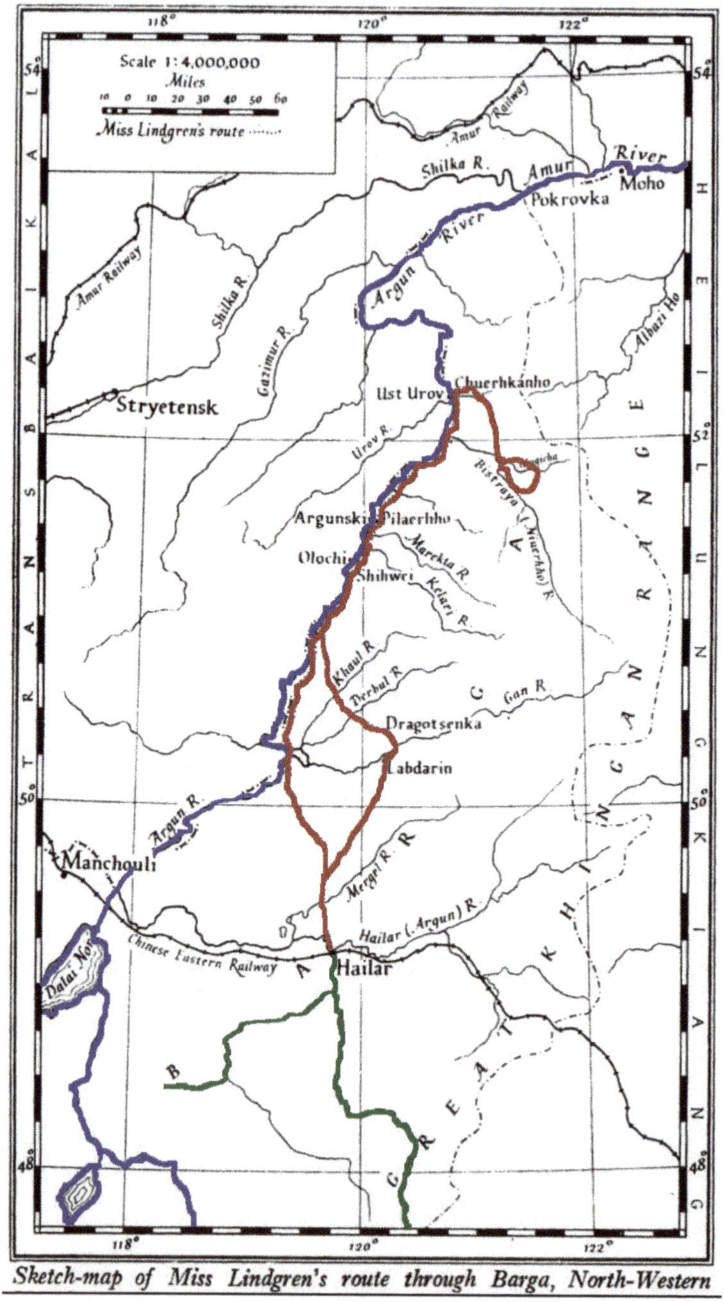

Fig. 7.12 Lindgren and Mamen's expedition routes in former Northwest Manchuria, 1929–1932 (author's highlighting) (MAA MN0082). © Museum of Archaeology and Anthropology, Cambridge

now known as Hūlúnbèiěr, Inner Mongolia. As with the Shirokogoroffs, Lindgren and Mamen also made a large number of field reports and Lindgren collected over 200 material artefacts.

Ethel John Lindgren was born in Illinois in 1905 to a Swedish-American family, but spent much of her youth in Asia accompanying her stepfather, Henry Eichheim, the composer and ethnomusicologist, on his tours. In November 1917 she saw Central Asia for the first time, writing later,

> Standing on an inner great wall, above Kalgan, I saw the dun-coloured land continuing to the horizon and thought it was the desert.
>
> I had a great *feeling,* one of serenity, of eternity — a feeling of the ground (JLA 1987).

At that moment, Lindgren vowed to return to find out as much as possible about Central Asia — both Chinese Turkestan and Outer Mongolia — with a view to the possibility of entering these territories and doing ethnographic work within them.

Lindgren had learnt Chinese and Japanese during these visits and these, along with experimental psychology, were the subjects of her initial studies at Cambridge. Upon transferring to anthropology, and with a growing interest in the social psychology of cultural groups, working under the supervision of Ellis Minns, Lindgren fulfilled her wish to conduct ethnographic fieldwork in Mongolia. Lindgren arrived in Běijīng in December 1927, but it was not until March 1928 that she was able to find a suitable travel companion and the necessary visas to travel on to Urga (now Ulaanbaatar) (Fig. 7.13).[11]

For many anthropologists about to embark on expeditions, we normally find a shopping list of equipment. For Lindgren this list consisted of one item only: a shotgun with 500 rounds of ammunition and its licence, issued by the US Legation (JLA 1928a). She also packed a camera, which she probably saw equally as a scientific tool to document her fieldwork — as recommended in *Notes and Queries in Anthropology* (Marreco and Myres 1912: 353-59) — and a means of recording images for her personal memoirs. Ironically, as Lindgren wrote to

11 Lindgren's first travel companion had withdrawn from the trip over safety concerns and others — like Roy Chapman Andrews and Sven Hedin who Lindgren met in Beiping as they were leading expeditions out to Mongolia — were unwilling to have a young female on their teams (JLA 1928a; 1928c).

Fig. 7.13 "E. J bartering at our camp with R. T. woman, Listvi͡anai͡a, near Bystrai͡a River". Photo by Oscar Mamen, 30 May 1932 (MAA N.23911.LIN). © Museum of Archaeology and Anthropology, Cambridge

her friend, after surviving military skirmishes and "so many bandits between here [Kalgan] and the missions [at Chabar] (which are near the border of Outer Mongolia) that it is unsafe to take anything with one" (JLA 1928b), the Mongolian border guards confiscated Lindgren's camera and gun as she entered the country. As Lindgren commented, "Mongolia was by then a satellite state of Russia", and therefore not only was photography banned, her movements were restricted to the city boundaries of Ulaanbaatar, meaning that she was unable to undertake the anthropological fieldwork as she had hoped (JLA 1932a). Lindgren did not own a camera again until 1931. Instead, all her photographs relating to Mongolia were given to her by friends. During her 1929 and 1930 expedition and residence in Northwest Manchuria, Oscar Mamen took all of the photographs (Lindgren 1936, ii).

Lindgren first met Mamen while in Ulaanbaatar, writing to a friend that Mamen was:

> a giant figure [...] of whom I have heard so much [...] He has clear blue eyes, grey-white hair, & that hawk-like explorer profile and gaunt figure one knows in travelling Norwegians —speaks excellent English, has good stories, & [enjoys] the pleasures of wine — in this case cognac is the only adequate consolation, women (in this case all memories) and song: the gramophone. So are the old pleasures modified & reproduced in Urga (JLA 1928d).

Oscar Mamen was born in June 1885 to a farming family in southern Norway and grew up enjoying outdoor pursuits. In 1911, on the invitation of his cousin, Alfred Rustad, Mamen travelled to Ulaanbaatar in order to help set up an office of the British American Tobacco Company. Mamen had travelled to Outer Mongolia (Republic of Mongolia) in search of adventure and riches. Instead he developed a love affair with a place and cultures that he extensively documented visually and literarily. Mamen never trained as a surveyor, geographer, or anthropologist, but he assisted other explorers who travelled to Mongolia and embraced many of their techniques and practices.[12] Thus, at around the same time the Shirokogoroffs were travelling with their camera to Siberia, Mamen obtained and travelled with a camera to remote areas of Outer Mongolia. For Mamen, photography was an artistic hobby and personal record, although he also at times utilised it as a scientific tool to evidence reality (Fig. 7.14).

Fig. 7.14 "Khavan examines movie, Elingui". Photo by Ethel Lindgren, 27 August 1931 (MAA N.40453.LIN). © Museum of Archaeology and Anthropology, Cambridge

12 Mamen features in several books written by travellers to the area, including Roy Chapman Andrews (1921).

Six months after their first meeting, Lindgren, Mamen, and all other foreign nationals were expelled from Mongolia after the political coup in February 1929. In their final days in Mongolia, Mamen was recommended to and employed by Lindgren as a guide and photographer for her proposed new fieldwork site of Northwest Manchuria. Mamen and Lindgren married in January 1930.

Relocating to Inner Mongolia, Lindgren and Mamen went in search of what Lindgren described as "a little-known tribe of Reindeer-Tungus" (Lindgren 1930: 518), writing:

> It was with incomplete and largely misleading information about the Northern Barga, its modes of communication, and where and how the Reindeer Tungus were to be found, that I set out to investigate this remote tribe in June of [1929] (Lindgren 1930: 527).

Lindgren's fieldwork was conducted during a transition period from the classical practice of exploration and ethnographical collecting (hence her first visit had undercurrents of salvage ethnography) to the new modes of immersive field research. During her first expedition, Lindgren had met and become friends with Olga Dmitrievna Kudrina, an Ewenki shaman (Fig. 7.15). At Olga's invitation, Lindgren returned to stay at Olga's camp during her second and third expeditions. This intensive time with Olga provided invaluable information that was to become the basis of Lindgren's doctoral thesis, "Notes on the Reindeer Tungus" (Lindgren 1936). A large number of photographs in the collection are of Olga, including images of her dressed in her shamanic costume, her relatives, and her camp, but vexingly, as with the Shirokogoroffs, there are no photographs of Olga performing as a shaman. Lindgren's thesis is significant for its early analysis of the functions of shamanic healing rituals and as a precursor to later reflexive methodologies (Lorimer 2006: 508).

Mamen is the unsung hero in this story of the success of Lindgren's fieldwork. Lindgren's previously mentioned description of Mamen demonstrates his immense popularity and sociability (JLA 1928d). At six feet, four inches tall, with blond hair, he equally had a physical presence, as well as being a figure of curiosity, particularly for children (Lindgren was six feet, one inch tall with ginger hair). Mamen was also a polyglot, fluent in Mongolian, Chinese, English, Norwegian, and conversant in Russian, German, French, and eventually Ewenki. His non-verbal communication was also effective. After six weeks on the trail of the "elusive and mysterious Ewenki", on their first encounter

Fig. 7.15 Olga Dmitrievna riding reindeer held by her husband, Nikolaĭ Larionovich. Ochilda, Upper Bystraia͡. Note Mamen's tent in the background. Photo by Oscar Mamen, 29 November 1931 (MAA N.23654.LIN). © Museum of Archaeology and Anthropology, Cambridge

Fig. 7.16 "Meeting the 1st R. T. on Ulugicha River". Nikolaĭ Ivanovich Kokeroff [Kokarov] with Lindgren at their joint camp. Photo by Oscar Mamen, 25 July 1929 (MAA N.126084.LIN). © Museum of Archaeology and Anthropology, Cambridge

with such an individual, Mamen writes, "shaking hands, gave him vodka and starting talking around our caperkelzie [sic] breakfast" (HILA Mamen 3-16: 25 Jul. 1929). Over the next five days at Nikolaĭ Ivanovich Kokeroff's camp (Fig 7.16), Mamen went hunting and fishing with the men, sharing both his catch and meals with them (HILA

Mamen 3-16: 26–30 Jul. 1929). It was probably Mamen's ability to hunt that aided Mamen and Lindgren's acceptance at the camps: in 1929 there were severe food shortages, with several deaths due to starvation being noted (Lindgren 1936: xxxi). Mamen wrote,

> The food question is becoming serious with us, and the Avankies [sic] have nothing to spare. I went twice out hunting but saw nothing. Finally managed to buy some flour, 10 Russian pounds for $3 (HILA Mamen 3-17: 2 Aug. 1929).

Lindgren certainly would not have been able to survive in the snow forests without Mamen's ability to procure food (Lindgren 1936: ii). Mamen's stories and photographs of hunting subsequently proved critical in engaging today's Ewenki and Oroqen men with the images during our digital sharing project (Fig. 7.17).

Fig. 7.17 "Three Tungus hunters from behind, Mid Martielkoi, Barga, N. Manchuria". Photo by Oscar Mamen, 27 November 1931 (MAA N.23611.LIN). © Museum of Archaeology and Anthropology, Cambridge

Mamen was responsible for all the expedition photography in 1929 (379 negatives), and for the majority of images from the 1931 and 1932 trips (1,650 and 1,320 negatives respectively). He also made about 1,500 feet of 16 mm cine film (MAA F.126021.LIN-F.126029.LIN). From Mamen's first photographic endeavours in 1913 he used folding-bed cameras with 127-roll film. These cameras were light and portable and Mamen utilised them for making both instant and sequential imagery. Unlike the Shirokogoroffs, it appears that Mamen did not have difficulties accessing or affording photographic material, and he amassed an impressively large archive for this time period.

In 1929, Mamen was using a Piccolette camera with a 4 x 6.5 cm negative that had been purchased by Lindgren for the expedition, and he was processing and distributing prints of "all those I snapped" while on the trail (HILA Mamen 3-16: 15 Jul. 1929). In 1931, Mamen had updated his equipment to a Zeiss Kolibri camera and Lindgren was using Mamen's old Kodak Vest Pocket Camera. A year later, Mamen was experimenting with a Leica 35 mm camera, although Lindgren wrote to her doctoral supervisor, Professor Minns,

> In many ways the much advertised Leica and Kolibri cameras have proved a disappointment. The ideal picture can be enlarged indefinitely: but if the film itself has some structural flaw (and unfortunately many have) an enlargement of course magnifies it to such a point that the print cannot be used for reproduction without much retouching (JLA 1933).

Mamen made a diverse portfolio of images: primarily informal portraits of his expedition companions, the lands they travelled, and the events they attended. He also used the camera to evidence "we were here", such as their first encounter with an Ewenki person (MAA N.126084.LIN), and as explanatory illustrations for his writings on events attended and new technologies encountered (HILA Mamen M.63) (Fig. 7.18).

Fig. 7.18 "3 women & 2 little girls, Omul-ail (W)". The girl in the middle is named Laorgao and her mother is holding her. On the right is Xiaonian, aged four, and her six-year-old sister is standing in the doorway too shy to be photographed. Information from Laorgao, July 2015. Photo by Oscar Mamen, 23 May 1929 (MAA N.39838.LIN). © Museum of Archaeology and Anthropology, Cambridge

The taking of anthropometric frontal and profile portraits was a new genre for Mamen in 1929, and as this practice primarily included Ewenki "types" it was probably done at Lindgren's request. Many of these portraits are similar to the Shirokogoroffs', although the inclusion of informal social elements at the edges of the frame of the anthropologist's posed and controlled portrait seems more deliberate than with the Shirokogoroffs (Fig. 7.19). After Lindgren obtained her own camera and was taking her own "type" studies, Mamen repositioned his camera to make more informal character studies that show a comradeship and partnership between those in front of and behind the camera.

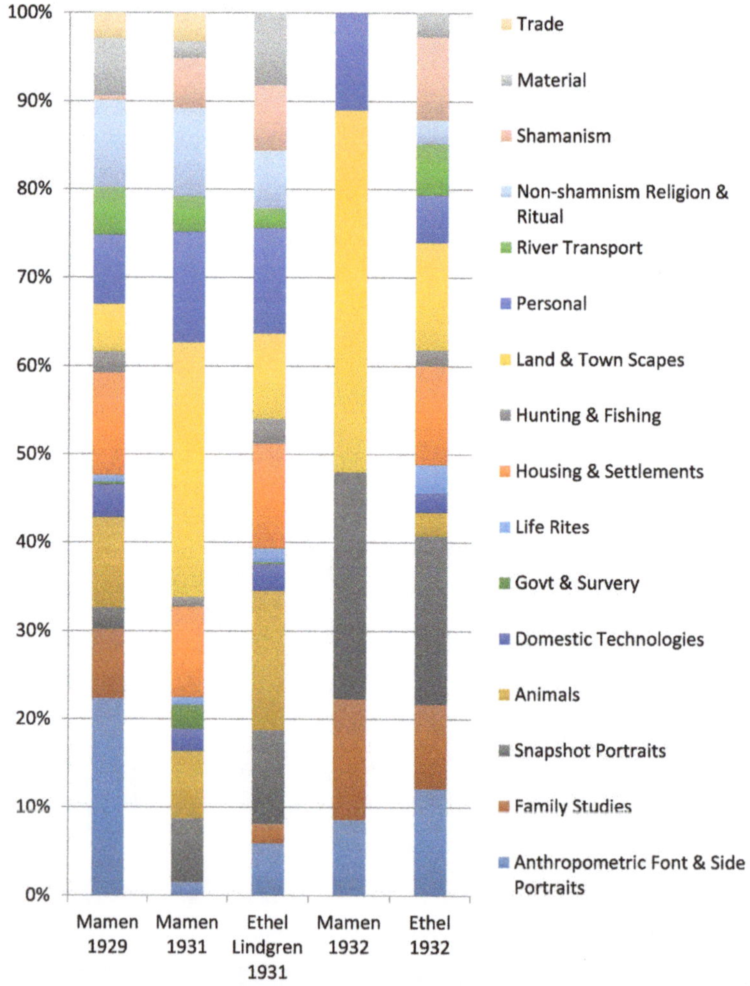

Fig. 7.19 The genres of photography undertaken by Oscar Mamen and Ethel Lindgren, 1929, 1931–1932, graph by Jocelyne Dudding

The Lindgren-Mamen collection is extremely important as it documents the changing conditions in Northwest Manchuria and Mongolia at a crucial stage in its political, social, and economic history. The Manchu Empire collapsed in 1911 and the Mongols in what was then Outer Mongolia undertook to create an independent nation state. A number of photographs depict the political movements of Mongolian nationalists in the Barga region at the time. Inner Mongolia made several attempts at independence, autonomy, or union with Outer Mongolia, but these were unsuccessful for various political reasons. Other photographs and Mamen's diaries record the Japanese invasion of Harbin in 1932, after which they considered it unsafe to remain in China. Unlike the Shirokogoroffs, who settled in China for the rest of their lives, Lindgren was never to return to Manchuria.

Due to concerns about the political situation and the safety of her friends and colleagues remaining in Manchuria, Lindgren published very little of her research. She also deliberately concealed the identity of specific individuals, particularly informants, to ensure their safety (Whitaker 1988: 255). Hence in her thesis, Russian traders are simply referred to as "Trader A.", "Trader B.", etc. (Fig. 7.20).

Fig. 7.20 "Alekseĭ Filippovich Kaĭgorodov", identified as "Trader B." in Lindgren's doctoral thesis. Photo by Oscar Mamen, Muchikan, 14 August 1929 (MAA N.21765.LIN). © Museum of Archaeology and Anthropology, Cambridge

Evolving Museology

The collections of these two couples now reside primarily in two institutions. The Shirokogoroff archive is held in the Peter the Great Museum of Anthropology and Ethnography (MAĖ) in St Petersburg. The collection is fragmentary, consisting of only the 810 photographs that have been discovered at present.[13] This collection itself was not well known for many reasons. Part of its obscurity might be due to the fragmented nature of the archive and partly due to the controversial status of these émigré scholars in the former Soviet Union. Nevertheless, prints made from their glass negatives were mounted onto captioned cards and used as a research archive for internal and visiting scholars (Fig. 7.21a). In addition to the photographs and field reports, the couple collected artefacts, physical anthropological measurements, and archaeological specimens.[14] Combined together, they make up the largest single collection in the museum (Sirina and Davydov 2017). Eleven wax cylinders recorded by Elizaveta Shirokogoroff are held at Institute of Russian Literature (Pushkin House) (FA IRL RAN 3271–3289), and many of their manuscripts are held in the Archive of the Academy of Sciences in the same city, with the remainder dispersed across Eurasia.

Lindgren and Mamen's photographs entered the photographic collections of the MAA in two separate events; first, in 1935 Lindgren sent 130 prints for inclusion in Haddon's teaching collection (Fig. 7.21b). Then, four years after her death, her son, John Lindgren, donated her photographs and papers to the museum in 1992. The collection is officially accessioned as the "Lindgren Collection" although the majority of photographs (sixty per cent) were made by Mamen.

Although both the MAĖ and the MAA actively sought photographs from Shirokogoroff and Lindgren at the time of their creation, their subsequent positioning within these institutes has been ambiguous. With the falling out of fashion of such anthropological teaching and research visual aids after the 1940s, and with what Elizabeth Edwards and Chris Morton describe as the "redrawing of collections

---

13 The collection in the MAĖ's archive consists of 501 negatives and 280 prints. Another 159 prints were registered by the MAĖ in the 1920s, but their location is not currently known.

14 "Archaeological excavations at the Amur river in Blagoveshchensk district" (photographic series MAĖ 2638) [RA IIMK 1/1(1916)/162].

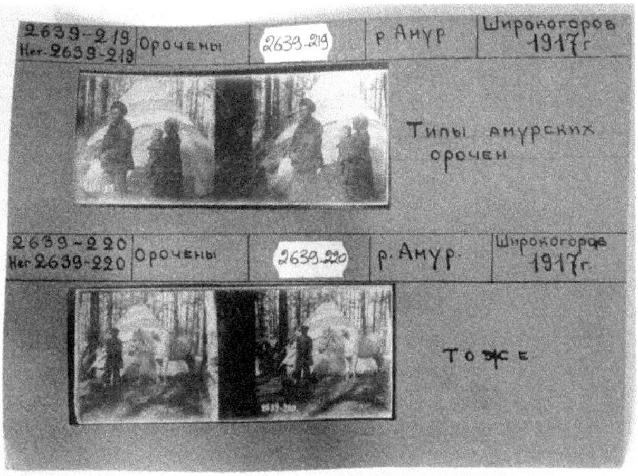

Fig. 7.21a "Types of Amur River Orochen". A mounted board from Shirokogoroff's Printed Collection. Photo by Sergei Shirokogoroff, likely July 1915. Orochens: Likely Bystraîa River camp (MAÈ 2639-219 and 2369-220). © Peter the Great Museum of Anthropology and Ethnography, Russian Academy of Sciences, St Petersburg

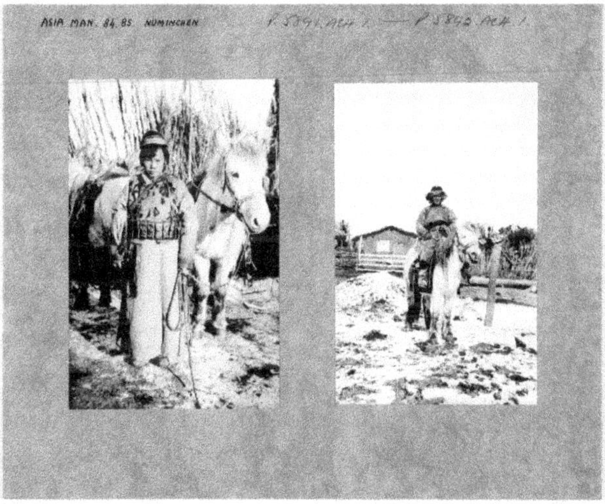

Fig. 7.21b "Numinchen" and "Kumarchen – Garsand, living among the Numinchen". A mounted board from the MAA's Teaching Collection and related catalogue card. Photos by Oscar Mamen, Imin River, 21 March 1932 (MAA P.5891.ACH1 and P.5892.ACH1). © Museum of Archaeology and Anthropology, Cambridge

boundaries and curatorial territories", these teaching collections were transferred — often divided — and left to languish in boxes in libraries, basements, cupboards, under stairs, etc. (Edwards and Morton 2015:

8). More recently, with developments in representation theories and alternative historical narratives — combined with the introduction of digital technologies — there has been an upsurge in interest in photographic collections cared for by museums. It was this changing academic context and the enthusiasm in the original communities that led our group to initiate a digital sharing project with the photographic collections of the two couples.

At the time of their fieldwork, both Lindgren and Mamen recognised the social importance of their photographs to the people they met. Lindgren wrote, the Ewenkis "were most anxious for copies of their photographs, which I trust have since reached them safely through the trading station" (Lindgren 1930: 534). It is not known whether any of these prints reached the Ewenki camps in 1929, and to date no one has mentioned seeing surviving prints within the Ewenki community. This return of photographs was not an isolated undertaking for Lindgren and Mamen. As Mamen recorded in his diary:

> Thursday, 23rd [May]. Hailar. Clear, warm weather. Been to the second Dagur village, Omul Ail, most of the day and taken a lot of snaps, etc.

and five days later:

> Tuesday. 28th. Hailar. Clear, hot weather. Been to Dagur village, Omul Ail, with Haisan and distributed photos, etc (HILA Mamen 3-16: 23 and 28 May 1929).

These early exercises in the sharing of prints open up the question, as we shall see below, of the different ways that images can be interpreted.

Affection for and Recognition of Northwest Manchuria in the Twenty-First Century

Almost a century has passed since the Shirokogoroff photographic archive was created, as well as some eighty years since Lindgren and Mamen assembled their archive. Between 2014 and 2017 all the images from both collections were shared and discussed with Ewenkis and Oroqens by myself and other scholars in China. The formal diffusionist and evolutionist frames that had encouraged the Shirokogoroffs and Lindgren and Mamen to compose their photographs had, in many cases, been forgotten both by scientists and by local people. Nevertheless the photographs were evocative and recognizable to descendants of the many cultural groups portrayed in the archives. In general, the better composed and somewhat fresher Lindgren-Mamen photographs had greater appeal for Manchurian audiences. However, photographs of the artefacts collected by the Shirokogoroffs, along with their wax cylinder recordings, evoked a similarly strong interest.

The long interval between the collection of this material and their return plays an important part in this story. Revolution, civil wars, and geopolitical tension were key factors in isolating these archives from their source communities. New digital technologies have helped bring them together again. Today we are able to digitize the plates at a high resolution, adjust and recover details in files, and thereafter to create proxies that after are often clearer and more legible than the originals. However, the most important element that fuels curiosity today is the search by local people for a cultural identity after the end of the Cultural Revolution. The incessant pace of modernization, industrialization, and change in the People's Republic of China has made these images especially evocative. Very few of our audiences possessed, or had even seen, historical photographs of their own ancestors, let alone images dating to the times of Lindgren-Mamen or the Shirokogoroffs.

Among the contemporary peoples of Inner Mongolia, the first question nearly always was: What group is this — are they Oroqen or Ewenki? The next question was then: Do you know the person's name? These questions illustrated a desire on the part of contemporary observers to connect and identify with the image. In many ways it also illustrated how these viewers felt a loss of their heritage when they were not able to identify which group was represented in a photo. The recalling and recording of individuals' names was important to many viewers as a way of making a connection with those portrayed. Working with the photographs enabled a sense of agency and ownership, and for many elders, an appreciation that their memories and histories were important — a recognition that they were the holders of knowledge with a responsibility to relay this information on to the next generations. Their enthusiasm to remember went to such a level that sometimes elders "recalled" memories which were not shared by others who were present, sometimes creating tension or debate.

Lindgren and Mamen's careful recording of names was therefore a crucial point of entry for many viewers. Some difficulties arose in that Lindgren and Mamen often recorded the Orthodox Christian Russian names adopted by Ewenkis, which might differ from the Ewenki or Chinese names by which they now may be more commonly known. Lindgren wrote that Ewenkis had adopted Russian names from "when the Reindeer Tungus now in Manchuria were still in Siberia", and continued favouring them due to their continued trade with their Russian *andaki* (trader-friends) (Lindgren 1936: 32; Kolås and Xie 2015: 2). Lindgren does note that most adult Ewenkis, as well as some children, had Tungus names, but these were not disclosed to her — a practice that she rightly or wrongly associated with a desire to avoid the displeasure of the Russian Orthodox Church (Lindgren 1936: 32). Further, Lindgren and Mamen also recorded names using a non-standard phonetic transcription, which complicates making links to the way these names are pronounced today.

The Lindgren and Mamen naming conventions enabled us to create some very direct and moving links between contemporary individuals and their ancestors. One contemporary Ewenki woman, Āntè Bù, who we met at Áolǔgǔyā in April 2015, immediately recognised the name of her father, but not his image, as he had died young and she had never seen a picture of him (Fig. 7.22). Using the name, we were then able to find photos of her grandparents, and her uncle, aunt, and brother. The Lindgren attributions contained the information that her grandparents had adopted her mother, a fact that Anta was not aware of. Having seen these images, she shared memories of and information about her ancestors with her own son and grandson. Later that night, Anta arranged for lieba (*khleb*), the Russian-style pan-baked bread we had identified in the photographs of, to be baked for dinner.

On the other hand, the archival recording of names could sometimes bring up uncomfortable issues and memories. Early in our fieldwork, David G. Anderson, a member of the project, raised the issue that Evenkis living in Siberia might be uncomfortable pronouncing the name of a deceased clan member in case the speaking of the name entices a departed spirit to return to the middle world and linger. Different authorities debated this point during the fieldwork on the Chinese side. According to Mèng Sōnglín, a senior Daur, Ewenkis do not practice special avoidances when pronouncing the names of their deceased

Fig. 7.22 Āntè Bù holding a portrait of her father, Piotr Buldorovskiĭ (MAA N.21681.LIN). Photo by Jocelyne Dudding, Áolŭgŭyā, September 2015

parents and relatives: they can directly call their grandparents' and ancestors' names. Or when they have been asked about these individuals, they can say who is from where, or who is from which family because there are many repeated names among these minorities (Sōnglín, pers. comm., 2 Nov. 2016). His comments reflect the importance and respect given to extensive genealogical knowledge among many Mongolian peoples, and he may be speaking about general Inner Mongolian norms. However, Sū Rìtài, an anthropologist working with Ewenki, does note that Mongolian shamans still practice such avoidances. For example, when someone's father died, if the person said,

> Dad come back, the spirit will return. However, if the person has been asked who your father is, he can directly call his father's name to tell them, especially when the person have been asked or to is required to complete registrations in police or official departments, they can say their names (Sū Rìtài, pers. comm., 2 Nov. 2016).

As I travelled to Inner Mongolia as a guest of the Hūlúnbèiěr Museum and was accompanied by a member of the Propaganda Department, it is conceivable that I was seen in an official capacity and therefore was able to request and be provided with individual names. Regardless of the context, when unnamed individuals could be identified with their Chinese, Russian, or Tungus name, there was an incredible sense of pride and ownership.

Lindgren's naming conventions for the different nationalities were mainly driven by her ideas of cultural evolution, but it is also clear that she was often concerned to record the names and deeds of friends and assistants. This identification allowed individuals to be placed within their social group and retain connection within local histories, which, as Laura Peers and Alison Brown describe, enables self-determination and cultural preservation, particularly after periods of government assimilation policies (Brown and Peers 2006: 273).

A striking example of how local histories can overwrite anthropological framings is the photograph of a mother, who we now know was called Pingrui, with her infant in a traditional cradle in the community of Omul Ail, now named Nántún, on 19 July 1932 (Fig. 7.23). Lindgren and Mamen left a copy of the print with the mother. This print remains with Pingrui's descendants and is considered a family treasure.

Fig. 7.23 Pingrui holding her "Dagur cradle & 3 months baby, Omul Ail". Photo by Oscar Mamen, 19 July 1931 (MAA P.10943.ACH1). © Museum of Archaeology and Anthropology, Cambridge

The difference in interpretations between the early twentieth century ethnographer and the people's lives that they touched can be read in Lindgren's caption:

> Two photographs of a Dagur cradle taken at Omul-ail, a Dagur settlement south of Hăilāĕr. The Dagur cradle is very much like [that of] the Numinchen, which I believe to derive from the former. The bulk of the Dagur population of Manchuria lives along the Nonni river, where for over two and a half centuries they have been the chief, almost the sole, traders dealing with the Numinchen and other Khingan Tungus tribes (MAA P.10943.ACH1).

Lindgren's description betrays her training in how to illustrate anthropological theories with images. She understands the cradle in this caption as being positioned within a system of diffusion whereby the artefact, which could be empty of mother and child, illustrates the way that one ethnic group derives from another. In Lindgren's manuscripts and letters, she wrote of how she used and planned to publish her photographs as tools in the study of social groups (see LCC 1931: 19 and 55; JLA 1932b). However, the magic of this tool is that the image, in Edward's terms, has the ability to lead multiple lives within which it can record parallel realities (Edwards 2003: 83). For the descendants of the mother and child, the image displayed a vibrant connection to the past:

> This is Pingrui, we don't know which baby this would be. The cradle is called a "Darde" (Daur language). There is some decoration at the back of the cradle, normally it's made from the small ribs of lambs, and on the top it is suede. The upper design is an auspicious pattern called Naires (Sudure Mani and Dambu 2015).

The striking difference between Lindgren's caption and the Nántún residents' description illustrates that, for originating communities, the photographs' social set of meanings or "other realities" is what is important (Brown and Peers 2006: 265).

Sometimes recognition was experienced without a tangible genealogical link to a particular individual. Of the photographs that drew the most comment, one portrait of "an old woman" was the most popular and was greeted with "She looks just like my grandmother" (Xú Giŭ, February 2015). For many it did not matter whether the woman was Oroqen or Ewenki, or that we didn't know her name. Instead, it was the memories of childhood and growing up while being looked after by their grandmother that the image conjured that were significant (Fig. 7.24a). This one photo evoked numerous stories of childhood.

The second favourite photo was that of a baby in his cradle, which prompted the exchange:

> "He's so grumpy".
>
> "So would you be if held up like that".
>
> "But with those cheeks he's obviously healthy" (Liú Xiá and Bái Yíng, February 2015).

The photo not only prompted comments on the baby's expression, but it also sparked stories of what their own cradle looked like (Fig. 7.24b). Based on these responses, and their universal appeal, these became the lead photographs in the projects' resulting exhibitions and catalogues.

Fig. 7.24a (left) Old mother, daughter and grandchild, Ikhe Bebe (MAA N.40513. LIN). © Museum of Archaeology and Anthropology, Cambridge

Fig. 7.24b (right) Child in cradle: middle wigwam of East group, Ikhe Bebe. Photo by Ethel Lindgren, 1 September 1931 (MAA N.40504.LIN). © Museum of Archaeology and Anthropology, Cambridge

In other instances, the recognition of a significant individual could elicit reactions to complex and tragic historical events. The recognition of the Wampuyen is a case in point. In March 1932, Lindgren and Mamen conducted an expedition south along the Yĩmĩn River during which they stayed for two nights at Ango Holis (now known as Anggo Xolis). Amongst the 200 photos they made during this stay were twelve portraits of a young woman whom Mamen identified as "Wampuzan" and Lindgren as "Wampuyan" (Figs. 7.25a and 25b).

Fig. 7.25a (left) "Wampuzan, young girl, Ango Holis". Photo by Oscar Mamen, 22 March 1932 (MAA N.21652.LIN). © Museum of Archaeology and Anthropology, Cambridge

Fig. 7.25b (right) "Wampuyan calling others, Ango Holis". Photo by Ethel Lindgren, 22 March 1932 (MAA N.80589.LIN). © Museum of Archaeology and Anthropology, Cambridge

As a result of the digital sharing and the public displays of these photographs in 2016, there has been a retelling of the tragic history of the Yĩmĩn River massacre that took place a few years after Lindgren and Mamen's visit. According to these oral accounts, an entire village was attacked and killed following a conflict between Burĩats and Yĩmĩn Oroqen in 1935. According to these accounts, only two girls survived.

One was Wanpuyen, who survived due to the fact that her thick braid stopped her attacker's blade on the back of her neck (Fig. 7.25b). Wampuyen was subsequently adopted by Déhǎi Bàiyer, but she later died from the plague Déhǎi Bàiyer's son, Mènghé Bātú, provided these details upon seeing Lindgren and Mamen's photos. These portraits of Wampuyen unlocked more than memories (Binney and Chaplin 2003); they created a dialogue that had been previously unheard and differed from official accounts. Orochon elders from Yīmǐn village recounted how the Buri͡ats attacked before dawn using machetes to behead men, women, and children. It is estimated that over 200 people died in the attack. Lindgren, who had acquired a shaman costume from Doshincha, the former chief of Anggo Xolis, in 1932, provides another perspective, writing in 1935 that the chief and entire village had been killed "by Buri͡ats tired of the Numinchen's continuous horse and cattle rustling" (Lindgren 1935). Families in nearby villages adopted the two girls who managed to escape and Anggo Xolis was abandoned. Mènghé Bātú commented that each time he and his friends saw and talked over the photos of Anggo Xolis, they remembered more details of the villagers and the attack.

These discussions, along with the inclusion of the photos and with their commentary in the exhibition "Dialogue Across the Century" in Nántún, July 2016, was seen by the community as being somewhat cathartic and a means of addressing past injustices (Fig. 7.26). Mention of the attack is made in official accounts, but neither the details nor the number of people killed are recorded in these documents. While showing the portraits of Wampuyen and others from Anggo Xolis brought painful memories to many, the images also brought the recovery and legitimization of the history for the Oroqen living on the Yīmǐn River. Official histories were questioned, and while there are no photographs of the actual attack or aftermath, Lindgren and Mamen's photographs provide support to examine previously written accounts. A second major theme in the sharing of the collections was a fascination with the elements of everyday life and material culture that were portrayed in the images along with the people. This applied equally to the much older Shirokogoroff collection and to the Lindgren-Mamen collection.

Many of the portraits in both collections are informally anthropometric in their paired front and side poses, with the resulting

Fig. 7.26 "Dialogue Across the Century" exhibition, Ewenki Museum, Nántún, July 2016. Photo by Jocelyne Dudding

portraits often appearing slightly awkward and frozen when compared to more journalistic or snapshot styles of photography. When these photographs were shown to contemporary audiences, people were curious about the awkward poses and asked why they were taken this way. When the theoretical context was explained — about how scholars sought to understand the physical form of an individual in order to better understand how identities evolved from one to another — the viewers quickly understood. To some degree, official government policies are still developmentalist and evolutionist, but just as quickly, these meanings were swept aside and the photographs reclaimed as cultural objects with their biographies and histories reattached.

Some participants were immediately able to see the humour behind some of the forced poses. For example, in the Shirokogoroffs' very first expedition to Zabaĭkal'e in Siberia, either the locals dressed in their "best" for the camera, or the couple asked locals and their Cossack guides to pose in traditional Oroqen hunting costumes (Fig. 7.27). There was great amusement when there was the realisation, or what Barthes (1984) calls the punctum, that the man wearing the winter furs on the left was wearing summer boots, and vice versa on the right. Speculation continued as to whether the men had deliberately dressed for the camera wearing the incorrect boots, or whether Shirokogoroff had asked the men to pose in clothing not their own and either the boots did not fit or they did not realize their mistake.

Fig. 7.27 "Men in winter hunting costumes". Photo by Sergei Shirokogoroff, Chita Region, June 1912 (MAĖ 2002-92). © Peter the Great Museum of Anthropology and Ethnography, Russian Academy of Sciences, St Petersburg

This particular photograph was significant since it also bridged a kind of gender divide of interest in photographs of material culture. While scenes of hunting were a visual focus for the men, scenes of domestic life became a focus for many women. Shirokogoroff's photographs of the two hunters overlapped this gendered interest. The men were interested primarily in the rifles and rifle tripods, and secondarily, along with the women, the purposes of the articles of clothing and what furs or materials they were made from.

More broadly, the photographs from both collections that documented Oroqen hunting equipment and clothing touched on contemporary political issues in another way. Hunting was a particularly sensitive topic for Oroqens, and most highly illustrated their sense of loss of traditional ways of life. During interviews undertaken in preparation for the exhibition "River Stars Reindeer", Nieren and Zhāng Róngdé commented,

> Hunting is highly valued amongst Oroqens and is an essential way through which traditional skills and knowledge are passed from fathers to sons.
>
> In 1996, all hunting was banned by the Chinese state on the grounds of animal preservation. As part of this, we were ordered to hand in our hunting guns, which for us is the symbol of our identity. While many recognise the need for the ban, the loss of hunting has had a huge social impact on us (Richard Fraser, pers. comm., Feb. 2015).

Photographs of camp life, and the material culture surrounding it, also spurred curiosity about lost lifeways. Recent policies of resettlement, and, in the case of Áolŭgŭyā Ewenkis, multiple resettlements, have been associated with the loss of culture and traditions. The greatest impact was on former hunters who had been permanently relocated to Áolŭgŭyā and disliked their increased separation from the forest and traditional ways of subsistence: hunting and herding. As Richard Fraser, one of the project facilitators, explained based on his interviews, "The hunters' lives in the town but he wishes to be in the forest. He is always pinning for his days as a hunter. Now all he can do is drink every day" (Fraser 2010: 327). Particularly for those who had been resettled to Áolŭgŭyā, images of older lodges and conical dwellings brought up links to the past and the manner in which newly urbanized settlements pose new challenges not suffered in the older dwellings.

It is fascinating that the debate on housing is an old one, and in the writings of both the Shirokogoroffs and of Lindgren we can see evidence that people struggled to define the best sort of dwelling for their times. In this interesting excerpt from Lindgren's unpublished diary, written during her expedition to the Chol River in 1931, she encapsulated a debate on the quality of housing materials and nostalgia over the loss of certain techniques:

> Birch-bark Wigwam Covers: Khavan spoke of birch-bark as far superior to reeds and said that there was no one who knew how to do it any more. "We have become useless", he said. He was delighted with photos of N. people and said that when he was young they all had birch-bark — "tikšã(n) ǰu". In winter they have roehide. He does not live in a house in

> winter, but he said "a few have". Spoke of houses as warmer. He said they kept their heavy winter things "in the mountains" but in the winter they lived far from the hills, by the river, where it is warmer. Work of preparing "tikšã(n)" he spoke of as heavy: you have to find the right pieces, cut them, then boil them. So they have given it up. The reed bands are easy to prepare (LCC 1931: 19) (Fig. 7.28).

Fig. 7.28 "[Reed] Wigwams & houses at the Orochen settlement at Öru Kere, Upper Yīmīn River". Photo by Oscar Mamen, 20 March 1932 (MAA N.21615.LIN). © Museum of Archaeology and Anthropology, Cambridge

Writing two decades before Lindgren in her published field report, Elizaveta Shirokogoroff worried about cultural assimilation brought on by the architecture of modern dwellings:

> The Amur Orochens, like most Orochens, live in conical yurts that are covered in the summer with panels made of boiled bark, and in the winter with warm coverings sewn out of skins. Now it seems this way of life is no longer valued by them in the winter and they have started to build log cabins [*zimov'i͡a*] of a Russian design. At the present moment there are already three such cabins (although two of them were built by the same Orochen [hunter]). [The residents] have gone so far into the Russian lifestyle that they have started to take on agriculture by settling in the middle sections of the Bystrai͡a River valley and planting there oats and wheat — and are demonstrating good results (Shirokogorova 1919: 20).

For the younger generations today, the stark visual contrast between the conical dwellings of the past and the brick multiple storeyed flats of today was an eye-opener that prompted discussions about the advantages and disadvantages of their lives over their grandparents' generation. The loss of their cultural heritage, especially the intangible heritage of language, song, and dance, was keenly felt by all generations. This was linked to government policies, which still continue, that push for constant resettlement into increasingly modern dwellings. At the same time, many viewers expressed frustration with the way that traditional dwellings were relegated to museums, or their elements were incorporated into modern brick and concrete architecture in order to try to encourage some monetary economic benefit to the region out of tourism. A classic case-in-point is the troubled story of the Ewenki "village" of Áolŭgŭyā, which has been resettled by government planners three times since 1950 (Xie 2015). Many community members told of how their grandparents refused to live in the new housing, instead sleeping in their traditional *d'īū* (conical lodge) and using the house for storage. Shirokogoroff writes personally of the inadequacies of the government houses, describing how they had to pitch their tents inside their allocated government house in order to keep warm (SPF ARAN 142-1(1918)-68: 127).

Again, it is fascinating that the story of government-induced wholesale resettlements is an old story, one that troubled observers as early as 1915. Elizaveta Shirokogoroff worried about centrally planned Oroqen resettlements (Fig. 7.29):

> Undoubtedly in the near future the Kumar Orochens will switch to a different manner of subsistence, and likely to agriculture, just like their neighbours have done who live more to the south and east near the Amur River. Around the city of Mergen there are already a few newly formed Orochen villages, and the Orochens there are ploughing the land. The Chinese government is trying in every sort of way, including the use of force, to convert their Orochen subjects to agriculture and to a life in villages planned out according to a Chinese template. They have built new centrally financed villages with 10–15 *fanzas* [Manchu-style semi-subterranean huts] to begin with and have begun resettling Orochens in them. The Chinese government even built an entire city called Sin-an — and filled it with Orochens who likely will scatter and run away. [...] I should mention that this transfer to a new form of economy will be suffered painfully by the Orochens (Shirokogorova 1919: 37).

Fig. 7.29 "An Orochen residence in the forest". Photo by Sergei Shirokorogoff, Autumn 1915. Orochens: Upper Amur basin, Manchuria (MAĖ 2638-69). © Peter the Great Museum of Anthropology and Ethnography, Russian Academy of Sciences, St Petersburg

There are of course many sides to the debate. The government likely forced resettlement onto Oroqens with a sincere desire to improve the health and well-being of the population. Different generations of government officials felt that traditional dwellings were unhealthy and vulnerable to the elements. Lindgren, some decades later, documented the continual problems caused by summer flooding and the linked problem of shortages of clean water that, combined with traditional hygiene patterns, contributed to the spread of epidemic diseases. The severe flooding of 1929 was one of the justifications given by the Chinese government for building permanent houses for Ewenkis. The vulnerability of traditional structures to flooding and epidemic disease was partly to blame for high rates of infant mortality in traditional camps — a feature of traditional life that contemporary viewers also commented on. For example, Āntè Bù was able to identify the portrait captioned "Wife of Innokentiĭ Nikolaevich Buldotovskiĭ, [Buldorovskiĭ?] with baby. Beremekan Camp. 3/8" (MAA N.21706.LIN) as Oksa[na], her aunt, but when asked who the baby was, Āntè Bù replied, "There were lots of children, and so many died while young, that I don't remember all their names. I don't know which child this would have been" (Figs. 7.30a and 7.30b).[15]

15 Interview with Āntè Bù, Áolŭgŭyā, 1 April 2015.

Fig. 7.30a (left) "Wife of In[n]okentiĭ Nikolaevich Buldotovskiĭ [Buldorovskiĭ?], with baby. Beremekan Camp". "Oksa[na], wife of Churin Buldovskiĭ [Buldorovskiĭ?] (which means "blue-eyed", like Russians), Āntè Bù's uncle. The infant's name is unknown". Information from Anta Bu, 1 April 2015. Photo by Oscar Mamen, 3 August 1929 (MAA N.21706.LIN). © Museum of Archaeology and Anthropology, Cambridge

Fig. 7.30b (right) "Valentina, daughter of Kostenkin [Konstantin] Kudrin, tied in her cradle preparatory to being packed on deer. Note block of ice for water on the left". Photo by Ethel Lindgren, Martielkoi River, 27 November 1931 (MAA N.24479.LIN). © Museum of Archaeology and Anthropology, Cambridge

Lindgren recorded the personal details of only one infant death, that of Valentina, the nine-month-old daughter of Tatiana Petrovna and Kostenkin [Konstantin] Dmitrievich Kudrin, who Lindgren had nomadised with during all three of her expeditions. Lindgren included three photographs of Valentina in her doctoral thesis (Lindgren 1936: 160–62, plates 27–9), and the understatedness of the third caption emphasises the reality: "Cradle, with Valentina in it, being loaded on a deer by the child's mother and another woman. The reindeer in the right foreground was slaughtered when the child died, 18 days later" (Ibid: 162, plate 29).

The combination of Valentina's four portraits, along with her and her family's names, details, and photographs, and her importance to the family being demonstrated by her father "Kostenkin relat[ing]

that on the occasion of his infant daughter Valentina's death they had killed a 'good reindeer' and made 'a very high *delken* [storage cache]'" (Lindgren 1936: 159), meant the photographs had a greater resonance that drew comments from several community members. As Binney and Chaplin note, the return of photographs does not always evoke happy or positive memories (Binney and Chaplin 1991: 431–32).

Unarguably, the highlights of both collections were the images of shamans and shamanistic costumes. Both the Shirokogoroff and Lindgren-Mamen photographic collections are complemented by entire shaman costumes they purchased and are now held in the respective museums. As mentioned previously, the shaman Olga Dmitrievna Kudrina played a special role in the Lindgren collection and indeed in Lindgren's research (Fig. 7.31a). It is perhaps not unimportant to understanding the friendship between Ethel and Olga that in the past the Kudrin family for many generations had supported visiting researchers. The name of one of Olga's ancestors, Grigoriĭ Vasil'evich Kudrin, appears in Sergei Shirokogoroff's field diary of the 1915–1916 expedition while they stayed at Ust' Urov on the Bystraia River [TumA 1916/16: 94]. Shirokogoroff photographed Grigoriĭ Vasil'evich Kudrin' *zimov'e* (winter cabin) and attributed it to the family — a prominent exception to the rule of his scarce documentation (Fig. 7.31b).

Fig. 7.31a "Olga Dmitrievna dressed as shaman, with Nic. and Stepan P., middle Martielkoi, near the Upper Bystraia River". Photo by Oscar Mamen, 26 November 1931 (MAA N.23609.LIN). © Museum of Archaeology and Anthropology, Cambridge

Fig. 7.31b Grigoriĭ Vasil'evich Kudrin's cabin. Photo by Sergei or Elizaveta Shirokogoroff, Priamurskiĭ Kraĭ, 1915–1916 (MAĖ 2639-157). © Peter the Great Museum of Anthropology and Ethnography, Russian Academy of Sciences, St Petersburg

Following in the footsteps of both Shirokogoroff and Lindgren, the later Soviet-era ethnographer Anatoliĭ Kaĭgorodov was also hosted by the Kudrin family, who organized his fieldwork in the Three Rivers region (Kaigorodov 1968; Heyne 2009). Indeed, one could try to reverse the interpretation and argue that the support of the Kudrin family, and Olga in particular, might be closely associated with the development of the themes of shaman-studies and shamanism in Europe.

In Inner Mongolia, the attitude towards shamanism has shifted dynamically. During the Cultural Revolution, religious practices, including shamanism, were banned. In the course of our fieldwork we heard several stories of how, during the period, shamans hid their costumes in the forests to prevent them from being confiscated. Unfortunately, many died before they were able to retrieve their regalia and their costumes were subsequently found by hunters or loggers and deposited in local museums. Since China ratified the UNESCO 2003 Convention on Safeguarding Intangible Cultural Heritage in 2005, there has been a surge in the numbers of shamans and shamanic practices. With the increased cultural ownership of shamanism there has been a move towards a more private and respectful approach, and on my last visit to Inner Mongolia in 2016, I saw for the first time a notice requesting that visitors not photograph the shaman's hut on display in the Inner Mongolian Museum, Hohhot, out of cultural respect. To date there has been no request for any photographs of shamans by Shirokogoroff or Lindgren-Mamen to be restricted as secret/sacred, but it is probably only a matter of time.

Conclusion

Lindgren's, Mamen's and the Shirokogoroffs' photographs ended up in museum collections with captioning that, in many ways, provides a greater understanding of anthropological histories than the content of the image. These photographs retain a "communicative knowledge", that is information communicated visually, but as Edwards notes, their conjunctive knowledge, which relies on social embeddedness, is restricted (Edwards 2001: 89). The process of digitally sharing the photographs with their originating communities enabled them to be recirculated, held, talked about, and viewed in a cultural setting unencumbered by any institutional context. As a result, their conjunctive knowledge was reanimated.

The notion of the photograph being a carrier of a person's spirit is based on the idea that the dead are still with us, and rather than fixing a shadow, photography preserves what John Berger describes as being a "likeness":

> What is a likeness? When a person dies, they leave behind, for those who knew them, an emptiness, a space: the space has contours and is different for each person mourned. This space with its contours is the person's likeness and is what the artist searches for when making a living portrait. A likeness is something left behind invisibly (Berger 2001: 19).

Using this definition aids our understanding of why a photograph represents something different for each viewer at a particular time and place. Even when the viewer may not have known the individual portrayed personally, there is often a mythical or social memory (French 1995) based on family, community, or historical stories that provides an emotional outline for viewing the photographs.

This process also emphasizes the responsibility that museums have not only to preserve and document collections, but also to make them accessible to communities in meaningful ways. For both the Shirokogoroff and Lindgren-Mamen collections, this was particularly important due to political, economic, and technological restrictions that made the photographs difficult for originating communities to access. During this project, we showed digital copies of the Shirokogoroffs' photographs and directed individuals to the MAĖ website[16] for access to low-resolution images and related information and this did change the nature of reciprocity in our fieldwork. For the Lindgren-Mamen collection, the MAA provided high-resolution jpeg files of the entire collection to six community museums and universities, and single files to individuals who engaged with specific images. We also carried a small number of prints, although these proved unnecessary as — from the oldest to the youngest — all community members engaged in viewing the digital images and had no difficulty in navigating through files on either the project's iPad or laptop.

The MAA has a long history of returning photographs to their originating communities, beginning with Alfred Haddon, who took prints from his first Torres Strait expedition (1888–1889) back to the islands during his second expedition (1898–1899). Haddon undertook this action recognising the social importance of the photographs, particularly when the photographs included family and friends who had died in between the trips. Haddon recommended this process in *Notes and Queries* in 1899 and 1914, as well as teaching this practice in his courses in anthropology at the University of Cambridge. It was within this context that Ethel Lindgren completed her studies and she certainly undertook the same practice of sharing prints made on previous expeditions with those she met again. Oscar Mamen, who did not have the same anthropological training, but appeared to have a working interest in exploration, surveying, and people, also ensured that he "printed a lot of photos for the people whom we had snapped" (HILA Mamen: 15 Jul. 1929).

Subsequent to the sharing of photographs by Lindgren and Mamen, a set of photographs was taken back to Evenki communities in Siberia by David Anderson during his doctoral research in 1996. This return was within the remit of "photo elicitation", that is, the showing of photographs to community members in order to elicit information. In the 2000s, the process had evolved into "visual repatriation", that is, the return of copies of photographs held in museum collections as museums and communities increasingly became aware of the intrinsic

16 http://collection.kunstkamera.ru/entity/ALBUM/1242177864?index=14

claims of descendants (Buijs and Jakobsen 2011). My issue with the term "visual repatriation" is that it implies a one-way process of museums giving back to communities, yet the original photographs are not returned and the process does not alter the museums' proprietary rights over the photographs. The term "repatriation" is also highly charged and politicised. For this project the term "digital sharing" was designed to identify that, along with a recognition of the cultural ownership of these images, it was a two-way process of sharing digital copies of the photographs and their related information cared for by MAA with communities. In exchange, there is increased circulation and access to the images and sharing of knowledge and ways of caring for both that knowledge and the images themselves. For the Lindgren project the MAA has also received a number of new photographs created in response to Lindgren's original photographs for our collections. Thus the project was a collaboration where each partner contributed equally to the sharing of Lindgren and Mamen's photographs.

Berger instructs us that photographs always need language and require a narrative of some sort to make sense (Berger 1980: 51), and this is certainly true for the Shirokogoroffs' and Lindgren-Mamen's photographs. Their photographs contain forensic evidence that relates basic information, and often provides the studium, that is an average effect of liking the photographs (Berger 1981: 26). A significant part of this studium was found not in the photographs' value, nor in what they visually represented, but in what they are in and of themselves: many individuals within the source communities seemed to want to see the photos because they desired to be part of the collective who had seen and commented on them (Berger 1981: 21). But the punctum, that which grabs the attention and makes a person entranced with an image, was present in moments when, for example, the Ewenki Headman recognised his family's bridle, or the Yīmǐn River community spotted the braid that saved Wampuyen from being beheaded.

This digital sharing project centred upon supporting the agency of local populations in interpreting and utilising the photographs of these two ethnographic couples for their own local heritage and culture. The project was run in conjunction with the Hūlúnbèiěr Museum, a municipal museum that oversees the Ewenki, Áolǔgǔyā, and Genhe local museums, and sought to promote advancement of museum practices and engagement with their local communities. The sharing of the photographs and the resulting discussions had a greater impact than just creating dialogue between individuals and across generations; it also started discussions about museums' roles in exploring continuing socioeconomic, education, and health issues. A second Mongolian heritage project is now being proposed that will continue the work of exemplifying partnerships with local museums and stakeholders.

In terms of the Shirokogoroffs, and Lindgren and Mamen, we have collated a more complex understanding of their work in Manchuria. Academic judgements have been consistently levelled against Shirokogoroff due to the lack of contextual information in his writings, and Lindgren due to her lack of publications, but it cannot be underestimated how much global politics influenced their arrival and departure from Manchuria. The Shirokogoroffs' exile separated them from their friends and family, and one gets a sense that neither fully settled in China. Lindgren chose not to publish immediately after her expulsion due to her concerns for the safety of her friends and colleagues that remained in Hǎilāěr — many of whom were imprisoned or killed in the following years of warfare. By the time that the political situation had stabilised in the 1950s, Lindgren was working as an editor at the Royal Anthropological Institute and developing her Cairngorm Reindeer Herd project with her second husband, Mikel Utsi. Lindgren never returned to Inner Mongolia, despite a desire to. In many ways, her photographs have become her legacy. Her collection provides invaluable cultural heritage for Ewenki and, quoting the headman of Áolǔgǔyā Camp 1, "finding and sharing these photos will bring knowledge and personal meaning for Ewenki in a time of crisis of diminishing customary ways of life and identity".[17]

17 Gě Jùn Gǔ, Headman, Áolǔgǔyā Camp 1, 8 April 2015.

Published References

Anderson, D. G. and D. Arzyutov. 2016. 'The Construction of Soviet Ethnography and "The Peoples of Siberia"', *History and Anthropology* 27 (2): 183–209, https://doi.org/10.1080/02757206.2016.1140159.

Andrews, R. C. 1921. *Across Mongolian Plains: A Naturalist's Account of China's "Great Northwest"* (New York: D. Appleton).

Arzi͡utov, D. V. 2017. 'Nabli͡udai͡a za nabli͡udateli͡ami: o vizual'nykh tekhnikakh teoretizirovanii͡a Sergei͡a i Elizavety Shirokogorovykh', *Ėtnograficheskoe obozrenie* 5: 32–52.

Barthes, R. 1984. *Camera Lucida: Reflections on Photography* (London: Fontana).

Berger, J. 1980. *About Looking* (London: Writers and Readers' Publishing Co-operative).

—. 1981. *Camera Lucida* (New York: Hill and Wang).

Binney, J. and G. Chaplin. 1991. 'Taking the Photographs Home: The Recovery of a Maori History', *Visual Anthropology* 4 (3–4): 431–42.

—. 2003. 'Taking the Photographs Home', in *Museums and Source Communities: A Routledge Reader*, ed. by L. L. Peers and A. K. Brown (London: Routledge), 100–10.

British Association for the Advancement of Science. 1909. *Anthropometric Investigation in the British Isles: Report of the Committee (being the final report on anthropometric method)* (London: The Royal Anthropological Institute).

Brown, A. K. and L. L. Peers. 2006. *'Pictures Bring Us Messages' / Sinaakssiiksi Aohtsimaahpihkookiyaawa: Photographs and Histories from the Kainai Nation* (Toronto: University of Toronto Press).

Buijs, C. and A. R. Jakobsen. 2011. 'The Nooter Photo Collection and the Roots2Share Project of Museums in Greenland and the Netherlands', *Études/Inuit/Studies* 35 (1–2): 165–86.

Czaplicka, M. A. 1914. *Aboriginal Siberia: A Study in Social Anthropology* (Oxford: Clarendon).

Edwards, E. 2001. *Raw Histories: Photographs, Anthropology and Museums* (Oxford: Berg).

—. 2003. 'Talking Visual Histories: Introduction', in *Museums and Source Communities: A Routledge Reader*, ed. by L. L. Peers and A. K. Brown (London: Routledge), 83–99.

Edwards, E. and C. Morton, eds. 2015. *Photographs, Museums, Collections: Between Art and Information* (London: Bloomsbury).

Fraser, R. 2010. 'Forced Relocation amongst the Reindeer-Evenki of Inner Mongolia', *Inner Asia* 12 (2): 317–46.

French, S. A. 1995. 'What is Social Memory?', *Southern Cultures* 2 (1): 9–18.

Henriot, C. and W.-H. Yeh. 2012. *Visualising China, 1845–1965: Moving and Still Images in Historical Narratives* (Leiden: Brill).

Heyne, F. G. 2009. 'Among Taiga Hunters and Shamans: Reminiscences Concerning my Friend, the Scholar of Manchuria, Anatolij Makarovich Kaigorodov (1927–1998)', *Shaman: Journal of the International Society for Shamanistic Research* 1/2: 53–78.

J. M. 1932. 'Woman Explorer in Mongolia Travels With Nomadic Tribes', *The Christian Science Monitor* (23 Dec 1932): 3.

Kaigorodov, A. M. 1968. 'Evenki v Trekhrech'e (Man'chzhuriia)' *Sovetskaia͡ Ėtnografiia͡* 4: 123–31.

Kolås, Å. and Y. Xie. 2015. *Reclaiming the Forest: The Ewenki Reindeer Herders of Aoluguya* (Oxford: Berghahn).

Lindgren, E. J. 1930. 'North-Western Manchuria and the Reindeer-Tungus', *Geographical Journal* 75 (6): 518–36.

—. 1935. 'The Shaman Dress of the Dagurs, Solons and Numinchens in N. W. Manchuria', *Geografiska Annaler* 17 (Supplement: Hyllningsskrift Tillagnad Sven Hedin): 365–78.

—. 1936. *Notes on the Reindeer Tungus* (unpublished doctoral dissertation, University of Cambridge).

Livingstone, D. N. and C. W. J. Withers. 2005. *Geography and Revolution* (Chicago, IL: University of Chicago Press).

Lorimer, H. 2006. 'Herding Memories of Humans and Animals', *Environment and Planning D: Society and Space* 24 (4): 497–518, https://doi.org/10.1068/d381t.

Marreco, B. F. and J. L. S. Myres, eds. 1912. *Notes and Queries on Anthropology* (London: The Royal Anthropological Institute).

Matiasek, K. 2016. 'A Mutual Space?: Stereo Photography on Viennese Anthropological Expeditions (1905–45)', in *Expeditions as Experiments: Practising Observation and Documentation*, ed. by M. Klemun and U. Spring (London: Palgrave), 187–212.

Shirokogoroff, S. M. 1923a. 'Ethnological Investigations in Siberia, Mongolia, and Northern China Part 1', *The China Journal of Science and Arts* (*Shanghai*) 1 (5): 513–22.

—. 1923b. 'Ethnological Investigations in Siberia, Mongolia, and Northern China Part 2', *The China Journal of Science and Arts* (*Shanghai*) 1 (6): 611–21.

—. 1925. *Anthropology of Eastern China and Kwangtung Province* (Shanghai: Commercial Press).

—. 1935. *Psychomental Complex of the Tungus* (London: Kegan Paul).

Shirokogorova, E. N. 1919. 'Severo-Zapadnaia͡ Man'chzhurii͡a (geograficheskiĭ ocherk po dannym mashrutnykh nabli͡udeniĭ)', *Uchenye zapiski istoriko-filologicheskogo fakul'teta v Vladivostoke* 1: 109–46.

—. 1936. 'Narodnai͡a muzyka v Kitae', in *Sbornik materialov po ėvenkiĭskomu (tungusskomu) fol'kloru*, ed. by G. M. Vasilevich (Leningrad: Izdatel'stvo Instituta Narodov Severa), 283–86.

Sirina, A. A. and V. N. Davydov. 2017. '"Prodavavshai͡a ledi plakala... kogda pokupku unosili": ėtnograficheskie kollekt͡sii S. M. i E. N. Shirokogorovykh', *Ėtnograficheskoe Obozrenie* 5: 9–31.

Sontag, S. 1978. *On Photography* (London: Penguin).

Talbot, W. H. F. 1839. *Some Account of the Art of Photogenic Drawing, or The Process by Which Natural Objects May be Made to Delineate Themselves Without the Aid of the Artist's Pencil* (London: R. and J. E. Taylor).

Whitaker, I. 1988. 'Obituaries: Ethel John Lindgren', *Asian Affairs* 19 (2): 254–55, https://doi.org/10.1080/03068378808730312.

Xie, Y. 2015. *Ecological Migrants: The Relocation of China's Ewenki Reindeer Herders* (Oxford: Berghahn).

Archival References

HILA: Hoover Institution Library and Archives, Stanford University, California

HILA Mamen 3-16, Mamen Box 3, folder 16. Field Diary of Oscar Mamen, folio dated 25 Jul. 1929.

HILA Mamen 3-17, Mamen Box 3, folder 17. Field Diary of Oscar Mamen, episode dated 2 Aug. 1929.

HILA Mamen 1-M63, Lindgren Box 1, folder M.63. Field diary of Oscar Mamen, 1929.

HILA Mamen 15.7.1929, Lindgren Box 3. Field diary of Oscar Mamen, 1929.

FA IRL RAN: The Phonograph Archive of the Institute of Russian Literature (Pushkin House) of Russian Academy of Sciences, St Petersburg

FA IRL RAN 3271 – 3289. Fonograficheskie valiki Sergei͡a i Elizavety Shirokogorovykh, 1915–1917.

JLA: John Lindgren's Personal Archive

JLA 1928a. Letter from Ethel Lindgren to Ethel Eichheim, 9 Mar. 1928.

JLA 1928b. Letter from Ethel Lindgren to Signe Laven, 3 Mar. 1928.

JLA 1928c. Ethel Lindgren's field diary, 6 May 1928.

JLA 1928d. Letter from Ethel Lindgren to Signe Laven, 23 Aug. 1928.

JLA 1932a. Annotations of Ethel Lindgren on an article published by *The Christian Science Monitor* on her travels, 23 Dec. 1932 (J. M. 1932).

JLA 1932b. Letter from Ethel Lindgren to Prof. Ellis Minns, 22 Feb. 1932.

JLA 1933. Letter from Ethel Lindgren to Prof. Ellis Minns, 31 Jan. 1933.

JLA 1987. Letter from Ethel Lindgren to John Lindgren, 30 Apr. 1987.

LCC: Archive of Lucy Cavendish College, Cambridge

LCC 1931 - A2012/001/11. Lindgren, E. "Chol Trip 1931" (unpublished manuscript).

MAA: Museum of Archaeology and Anthropology, Cambridge

MAA F.126021.LIN - F126029.LIN. 16 mm films by Oscar Mamen.

MAA N.126084.LIN. Meeting the 1st R. T. [Reindeer Tungus] on Ulugicha River. Nikolaĭ Ivanovich Kokeroff with Lindgren at their joint camp. Photo by Oscar Mamen, 25 Jul. 1929.

MAA P.10943.ACH1. Pingrui holding her "Dagur cradle & 3 months baby, Omul Ail". Photo by Oscar Mamen, 19 Jul. 1931.

MAĖ: [Numbered Collections of] Peter the Great Museum of Anthropology and Ethnography, Russian Academy of Sciences, St Petersburg

MAĖ 2002. Stekli͡annye negativy Sergei͡a i Elizavety Shirokogorovykh, Zabaĭkal'skai͡aoblast, Chitinskiĭ uezd October 1912 179 x 129". 116 plates.

MAĖ 2500. Stekli͡annye negativy Sergei͡a i Elizavety Shirokogorovykh, Priamurskiĭ kraĭ 1915, 1050 x 440 mm. 149 plates.

MAĖ 2638 Stekli͡annye negativy Sergei͡a i Elizavety Shirokogorovykh, Priamurskiĭ kraĭ, basseĭn verkhnego Amura, 44 x 107 mm [verascope]. 81 plates.

MAÉ 2639. Steklîannye negativy Sergeîa i Elizavety Shirokogorovykh. Verascope, Amurskiĭ okrug i Manchzhuriîa 44 x 107 mm [verascope]. 604 plates.

RA IIMK: Manuscript Archive of the Institute of the History of Material Culture, Russian Academy of Sciences, St Petersburg

RA IIMK 1-1(1916)-162: 1. Otnoshenie V. V. Radlova v Imperatorskuîu Arkheologicheskuîu komissiîu (12 Jul. 1916). 4 folios.

RA IIMK 1-1(1916)-162: 2–2v. Soprovoditel'noe pis'mo grafa A. A. Bobrinskogo k otkrytomu listu S. M. Shirokogorova (2 Jul. 1916).

SPF ARAN: St Petersburg Filial of the Archive of the Russian Academy of Sciences

SPF ARAN 849-5-803. E. N. Shirokogorova. Polevoĭ. Polevoĭ dnevnik, 1912.

SPF ARAN 142-1(1918)-68: 124–27. Pis'mo S. M. Shirokogorova L. ÎA. Shternbergu, 30 Nov. 1916.

TumA: Donald Tumanisonis's Personal Archive, Horten, Norway

TumA 1915/16. Photocopied Field Diary of Sergei Shirokogoroff, 1915–1916.

8. "The Sea is Our Field": Pomor Identity in Russian Ethnography

Masha Shaw and Natalie Wahnsiedler[1]

"The sea is our field" is a popular old saying among a group of northern Russians who became known as Pomors. "If God gives us fish, he will give us bread, too", the saying continues (Maksimov 1857: 247). This saying captures one of the key axes around which identity is expressed in this far northern extreme of Russian settlement. Russian identity is traditionally linked to cereal agriculture and to steppe landscapes. The term Pomors, by contrast, derives from the Russian words *po mori͡u*, meaning "by sea". It indirectly indexes the fact that the people living along the White and Barents Seas have traditionally thrived on fishing and hunting of sea mammals — a subsistence strategy which would grow to have great importance for Pomor identity movements in the late twenthieth and early twenty-first centuries.

In this chapter we explore how material, linguistic and ecological factors underscore the way identity is expressed along the northern

1 We are grateful to the chairmen of several fishing collective farms who provided a great administrative support and shared their knowledge wherever possible. The people of Arkhangelsk oblast′ were very generous and hospitable and shared with us their time and many cups of tea. Scholars of the Northern (Arctic) Federal University gave us valuable advice especially upon our arrival to the field and facilitated our further research in Arkhangelsk oblast′.

 https://doi.org/10.11647/OBP.0150.08

boundary of European Russian settlement. These narratives, both historical and contemporary, illustrate the way that an *etnos* can be seen to derive its identity from an evocative landscape. As we shall see, the ecological conditions of Pomor identity provide a strong pull which contemporary activists use to defend Pomor resilience. This ethnographic example, from the far north of Russia, illustrates the "biosocial" component to *etnos* thinking as outlined in chapters 1 and 2. Although relatively small in population, Pomors have played a significant role in thinking about identity and Russian ethnography, in particular its unique *etnos* theory. Pomors have been described as the "most authentic Russians", as an ambiguous sub-group or *subetnos* of Great Russians, and as a "less-numerous indigenous minority".

It is interesting, and perhaps not insignificant, that examples of the distinctive quality of Pomor lifeways go back to the very foundation of Russian ethnography in the eighteenth and nineteenth centuries — a curious case where ethnographic examples have played a role in forming the discipline that documents them. Further, it is remarkable that the status of identity at this very northern extreme of Russian settlements tends to mirror similar arguments made about the status of southern Slav settlements in the region now known as Ukraine. In this chapter, we identify some general themes in the description of Pomor life which reflect back upon the way that Great Russians are identified as a nation.

The Pomor example has a further ironic twist to it, which has been part and parcel of recent political movements. The intimate familiarity that Pomor seafarers had with sea-going technology gave them a special role in facilitating the expansion of the Novgorod state first along the White Sea coast, then to the Arctic islands of the Barents Sea, and finally across Siberia. The sea-going quality of Russian expansion across Eurasia gives Pomors a unique status as a people hosting a special type of indigenous political and ecological adaptation, while at the same time playing a key role in colonization across Eurasia. This double-bind in the definition of Pomor identity, as we will show, plays an important role in how Pomors today are perceived as being part of the Great Russian identity project and simultaneously different from it.

The chapter is based upon fieldwork in Pomor villages and interviews with representatives of the Pomor intelligentsia in 2014–2016 in the city of Arkhangelsk and several villages in Mezenskiĭ, Primorskiĭ and Onezhskiĭ raions of Arkhangelsk oblast'. Fieldwork included taking part in informal activities, such as fishing and berry picking, as well as participating in various festive events in the city and official celebrations of fishing collective farms in several villages.

Pomor Landscapes and the History of Slavic Ethnography

Pomors have inspired the curiosity of travellers and ethnographers since the late eighteenth century. Early ethnographic accounts of Pomors belong to scholars who worked in a holistic tradition with no clear boundaries between disciplines. The earliest ethnographic accounts of the Russian north were written by natural scientists or scholars who worked across several subject areas. Their descriptions of Pomor'e and its inhabitants were interspersed with descriptions of animals and plants, and geology (Chelishchev 1886; Fomin 1797; Lepekhin 1805). Imperial ethnography tended to distinguish northern Russians in terms of their distinct livelihood, dialect, material culture, and relationship to the state. Soviet ethnographers continued to treat Pomors either heroically, as pioneers of Russia's northern frontier, or as exceptions embedded into a hierarchical classification of identities. Perhaps unique to the Pomor case is that through the process of thinking and writing about Pomor society, Russian ethnography came to define itself.

Pomor landscapes, or rather seascapes, appeared quite early as a marker of identity. Afanasiĭ Shchapov — himself a famous liberal Siberian regionalist who argued for the autonomy and self-government of regional groups — cited Pomor lifeways in an influential essay on the affordances of oceans and mountains to shape peoples:

> In Northern Pomor'e, in severe polar climate, on dull barren polar soil, nature has designed its great economy in such a way, so that to harmonize the polar cold, the polar accelerated and heavy inhaling of oxygen with the demand for, and quantity and quality of polar food; it harmonized the demand for and intensity of polar movement with the intensity and movement of life. [...] What was available there for a stable and reliable provision for Pomor colonization and life? What could support the dominant population, dominant physiological and ethnographic development and a dominant people? The sea, only the ocean-sea, with its inexhaustible vital content. [...] The sea became a vital

> element for them, the sea is everything for them. Ancient biographies of Pomor saints tell almost exclusively about maritime life and activities, sea fishing and hunting, Novgorodian Pomor settlers and sea storms. These tales are full of legends about sea wonders performed by Pomor saints, who are portrayed as some sort of sea heroes and half-gods. The sea was the most poetic and spiritual subject for Pomor writers (Shchapov 1864: 112–14).[2]

It is a curiosity of Pomor ethnography that this group is further subdivided according to the qualities of the coasts (*berega*) on which they live. Thus, for example, there are seven named "coasts" on the White Sea coastline: Zimniĭ, Letniĭ, Onezhskiĭ, Pomorskiĭ, Karel'skiĭ, Kandalakshskiĭ, and Terskiĭ *berega.* Some names reflect local climatic conditions — such as Zimniĭ (Winter) and Letniĭ (Summer) *berega* — while others are named after local geographical objects such as rivers or settlements. The names are still largely in use. Bernshtam (1978) differentiated the White Sea coasts according to the degree of Pomor self-identification among local population. She argued that by the beginning of the twenthieth century, people on Pomorskiĭ coast had the strongest Pomor identity, as they connected Pomor identity to Murmansk sea fisheries (which gave rise to the very name *Pomor*) and considered only themselves as true Pomors. By contrast, the weakest Pomor identity was to be found among the population of Karel'skiĭ, Terskiĭ, Kandalakshskiĭ, and Onezhskiĭ coasts, as they were only called Pomors by people from neighbouring regions located far away from the sea. Such differences between the coasts are less pronounced today. However, it is still possible to come across an opinion that populations of some coasts are more Pomor than of the others.

This geographically-grounded curiosity in northern Russians in the early nineteenth century would continue to reverberate through the Imperial period and into the Soviet period itself. Thus, in the sixth volume of the authoritative Soviet-era ethnographic encyclopaedia *Peoples of the World*, Pomors were represented as a "historical-cultural group of the Russian people" differing from other northern Russians mainly in their subsistence as "brave seafarers, sea hunters and fishers" (Tolstov 1964: 145). The key theoretical term in this volume — the "historical-cultural group" — was further described as being "more geographical than ethnographical" and was applied exclusively to the

2 All translations from Russian to English are by Masha Shaw.

dwellers of the northern seashore. Similarly, in Tokarev's textbook *The Ethnography of the Peoples of the USSR*, Pomors were represented as a "cultural-geographic type" of the Russian population who displayed a unique "cultural and economic (*khozi͡aĭstvennyĭ*) type" based on fishing and sea hunting (Tokarev 1958: 31).

As we shall see, important elements of this geographically-defined identity structure would flow into the concept of Pomor indigeneity at the end of the Soviet period. These geographical examples also illustrate what Nathaniel Knight noticed as a strong geographical turn to thinking about identity within the Russian academy in general (Knight 2017). It is perhaps not insignificant that Karl von Baer, the founder of the ethnographic section of the Imperial Russian Geographical Society, came to respect geographical influences on identity after his travels with Pomors (Ibid).

Between these two sets of descriptions in the mid-nineteenth century and the mid-twenthieth century, many generations of ethnographers added specific observations on the uniqueness of Pomor culture and its link to their northern homeland. That uniqueness usually was transformed into the interpretative schemes of ethnographers involved in "*etnos* thinking" which underlay the *etnos* theory (see chapter 2). Thus, material culture and language as categories were not only especially important for theoretical thinking but also conjoined with field ethnographic data.

Material Culture

> Generally, Pomors are hospitable, sturdy, healthy people. Their faces are broad and always red since they spend most of the year outside, at sea. Men wear caps [*kartuzy*], jackets [*pidzhaki*] and leather boots in the summer; boot covers [*bakhily*] and Norwegian jersey-jackets [*kutrki-fufaĭki*] for fishing and hunting, and in winter they wear felt boots and sheepskin coats [*tulupy*]. Women wear bright colorful sarafans. Their houses are mostly spacious and rather clean. Every house has a samovar, and tea- and tableware. The main fishery that feeds Pomors is Murmansk fisheries (Ėngel'gardt 2009 [1897]: 52–3).

By the late nineteenth century, the study of material culture was a significant research focus in Russian ethnography through which it was thought that peoples (*narody*) could be distinguished. These early studies focussed on rural populations and in particular on Russian peasant communities. It was thought that rural peasants preserved in their lifeways ancient customs and beliefs (Leskinen 2012: 250).

The analysis of clothing and traditional dress was a classic method for distinguishing local populations. There was a particular emphasis on women's clothing as a marker of identity similar in style to other Slavic regions. Sluchevskiĭ (2009) described Pomor women as well dressed regardless of their social and economic status, wearing long colourful *sarafany*, and beautifully decorated headwear called *kokoshnik* and *povoĭnik*, as well as extensive neck decorations. Sluchevskiĭ noted the absence of an otherwise typical *kokoshnik* in women's clothing in Mezen' region, which neighboured the reindeer-herding Nenets population. Instead, Mezen' women wore kerchiefs "with two ends tied above the forehead like two little horns which dangled in the most peculiar way" (Sluchevskiĭ 2009: 156). A distinctive feature of women's clothing in some parts of Pomor'e was an extensive use of pearls extracted from local rivers. Sluchevskiĭ was particularly impressed by the light and skilful movements of Pomor women in their long and richly decorated dresses as they steered their boats in rough and roaring waters. In the authoritative Soviet-era volume *Peoples of the European Part of the USSR*, the Pomor women's *sarafan* of the late nineteenth century was distinguished from those in all other regions for being made of silk (Aleksandrov et al. 1964: 372) (Fig. 8.1).

However, in line with the emphasis on landscape, Pomor winter outerwear also created a special arena to explore difference. Scholars often noted peculiar types of clothing among the White Sea coast population. They also stressed that this clothing was conditioned by the harsh environment and the wearers' ways of life. Many studies have emphasised the Norwegian and Nenets influences on Pomor clothing; Maslova, for instance, writes that the so called *zi͡uĭdvestka* was a typical hat of Pomor fishermen (Maslova 1956: 557). This Norwegian style of hat was made of leather or textile and had flaps to protect the ears. Other characteristic types of clothing for Pomors were the *mali͡tsa* and *sovik* made of reindeer skin (Maslova 1956: 712). This clothing came from Nenets culture where it is known as *mal'cha/mal'tsa* and *săvăk* respectively (Fig. 8.2).

Fig. 8.1 Pomor women's clothing illustrating three types of headwear (from left to right): *povoĭnik* (under the scarf), *kokoshnik*, and kerchief with "dangling horns". Photo by Nikolaĭ A. Shabunin (MAĖ 974-54). © Peter the Great Museum of Anthropology and Ethnography, Russian Academy of Sciences, St Petersburg

Again, in the same Soviet-era encyclopaedia that summarized classifications of the peoples of the European part of the USSR, the traditional Pomor peasant dress was contrasted with those of the central regions of Russia because of its incorporation of designs from neighbouring reindeer-herding peoples (Aleksandrov et al. 1964: 377) (Fig. 8.3). These two types of parkas are generally characteristic of the reindeer-herding Nenets people. These examples of creole forms of clothing — outerwear which blends Slavic and indigenous styles — foreshadow the late twentieth century debate on the status of Pomors as perhaps an indigenous people.

Fig. 8.2 A group of peasants in Arkhangelsk province at the turn of the twentieth century. Nearly all men and two younger boys wear a type of parka made of reindeer skin: either *malitsa* (fur facing inwards) or *sovik* (fur facing outwards). One man (far left) and a younger boy at the back wear other types of coats made of cloth. Photo by Nikolaĭ A. Shabunin (MAÈ 974-41). © Peter the Great Museum of Anthropology and Ethnography, Russian Academy of Sciences, St Petersburg

Although Pomors from the very beginning were associated with the ocean, it was only late in the Imperial period that scholars cast a glance to the way that they set out to sea. Sluchevskiĭ conducted a detailed description of the *shnîaka* — a shallow and narrow sailboat with wide sails designed for ocean fishing in the season just after the ice on the White Sea breaks up (Sluchevskiĭ 1886: 51). In comparison to later accounts, Sluchevskiĭ's observations on the *shnîaka* read ironic if not paternalistic where the word "brave" is used as a synonym for "foolhardy" to describe sailors using such a dangerous and unstable boat.

Nikolaĭ Zagoskin gave the first comparative description of northern sea-faring knowledge in his encyclopaedia of Russian river and sea routes. Zagoskin's description of Pomor sea-faring is summarised within a section on the expansion of Novgorod colonizers across the White Sea (Zagoskin 1910: 153ff). His idea of sea-knowledge as

1
2
3
4
5
6
Крестьянская мужская и женская одежда начала XX в.:
1—2 — крестьяне (Московская губ.), 3 — помор (Архангельская губ.), 4 — женская одежда с сарафаном (Нижегородская губ.), 5 — с полосатой юбкой (Тульская губ.), 6 — с поневой (Воронежская губ.)

Fig. 8.3 Comparative illustration of peasant costumes distinguishing Pomor costumes (far right) from that of other central Russian peasants (Aleksandrov 1964: 377)

colonization-knowledge would be evocatively encapsulated in the Soviet period in Mikhail Belov's ethno-archaeological reconstruction of a Pomor *koch* — reconstructed on the basis of archaeological remains in the former fur-trade fort of Mangazei in north-central Siberia (Belov 1951). This peculiar round, keel-less sailboat was especially designed to be dragged overland to allow fishermen or explorers to move from one watershed to another overland.

Belov, in contrast to others, is one of the first to associate Pomor sea knowledge with a heroic set of qualities that give credit both to the ingenuity of the people and their place in the history of Russian imperialism. The *koch* in his account was an ingenious sort of vessel that allowed the Russian nation to expand overland across Eurasia. His nationalist reconstruction is spectacular with its detailed drawings of the vessels and quotations from diaries of those who sailed upon them (Fig. 8.4). It is striking that this technological and geographic interest in the *koch* does not seem to have captured the imagination of imperial ethnographers.

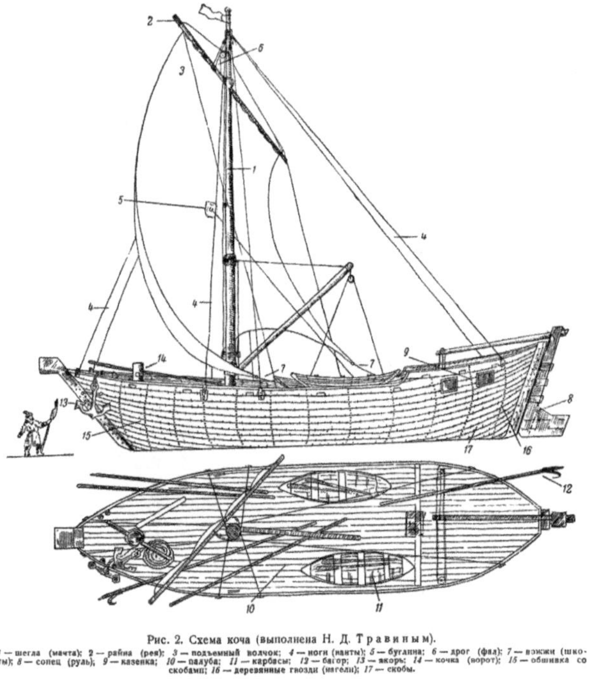
Рис. 2. Схема коча (выполнена Н. Д. Травиным).
1 — шегла (мачта); 2 — райна (рея); 3 — подъемный волчок; 4 — ноги (ванты); 5 — бугапна; 6 — дрог (фал); 7 — вожжи (шкоты); 8 — сопец (руль); 9 — казенка; 10 — палуба; 11 — карбасы; 12 — багор; 13 — якорь; 14 — кочка (ворот); 15 — обшивка со скобами; 16 — деревянные гвозди (нагели); 17 — скобы.

Fig. 8.4 Schematic drawing of a Pomor *koch* (Belov 1951: 75)

Traditional Pomor vessels, such as the *koch,* continue to exercise a hold on the imaginations of contemporary intellectuals living in Arkhangelsk. For example, in our interviews, an Arkhangelsk museum worker and historian asserted that Pomor traditional boats should be restored in order for Pomor identity to be truly preserved. In the late 1980s, in Petrozavodsk, a city in the Republic of Karelia, a group of enthusiasts recreated the historical *koch,* which they called "Pomor". This vessel was used for several navigation trips from Arkhangelsk to the Solovki Islands and up to the Kanin Peninsula. Another navigation expedition that intended to repeat the ancient route of Russian explorers using historically reconstructed vessels took place in 2011 and 2012. Its members aimed to follow the routes of Russian pioneers along the Arctic Ocean and down the Lena River.

A final area of intensive research was on the architecture of dwellings, which gave ethnographers an overview of large-scale differences between northern and southern regions. For instance, scholars argued that smaller villages were common in the north, while larger villages prevailed in the south (Tolstov 1964: 144). The way that space was structured and enclosed was another significant topic, with many ethnographers noting that southern communities tended to fence off private land while Russians in the central region tended to use land communally. From this angle, Pomor Russians were unique again. For example, in 1970, ethnographers of the Moscow Academy of Sciences published the volume *Russians* (Kushner 1970) which presented individual sections on the architecture of peasant dwellings and their internal design. Chizhikova (1970) argued that the dwellings in the north of the European part of Russia distinguished themselves by large building structures that included in one complex rooms for humans but also containing under one roof spaces for animals and for storage (Fig. 8.5).

Fig. 8.5 Example of a peasant's house. Photo by Nikolaĭ A. Shabunin (MAĖ 974–88). © Peter the Great Museum of Anthropology and Ethnography, Russian Academy of Sciences, St Petersburg

These large, multi-functional constructions differed sharply from peasant yards in central and southern regions where separate outhouses would be built for animals and storage. As discussed in chapter 3, a major theme in the pan-Slavic typologies of Nikolaĭ Mogilīanskiĭ was the built structure of the village. Mogilīanskiĭ distinguished between the southern Slavic village of neatly constructed courtyards (*dvor*) and fences dividing extended families from one another, and the open and somewhat messy structure of a Great Russian village, which lacked fences and courtyards.

Tat'iana Bernshtam — one of the most well-known ethnographers of Pomors — was one of the first to draw attention to the distinctive outbuildings of Pomor fishing spots. For instance, she outlined that some Pomor dwelling structures distinguished themselves from other houses of northern Russians by having extra facilities for fishing and seal hunting equipment (Bernshtam 2009: 47–8). In addition, wealthier families had their own icehouses (*ledniki*, i.e. places for storing fish and the fat of animals, mostly built as pits) and fish-drying racks nearby the house. These observations have come together as a description of a unique architectural ensemble known as the *tonīa* — again, a geographic-technical object which, while mentioned by imperial observers, would gain a special importance in the post-Soviet period. According to a recent account, *tonīas*:

> were specially outfitted for fishing and the initial processing of fish (and sea mammals). A *tonīa* would be built of a hut (in which fishers and sea mammal hunters would live during the fishing and hunting seasons), a steam-bath, storage shelters for provisions, fishing equipment and salt, ice houses for the preservation of fresh fish, hanging structures to untangle and dry nets, a special windvane (*flīuger*) to determine the direction of the wind, and special equipment (*lebedki, vorota*) for hauling boats and nets onto the beach. Many *tonīas* would have large wooden crosses. Larger *tonīas* might even have their own chapels (Laĭus and Laĭus 2010: 24–5).

An important aspect of the *tonīa*, aside from its economic significance, was its role in consolidating cultural transmission during the intense periods of fishing of the high season.

Material culture, ranging from clothing to architectural ensembles, have been markers of Pomor identity for over 150 years and continue to structure the way that Pomors see themselves. This is an important illustration of the way that material artefacts have been used to define *etnos* starting from the first work of Fëdor Volkov at the end of the nineteenth century (see chapter 3).

Northern Russian folklore and *Pomor'ska govori͡a*

> I could barely understand my companion's speech, due to its many provincialisms. Yet, it was not as obscure and confusing for me as was, for example, the speech of distant Pomors. The lasher's dialect must have been influenced by the proximity of the province's capital and by the communication with travellers. In a distant part of Pomor'e, especially in places far away from towns, I often found myself at a dead end while trying to understand a Russian person speaking in my native tongue. Listening later to the language of Pomors, I came across words — alongside Karelian and old Slavic words — that were astonishing in their striking accuracy of expression. Take for example, the word "undead" (*nezhit'*), which is a collective noun for all spirits of folk superstition: water, house and forest spirits, mermaids and everything that does not live a human life (Maksimov 1871: 43–4).

The Russian north also attracted the attention of ethnographers, folklorists and linguists keen to discover ancient epic songs called *byliny* and to document the special dialect spoken in the region. Ethnographic expeditions to the Russian north in the second half of the nineteenth century discovered a rich repertoire of *byliny*.

Byliny were at first regarded as part of a wider range of texts, not necessarily related to heroic epics, called *stariny* ("old songs" or "songs about ancient times") (Panchenko 2012: 430). This folklore genre was thought to represent a form which started to become extinct in the middle and southern parts of Russia already in the twelfth century (Kozhinov 1999). In line with its severe landscape, the north has since been viewed as a "natural preserve" of the epic. The Russian north was therefore the place where most *byliny* have been recorded. Scholars assumed that *byliny* and *stariny* have preserved the "voice of medieval Russian people" (Panchenko 2012: 430). This discovery defined the nature of ethnographic interest in the area for many decades to come. Until now, the White Sea coast attracts numerous folklore expeditions. Villagers see almost any ethnographer who comes to their place as first and foremost a folklorist and immediately direct them to village elders who can still remember old tales.

One of the folklorists to travel to the north with the aim of recording *byliny* was Alekseĭ Markov. In 1898, he spent several weeks in the village Zimni͡ai͡a Zolotitsa where he especially worked with storytellers (*skaziteli*) Kriukovy (Markov 1901: 1). Markov believed that the remarkable survival of *byliny* on Zimniĭ Bereg (Winter Coast) was directly linked to the particular *byt* (lifestyle) of the locals (Ibid: 8–9). The scholar concluded that peasants in Zolotitsa learned the old songs as they spent extended periods far away from their homes in distant fishing huts while fishing for salmon in summer, and during their hunting trips for sea mammals or shorter hunting trips in the forests (Ibid). Geography and isolation played a big role in framing these traditional skills. As Markov wrote:

> Even now, with the improvement of communication ways in the introduction of mail services and telegraphs to a large degree [...] Even now, it takes a long time for the Russian news to arrive on the White Sea coast, and these news do not impress the peasants (Ibid: 11).

The assumption that the Russian north was isolated would come to be challenged late in the Soviet period by the ethnographer Svetlana Dmitrieva who pointed out that the area had intensive trade and cultural connections with Scandinavia (Dmitrieva 1972: 70–2). She further argued that a look at biographies of *skaziteli* (tellers) of *byliny* reveals that many of them were literate and had lived and worked in cities like St Petersburg and Novgorod. Narrators from the White Sea coast, Mezen' and Pechora travelled as far as Scandinavia.

Another characteristic of the region was its special dialect. The different Russian dialects became a focus of ethnographic and linguistic research with a general interest in Russian culture in the nineteenth century. Nadezhdin, for instance, criticised linguists for having so far focused on the official Russian *rossiĭskiĭ* (language), while local spoken languages remained unstudied. He drew attention to different types of the Russian language: the Great-Russians' language, the Small-Russian, and Belorussian (Anuchin 1889: 14–5). Mid-twentieth century ethnographers usually differentiated between southern and northern dialects, with the distinctive feature being the phonetic peculiarity of vowels [o] and [a]. They argued that in the northern regions the

Fig. 8.6 Front cover of the dictionary *Pomor'ska govori͡a* (Moseev 2005)

okai͡ushchiĭ dialect prevailed, while in the south the *akai͡ushchiĭ* dialect was more common (Aleksandrov et al. 1964: 153, 155). Moreover, in the 1964 Soviet-era encyclopaedia ethnographers published very few scattered examples of Pomor distinctiveness, but the sections on the Pomor dialect were uncharacteristically prosaic in distinguishing not only vowels but also sets of lexica that were unique to the region. In terms of ethno-national representation, the group was sketched out on a map of northern Europe according to the extent of its dialect (Ibid).

The northern dialect, with its unique pronunciation, as well as peculiar vocabulary related to environmental knowledge also attracted the attention of scholars. Already in the second half of the nineteenth century, the ethnographer and historian Aleksandr Podvysot͡skiĭ composed a dictionary of Arkhangelsk province's local dialect (Podvysot͡skiĭ 1885). This work was continued by Kseni͡a Gemp (2004) and I. M. Durov (2011) among others. In the 2000s, these descriptions gave ground for Arkhangelsk activists to outline the northern dialect as a separate language. Together with other activists, Ivan Moseev published a dictionary called *Pomor'ska govori͡a* (Moseev 2005) (Fig. 8.6). Words and phrases presented in the dictionary were collected in Arkhangelsk region mostly by non-linguists. In an interview with Anna Pyzhova, Moseev emphasised the role of Pomor language: "Today, I am among the few northerners who are relatively fluent in their language — Pomorskai͡a govori͡a. This is my first language, the language of my childhood, the language of my parents, relatives, neighbours, and therefore my native language" (qtd. in Pyzhova 2011). While Arkhangelsk scholars criticised Moseev's dictionary as non-scientific and a work of an amateur, it turned out to be quite popular among Arkhangelsk townspeople and even inspired similar projects in other parts of Arkhangelsk oblast.

Pomor Distinctiveness in a Pan-Slavic Frame

Russian ethnography in the Imperial period, and throughout the Soviet period, placed differing emphases on the distinctness of Pomors from other Slavic groups. This discourse of difference reflects a certain awkwardness within which Pomors fit into standard genealogies and typologies of Slavic people. As we have seen in chapter 3, the way that Great Russians were defined to a large extent was calibrated on how the northern and southern frontiers of Slavic settlements were described. The reports of travellers and ethnographers tend to alternately fit Pomors sometimes close to Great Russians, sometimes with the traditions of northern indigenous peoples, and sometimes as part of a distinct northern European or Fennoscandian culture. This ambiguity is also reflected in some minority opinions.

For example, Dmitriĭ Zelenin, in his *East Slavic Ethnography* (published in German in 1927 and translated into Russian for the first time in 1991) classified the "Pomor dialect" as a sub-group within north Russian dialects (Zelenin 1991). He also put forward a controversial theory of there being "two peoples" (*narodnost'*) within the Great Russians. He distinguished north and south Great Russians on the basis of their dialects, and demoted the central Russian groups to a sort of interstitial group. Further, following the acclaimed linguist A. Shakhmatov,

Zelenin considered northern Russian dialect groups to be descendants of the ancient Slavic tribes of Slovene and Krivichi — giving northern Russians (and Pomors in particular) a genealogy of being the purest type of Great Russians. This linguistically-driven theory sits in contrast to another widely held view that the Pomors were descendants of the Novgorod Slavs mixed with Finnish Karelians (Leskinen 2016: 528–29).

This powerful ambiguity as to whether or not northern Russians represented one pole of Slavic cultural difference as compared to southern Russians, or if they were "pure" or "mixtures", would prepare the ground for Pomors to become a controversial example in Soviet ethnography. Since Pomors distinguished themselves from other Russians by their way of speaking, material culture, and way of life, ethnographers had to find a special place for them in ethnographic theory. However, they struggled to represent the unique quality of Pomors as being somehow the most pure, original or distinctive representatives of the Great Russians. This clumsiness is similar to that faced by the Shirokogoroffs during their Zabaĭkal′ fieldwork in 1912–1913 (see chapter 5). The Shirokogoroffs were puzzled by creole categories they recorded instead of pure ethnic categories their mentors had told them to expect. This general discomfort with hybridity came to haunt Soviet etnnographers generation after generation. Their unease led to the evolution of the discrete category of the "subetnos" with its marked continuities with earlier imperial studies of material culture.

Pomors as *Subetnos*

As several chapters in this volume attest, *etnos* theory became an important arena for weighing identity claims in the late Imperial period and the height of the Soviet period. *Etnos* theory differs from its cognates in American and European anthropology for its distinct interest in ethnic origins (*etnogenez*) — a quality often linked to its purported primordialism (Banks 1996: 17). The unique way that Pomor lifestyles have been documented produced odd anomalies within Soviet *etnos* theory. If other nations were pure *etnoses*, Pomors in some sources became a primary example of a *subetnos*.

A key feature of *etnos* theory was the idea of a hierarchical classification of ethnic communities. The head of the ethnographic department of the Russian Academy of Sciences and Director of the Institute of Ethnography, I͡Ulian Bromleĭ was one of the scholars who excelled in sketching out hierarchical distinctions. His somewhat baroque classification system laid-out a set of "meta-ethnic communities" at the top of this taxonomy (Bromleĭ 1983). At the bottom, he sketched out a smaller unit, which he described as a *subetnos*. Within the hierarchical taxonomy of *etnos* theory, Bromleĭ placed Pomors as a classic example of the *subetnos* of Russians.

Bromleĭ's classification was intended to replace what we noted above as Tolstov's "historical-cultural group" (Tolstov 1964: 145) and Tokarev's "cultural-geographic type" (Tokarev 1958: 31). Bromleĭ argued that one person could simultaneously belong to several ethnic groups of different orders. For example, one person could consider themselves to be Russian (main ethnic unit), a Pomor (*subetnos*), and a Slav (*meta-ethnic community*) (Bromleĭ 1983: 84). The idea of larger groups comprising smaller groups gained increasing popularity in Soviet ethnography, especially from the 1980s. This model reminds one of the Russian *matreshka* dolls, a set of wooden nesting dolls of different sizes that can be placed one inside another.

Alongside Bromleĭ, charismatic geographer and historian Lev Gumilëv developed an independent theory of *etnos* and *subetnos*, where Pomors also served as a prime example. His work, although initially very controversial, later gained popularity in Russian post-Soviet scholarship as well as in the wider community. Gumilëv's writings have become especially popular among local Pomor historians in the late Soviet period, and arguably Pomor activists borrowed more widely from Gumilëv's vibrant prose than from Bromleĭ. Gumilëv regarded *etnos* as a living organism that like any other organism is born, matures, grows old, and dies (Shnirel'man 2006). This basic assumption allows one to calculate different stages and their characteristics of an *etnos*. In Gumilëv's theory, an *etnos* is closely connected to the environment where it develops — which again is a strong theme in Pomor scholarship.

Moreover, Gumilëv believed in a hierarchy of *etnoses*. Like Bromleĭ, he developed a hierarchical taxonomy where he distinguished between a "superetnos", "etnos", and "sub-etnos". Gumilëv argued that an *etnos* possesses a mechanism of self-regulation. For instance, an *etnos* is able to increase its own complexity to defend itself from external impacts.

Therefore, according to Gumilëv, the Great Russian *etnos* itself started to produce subethnic divisions in the fourteenth and fifteenth centuries that sometimes took the form of estates (Gumilëv 1989). This resulted in the segregations of Cossacks in the south and Pomors in the north.

Scholarly discussions and definitions of *etnos* and *subetnos* have been incorporated into public narratives on Pomors, often with a degree of terminological confusion. The following quote and a subsequent paragraph show how a discussion about Pomors' status can go full circle from Pomors being seen as a separate *etnos* within the Russian people to them actually being Russian:

> What do you mean [Pomors] are not recognised. How shall I put it — not recognised. So, the Pomor *etnos*, i.e. a special people among the Russians, the Pomor *etnos*, the *etnos is* recognised. [...] [Pomors are] called *etnos* everywhere now. [...] *Etnos* is such a special characteristic. [...] Cultural, economic, all sorts. Let's have a look [in an encyclopaedia] what *etnos* is (Male, 75 years old, Arkhangelsk, Russia, 2014).

Another example of the same circular thinking was provided by a discussion surrounding an encyclopaedia entry for the term *etnos*. This entry referred the reader to another term — *ėtnicheskaia͡ obshchnost'* (ethnic community) instead. The definition described *ėtnicheskaia͡ obshchnost'* as a "historically developed type of a stable social group of people, represented by a tribe, *narodnost'* (nationality/people), nation" (Bol'shoi ėntsiklopedicheskiĭ slovar' 2000). It continued to say that the term *ėtnicheskaia͡ obshchnost'* is ethnographically close to the notion *narod* (people). The subsequent discussion about how this applies to Pomors made the interviewee say that "a separate people does not sound very nice. They [Pomors] are Russian, that's the thing" (Male, 75 years old, Arkhangelsk, Russia, 2014).

Local Ideas

Among the classic Pomor ethnographers, it is arguably Tat'ia͡na Bernstham who most closely engaged with the hierarchical themes outlined by Bromleĭ and Gumilëv, even though she did not use the term *subetnos*. She promoted the idea of "local groups" as an alternative approach to the study of *etnos* in her later work. In the introduction to a collective volume on the Russian north (Bernshtam 1995), she suggested developing new approaches to the theory of *etnos*. According to Bernstham, ethnographers have so far engaged in the development of theories regarding ethnogenesis and scales of hierarchies of ethnic groups. However, she notes that ethnographers have also realised that the reality of ethnic borders, languages, and other elements of culture do not necessarily correspond with these theories. Bernshtam suggested that studying "local groups" could contribute to finding new approaches for the theory of *etnos* (Bernshtam 1995: 5). While her "local groups" approach does not contradict *etnos* theory, it seems to encourage a new methodology. Instead of trying to match theory and empirical findings, Bernshtam argued for inductive methodologies, whereby scholars should document people's local ideas (*narodnye lokal'nye predstavleniia͡*) and gradually assemble them to identify groupings. These local ideas, according to her, would reflect the entire array of a group's sacred and mundane connections to the surrounding universe (Bernshtam 1995: 208). This methodological shift brought Bernshtam to highlight the importance of studying people's religious beliefs and practices, and the perception of space and place.

Bernshtam studied local ideas among the rural population of Arkhangelsk and Vologda oblasts in the Russian north (Bernshtam 1995). She structured her analysis of the ethnographic data using categories that she saw as key for the study of local groups: endonyms and exonyms of people and places; intra- and inter-group differences; culture and economy; wedding rituals; folk legends about first settlers and sacred places. Bernshtam paid particular attention to topoethnonyms — groups' names derived from a geographical object — because a topoethnonym "unites a group and locus into a secular-sacred nature-culture unit — one's own world" (Bernshtam 1995: 308–9). She then attempted to trace ethnogenetic and cosmological origins of main local ideas, which she saw grounded in the social and Orthodox history of the region. She argued that the stability of local forms of Orthodox beliefs played an important role in preserving socio-cultural and spiritual specificity of local groups.

Bernshtam's cosmological approach to studying local groups led her to explore people's ideas about space, "us-them", the ancestral home, and destiny. Without such reconstruction of people's worldview, she argued, the very ethnographic project of studying local groups is futile (Bernshtam 1995: 208).

Within this range of writing on the hierarchical way that Pomor lifeways fit with those of other Slavic peoples, the topic of Pomor ethnogenesis deserves a special focus.

Theories of Pomor Origin

Pomors are commonly believed to have originated from the territory of Novgorod Republic — a separate unit within the Russian state during the twelfth to fifteenth centuries. Novgorod city was located at the crossroads of major trading routes as trade played an important role in Novgorod Republic's prosperity. The nineteenth-century travel accounts often trace Pomors' origin back to Novgorod by highlighting their distinct disposition: "Descendants of freedom-loving Novgorodians, Pomors have still preserved the spirit of enterprise, unrestraint and courage of their ancestors" (Ėngel'gardt 2009: 48). As mentioned above, a lineage of descent to the Novogorod state also linked Pomors to the role of sea-faring colonizers who extended Russian influence eastwards across Eurasia.

Bernshtam and other scholars have advocated for a more complex picture of Pomor origin and argued that there were two colonization waves, from Novgorod and the Upper Volga region. Descendants from Novgorod colonized mainly the western part of the Russian north, whereas settlers from the Volga region colonized primarily the eastern part (Bernshtam 1978: 31). Contemporary popular representations of Pomors, however, continue to portray them as courageous, enterprising and independent people, thus contributing towards creating a timeless image of a people with a unified Novgorodian origin.

Referring to the settlement of Slavic people in the north, Russian scholars often use the term "colonization" (*osvoenie*). It is commonly assumed that when moving north, the Slavs encountered other nations; but scholars dispute the extent to which the groups have mixed with the local Finno-Ugric groups. There has therefore been difficulty in specifying the role of the Finno-Ugric groups in the formation of northern Russians. Bernshtam argued that the population settling the territories of the Russian north from Novgorod and Upper Volga areas was already ethnically heterogeneous, and that the new settlers did mix with the local Finno-Ugric groups (Bernshtam 2009: 220). In Soviet ethnography, scholars usually argued that the colonisation of the Russian north took place without conflicts and was characterised by a peaceful relationship between Slavs and Finno-Ugric groups "contributing to mutual influence and mutual enrichment of cultures" (Vlasova 2015: 16). However, scholars also assumed that Slavs became the dominant ethnic group and often assimilated the local population. By the seventeenth century, migration and the colonization of the north decreased and the composition of the population became more constant. By this time, according to Vlasova, the northern Russian population had developed into an ethnic-territorial community with particular cultural-economic features (Ibid: 36–7).

The question of miscegenation (*metisatsii͡a*) was often discussed when it came to explanations of how different branches of Russians emerged. In the case of Great Russians, scholars were concerned with the influence of Finno-Ugric heritage on their physical appearance (Leskinen 2012: 249).

In the Russian north, beliefs about mythical ancestors called "Chud'" have been widespread. For example, Pëtr Efimenko noted that the village Zolotit͡sa on the Winter Coast was originally founded by a tribe called Chud'. According to Efimenko, locals used to talk about a place nearby the village called "Chudskai͡a pit" where this tribe had settled originally, and it was believed that the Chud' merged with the Slavic people who arrived from the south (Efimenko 1877: 10–1). Today, scholars assume that the term Chud was a collective term for native groups such as Meri͡a, Ves' and others that Slavic people encountered while moving north (Vlasova 2015: 30–1).

The Russian natural scientist Nikolaĭ Zograf wrote an account of people inhabiting European Russia. He noted that, across the north, Russian settlements are located in forests, tundra, and along the shores. Zograf called the Russians the "rulers" of these lands (Zograf 1894: 8), and argued that there are two types of Russian people inhabiting the north. The first group, which is the minority, settled along the rivers of Sukhon, northern Dvina, Onega and near the mouth of Mezen', as well as along the seashore. He described them as tall, strong, and beautiful, with dark blond to brown hair, and blond bushy beards. These Russians were mostly sailors, fishermen and traders, or navigators. Many of them considered themselves descendants of the first inhabitants of the region — the first settlers from Novgorod (Ibid: 9). The other group, according to Zograf, were the peasants living in Arkhangelsk and Vologda province in the places along smaller rivers, or far away from the large waterways. These Russians were of lower stature; their eyes narrower compared to the other group, their facial features less proportional, and their hair colour darker. According to Zograf, all this suggests that these peasants were not the pure descendants of Novgorod Russians, but a mixed-blood people with a tribe called Chud'. This tribe is believed to have disappeared; however, it is mentioned in chronicles, epics and legends (Ibid: 9).

Academic works on Pomors' ethnogenesis found a strong resonance in recent claims about Pomor indigeneity. Drawing on the concepts of *etnos* and *subetnos* and arguments about Pomors' descent from mixed populations of Russian and Finno-Ugric groups, activists from the city of Arkhangelsk promoted the idea of Pomors as a separate indigenous group that deserves a protected status and special rights to natural resources. To further support their claims, they quoted the results of a research on a gene pool of Russians, which was carried out by the Institute of Molecular Genetics and the Russian Academy of Medical Sciences in cooperation with British and Estonian scholars (Balanovsky et al. 2008). The activists referred to results of this investigation as proof that Pomors are not incomers from southern parts of Russia, but an indigenous population of the north. In particular, they referred to the fact that the gene pool of Pomors is more related to Finno-Ugric than to the Russian people.

Other supporters of Pomor indigeneity declared to us during informal conversations that Pomors have a number of physiological features that distinguish them from the Russian people: for example, that the Pomor skull is of a different shape and their arms are longer. Although it would be difficult to find academic literature to support these generalizations today, this discourse of physical difference builds on a set of old stereotypes of the distinct physical form of the Pomor population. Leskinen in her monograph on the "construction" of the idea of the Great Russians writes that several decades of description of Pomors can be summarized as a play of contrasts between an ideal of what an ancient Slavic type should be (tall, strong, light-haired) intermixed with the cardinal opposite of the stereotype of a Finnish type (short, gnarled, dark haired) (Leskinen 2016: 533). She links this play of opposites to a not-so-subtle construction of regional ethnic hierarchies.

A leader of a Pomor organization in Arkhangelsk appealed to the concept of Chud′ as a proof of Pomors′ distinctiveness and mixed origin:

> Since Chud′ tribes used to live here, where would pure blood Slavs come from? [...] It is not surprising that people here are different according to some anthropological [*antropologicheskim*] parameters too. There are darker people here, and with narrower eyes. [...] Chud′ tribes are indigenous proto-Pomor tribes. The ones that gave birth to the Pomors, [...] Saami, Karels, Vepses [...] and other Finno-Ugric peoples. Later, Slavic people came here, and assimilation, inter-marriages and mixture of cultures occurred. The Pomors probably emerged at the interface of all this. They are a mixed people. Therefore, to bang one's chest and shout that we are pure Russians, is not quite correct (Male, 40 years old, Arkhangelsk, Russia, 2014).

Pomor indigeneity claims caused a lot of controversy among the scholarly community and wider Russian society, as they seemed to challenge the established concept of ethnogenesis and the very integrity of the Great Russian identity project.

Recent Pomor Identity Movements

Over 150 years of debate on the identity of Pomors, and the northern Slavic zone, has had a powerful effect on local communities. With the reforms of perestroika, and the fall of the Soviet Union, ethnic identity movements came to be one of the major vectors by which local people expressed their sense of belonging and rights. These movements have taken a number of forms, ranging from very localized initiatives — often led by a single individual — to document and preserve artefacts and items of clothing in local museums, to the vociferous and sometimes surprising attempts to have Pomors recognized as an indigenous people.

A Museified Approach to Culture

Pomor material culture is still appreciated in villages, which is often manifested in local museums run by a group of people or a single person. Such museums exist in many villages on the White and Barents Sea coasts. Some of them are curated with the help of official institutions such as the Houses of Culture or larger museums; others are run by local people who usually have no professional background. These museum collections are aimed at preserving the Pomor heritage. Collectors consider the conservation of material culture as significant for preserving the memory of those Pomors who used to go on extensive fishing and sea mammal hunting trips at the sea.

This preservation of material culture is all the more important as local people often feel that Pomor culture has undergone significant changes that mean Pomors of today are not the same as their ancestors:

> We used to have Pomors — those who used to go to the Kanin [Peninsula] to fish. To Morzhovet͡s [Island, for seal hunting], to Novai͡a Zemli͡a. Those used to be Pomors. Previous old men. I almost do not remember true Pomors. Although I do remember some old men. They always [...] went to hunt seals (Female, 75 years old, Arkhangelsk oblast, Russia, 2014).

The professionalisation of fishing and sea mammal hunting, which began with the collectivisation of work in the countryside in the 1920s–1930s, might explain a wide spread opinion among villagers today that there are "no Pomors left", since locally-run collective farms (*kolkhozy*) do not run seal hunting anymore, and their coastal fisheries are only a fraction of what they used to be. Some *kolkhozes* still run salmon fisheries at *toni͡as* — often at a loss, because fishing quotas are very low and income from the catch does not cover the costs (Figs. 8.7 and 8.8). *Kolkhozes* maintain these fisheries mainly for social reasons, as they provide local people with access to employment and traditional food (as they sell part of the catch in village shops). When people in the village say that there are few fishermen left, they often refer to those who work at *toni͡as*. *Toni͡as*, therefore, remain a key material expression of fishing as a livelihood and source of identity.

Through the creation of museums and the collection of historical material artefacts, some locals establish a connection to Pomor heritage. For instance, there is a rather extensive collection of various Pomor objects and clothing in a village on the Winter Coast, gathered by a woman who is originally from the village but has now lived in the city for many years. The woman keeps the collection in her village house which she visits once a year for a couple of months in the summer.

Fig. 8.7 *Toni͡a* Kedy. Photo by Natalie Wahnsiedler

Fig. 8.8 Salmon fisheries at *toni͡a* Kedy. Photo by Natalie Wahnsiedler

She has been collecting the items for many years and arranged them in groups in the uninhabited part of her old wooden house (*povet'*).[3] According to the general museum practice, she labelled the items with short texts. Her large collection comprises clothing, fishing nets, various kinds of old dishes, spinning wheels, and other artefacts. Other local museum collections have a more specific focus according to the collector's interests, such as, for example, a collection of Pomor seafaring instruments in a barn.

The "museified" approach to Pomor identity stands in contrast with a more hands-on view of Pomorness widely held in villages. Village dwellers connect Pomor identity to fishing as an active practice — often as part of an official profession — as the following quote from fieldwork interviews suggests:

> I used to be [Pomor], until I got married. I then became a housewife and stopped fishing (Female, 60 years old, Arkhangelsk oblast, Russia, 2014).

The "museified" approach is often held among people who have come to the village from elsewhere, or among former permanent residents who now live in the city and visit their home village occasionally. Permanent dwellers, on the other hand, often have a practice-based approach to Pomorness. Masha Shaw looks at a similar distinction between permanent residents, seasonal in-migrants and casual incomers in a different part of the White Sea coast. She argues that for incomers, the activity of collecting and formalizing historical data about the village serves as a compensation for their separation from their home place. It allows them to reengage and reconnect with their home village. In contrast, people who live in the village permanently "do not have a need to reify the village's history and culture, because they are in the place, and this constantly keeps them busy with various everyday concerns" (Nakhshina 2013: 219). Fishing is still a vital everyday activity for many villagers on the White Sea coast, although some practices have been long gone. This is reflected in the wide array of opinions on Pomorness held among villagers, from "there are no true Pomors left anymore" to "everyone here is a Pomor".

---

3 A *povet'* is the non-residential part of a typical northern peasant house which was used for the storage of household items, fishing equipment, carts, etc.

Pomor crosses

While few attempts are made to reconstruct the fishing *toni͡as*, more recently a new movement of reconstructing old and constructing new Pomor wooden crosses emerged. The wooden crosses are a widespread phenomenon along the White Sea coast in northwest Russia. Although often referred to as "votive", these wooden crosses had multiple functions. Russian scholars emphasize that the tradition of wooden crosses must be conceptualized within the maritime culture of the region. Along the seashores, the crosses functioned as navigation marks (Okorokov 2005). Often, they were placed at important places along the roads — at the crossroads or river crossings — and were constructed on visible spots, on hills, and high riverbanks and seashores (Fig. 8.9). The votive crosses were built following a promise to God, a sign of gratitude for something good, or for deliverance from something evil. The vows were given on some special occasion, usually associated with hardships such as illness, death, or disappearance of a family member, famine or crop failure (Shchepanskai͡a 2003). Although, the wooden crosses can be found throughout the territory of the Russian north, they are more frequent and visible along the Mezen' River and northeast coast of the White Sea.

Locals build new crosses nearby their outdoor cabins in a way that echoes the former tradition of erecting crosses near a *toni͡a*. They consider it to be a way to show respect to their ancestors. Old crosses are carefully maintained. One such cross is located between the villages of Koĭda and Dolgoshchel'e. According to a local story, this cross was erected by a group of fishermen who were returning home from fishing and got lost on the way. However, when they reached this location on the hill, they were able to find the direction to their village. Therefore, they made a promise to build a cross. Travellers who pass this way usually stop by the cross and leave some coins or other little things like empty bullet casings.

A group of Pomor artists and intellectuals, supported by *kolkhoz* chairmen, committed themselves to build a cross in the Norwegian municipality of Vardø. The cooperation between Arkhangelsk and Vardø had begun already in the late 1980s and early 1990s with cultural exchanges that resulted in the opening of a Pomor museum in Vardø. The cross was constructed by a local artist in Arkhangelsk and then

Fig. 8.9 Old Pomor cross at *toni͡a* Kedy. Photo by Masha Shaw

brought to Norway by car. It was erected nearby the place of an old Pomor cemetery.

The movement of (re)constructing Pomor wooden crosses points towards the wider identity claims on behalf of Pomor activists. Although the crosses point literally to the importance of Russian Orthodox Christianity to Pomor traditions — and in particular to those parts of their traditions that link them to the wider Russian nation — the crosses symbolically point to their reverence for the places and seascapes where Pomors traditionally reside. Thus while serving as a religious and to some extent nationalist monument, the crosses perform a double function of pointing to Pomor rootedness. This quality would come to play an important role in recent years.

Indigeneity Claims

In the 2000s, a group of activists from the city of Arkhangelsk claimed that Pomors should be recognised as a less-numerous minority (*korennoĭ malochislennyĭ narod*). The term *korennye malochislennye narody*

(KMN), usually translated as "less-numerous indigenous peoples", was introduced into the Federal Law in 1999. Within Russia today, 47 peoples are officially recognised as KMNs of the Russian Federation (Pravitel'stvo 2015) who "qualify for the rights, privileges, and state support earmarked for indigenous peoples" (Donahoe et al. 2008: 993).

The concept of KMN goes back to imperial understandings of ethnic diversity and is related to the expansion of the Russian state and the acquisition (*osvoenie*) of new territories (Sokolovskiĭ 2001: 76). In the Imperial period, the term *inorodt͡sy* was frequently used in the administrative practices of the Russian Empire (Ibid: 86). In the Russian language, the term semantically means to "be born of another kind". Therefore, it implements the notion of a division between "the own people" and "the others" (Ibid: 89). In the early Soviet period, the imperial legacy merged with "the paternalistic idea of there being 'small peoples' [*malye narody*], diminutive in *both* world-historical importance and population" (Anderson 2000: 79). This fracture between being part of a majority group, and being a peculiar or special population deserving of paternalistic support, seems to be a constant theme in how northern Slavic populations have been described. However, this particular term has an additional twist in that it has been historically applied to (Siberian) hunter-gatherer societies — a group of people who in the minds of many urban intellectuals might be thought to be the antithesis of urban Russians. Hence it is with great irony that this term was employed by a group of activists for a population that has been considered as Russian, and sometimes even as "the most authentic Russians".

While the idea to officially recognise Pomors as an indigenous group was rather new, an increasing interest in Pomor culture and heritage emerged already in the late 1980s and early 1990s. Perestroika and the dissolution of the Soviet Union opened up new possibilities for civil engagement. A new interest in ethnicity and indigeneity developed, sometimes leading to the formation of ethno-political organizations (Shabaev and Sharapov 2011: 107). In Arkhangelsk oblast, one such organization, called "Pomor Revival" (*Pomorskoe vozrozhdenie*), was founded in 1987. In the early 2000s, the national-cultural organization "Pomor Autonomy" was formed at about the same time with the "Pomor Obshchina". The interest in Pomor culture developed along with the interest in international projects and cooperation, especially with Norway. The awareness of historical connections between Russia and Norway in the sphere of fishing and trade played an important role.

As Russia transited from the planned state economy to market economy and liberalism, most *kolkhozes* in Arkhangelsk oblast collapsed. The remaining fishing *kolkhozes* on the White Sea Coast are not able to provide the same employment opportunities and social support as before. Therefore, many villagers have to rely on subsistence economies of which fishing is the most important. However, strict restrictions apply, especially to fishing salmon, which is the most valuable species. Since Atlantic salmon spawns in several rivers of Arkhangelsk oblast, fishing with nets is entirely forbidden both in rivers and the White Sea to avoid salmon bycatch. Some restrictions are lifted for recreational fishing on a few officially organized fishing grounds. However, in rural areas, obtaining licenses is considered too costly. In addition, coastal residents often have their traditional inherited fishing grounds and they do not wish to fish in other places.

Locals do not consider fishing as a leisure activity, but as a source of livelihood. Activists argue that the situation is different in the neighbouring Nenets Autonomous District where Nenets people are recognized as an indigenous less-numerous minority and are therefore entitled to traditional fishing rights. Activists highlight the unfairness of the situation when Pomors and Nenetses live in similar climatic and socio-economic conditions, and yet do not have the same access to resources. They argue that the recognition of Pomors as a small-numbered indigenous people would allow Pomor fishermen to conduct their traditional economies and improve their living conditions.

Activists' persistent appeals for Pomors' recognition resulted in a response at a state level when the federal government held a meeting in 2007 that looked into the social and economic support of Pomors. The government also requested an expert opinion on Pomor identity from several prominent Russian anthropologists. Scholars responded by not advising the government to support activists' claims for Pomors to be recognised as a separate ethnic group. They argued that Pomors are a regional subgroup of Russian people, since they do not speak a separate language and their material and spiritual culture has always been very close to that of the majority of the Russian people (Nakhshina 2016: 313).

The main resolution of the 2007 meeting was the federal government's recommendation to regional governments of those administrative units where Pomors live to take measures to improve Pomors' social and economic conditions. It also proposed changes to the federal law on fisheries that would allow Pomors to conduct their traditional way of life. Since the resolution was merely a recommendation, regional governments did not act on it. Pomor activists made further appeals to the government but did not manage to achieve any formal recognition of Pomors as a separate indigenous group of the Russian Federation (Nakhshina 2016).

Fieldwork research in Arkhangelsk oblast in 2014–2016 revealed a coexistence of highly contested views on Pomor identity. One position was represented by Pomor activists who claimed that Pomors are an indigenous group and thus a separate *etnos* within the Russian Federation. Activists pointed out the distinctiveness of the Pomor group, basing their arguments on the scholarly understanding of what characterises an *etnos*, i.e. a distinctive language, culture and identity. The identity factor allowed for some of them to have a very broad and inclusive approach to Pomorness, as in the following view held by a Pomor organisation's leader:

> [Pomors] are those who care for this culture, this way of life. [...] However, we should not confuse Pomors with fishermen. The same way that we should not confuse Nenetses with reindeer herders. Nenetses now work in prosecution, and in other sections of governance. They do not have to be herders. Everyone here for some reason sees a Pomor with a fishing net over the shoulder. [...] But historically this is not the dominant way of subsistence anymore. [...] Those who know ornament patterns, singing culture, Pomor fairy tales and other stuff. All this comes together if you care about it. [...] People tell me, I myself come from Ukraine, came here twenty years ago. But I don't feel myself as a Ukrainian. I feel myself as a Pomor. May I? Why not? I always give this example: Pushkin, the dearest writer for the Russian reader. But he is so Ethiopian. But if you have done more for the Russian people, then you are probably a Russian. If you feel yourself good in Pomor'e, it probably means you are a Pomor. At least we do not measure skulls here and do not take blood tests (Male, 40 years old, Arkhangelsk, Russia, 2014).

The approach to Pomors as a separate indigenous group was on the rise until one of the most prominent Pomor activists, Ivan

Moseev, underwent a court trial where he was charged with "the incitment of national hatred". The accusation was based on an online comment — allegedly made by Moseev — which singled out Pomors as an ethnic group and implied their superiority over the Russians. Moseev denied the accusations and subsequently withdrew from public activities. His case was widely covered in local newspapers and even in the international *Barents Observer* and left behind a degree of uncertainty among urban intellectuals and artists who supported the claim that Pomors are a separate *etnos* and not just a sub-group of Russians. Many started to classify Pomors in less "separatist" terms and switched to more academically sanctioned and officially recognised concepts such as *subetnos* or ethnic community (*ėtnicheskai͡a obshchnost'*).

Some Arkhangelsk intellectuals who sympathised with the idea of Pomor indigeneity simultaneously insisted on the uniqueness of Pomors in their Russianness. According to one local thinker and a dedicated Orthodox believer, Pomors and the Russian north more widely have preserved certain spiritual qualities, and therefore could serve as a gene pool for true Russian values. This apparent incongruity whereby Pomors are indigenous and Russian at the same time, often emerged during conversations with people in Arkhangelsk, perhaps pointing towards some inherent contradictions within the *etnos* concept itself.

Claims about Pomor indigeneity were confronted by other Arkhangelsk scholars and intellectuals, who argued that Pomors are a historically developed identity of the White Sea coastal dwellers. They saw Pomors' specificity in their economy and some even found the factor of ethnicity altogether insignificant:

> It seems that Pomors have an economic rather than ethnic foundation. In other words, it is not important whether it were Finno-Ugric or Slavic people who settled here, but their traditional way of life based on [...] sea fishing and hunting, salt making and subsidiary crop farming and animal husbandry — in other words, agriculture — because just fishing and hunting was not enough. It was a natural phenomenon, this Pomor complex economy. [...] These Pomors, their status had never been marked as that of a separate ethnic group, neither before the revolution, nor during the Soviet period. [...] All this national underpinning of the current Pomor question is mainly connected to contemporary events (Male, 45 years old, Arkhangelsk, Russia, 2014).

In villages along the White Sea coast, many people have never heard of Pomor organisations in Arkhangelsk fighting for their rights to resources. Most interviewees considered Pomors to be Russian people; yet, many of them supported the idea of granting Pomors a status of a less-numerous minority, in order for them to obtain official access to their traditional fishing grounds.

The turmoil caused by Pomor activists in Arkhangelsk was hardly noticed in the village for two main reasons: firstly because Pomor activists failed to establish connections with rural residents; and secondly because villagers have a profoundly different understanding from the activists of what it means to be a Pomor. For the majority of people in the coastal villages of Arkhangelsk oblast, being Pomor means to be actively engaged in activities connected to the sea. Many people take pride in being descendants of the historical seafarers and *promyshlenniki* (fishers and hunters) that have been so vividly described in ethnographic and fictional literature.

Conclusion

Pomor identity has proven to be a challenge for both imperial and Soviet scholars. Pomors have been cited as the "most authentic Russians", as an ambiguous sub-group (*subetnos*) of Great Russians and an indigenous minority. This ambiguity and uncertainty regarding Pomor identity seems to have its origins in Pomors' unique settlement at the borders of the Russian Empire and the Soviet Union as well as their historical portrayal as explorers and pioneers and their unique ways of livelihood.

While folklorists considered the territory of Pomor'e as an isolated region, its history shows its importance in both geopolitical and ethnographic discussions. In political and historical narratives, Pomor'e was regarded as the "window to Europe" due to the importance of Pomor seafaring and trading relations. At the same time, Pomors' historical connections to the Novgorod Republic facilitated the idea of Pomors as "authentic Russian people". Pomors' ability to travel the sea and rivers gave them a special role in the expansion of the Slavic population not only along the White Sea coast but also across Siberia. Pomors' movement to the east was the first wave of Russian colonisation and resulted in the formation of mixed settler communities along the Arctic sea cost such as tundra peasant settlements in Taymyr (*zatundrennye krest'i͡ane*), a creole community in Yakutia (*russkoust'int͡sy*) and others. Along with this west-east dichotomy, the Pomors were also looked at from the perspective of an academic construction of the north-south dichotomy, an attempt to categorise the Slavic population by ethnographers (see chapter 3). Both views shaped a central-peripheral flexibility of Pomors in public discourses.

Soviet historians and ethnographers enthusiastically employed these historical and geopolitical ambiguities to develop a comprehensive ethnic theory. In these academic discussions, Pomors appeared as an important example of ethnic hierarchies. As the editors of this volume show in their introduction, the core of those debates was the theory of *etnos* which flourished as part of Soviet identity politics during the Cold War. Trying to make the theory practical for ideologically biased reconstructions of history and ethnographic classifications, Soviet ethnographers coined a number of alternative terms related to *etnos*. One of them was the term *subetnos*, which was applied to Pomors. In ethnographic volumes, Pomors were introduced along borderland groups such as Cossack and, ironically, Siberian communities, whose descent has been drawn from Pomors. Such subentry in official identity classifications facilitated indigeneity claims of Pomor activists in the beginning of the twenty-first century.

Russian scholars and policy makers based their classifications on a set of identity characteristics such as material culture, language, and physical appearance which varied in different periods and knowledge ecologies. In recent debates about Pomor indigeneity, these identity characteristics have been incorporated and "naturalised" in making claims about Pomors' distinctiveness from Russians. This shift from academic descriptions and constructions to the knowledge appropriated by local intelligentsii͡a allows us to see the fluidity of historical anthropological ideas and their social life within local communities. The Pomor case — taken from the margins of the former empire — introduces us to a field of northern studies where one can account for no border between academic constructions and local knowledge.

Published References

Aleksandrov, V. A. 1964. *Russkoe naselenie Sibiri XVII–nachala XVIII v. (Eniseĭskiĭ kraĭ)*. Trudy instituta ėtnografiĭ AN SSSR (Novaı͡a serii͡a) 87 (Moscow: Nauka).

—. K. G. Guslistyĭ, A. I. Zalesskiĭ, V. K. Sokolova, and K. V. Chistov, eds. 1964. *Narody Evropeiskoĭ chasti SSSR*. Narody Mira (Moscow: Izd-vo AN SSSR).

Anderson, D. G. 2000. *Identity and Ecology in Arctic Siberia: The Number One Reindeer Brigade* (Oxford: Oxford University Press).

Anuchin, D. N. 1889. 'O zadachakh russkoĭ ėtnografii', *Ėtnograficheskoe obozrenie* 1: 1–35.

Balanovsky, O., S. Rootsi, A. Pshenichnov, T. Kivisild, M. Churnosov, I. Evseeva, E. Pocheshkhova, M. Boldyreva, N. Yankovsky, E. Balanovska, and R. Villems. 2008. 'Two Sources of the Russian Patrilineal Heritage in their Eurasian Context', *American Journal Of Human Genetics* 82 (1): 236–50, https://doi.org/10.1016/j.ajhg.2007.09.019.

Banks, M. 1996. *Ethnicity: Anthropological Constructions* (New York: Routledge).

Belov, M. I. 1951. 'Arkticheskie plavanii͡a i ustroĭstvo russkikh morskikh sudov v XVII veke', in *Istoricheskiĭ pami͡atnik russkogo arkticheskogo moreplavanii͡a XVII veka*, ed. by A. P. Okladnikov and D. M. Pinkhenson (Moscow: izd. Glavsevmorputi), 63–80.

Bernshtam, T. A. 1978. *Pomory* (Leningrad: Nauka).

—. 1995. 'Vvedenie', in *Russkiĭ Sever. K probleme lokal'nykh grupp*, ed. by T. A. Bernshtam (St Peterburg: MAĖ RAN), 3–11.

—. 2009. *Narodnai͡a kul'tura Pomor'i͡a*. (Moscow: OGI).

Bol'shoi ėntsiklopedicheskiĭ slovar'. 2000. 'Ėtnicheskai͡a obshchnost'', http://dic.academic.ru/dic.nsf/enc3p/338586

Bromleĭ, I͡U. V. 1983. *Ocherki teorii etnosa* (Moscow: Nauka).

Chelishchev, P. I. 1886. *Puteshestvie po severu Rossii v 1791 godu* (St Peterburg: Tipografii͡a Balasheva).

Chizhikova, L. N. 1970. 'Arkhitekturnye ukrashenii͡a russkogo krest'i͡anskogo zhilishcha', in *Russkie. Istoriko-ėtnograficheskiĭ atlas*, ed. by P. I. Kushner (Moscow: Nauka), 7–60.

Dmitrieva, S. I. 1972. 'O spet͡sifike kul'turnogo razvitii͡a Russkogo Severa (Byl li Sever glukhoĭ okrainoĭ Rossii?)', *Sovetskai͡a ėtnogafii͡a* 2: 68–73.

Donahoe, B., J. O. Habeck, A. E. Halemba, and I. Sántha. 2008. 'Size and Place in the Construction of Indigeneity in the Russian Federation', *Current Anthropology* 49 (6): 993–1020.

Durov, I. M. 2011. *Slovar' zhivogo pomorskogo i͡azyka v ego bytovom i ėtnograficheskom primenenii* (Petrozavodsk: Karel'skiĭ nauchnyĭ t͡sentr).

Efimenko, P. S. 1877. *Materialy po ėtnorafii russkogo naselenii͡a Arkhangel'skoĭ gubernii. Chast' I. Opisanie vneshnego i vnutrennego byta* (Moscow: Tipografiia Millera).

Ėngel'gardt, A. P. 2009. *Russkiĭ Sever: putevye zapiski* (Moscow: OGI).

Fomin, A. 1797. *Opisanie Belogo mori͡a* (St Peterburg: Imperatorskai͡a akademii͡a nauk).

Gemp, K. 2004. *Skaz o Belomor'e. Slovar' pomorskikh recheniĭ* (Moscow: Nauka).

Gumilëv, L. N. 1989. *Ėtnogenez i biosfera Zemli* (Leningrad: LGU).

Knight, N. 2017. 'Geography, Race and the Malleability of Man: Karl von Baer and the Problem of Academic Particularism in the Russian Human Sciences', *Centaurus* 59 (1–2): 97–121, https://doi.org/10.1111/1600-0498.12154.

Kozhinov, V. V. 1999. *Istorii͡a Rusi i russkogo slova* (Moscow: Algoritm).

Kushner, P. I., ed. 1970. *Russkie. Istoriko-ėtnograficheskiĭ atlas* (Moscow: Nauka).

Laĭus, I͡U. A. and D. D. Laĭus, eds. 2010. *"More — nashe pole" Kolichestvennye dannye o rybnykh promyslakh Belogo i Barent͡seva moreĭ XVII–nachala XX vv.* (St Peterburg: Izdatel'stvo Evropeĭskogo universiteta v Sankt-Peterburge).

Lepekhin, I. 1805. *Puteshestviia akademika Ivana Lepekhina v 1772 godu. Chast' IV* (St Peterburg: Imperatorskai͡a akademii͡a nauk).

Leskinen, M. V. 2012. '"Malorossiĭskai͡a narodnost'" v rossiĭskoĭ nauke vtoroĭ poloviny XIX v. Problemy ėtnograficheskogo opisanii͡a', in *Russkie ob Ukraine i ukraint͡sakh*, ed. by E. I. Borisenok (St Peterburg: Aleteĭi͡a), 244–83.

—. 2016. *Velikoross/velikorus. Iz istorii konstruirovanii͡a ėtnichnosti. Vek XIX* (Moscow: Idrik).

Maksimov, S. V. 1857. 'Murman. Promysly na russkom laplandskom beregu', *Morskoĭ sbornik. Chast' neofit͡sal'nai͡a 32* 12: 237–74.

—. 1871. *God na severe* (St Peterburg: Tipografii͡a A. Transheli͡a).

Markov, A. 1901. *Belomorskie byliny* (Moscow: A. A. Levinson).

Maslova, G. S. 1956. 'Narodnai͡a odezhda russkikh, ukraint͡sev i belorusov v XIX–nachale XX v.' (Moscow: izd-vo Akademii Nauk SSSR), 543–757.

Moseev, I. I. 2005. *Pomor'ska govori͡a. Kratkiĭ slovar' pomorskogo i͡azyka* (Arkhangel'sk: Pravda Severa).

Nakhshina, M. 2013. 'The Perception of the Built Environment by Permanent Residents, Seasonal In-migrants and Casual Incomers in a Village in Northwest Russia', in *About the Hearth: Perspectives on the Home, Hearth and Household in the Circumpolar North*, ed. by D. G. Anderson, R. P. Wishart, and V. Vate (New York: Berghahn), 200–22.

—. 2016. 'Constraints on Community Participation in Salmon Fisheries Management in Northwest Russia', *Marine Policy* 74: 309–15.

Okorokov, A. V. 2005. 'Pomorskie kresty v sakral'nom landshafte', in *Kul'tura russkikh pomorov. Opyt sistemnogo issledovaniia͡*, ed. by Ė. L. Bazarova, et al. (Moscow: Nauchnyĭ mir), 241–48.

Panchenko, A. 2012. 'Russia', in *A Companion to Folklore*, ed. by R. Bendix and G. Hasan-Rokem (Malden: Wiley-Blackwell), 426–41.

Podvysot͡skiĭ, A. 1885. *Slovar' oblastnogo Arkhangel'skogo narechii͡a v ego bytovom i ėtnograficheskom primenenii* (St Peterburg: Tipografii͡a imperatorskoĭ akademii nauk).

Pravitel'stvo Rossiĭskoĭ Federat͡sii. 2015. 'O Edinom perechne korennykh malochislennykh narodov Rossiĭskoĭ Federat͡sii (s izmenenii͡ami na 25 avgusta 2015 goda). Postanovlenie ot 24 marta 2000 goda N 255', http://docs.cntd.ru/document/901757631

Pyzhova, A. 2011. 'Politizat͡sii͡a ėtnichnosti na primere pomorov', http://www.gumilev-center.ru/politizaciya-ehtnichnosti-na-primere-pomorov-arkhangelskojj-oblasti

Shabaev, I. and V. Sharapov. 2011. 'The Izhma Komi and the Pomor: Two Models of Cultural Transformation', *Journal of Ethnology and Folkloristics* 5 (1): 97–122.

Shchapov, A. 1864. 'O vlii͡anii gor i mori͡a na kharakter poseleniĭ', *Russkoe slovo* 6 (3): 105–16.

Shchepanskai͡a, T. V. 2003. *Kul'tura dorogi v russkoĭ miforitual'noĭ tradit͡sii XIX–XX vv* (Moscow: Indrik).

Shnirel'man, V. A. 2006. 'Uroki Gumileva: blesk i nishcheta teorii ėtnogeneza. Vvedenie', *Ėtnograficheskoe obozrenie* 3: 3–7.

Sluchevskiĭ, K. K. 1886. *Po severu Rossii* (St Peterburg: Tipografija Èduarda Goppe).

—. 2009. *Poezdki po severu Rossii v 1885–1886 godakh* (Moscow: OGI).

Sokolovskiĭ, S. V. 2001. *Obrazy drugikh v rossiiskikh nauke, politike i prave* (Moscow: Put').

Tokarev, S. A. 1958. *Ėtnografii͡a narodov SSSR; istoricheskie osnovy byta i kul'tury* (Moscow: Izdatel'stvo Moskovskogo universiteta).

Tolstov, S. P. 1964. *Narody evropeĭskoĭ chasti SSSR* (Moscow: Nauka).

Vlasova, I. V. 2015. *Russkiĭ Sever. Istoriko-kul'turnoe razvitie i identichnost' naselenii͡a* (Moscow: IEA RAN).

Zagoskin, N. P. 1910. *Russkie vodnye puti i sudovoe delo v dopetrovskoĭ Rossii. Istoriko-geograficheskoe issledovanie* (Kazan: Izdanie upravlenii͡a vodnykh puteĭ i shosseĭnykh dorog).

Zelenin, D. K. 1991. *Vostochnoslavi͡anskai͡a ėtnografii͡a* (Moscow: Nauka).

Zograf, N. I. 1894. *Russkie narody* (Moscow: Tipo-litografii͡aVysoch. utv. T-va I. N. Kushnerev i K.).

Archival References

MAĖ: [Numbered Collections of] Peter the Great Museum of Anthropology and Ethnography, Russian Academy of Sciences, St Petersburg, Russia

MAĖ 974. Photo collection of Nikolaĭ A. Shabunin.

9. Epilogue: Why *Etnos* (Still) Matters

Nathaniel Knight

The concept of *etnos* occupies a liminal, contested, yet remarkably durable niche in the array of categories of identity. *Etnos* was first articulated in the Russian context in the waning days of the old Tsarist Empire as a fusion of sorts joining an ethnographic tradition rooted in the humanities, with a cluster of fields in the natural sciences seeking to understand human diversity on the basis of bodily features. The most fervent promoters of *etnos,* Nikolaĭ Mogilīanskiĭ and Sergei Shirokogoroff, were of a rising generation of ethnographers, trained internationally, with substantial research experience, and poised to move into leading positions in the field. Both focused on areas at the periphery of the empire, and in the aftermath of the revolution found themselves cast into these peripheral regions, where they participated in political movements in opposition to the Bolshevik regime, before being forced into emigration. Consequently, the concept of *etnos* took shape in the 1920s and 1930s outside the emerging field of Soviet ethnography within which it came to be seen as ideologically suspect.

Yet *etnos* eventually did penetrate into Soviet parlance, tentatively at first in the post-war years and with greater force by the 1960s. By the 1970s, it had been officially enshrined as a central tenet of Soviet ethnography, largely through the efforts of I͡Ulian Bromleĭ, director of the Academy of Sciences Institute of Ethnography (Bromleĭ 1973). The concept attained still broader circulation in the late 1980s and 1990s

 https://doi.org/10.11647/OBP.0150.09

with the publication of the semi-suppressed works of Lev Gumilëv (Gumilëv 1989). But no sooner had *etnos* gained a foothold in the Russian public sphere than it was subjected to a blistering critique by post-Soviet ethnographers led by Valeriĭ Tishkov, Bromleĭ's successor at the Institute of Ethnography (Tishkov 2003). Tishkov's "requiem for *etnos*", however, proved premature — the deceased was alive and well and living in Astana, Bishkek, Ulan Bator, Iakutsk, and any number of other locations in the post-Soviet space, including Moscow itself. Not only is *etnos* well established in public discourse, it has been embraced with particular fervour by minority groups in the very peripheral regions that gave rise to the concept at its outset.

The continuing vitality of the concept of *etnos*, despite its sporadic rejection within the academic sphere, is a phenomenon that deserves serious and careful consideration. It is not enough simply to label *etnos* as a "category of practice", as Rogers Brubaker suggests — a kind of ethnographic false consciousness, colouring the way that the uninitiated view the world, but unworthy of application as an authentic "category of analysis" (Brubaker 2004; 2002). And while *etnos* may have a certain value in legitimatizing claims both symbolic and material on the part of minority groups, an "instrumental" reading of the concept as a tool in the hands of ethnic entrepreneurs is insufficient to explain its pervasiveness and persistence (O'Leary 2001). Even if we resist the temptation to reify *etnoses* — viewing them, in the style of Gumilëv, as quasi-sentient beings — we must acknowledge that the concept would not persist if it did not have a certain elemental traction, an explanatory power that cannot easily be evoked through other means. This is all the more true if we extend our view, as the authors of this collection suggest, from the actual term *etnos* to a broader "*etnos* thinking".

Simply put, *etnos* offers a middle ground. Free from the rigid, hierarchical, and anti-humanistic connotations of biological determinism associated with the concept of race, *etnos*, at the same time, is not so contingent and ephemeral that identity becomes purely a matter of individual choice. It is this niche that Teodor Shanin had in mind in identifying *etnos* as the "missing term" lacking in the existing array of sociological concepts (Shanin 1986). An *etnos* is hard and durable, persisting over multiple generations, yet it is not immutable. It has a history and an origin, changing over time and facing the prospect of eventual disappearance. Thus the common characterization of *etnos* as a "primordialist" concept built around the notion of a fixed unchanging essence may not be entirely justified.

In relation to individuals, *etnos* can be deployed in complex and dynamic patterns. The concept itself is sufficiently commodious to accommodate a range of interpretations, variations, and nuances. Not only do monolithic understandings of *etnos* tend not to gain footing, even clear definitions are often hard to come by. Nonetheless, *etnos* offers a kind of structured flexibility in explaining how individuals accommodate themselves to larger collectivities. Thus in chapter 8 we learn from Masha Shaw and Natalie Wahnsiedler that the Pomors of the Russian north can consider themselves part of their own distinctive *subetnos* without diminishing their broader identify as Russians — in fact, the Pomors are sometimes seen to embody a deeper, purer essence of the Russian *etnos*. Depending on the context and contingency, individuals can accentuate their closer local identity without negating their belonging to a larger overarching *etnos*. Nor is it beyond the realm of possibility for individuals to pass from one *etnos* to another or even maintain separate *etnos* affiliations concurrently. What is firm and persistent about *etnos* are the categories themselves, leaving individuals the opportunity to identify with these categories in more nuanced, contingent ways. It was precisely in an effort to move beyond the inconsistencies and unpredictability of individual identity, that Sergei Shirokogoroff gravitated toward the notion of *etnos* as a means to articulate a transcendent essence of identity existing above and beyond the individuals who might comprise it.

Why, however, should we as scholars lend credence to this notion of *etnos*, given its tangled history and the problematic strains it has been seen to engender? Why not simply embrace the notion of hybrid individual identities and leave it at that (Ab Imperio Editorial Board 2018)? Yet even acknowledging the prevalence of hybrid identities in the modern world, one still needs to account for the elements out of which hybrids are formulated. A hybrid can only exist, after all, when it is composed of identifiable components; otherwise, it becomes a thing in itself and loses its hybrid features. Thus essentialist categories may not be so easy to evade. *Etnos*, moreover, need not be seen as a monolithic formation. In so far as *etnos*, in practically all of its renditions, denotes a totality of distinctive elements — language, material culture, religious beliefs, folklore and traditions, as well as physical features — it can encompass variation, differing combinations and hues, without ceasing to comprise an integral whole. *Etnos* implies recognisability, not absolute purity.

Most of all, however, *etnos* thinking deserves to be taken seriously because it offers a mode of understanding the social world that, regardless of the views of scholars, is compelling to large numbers of individuals and communities throughout the world. However much we may wish the world to be otherwise, *etnos*, particular for minority populations who face the threat of assimilation, is a reality that cannot be sacrificed. Like the related concepts of nation, tribe, and ethnicity, *etnos* engenders a sense of connectedness that gives rise to social meaning. For the present day Evenki and Orochen — to whom Jocelyn Dudding showed photographs taken by early twentieth-century ethnographers (see chapter 7) — it was a matter of fundamental importance that they shared an ethnic identification with the individuals depicted. *Etnos* provided for them a pathway into the past, a link to their ancestors, a repository of lost knowledge that amounted to a tangible asset, such that inability to recognize the markers of *etnos* constituted a palpable loss. Likewise, the diachronic ties of *etnos* stretching over time engender synchronic links among individuals sharing connections to past ancestors and enacting common cultural traits and ways of life rooted in the past. As recent events continually show, despite technological tools that allow the creation of virtual communities transcending the bounds of culture, locality, and even language, the call of *etnos* has not lost its force.

***

The authors of the essays in this volume focus particular attention on the context and milieu in which the concept of *etnos* took shape in its initial iterations — *etnos* 1.0, if you will. In chapter 4, Sergei S. Alymov and Svetlana V. Podrezova pinpoint quite convincingly the St Petersburg anthropological school of Fëdor Volkov as the seedbed upon which the concept of *etnos* first took root. In chapter 3, Alymov shows as well how the Ukrainian national movement which inspired both Volkov and his protégé Mogilı͡anskiĭ added a critical element which led these scholars to infuse the biological models drawn from the French anthropological school of Paul Broca with a strong ethno-national awareness. In chapters 5 and 6, David G. Anderson and Dmitry V. Arzyutov trace the fieldwork of Sergei and Elizaveta Shirokogoroff, showing how they turned to the concept of *etnos* as a means of bringing order to the chaos of ethnographic nomenclature based on untidy, overlapping criteria of language, lifestyle, religious observances, and other traits. By reducing complex identity to an essence of *etnos*, Sergei Shirokogoroff believed he could reveal the underlying equations that govern ethnic relations and express them with mathematic precision. In chapter 6, Arzyutov in particular shows how Shirokogoroff's vision of *etnos* seeped into the political realm. Allowed to function unhindered, Shirokogoroff suggested, the dynamics of *etnos* would set in motion spontaneous processes of self-organization. Ethnic nations, thus, could realize their fundamental interests and enact the popular will without sinking into the destructive and divisive realm of politics. Shirokogoroff, who died in Chinese exile leaving his major works available only in English or unpublished altogether, might appear to have carved out an intellectual dead end, a scholarly path not taken. But ideas that appear obscure and neglected can have a surprising afterlife. This was certainly the case with Shirokogoroff's *etnos*, which left an imprint on Chinese and Japanese concepts of ethnic nationality (*mínzú*) and played a large role in the rediscovery of *etnos* by Bromleĭ and his associates in the 1960s and 1970s.

More could be said about the context in which *etnos* emerged and the timing of its appearance. While much of *etnos* was new and distinct, it emerged out of an ethnographic tradition directed toward the phenomenon of *narodnost'* — usually rendered as ethnicity or nationality in the cultural sense. Russia in the nineteenth century was a world of nations, in which ethnic difference served as a primary marker delineating the vertical contours of social space. *Narodnost'* — as defined by Nikolaĭ Nadezhdin, an early architect of the Russian tradition of ethnography — represented the totality of features allowing a population to be recognized as distinct. In turn the spirit of *narodnost'* found concrete actualization in peoples (*narody*), the natural units that structured the composition of the human race. The task of the ethnographer was to study *narodnost'* and peoples in their natural setting in order to identify their distinguishing features and establish their relationship to one another (Nadezhdin 1847).

The notion of ethnography as the science devoted to ethnic distinctiveness set the field in Russia on a somewhat different trajectory from the developing fields of anthropology and ethnology in western Europe, which were directed more toward general problems of the differentiation of the human race as a whole. With the rise of evolutionist theory, anthropology took as its subject a universal human culture divided into a set of discrete stages or levels expressed in particular cultural spheres. An evolutionist anthropologist might focus on a topic such as housing, transportation, musical instruments or religious practices and compare a broad range of artefacts from many different groups to show how the successive stages of cultural evolution were expressed in this particular area (Chapman 1985; Stocking 1995). Elucidating the distinctive features of particular ethnicities was at best a secondary task clearly subordinated to the challenge of tracing the universal trajectory of cultural evolution.

The tradition in Russia of ethnographic research focusing on ethnic distinctiveness remained well entrenched, but by the 1890s, evolutionist models had begun to make inroads. Moscow was particularly receptive to evolutionism. Maksim Kovalevskiĭ, the pioneering Russian sociologist, was an early and prominent proponent of evolutionist thought who remained influential despite the fact that he was obliged to leave his position at Moscow University for political reasons in the early 1890s and move to France (Glebov 2015). Dmitriĭ Anuchin, the polymath social scientist whose research encompassed the fields of physical anthropology, ethnography and geography, was somewhat more restrained in his evolutionist proclivities, but nonetheless adhered to aspects of the evolutionist model. Anuchin's protégé, Nikolaĭ Kharuzin, an indefatigable young ethnographer whose career was tragically cut short by his untimely death in 1901, was much less constrained in his embrace of evolutionist models. His posthumously published textbook on ethnography was a veritable manifesto of evolutionist theory and practice (Kerimova 2011; Knight 2008). In St Petersburg, the evolutionist camp was well represented by Lev Shternberg, the former political exile, known for his studies of the Giliaks of Sakhalin Island and for his collaboration with Franz Boas (Kan 2009).

The concept of *etnos* emerged, I would suggest, in the context of a backlash against evolutionist ideas and methods among Russian ethnographers. The two primary theorists of *etnos* in its earliest iteration, Mogilîanskiĭ and Shirokogoroff, both formulated their ideas in dialogue with specific evolutionist scholars, who served as foils against which the new ideas took shape.[1] Mogilîanskiĭ first made use of the term *etnos* in his 1902 review of Kharuzin's textbook, later published in 1908 (Mogilîanskiĭ 1908). In his expanded treatment published in 1916, Mogilîanskiĭ drew a sharp dividing line between his approach based on the centrality of *etnos* and evolutionist scholars such as Kharuzin and Shternberg who saw ethnography essentially as a history of culture writ large. "For a historian of culture", Mogilîanskiĭ wrote, "all of humanity as a whole stands in the foreground [...] A people, *etnos*, is a mere substrate on which some phenomenon or another takes place" (Mogilîanskiĭ 1916: 9). Specific examples from the real life of peoples, drawn from the most diverse and disparate groups are used merely to illustrate the larger patterns of human development. Mogilîanskiĭ proposed that ethnography move in a different direction: "an ethnographer should not ignore the concept of *etnos*" (Ibid: 10).

Sergei Shirokogoroff's path to the concept of *etnos* is somewhat harder to trace given that in his theoretical works on the topic he neglected to acknowledge the precursors to his ideas or to place them in the context of the development of Russian ethnography. Anderson and Arzyutov, in their exhaustive research into Shirokogoroff's career and work presented in chapters 5 and 6, have, however, uncovered some suggestive hints. A key figure in the development of Shirokogoroff's thinking was undoubtedly Shternberg. A mentor, perhaps even a father figure, Shternberg served at the same time as an intellectual antagonist, a negative point of reference against which Shirokogoroff formulated his own thinking. In a 1932 letter to a Polish collaborator, cited in chapter 6, Shirokogoroff refers to Shternberg's evolutionism and notes with emphatic distaste Shternberg's embrace of the work of James George Frazer, whose magnum opus, *The Golden Bough*, exemplified the comparative method of "historians of culture". Had it been Shternberg who confronted the confusion of ethnic identities among the Tungus and Orochen of Zabaĭkal'e and Manchuria, he would likely have found it of little consequence and perhaps even seen it as confirmation of the position that "the individual elements that

1 Sergeĭ Glebov makes a similar argument about the reaction against evolutionism as a factor in the formation of Eurasianist theory (Glebov 2015).

appear in among separate peoples, do not act autonomously. They are always inextricably tied to [...] the evolutionary development of culture overall" (Zhurnal zasedaniîa 1916: 6). For Shirokogoroff, in contrast, identifying a distinct overarching Tungus and Orochen *etnos* was a critical imperative, necessary to distil a deeper truth out of the confusion of everyday nomenclature.

In asserting the primacy of *etnos* over the evolutionist "history of culture", Mogilîanskiĭ and Shirokogoroff were echoing the older tradition of ethnography as the study of *narodnost'*. For Shirokogoroff, who says little about his predecessors and addresses an international audience, the connection is implicit, but Mogilîanskiĭ is open in acknowledging the continuity. He writes of "preserving *etnos* as the basis for scientific ethnography", not introducing *etnos* as an innovation (Mogilîanskiĭ 1916: 11). Looking back to previous conceptions of ethnography, he cites the conceptions of Nadezhdin and Aleksandr Pypin envisioning ethnography as the study of *narodnost'* and refers approvingly to Anuchin's endorsement of detailed monographic studies of specific peoples as the central task of ethnography. "Ethnography", Mogilîanskiĭ concludes, "is above all the study of peoples (*narodovedenie*)" (Ibid: 12). Shirokogoroff in turn defines *etnos* in terms synonymous with *narodnost'* as a "group of people, speaking the same language, recognizing their common origin, possessing a complex of customs and a social system, which is consciously maintained and explained as tradition and differentiated from those of other groups" (Shirokogoroff 1924: 5). Just as Nadezhdin understood ethnography as the study of *narodnost'*, Shirokogoroff defined the field as the science that studies *etnos*.

Is *etnos* and ethnography as envisioned by Mogilîanskiĭ and Shirokogoroff, therefore, simply a matter of old wine in new bottles? The one aspect of both conceptions that appears distinct and innovative is the insistence that *etnos* be understood to include a biological component. But if *etnos* is, as the editors of this volume suggest in chapter 2, a biosocial concept, where exactly does the biological connect with the social? It would appear that Mogilîanskiĭ and Shirokogoroff each approach this problem from a different angle. Mogilîanskiĭ argued that biometric research — detailed studies characterizing the group from the perspective of physical anthropology and connecting it to larger racial categories — needed to be included as an integral component of *etnos*. Therefore ethnography, in his view, should be understood as a compound science, akin to archaeology, that draws on the skills of specialists from a range of fields to address its specific aim (Mogili͡anskiĭ 1916: 15). A model for Mogili͡anskiĭ's conception can be found in his friend and mentor Volkov's exhaustive and controversial two-volume study of the Ukrainian people which, above and beyond demonstrating the independent status of the Ukrainian language and the distinctiveness of Ukrainian folkways, depicted the Ukrainians as a single and separate anthropological type.[2]

Shirokogoroff in his early 1920s formulations of the concept of *etnos* was less insistent on the role of biometric classification. In an arrangement somewhat similar to the Boasian four-field system, he envisioned anthropology and ethnography as separate entities — one based in the natural sciences, the other in the humanities — which joined together with linguistics to form the overarching field of ethnology (Shirokogorov 2002 [1923]: ch. 2). Anthropology, in his view, was a purely biological science viewing humanity from a zoological perspective. But Shirokogoroff, perhaps influenced by his own attempts at anthropometric classification and analysis, came to question the value of racial classification. He notes the wide variety of schemes of racial divisions, the lack of stable definitions, and the disjuncture between racial types and recognized ethnic or national groups. Ultimately he concluded that the very idea of a limited number of races, which had guided research agendas and classification schemes up to that time, was "unsatisfactory in light of a closer acquaintance with separate peoples" (Ibid: 63). Biometric analysis, he added, was of more use in shedding light on the historical origins of modern populations, foreseeing, perhaps, the modern uses of genomic studies.

More important than biometric data in defining *etnos* was the nature of the *etnos* itself as an autonomous organic entity. *Etnos*, in Shirokogoroff's view, was the core unit through which humans adapted to their environment and engaged in the struggle for survival. As such, the *etnos* had the capacity for independent action and self-regulation above and beyond the volition of the individuals who composed it.

2 Volkov's study and the reaction it provoked is described in detail in chapter 3. See also Mogil'ner 2008: 138–44.

Shirokogoroff writes, "an *etnos* is always struggling for its existence, and, if it can oppose other *etnos*es and becomes victorious, it may continue expanding in territory, which is one of the external manifestations of its growth" (Shirokogoroff 1924: 7).

Shirokogoroff's conception of *etnos* easily spilled over into the realm of geopolitics, as nations, infused with the spirit of the *etnos*, competed with one another for dominance and survival. The *etnos*, in its reified form, engaged in this autonomous action through its psychological and cognitive capacities, the primary adaptive mechanism through which it engaged in the struggle for survival (Shirokogorov 2002 [1923]: 64). Thus, when Shirokogoroff spoke of *etnos* as a biological unit, he was referring not to the shared physical traits of a given population, but to the biological functions of adaptation and self-regulation that took place on the level of the *etnos* and insured the survival of the individuals who comprised it. Shirokogoroff's conception transcended the view of the organism as a metaphor and endowed the *etnos* with a hard ontological substance as a living being in its own right, with its own lifecycle and role as the essential actor in the process of human evolution.

Thus, we find, in Mogilianskiĭ and Shirokogoroff's conceptions, two contrasting views of *etnos*, one weighted toward the material sphere, the other arising out of the metaphysical realm. This duality could even be seen to have reappeared in *etnos* 2.0 — the models of *etnos* developed in the 1960s and 1970, particularly the contrasting visions of Bromleĭ and Gumilëv. To be sure, the parallel is by no means exact. Bromleĭ', for example, relied far less on the presence of shared biometric traits in his vision of *etnos* than did Mogilianskiĭ. Moreover, the two scholars differ in their placement of ethnography with the larger framework of the human sciences: Bromleĭ, in keeping with the Soviet tradition, situated ethnography within the humanities, while Mogilianskiĭ insisted on its close relation to the natural sciences, a position shared by Gumilëv. Yet the contrast persisted between views of *etnos* as an assemblage of distinguishing features and *etnos* as a reified organic whole.[3]

***

3 Bromleĭ, in fact, directly notes the correspondence between Shirokogoroff and Gumilëv's organic understandings of *etnos* (Bromleĭ 1973: 26).

A closer look at Mogilîanskiĭ and Shirokogoroff's concepts of *etnos* provides some insights as to why this concept has proven so controversial yet at the same time so resilient. Like other categories of identity, *etnos*, whether understood as a community defined by shared traits or as a social organism, retains the potential to evoke violence. Once the *etnos* is recognized as a conceptual object, it can serve as a point of reference: elements in the surrounding world are viewed from the perspective of the benefits or harm they confer on the *etnos*. The resulting interests of the *etnos* can attain the status of a moral absolute. Individual rights, respect for cultural diversity, maintenance of international order and stability, adherence to law and ethical standards all potentially yield to the overarching interests of the *etnos*. The events of the 1990s, from the massacres in the former Yugoslavia and Rwanda to the turmoil in the former Soviet republics, revealed the destructive potential inherent in visions of collective identity. The surge of ethno-nationalism and tribalism in the current political climate reminds us that this potential is far from exhausted.

Yet while the dangers of *etnos* are readily apparent, the remedies are far from clear. Is *etnos* itself the problem, or is it more appropriate to focus on the immediate causes — the hatred, xenophobia, and chauvinistic pride that so often infect ethnic consciousness? If *etnos* is an organism, are these maladies its diseases? In this case, is it not better to think about how to effect a cure? It is possible to envision a healthy incarnation of *etnos*, cleansed of its malevolent content? And what are the alternatives? Is it realistic to expect populations to abandon their terms of group identity, terms that often provide the basis for claims, both practical and symbolic, on state and society, in response to abuses for which they may feel no responsibility? Whether we view *etnos* as a dangerous illusion or a useful means to understand longstanding affinities based on shared culture and history, the phenomena of *etnos* thinking will continue to exist. Whether couched in the language of tribe, nation, ethnicity or *etnos*, individuals will continue to seek meaning and coherence by envisioning their lives in the context of larger collectivities whose roots in the past and trajectory into the future extend beyond the finite bounds of individual mortality. The concept of *etnos*, and the broader *etnos* thinking that accompanies it, offer a framework for describing and analysing these behaviours. Whatever the inconsistencies and weaknesses of the concepts developed by Mogilïanskiĭ, Shirokogoroff and their later Soviet successors, these are ideas that still speak to us in the present day.

Published References

Ab Imperio Editorial Board. 2018. 'The Impossibility of Pure Forms: Normative Hybridities as a "Banality of Life"', *Ab Imperio* 1: 15–9, https://doi.org/10.1353/imp.2018.0001.

Bromleĭ, I. U. V. 1973. *Ėtnos i ėtnografii͡a* (Moscow: Nauka).

Brubaker, R. 2002. 'Ethnicity without Groups', *European Journal of Sociology/Archives Européennes de Sociologie* XLIII (2): 163–89.

—. 2004. *Ethnicity Without Groups* (Cambridge, MA: Harvard University Press).

Chapman, W. R. 1985. 'Arranging Ethnology: A. H. L. F. Pitt Rivers and the Typological Tradition', in *Objects and Others: Essays on Museums and Material Culture*, ed. by G. W. Stocking (Madison, WI: University of Wisconsin Press), 15–48.

Glebov, S. V. 2015. 'N. S. Trubetskoi's Europe and Mankind and Eurasianist Antievolutionism: One Unknown Source', in *Between Europe and Asia: The Origins, Theories, and Legacies of Russian Eurasianism*, ed. by M. Bassin, S. Glebov, and M. Laruelle (Pittsburgh, PA: University of Pittsburgh Press), 48–67.

Gumilëv, L. N. 1989. *Etnogenez i biosfera Zemli* (Leningrad: LGU).

Kan, S. 2009. Lev Shternberg: Anthropologist, Russian Socialist, Jewish Activist (Lincoln, NE: University of Nebraska Press).

Kerimova, M. M. 2011. Zhizn', otdannai͡a nauke. Sem'i͡a ėtnografov Kharuzinykh. Iz istorii rossiĭskoĭ ėtnografii (1880–1930-e gody) (Moscow: Vostochnai͡a literatura).

Knight, N. 2008. 'Nikolai Kharuzin and the Quest for a Universal Human Science: Anthropological Evolutionism and the Russian Ethnographic Tradition, 1885–1900', *Kritika: Explorations in Russian and Eurasian History* 9 (1): 1–29.

Mogil'ner, M. 2008. *Homo Imperii: Istorii͡a fizicheskoĭ antropologii v Rossii (konet͡s XIX–nachalo XX v.)* (Moscow: Novoe literaturnoe obozrenie).

Mogili͡anskiĭ, N. M. 1908. 'Ėtnografii͡a i e eë zadachi', *Ezhegodnik Russkogo antropologicheskogo obshchestva* 3: 1–14.

—. 1916. 'Predmet i zadachi ėtnografii', *Zhivai͡a starina* 25: 1–22.

Nadezhdin, N. I. 1847. 'Ob ėtnograficheskom izuchenii narodnosti russkoĭ', *Zapiski Russkogo Geograficheskogo Obshchestva* (Tipografii͡a Imperatorskoĭ Akademii Nauk: Sankt-Peterburg), 61–115.

O'Leary, B. 2001. 'Instrumentalist Theories of Nationalism', in *Encyclopedia of Nationalism*, ed. by A. Leoussi (New Brunswick, NJ: Transaction), 148–53.

Shanin, T. 1986. 'Soviet Theories of Ethnicity: The Case of a Missing Term', *New Left Review* 158: 113.

Shirokogoroff, S. M. 1924. *Ethnical Unit and Milieu: A Summary of the Ethnos* (Shanghai: E. Evans and Sons).

Shirokogorov, S. M. 2002 [1923]. *Ėtnos — issledovanie osnovnykh prinfsipov izmeneniīa ėtnicheskikh i ėtnograficheskikh īavleniĭ* (Vladivostok: Izdatel'stvo Dal'nevostochnogo universiteta).

Stocking, G. W. 1995. 'Prologue: Tylor and the Reformation of Anthropology', in *After Tylor: British Social Anthropology, 1888–1951* (Madison, WI: University of Wisconsin Press), 3–14.

Tishkov, V. A. 2003. *Rekviem po etnosu* (Moscow: Nauka).

Zhurnal zasedaniīa. 1916. 'Zhurnal zasedaniīa Otdeleniīa a ėtnografii IRGO 4 marta 1916 goda', *Zhivaīa starina* 2–3: 1–11.

List of Illustrations

Chapter 3

Chapter 4

Chapter 5

Chapter 6

Chapter 7

Chapter 8

Index

This book need not end here...

Share

All our books—including the one you have just read—are free to access online so that students, researchers and members of the public who can't afford a printed edition will have access to the same ideas. This title will be accessed online by hundreds of readers each month across the globe: why not share the link so that someone you know is one of them?

This book and additional content is available at:
https://doi.org/10.11647/OBP.0150

Customise

Personalise your copy of this book or design new books using OBP and third-party material. Take chapters or whole books from our published list and make a special edition, a new anthology or an illuminating coursepack. Each customised edition will be produced as a paperback and a downloadable PDF.

Find out more at:
https://www.openbookpublishers.com/section/59/1

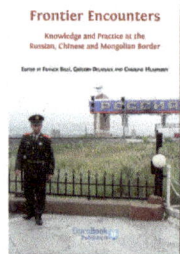

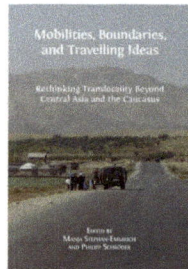

www.ingramcontent.com/pod-product-compliance
Lightning Source LLC
Chambersburg PA
CBHW050806270326
41926CB00026B/4561
* 9 7 8 1 7 8 3 7 4 5 4 4 9 *